THE NATURE OF NORTH AMERICA

THE NATURE OF NORTH AMERICA

A HANDBOOK TO THE CONTINENT
Rocks, Plants, and Animals

David Rockwell

Illustrations by Janet McGahan

B
Berkley Books
New York

THE NATURE OF NORTH AMERICA

A Berkley Book
Published by The Berkley Publishing Group
375 Hudson Street
New York, New York 10014

First edition: November 1998

Library of Congress Cataloging in Publication Data

Rockwell, David B.
    The nature of North America : A handbook to the continent : rocks, plants, and animals /
David Rockwell : illustrations by Janet McGahan.
       p.   cm.
    Includes index.
    ISBN 0-425-16548-5 (pbk.)
    1. Natural history—North America.   I. Title.
QH102.R63   1998   98-27182
508.7—dc21   CIP

Printed in the United States of America

10 9 8 7 6 5 4 3 2 1

To My Father

Contents

PREFACE

THE NATURE OF NORTH AMERICA IS GRANITE AND DOLOMITE. It's drumlin and kettle, meander scar and rift valley. It's Milbert's tortoiseshell and great spangled fritillary, wolf willow and yarrow. It's wandering tattler, blackfin cisco, and manatee. It's rock 3.96 billion years old and clones of aspen trees over a million years old. It's blind catfish dwelling 1,860 feet beneath the earth's surface and shrews with hearts that beat 22 times a second. It's Death Valley. Islands north of the Arctic Circle. Great Lakes. Rivers like the Yukon and Mississippi. Trees as grand as the giant sequoias.

An undisturbed acre of meadow hosts an estimated 666 million individual mites, 250 million springtails, 18 million beetles, and perhaps 135 million or so other arthropods. Those numbers, like the number of stars in the universe, are numbing, beyond human comprehension. But consider them anyway, and add to the sum all the plants, fungi, bacteria, amphibians, reptiles, birds, and mammals that might share that acre. Multiply the total by 5.8 billion, the number of acres in North America. Subtract the millions of acres under concrete or in cultivation if you wish. But do factor in the multifariousness of the continent's rocks, waters, and climates, and you begin to appreciate the dimensions of the North American continent.

Bewildered by abundance and diversity, your inclination, perhaps, is to step back and look for broad patterns and processes. That, in part, is the perspective this book takes. The complex array that makes up North America (from Greenland to Mexico) is synthesized and organized into geologic provinces, hydrologic regions, soil orders, climatic zones, and plant and animal communities. Processes responsible for these patterns are synopsized: How did the Rocky Mountains form? Why does the jet stream flow where it does? Why are fish in the west bigger, longer lived, and more fecund on the whole than fish in the east? Interspersed are the savory particulars: short articles that cover new discoveries; explanations of often misunderstood natural phenomena; and oddities. You will also find descriptions of species or communities of organisms that characterize regions. For a more complete preview, you might survey the table of contents preceding each part. Graphs, charts, line drawings, maps, and sketches complement the text throughout. In short, this book attempts to summarize information about the continent's natural foundations and to do so in a manner that appeals to the lay reader as well as the scientist.

My thanks to the many scientists, observers, and previous compilers that make a volume like this possible; to Rick Balkin for suggesting the book and for guiding its development; to Hillary Cige, my editor at Berkley, for her many contributions; to Steve Austad and Doug Macdougall for serving as scientific advisors; to Lee Esbenshade for her thorough copyediting and proofreading; and to Janet McGahan for the pen-and-ink art that graces so many of the pages. I owe a particular debt to Jerry McGahan for his careful reading of the manuscript and insightful criticism. As always, I am grateful to Nancy, Addy, and Isaac for their support and patience.

Part One
GEOLOGY

Part One Geology

STRUCTURE

LIKE A HARD-BOILED EGG, THE EARTH IS divided into a series of distinct concentric layers. On the surface, analogous to the shell of the egg, is a veneer of low-density rock called the crust. It encases the earth and makes up continents and ocean floors. Beneath, like the white of the egg, is the mantle, a thick region of denser rock. And at the earth's center, in the position of the yolk, is a metallic sphere called the core.

The crust accounts for only about 0.4 percent of the earth's overall mass. Surprisingly, only eight chemical elements comprise 98.5 percent of its weight. Continental crust is mainly made up of felsic rocks which are rich in silicon, oxygen, and aluminum. Oceanic crust is basalt, a denser rock rich in two relatively heavy elements, iron and magnesium.

Continental crust and oceanic crust differ substantially in thickness. Worldwide, continental crust averages about 25 miles in depth, oceanic crust 4.3 miles, so that the total continental crust exceeds oceanic crust in volume, even though oceans cover more than 70 percent of the earth's surface.

North America's crust varies from 15.5 to 34 miles in thickness and averages around 22 miles. The areas with the thickest crust include the Williston Basin of North Dakota and eastern Montana, the western Great Plains region, and Lake Superior. The thickest area is in eastern Montana, where the crust is some 36 miles deep; the thinnest spot is in western Oregon, only 11 miles deep. These two single-point measures are considered anomalies, the result of unusual events that took place as the crust evolved. As a general rule, North America is thickest in its interior and thinnest on the coasts. The crust on the east side is on average about 3 miles deeper than on the west side.

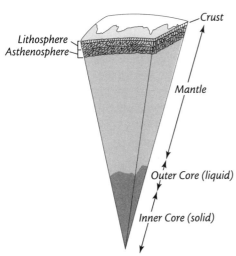

Cross section of the crust

Thickness of the crust in miles. Contours have been smoothed. Little data is available for Mexico, central and northern Canada, and much of Alaska.

The earth's crust is thinner where it is being stretched and thicker under mountain ranges. The latter is due to a phenomenon known as isostasy. Just as a ship sinks lower in water as more weight is added to it, those parts of the continent burdened with large mountain ranges sit deeper than those without mountains. The deep-sitting regions are called roots.

All of the crust and the uppermost part of the mantle are often referred to as a single unit, the lithosphere. Even though the crust

The Earth's Layers

Layers (compositional)

Crust
    Oceanic: 4.34 mi thick
      0 - 0.31 mi: sediments
      0.31 - 0.62 mi: basalt
      0.62 - 4.34 mi: gabbro
    Continental: 21.7 mi thick (average)
      0 - 0.62 mi: sediments
      0.62 - 18.6 mi: granite-granodiorite
      18.6 - 21.7 mi: gabbro
Mantle: 4.34 or 21.7 mi to 1798 mi of depth
    upper (to 415.4 mi): peridotite, pyrolite
    lower (415.4 - 1798 mi): pyrolite
Core: 1798 mi to center; iron (90%), nickel (9%),
    sulfur + phosphorus + carbon + oxygen (1%)

Layers (mechanical)

Lithosphere: rigid shell broken into plates
    Oceanic: 0 - 40.3 mi
    Continental: 0 - 74.4 mi
Asthenosphere: plastic; 40.3 or 74.4 mi
    to 124 mi
Mesosphere: rigid; 124 - 1798 mi
Outer core: liquid; 1798 - 2926.4 mi
Transition: mushy; 2926.4 - 3205.4 mi
Inner core: solid; 3205.4 - 3950 mi

and mantle are composed of different materials and have different densities, they are firmly attached. The lithosphere encases the earth like the shell of our imaginary hard-boiled egg, but this shell is cracked, broken into a number of pieces or plates that move with respect to one another. Some of the plates hold continents; others carry ocean crust; still others carry both. They are mobile because near the base of the lithosphere, the mantle material is hot enough to flow like warm plastic. This plasticlike part of the mantle is called the asthenosphere.

The plates, driven by convective forces in the mantle, glide over the asthenosphere at about the same rate as our fingernails grow—an inch or two a year. This does not seem very fast, but over millions of years, the plates travel tremendous distances. Over just the last 10 million years,

What's in the Crust?

Aluminum 8.1%
Iron 5.0%
Calcium 3.6%
Sodium 2.8%
Potassium 2.6%
Magnesium 2.1%
All other elements 1.5%

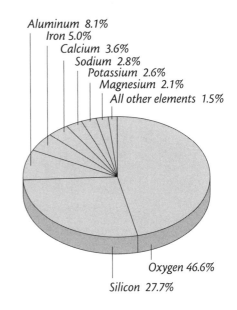

Oxygen 46.6%
Silicon 27.7%

for example, a plate traveling at 2 inches per year would travel more than 300 miles.

We still do not know how thick the lithosphere is at every point beneath North America, but estimates put it at between 40 and 75 miles, with the thickest portions under the oldest parts of the continent. The asthenosphere extends from the base of the lithosphere to a depth of 124 miles and makes up about 6 percent of the total thickness of the mantle.

COMPOUNDS IN THE CRUST

Compound	Continental (Upper)	(All)	Oceanic
SiO_2	66.00%	57.30%	49.50%
Al_2O_3	15.20	15.90	16.00
FeO	4.50	9.10	10.50
CaO	4.20	7.40	11.30
Na_2O	3.90	3.10	2.80
K_2O	3.40	1.10	0.10
MgO	2.20	5.30	7.70

Mantle Turnovers
Downwelling creates giant superswells

Recent computer models developed by Paul J. Tackley and others at the University of California are improving our understanding of how the mantle works to move the earth's plates. These models suggest that most of the time, the mantle's upper and lower layers circulate independently. Periodically, however, they intermingle as when a large amount of material in the mantle's upper layer cools, becoming dense enough to sink into the lower mantle. These immense downwellings, in turn, force hot rock from the lower mantle into the upper mantle. Scientists now speculate that these "superswells" account for periods of major geologic activity on the earth, adding material to continents and forming major mountain ranges. Mantle superswells may also release large amounts of carbon dioxide, which can raise the earth's temperature and affect living communities.

The Sum of the Parts

From a geologic perspective, North America has three main parts: the Canadian Shield, the Stable Interior, and the mountain belts.

The Canadian Shield is a vast area centered around Hudson Bay. Often described as the nucleus of North America, the Shield stretches 4,000 miles from east to west and 4,000 miles from north to south, making up almost a quarter of the continent. All

continents have shields—large areas of exposed Precambrian rocks, mostly granite and gneiss, that have not been folded or otherwise deformed since Precambrian time, the geologic interval that ended half a billion years ago. These stable, core areas of relatively rigid and ancient rock, the oldest exposed rock on earth, have few mountains and no volcanoes, and they seldom experience earthquakes.

Major structural components of North America

During the Precambrian interval, the Canadian Shield—the largest of all continental shields—underwent at least three episodes of mountain building and erosion. But by the end of Precambrian time, the major mountain ranges had eroded away; today, geologists detect only traces of them. The major structural features of the shield that remain are a series of broad basins and ridges. Today, the surface of the Shield is dotted with glacial features left during the last ice age, which ended just 15,000 years ago.

The second major part of the continent, the Stable Interior or Platform, encompasses both the central lowlands and the Great Plains. It surrounds the Shield on three sides and has as its foundation the same ancient core of bedrock that makes up the Shield. But the Stable Interior is coated with a veneer of undeformed sedimentary rocks, mostly limestone, sandstone, and shale. This layer, rich in marine fossils, becomes progressively thicker as one travels away from the Shield. The trend indicates that the underlying rock dips gently to the south, west, and east, although in places it, too, has been warped slightly into basins and ridges. Like the Shield, the northern parts of the Stable Interior have been glaciated.

The third and newest part of the continent lies along the margin. It is composed of three major mountain belts: the Cordilleran, the Appalachian, and the Arctic. Although each has a unique geologic history, all represent relatively recent episodes of mountain building brought on by the folding, squeezing, fracturing, and uplifting of rock. Together these mountain belts occupy the largest percentage of the continent's surface.

Foundations: The Geologic Provinces

Canadian Shield

The oldest part of the continent, the Canadian Shield, makes up about one third of the North American landmass and is the central nucleus around which the rest of North America is built. Most of modern-day Greenland, separated from the rest of the continent by the Davis Strait, started moving away from the Canadian Shield about 65 million years ago.

While the Shield does have some sedimentary rocks, most of it is what geologists call the "basement complex"—igneous and metamorphic rocks like granite and gneiss that make up the foundation of North America. At one time, sedimentary rocks covered this part of the continent, but they have eroded away; now only remnants remain.

The Shield has undergone three or more major episodes of mountain building, all during the Precambrian interval. Only traces of these early mountain ranges are left; erosion carried away the rest over half a billion years ago. Since then, the Shield has only seen major mountain building on its eastern rim, and has remained a relatively stable, rigid block. Because the Shield has been formed and deformed over the last 3 to 4 billion years, geologists have not yet fully deciphered the detail of its history.

Typically, the terrain of the Shield is low and rolling: mostly rounded hills dotted by countless lakes. Structural features include a series of enormous basins separated by ridges. The most significant of these are located at Hudson, Foxe, Ungava,

and James Bays; between Victoria Island and the Boothia Peninsula; in southeastern Saskatchewan; and between Lakes Michigan and Huron. Some of these basins hold almost 2 miles of sediment. The Torngat Mountains of Labrador lie along the eastern edge of the Shield and reach 5,000 to 6,000 feet in elevation. Other prominent geologic features left more recently by the glaciers of the last ice age include old meltwater channels, till, eskers, and glacial lake sediments. The glaciers scraped the Shield clean and exposed more of the basement complex than has been bared in hundreds of millions of years. Great Bear, Great Slave, Athabaska, Winnipeg, and Huron Lakes, all created by the ice sheets, are among the world's largest lakes.

Greenland

Greenland is the world's largest island. Most of it lies north of the Arctic Circle. It is basically a continuation of the Canadian Shield, although it is called the Greenland Shield. As such, it is mostly underlain by a similar basement complex of very old granite and gneiss, some of which was metamorphosed (altered by high temperature and pressure) about 3.8 billion years ago.

The mountain belt along Greenland's east coast is made of the same rock that makes up the mountains of the Caledonian province of Europe, evidence that Europe was once attached to Greenland. Similarly, a range that runs east to west across Greenland's northern margin was once connected to the northern mountains of Canada.

Geologic provinces of North America

Greenland's ice cap is 1,500 miles long, 450 miles wide, and up to 11,200 feet thick. It covers 90 percent of the island's surface. If it melted, its runoff would raise the world's oceans 20 feet. The ice sheet is so heavy that it has depressed the center of the island 1,200 feet below sea level. If the island did lose its ice cap, all that would remain of Greenland would be a ring of small islands.

The ice-free part of Greenland—a narrow rim along the coast mostly on the west side—is indented with many deep, glaciated fjords.

Appalachian Mountains and Plateaus

The Appalachian Mountains and Plateaus stretch for 1,200 miles along the eastern margin of North America (from Newfoundland to Georgia). They range from 3,200 to 6,500 feet in elevation and trend northeast to southwest. This system is older than the Cordilleran system in the west; its internal structures were formed more than 200 million years ago. However, the topographic or surface relief we see today is from relatively recent uplift and erosion. Although the geologic history of the Appalachian system varies considerably along its length, its creation involved three major mountain-building episodes or orogenies. The first, known as the Taconic, started when an island arc or microcontinent collided with eastern North America. The collision destroyed a vast carbonate platform that had built up along the coast, pushed up a chain of mountains, and added a microcontinent, what geologists refer to as an exotic terrane, to the continental margin. The second and third orogenies, known as the Acadian and Alleghenian respectively, occurred when North America collided with Baltica (the forerunner of Europe) and when North America collided with the supercontinent Gondwanaland. By 65 million years ago, however, erosion had leveled the mountains created by these collisions. The three gentle intervals of uplift and erosion that have occurred since then created today's rolling Appalachian topography.

The core of the system, what many nonspecialists call the Appalachian Mountains, is a subprovince known as the Valley and Ridge. It is actually the fold and thrust belt on the western margin of the much larger Appalachian system, a zone where large sheets of sedimentary rock were thrust inland and stacked, shinglelike. Another subprovince, the Piedmont, lies to the east and south. Its rock is metamorphosed and intensely crumpled. Between these two areas lies the narrow Blue Ridge, comprised of igneous rocks of the Precambrian basement. The Blue Ridge sports the highest mountains of the Appalachian system.

Central Lowlands

The Central Lowlands Province, which spans over 300,000 square miles and surrounds the Canadian Shield on three sides, is bordered by the Appalachians to the east and the Great Plains to the west. Most of it is low in elevation and has only minor relief. Elevations range from under 500 feet along the Mississippi to just under 2,000 feet at the escarpment in the west that marks the edge of the Great Plains.

The bedrock, hidden by a thin veneer of sediments, is Precambrian granite and gneiss, again part of the basement complex, but younger than the bedrock of the Shield. Warped gently into basins and ridges, it dips gradually to the south; water wells drilled in Iowa often hit bedrock, while much deeper oil wells drilled on the province's southern end never do.

The overlying sedimentary strata, mostly limestone, sandstone, and shale, are generally flat and have been disturbed little since they accumulated in the shallow seas that have repeatedly inundated the Central Lowlands. However, glaciers have done a good deal of reshaping of surface features. Major portions of the province are subdivided according to the age of the glacial drift that covers them.

Great Plains

The geologic structure of the Great Plains Province is similar to that of the Central Lowlands. Although the Great Plains are higher in elevation (elevations range from 1,600 to 4,900 feet above sea level), they, too, exhibit little relief. Their higher elevation is due mostly to the great sheets of sediment that eroded from the Rocky Mountains and accumulated over the ages. The Great Plains have also undergone some tectonic uplifting and tilting.

The Great Plains Province was arid during the Pleistocene—too arid for plants to form much of a protective cover. Winds worked surface sands into massive dunes with a northwest to southeast alignment. Those dunes designed drainage patterns. In some areas, the patterns remain.

Consisting of an elliptical dome of Precambrian basement rock and younger limestone, the Black Hills of South Dakota were uplifted during the Laramide Orogeny, a major mountain-building episode that started roughly 85 million years ago.

Rocky Mountains

The Rocky Mountain Province extends from just north of Alberta to near Santa Fe, New Mexico, and includes over one hundred mountain ranges. This massive belt of mountains varies in width from less than 60 miles in Canada to over 350 miles in the central U.S. Its highest peaks, which are over 14,400 feet above sea level, occur in Colorado. The Rockies also contain a number of large basins and fault-bounded troughs. An example is the Rocky Mountain Trench, a lowland that stretches along the western margin of the Canadian Rockies from the Yukon to Montana.

The geologic history of the region varies considerably from area to area and has produced a tremendous variety of rocks and structures. Despite the diversity, however, most if not all of the Rocky Mountain region was affected by the Laramide Orogeny between 85 and 35 million years ago. The Laramide was followed by major faulting and uplift that shaped much of the relief seen today.

The Rocky Mountain Province is usually divided into four subprovinces: Canadian, Northern, Middle, and Southern. Much of the Canadian and Northern Rockies formed on the western edge of an area that received huge amounts of sediment from the continent over a period of about 1 billion years. Later, compression caused by island arcs colliding with North America thrust huge slabs of this sedimentary rock eastward to create a series of steep, angular, parallel mountain ranges separated by long, narrow valleys. Ranges in the southern reaches of the Northern Rockies were formed by block faulting, when large blocks of rock moved up or down.

The Middle and Southern Rockies received less sediment early on than their northern counterparts because they were part of a stable platform. The mountains in these two subprovinces formed primarily as a result of uplift (although the Wasatch and Wyoming ranges formed by folding and thrust faulting). Individual ranges are separated by broad basins. Later, volcanic activity played a part in creating and shaping some of the ranges of this zone (such as the San Juans and Absarokas).

Many areas of the Rockies were sculpted to their present shape by the glaciers of the Pleistocene.

Interior Mountains and Plateaus

The Interior Mountains and Plateaus Province stretches from Alaska to California. Like the Rocky Mountains Province, it consists of a long belt of rugged mountains and high plateau topography and, similarly, is both high and diverse. The highest part of the province is the Sierra Nevada range. There, peaks rise to over 12,000 feet above sea level. Elevations are generally lower in Canada and Alaska.

The Alaskan portion of this province is composed of a complex collage of exotic terranes—marine sediments and volcanic island arcs that became attached to the continent. Massive intrusions of granite and metamorphic rocks comprise the Pelly, Omineca, Cassiar, and Columbia ranges in Canada. While those rocks formed, microcontinents collided with the continent just to the west. Millions of years later, large volumes of basalts erupted and flowed across vast areas of these exotic terranes in the Interior Plateau.

The subduction of the Pacific Plate under the western margin of North America created the prominent volcanic peaks of the Cascade Range. Volcanoes have been erupting here for at least 30 million years, although the volcanoes we see today have formed only within the last 2 million years or so. The Sierra Nevada Range just to the south of the Cascades is a massive fault block of granite uplifted to its present height of over 14,000 feet during the last 5 million years. It, too, has experienced several episodes of volcanism, especially on the northern end.

Columbia and Snake River Plateaus

The Columbia Plateau is misnamed; when considered in the context of the surrounding highlands, it is clearly not a plateau but a plain. The plain is roughly saucer shaped. Its lowest point at Pasco, Washington, is near sea level, whereas its rim varies from 2,000 to 6,000 feet above sea level. In the northeast, in an area known as the Channeled Scablands, broad channels cut by catastrophic flooding during the last ice age scar the plain. The southwest and southern reaches of the Columbian Plateau border the Basin and Range Province and are folded into valleys and ridges with as much as 5,900 feet of relief.

A huge volume of basaltic lava provides the unique underlay for the 141,000-square-mile Columbia Plateau. From 17.5 to 14.5 million years ago, great floods of lava erupted from vents in southeastern Washington and poured north and west across the province. Smaller but still significant flows continued for the next 7.5 million years. Ultimately, the layer of lava covering the plain reached a depth of 2.5 miles. This massive accumulation warped the underlying crust and, along with the collapsing of emptied lava chambers and a thinning or extension of the continental crust in the region, gave the plain its saucer shape. The basalt field has changed the drainage patterns of the region. The Columbia and Spokane Rivers, for example, have been forced around its northern edge.

A smaller and thinner basalt plain called the Snake River Plateau lies to the southeast of the Columbia Plateau. Lava has been erupting in this region for the past 5 million years. The North American Plate has moved so that the hot spot that created the field is now beneath Yellowstone National Park. The Snake River cuts directly through the lavas of this plain.

Basin and Range

The Basin and Range Province, a large region that extends from southern Idaho and Oregon to northern Mexico, is named for its relatively evenly spaced north-south mountain ranges and intervening valleys.

The province encompasses more than four hundred individually named mountain ranges. In Nevada, some peaks are over 11,400 feet in elevation, while the basins are generally at 5,000 to 6,000 feet. Most of the mountains are steep and deeply dissected. The basins contain sediment eroded from bordering ranges that is as much as 2 miles deep.

This relatively unique landscape has been formed by extensional faulting. Shearing along the San Andreas Fault in California has pulled and stretched the earth's crust as far inland as Utah and New Mexico. The earth's crust here is about half as thick as it is in the neighboring Colorado Plateau. The stretching or extension has produced numerous steep or high-angle faults to create each range and basin formation. Blocks of rock have slipped vertically along these faults. Some have volcanic activity associated with them.

Extension started in the province as much as 35 million years ago, but most of the topography we see today was created within the last 17 million years. The process, which could be described as broadly distributed rifting, continues today. It is estimated that extension has stretched the crust of the province by 65 to 100 percent.

One of the most prominent features in the Basin and Range Province is the arid Great Basin, which is not really a basin at all but a large bulge that sits above the surrounding terrain on three of its sides. The Great Basin is mostly internally drained; that is, because of evaporation or seepage, streams die out before they leave the basin. Part of the reason for the province's aridity is that it sits in the rain shadow of the Sierra Nevadas. South of the Great Basin, the province includes the Mojave and Sonoran Deserts.

Colorado Plateau

The Colorado Plateau is a large oval-shaped area of over 15,000 square miles that overlaps portions of Colorado, Utah, New Mexico, and Arizona. In general, the province stands about 1 mile above sea level, although it contains many plateaus of different elevations and a variety of terrains. The north-central Canyonlands section is dominated by gently folded sedimentary rocks; the western High Plateaus by thick accumulations of volcanic materials; the northern Uinta Basin and the south Grand Canyon sections by mountains and high cliffs; and the south-central Navajo section by isolated buttes, mesas, mountains, and volcanic structures.

A broad regional uplift that also affected both the Rocky Mountain and the Basin and Range Province elevated the Colorado Plateau about 10 to 8 million years ago. After a lull, another pulse of uplifting occurred 2 or 3 million years ago. The uplifts occurred when the earth's surface bobbed upward after erosion removed earlier mountain ranges.

The most famous feature of the Colorado Plateau Province is the Grand Canyon. The Colorado River (or its predecessor) was in place before uplifting started. As the land rose, the river cut through it, carving the steep-walled canyon. Most of the sculpting occurred during the last episode of uplift 2 to 3 million years ago.

Pacific Rim and Coast Ranges

The Pacific Rim and Coast Ranges Province stretches along the edge of the continent from southern Alaska to the U.S.–Mexico border. Elevations range from sea level to over 20,000 feet. Denali, the continent's highest peak, is in this province.

The interaction of the Pacific, Juan de Fuca, and Explorer Plates with the North American Plate accounts for almost all of the geology in this province. The portion of the province that lies in Alaska and British Columbia, for example, is mostly made up of exotic terranes that collected as the North American Plate moved west. Some of these terranes traveled well over 5,000 miles before welding to North America.

The biggest part of the province extends from the westernmost Aleutian Island to the Queen Charlotte Islands in British Columbia. It was shaped by the collision of the Pacific and North American Plates as well as by glaciation. One of the most seismically active areas in the world, the region also has many volcanoes. The Aleutian archipelago is a series of seventy-eight volcanoes formed by the subducting Pacific Plate; of these, sixty-six have been active in recent geologic times. The higher and more heavily glaciated Alaska Range to the north and east is considered part of the same system. To the south lies a lowland bordered by a parallel system of coast ranges—the Kodiak, Kenai, Chugach, St. Elias, and Fairweather. These mountains harbor the most extensive system of glaciers on the continent.

Coastal British Columbia also has high, rugged mountains with many glaciers, and it, too, is a mosaic of exotic terranes. Much of the area has been affected by the subduction zone to the west of Vancouver Island. Here, the Juan de Fuca and Explorer Plates slide under the North American Plate. Farther south, other mountain ranges, each with a different history, exhibit somewhat different structures: in Washington and Oregon the Olympics, the Coast Ranges, and the Klamath Mountains; in California the Coast Ranges, Transverse Ranges, and Peninsular Ranges.

In California, the single most important geological structure is the San Andreas Fault. Extending for 1,000 miles through western California, it and many associated faults remain active. The total movement along the San Andreas Fault over the last 5 million years has been more than 60 miles. Different segments of the fault may have moved at different rates.

Sierra Madre Occidental

The 120,000-square-mile Sierra Madre Occidental Province borders the Basin and Range Province and stretches for almost 950 miles along the west coast of Mexico. This province is characterized by a high plateau of volcanic rocks with a series of northwest to southeast depressions. The province is also dissected by steep, river-carved canyons. Its average elevation is 6,500 feet above sea level, although the highest peaks are over 11,000 feet.

The province has been shaped in part by the subduction of two small plates, the Rivera and Cocos, beneath the North American Plate. Volcanic activity started in the region about 25 million years ago and continued until about 5 million years ago. During that time, over 6,500 feet of volcanic rock accumulated—rock that now covers the Sierra Madre Occidental.

Impact Craters

Until recently, most people considered impact craters of minor importance in understanding geology. But geologists now believe that "impact" helped shape the early earth. The evidence comes from other planets and our own moon. The oldest surfaces on the moon are covered with impact craters dating back 4.6 to 3.9 million years, a time when both the moon and the earth were pelted with meteors at a rate 100 to 1,000 times greater than today. For the new earth, that many impacts had spectacular consequences.

The most widely accepted hypothesis for the origin of the moon, for example, is that a Mars-sized object hit the proto-earth; it vaporized and ejected immense clouds of material into orbit, clouds that eventually condensed to form the moon. Early impacts likely had consequences for the earth's atmosphere. Some geologists theorize that the heat generated by thousands of impacts released gases from the mantle and shaped the primordial atmosphere and hydrosphere. An unrelenting bombardment would have prevented the development and early evolution of life, because the largest impacts would have sterilized the planet.

Even after life gained a foothold and blossomed, the impacts brought major changes. A large object striking the earth probably resulted in the extinction of the dinosaurs. Many geologists now believe that unusual sediments at the level of the Cretaceous-Tertiary boundary in geologic strata, the point at which dinosaurs and

many other species vanished, came from a meteorite or perhaps an earth-comet collision. These K-T boundary sediments, as they are designated, are recognizable around the globe because they contain an abnormally high concentration of iridium (thirty times higher than sediments above or below). Iridium is extremely rare on earth but abundant in meteorites. The layer also contains particles called "shocked grains" that have been deformed by an explosive impact and are typically found only at impact sites.

How did these particles get distributed globally? Large impact events have the capacity to blow a hole in the atmosphere through which materials are ejected in an immense fireball. Carried above the atmosphere, the materials quickly encircle the globe and eventually fall back to the earth's surface. The actual impact site is thought to be a 65-million-year-old, 112-mile-diameter crater in the Yucatan called the Chicxulub Crater. Scientists estimate that the meteorite that made it was larger than the depth of the earth's atmosphere.

When a large object, say 6 miles in diameter or greater, hits the earth, the results are deadly. The impact ejects enough material into the atmosphere to shade the sun for several months or longer. During such an event, temperatures drop and deep snow accumulates, even at the equator. Dust circles the globe for years, perhaps decades. It reflects radiation and light back into space and keeps the earth cold. Such an explosion converts nitrogen in the atmosphere into acidic compounds that fall as acid snow and rain, a form of precipitation lethal to many organisms. Ultimately, the acid triggers change by dissolving carbonate rocks and releasing carbon dioxide into the atmosphere. The carbon dioxide reverses the cooling trend by way of the greenhouse effect.

Need humans worry about another K-T event? Estimates based on the earth's cratering rate, constant for the past 3 billion years, suggest such events happen only about every 50 to 100 million years, al-though smaller, more frequent impacts could also affect the earth's climate and biosphere. Every 2 or 3 million years, for example, a meteorite large enough to make a 12-mile-diameter crater hits the earth. An impact of that magnitude could create a situation analogous to a nuclear winter but probably would not cause mass extinctions. The last event of that size occurred only a million years ago. Even smaller impacting bodies, leaving craters 6 miles in diameter, would change the atmosphere. Models predict that the impact would vaporize enough

Impact structures in North America

material to cause a fivefold increase in the amount of sulfur in the stratosphere. Slightly larger events would probably lead to climate shifts and might destroy the ozone layer.

Meteorite impacts are more difficult to predict than other natural disasters. Consider that in March of 1989 an asteroid about a third of a mile in diameter passed within 435,000 miles of the earth. No one saw it until it had passed. Had it struck the earth, it would have left a crater 6 miles in diameter. Although 435,000 miles sounds like a great distance, a calculation of orbital velocities shows that the asteroid missed the earth by only hours. At least 1,000 extraterrestrial bodies larger than 0.6 mile in diameter periodically cross the earth's orbit.

Impact Structures

An object must weigh 350 tons or more to form an impact crater; smaller objects break up as they enter the atmosphere. The form an impact crater takes depends on the size of the object. This size-form relation is apparent in fresh craters on the moon. The smallest ones are bowl-shaped. As the diameter increases, slumping of the inner walls and rebounding of the depressed floor push out larger terraces on the crater's rim and make peaks in the center. The largest craters show one or more peak rings (called impact basins). This same effect is observed on planets throughout the solar system.

Meteorite fragments are found only in the smallest craters, which are usually quickly destroyed by erosion. Craters larger than about half a mile across lack meteorite fragments; the pressures and temperatures produced on impact melt and vaporize the meteorite and some of the rocks it hits. These craters do share characteristic types of rock and mineral deformations. The unique traits are generated by the high pressures and temperatures associated with impacts—geologists term the process "shock metamorphism."

IMPACT CRATERS IN NORTH AMERICA

Name	Location	Age (in millions of years)	Diameter (in miles)
Ames	Oklahoma, U.S.	470 ± 30	16
Avak	Alaska, U.S.	>95	12
Barringer	Arizona, U.S.	0.049 ± 0.003	1.2
Beaverhead	Montana, U.S.	600	60
Brent	Ontario, Can.	450 ± 30	3.8
Carswell	Saskatchewan, Can.	115 ± 10	39
Charlevoix	Quebec, Can.	357 ± 15	54

IMPACT CRATERS IN NORTH AMERICA (CONT.)

Name	Location	Age (in millions of years)	Diameter (in miles)
Chesapeake Bay	Virginia, U.S.	35.5 ± 0.6	85
Chicxulub	Yucatan, Mex.	64.98 ± 0.05	170
Clearwater East	Quebec, Can.	290 ± 20	26
Clearwater West	Quebec, Can.	290 ± 20	36
Couture	Quebec, Can.	430 ± 25	8
Crooked Creek	Missouri, U.S.	320 ± 80	7
Decaturville	Missouri, U.S.	<300	6
Deep Bay	Saskatchewan, Can.	100	50
Des Plaines	Illinois, U.S.	<280	8
Eagle Butte	Alberta, Can.	<65	10
Flynn Creek	Tennessee, U.S.	360 ± 20	3.5
Glasford	Illinois, U.S.	<430	4
Glover Bluff	Wisconsin, U.S.	<500	8
Gow	Saskatchewan, Can.	<250	5
Haughton	NW Territories, Can.	23 ± 1	24
Haviland	Kansas, U.S.	<0.001	0.02
Holleford	Ontario, Can.	550 ± 100	2.3
Ile Rouleau	Quebec, Can.	<300	4
Kentland	Indiana, U.S.	<97	13
La Moinerie	Quebec, Can.	400	50
Manicouagan	Quebec, Can.	214 ± 1	100
Manson	Iowa, U.S.	73.8 ± 0.3	35
Marquez	Texas, U.S.	58 ± 2	13
Middlesboro	Kentucky, U.S.	<300	6
Mistastin	Newfoun./Lab., Can.	38 ± 4	28
Montagnais	Nova Scotia, Can.	50.50 ± 0.76	45
New Quebec	Quebec, Can.	1.4 ± 0.1	3.4
Newporte	North Dakota, U.S.	<500	3
Nicholson	NW Territories, Can.	<400	12.5
Odessa	Texas, U.S.	<0.05	0.2

IMPACT CRATERS IN NORTH AMERICA (CONT.)

Name	Location	Age (in millions of years)	Diameter (in miles)
Presqu' Ile	Quebec, Can.	<500	24
Red Wing	North Dakota, U.S.	200 ± 25	9
Saint Martin	Manitoba, Can.	220 ± 32	40
Serpent Mound	Ohio, U.S.	<320	8
Sierra Madera	Texas, U.S.	<100	13
Slate Islands	Ontario, Can.	<350	30
Steen River	Alberta, Can.	95 ± 7	25
Sudbury	Ontario, Can.	1850 ± 3	250
Upheaval Dome	Utah, U.S.	<65	10
Wanapitei	Ontario, Can.	37 ± 2	7.5
Wells Creek	Tennessee, U.S.	200 ± 100	12
West Hawk	Manitoba, Can.	100 ± 50	2.4

A Falling Star

It's rare to find a meteorite, and it's even rarer to find a freshly fallen meteorite—one that hit the earth just moments earlier. But farmers Stéphane and Serge Forcier of St. Robert de Sorel, Quebec, happened to be home at the right time, just as a meteor exploded 6 to 12 miles above the earth's surface and sent a shower of fragments across southern Quebec.

People who witnessed the June 14, 1994 event in Ontario and the northern U.S. saw a fireball shooting across the sky accompanied by a sonic boom. The Forcier brothers, hearing "something tumbling through the air and hitting the ground," hurried outside and found their cows staring at a 6-inch hole in the ground. From that hole, the brothers dug out a cold, black stone the size of softball. It weighed 5 pounds.

The next day, geologists confirmed the stone was a meteorite from what has come to be known as the St. Robert Meteor Shower. The shower was the first on record in eastern Canada. The geologists took the piece to a lab where they began monitoring short-lived changes in the meteorite's chemistry to estimate the length of time it was in orbit and the age, size, and origin of the parent body.

Scientists are interested in meteorites because most date from the origin of the earth (4.6 billion years ago) and provide information about the origin of our solar system and the nature of the earth when it was young. Although most are thought to be fragments of asteroids, some are pieces of the moon or Mars or extinct comets. Whatever their origin, they provide valuable clues to the makeup of the universe.

PLATE
TECTONICS

SEVEN MAJOR LITHOSPHERIC PLATES AND a number of small ones encase the earth. Each one is about 50 miles thick. The plates move continuously relative to one another at rates varying from 0.3 to 5 inches per year. The pattern of movement is neither symmetrical nor simple: the plates fit tightly together, like the pieces of a puzzle, so that the movement of one affects the movements of others.

Moving plates are the agents of most geological change on the earth. Mountain building, rifting, volcanic eruptions, earthquakes, faulting—all are due to different types of interactions at plate boundaries. Geologists use earthquakes and volcanoes to map plate boundaries and to track plate movements.

The North American Plate carries North America, half of the North Atlantic Ocean, and a portion of eastern Siberia. On its eastern margin, it abuts the Eurasian and African Plates along the Mid-Atlantic Ridge, a deep-ocean ridge that runs north-south through the center of the Atlantic Ocean. Here, new molten rock constantly wells up from the mantle. Upon reaching the surface, the rock cools and

slides away from the ridge axis, adding itself to the plates. The addition of this new rock causes the continents riding on the plates to spread apart. Thus, North America is moving away from Europe and Africa at a rate of about an inch a year.

On its west side, the North American Plate bumps up against the Pacific Plate. Where they meet off the coast of northern Mexico, the two plates move away from each other along a spreading center much like the Mid-Atlantic Ridge. Farther north, off the coast of California, the Pacific Plate is sliding past the North American Plate, scraping against it as it moves northwest at a rate of about 2 inches a year. In California, everything west of the San Andreas Fault system is actually part of the Pacific Plate and is moving northwest with respect to the rest of North America. Movement along this boundary has had profound effects on the geography of the western U.S. It is, in essence, pulling the crust apart as far inland as Utah and creating the vast area known as the Basin and Range Province, a region replete with the equivalent of stretch marks—numerous north-south ridges and valleys. Continental crust in the Basin and

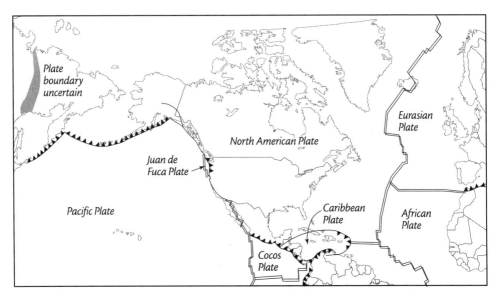

The North American and surrounding lithospheric plates. Black triangles represent subduction zones.

Range is as thin as it gets anywhere on earth and is still thinning.

These same two plates, the Pacific and the North American, meet in a very different way off the coasts of Alaska and eastern Siberia. Here, the Pacific Plate collides head-on with the North American Plate, and because oceanic crust is heavier than continental crust, the Pacific Plate slides beneath Alaska and Siberia where it is pulled into the mantle. This process, called subduction, generates both strong earthquakes and large volcanoes. The earthquakes are caused when fractures form in the still brittle plate as it descends into the mantle. Volcanoes occur when the plate sinks into the asthenosphere, where higher temperature and pressure cause water and minerals in the crust to flow into the mantle. Water lowers the melting temperature of the mantle and causes some of it to melt. Any molten rock less dense than the asthenosphere rises and can burst through the crust as a volcano. The Aleutian Islands are all volcanoes, their magma generated by the sinking of oceanic crust and the subsequent melting of mantle material.

Two other subduction zones are active along the west coast of North America. The Juan de Fuca Plate is subducting beneath British Columbia, Washington, and Oregon at a rate of about 0.6 inch a year. As a result, volcanoes like Mounts Rainier, Hood, and St. Helens occur in the Cascade Range. Farther south, the Cocos Plate subducts beneath Mexico and Central America at a relatively rapid rate, causing major earthquakes and big volcanoes.

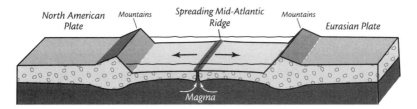

On its eastern margin, the North American Plate abuts the Eurasian and African Plates along the Mid-Atlantic Ridge.

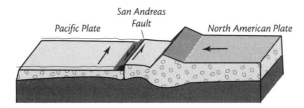

On its west side, the North American Plate bumps up against the Pacific Plate.

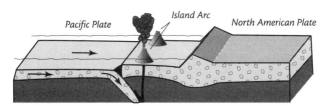

Off the coasts of Alaska and eastern Siberia, the Pacific Plate collides head-on with the North American Plate.

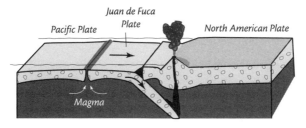

The Juan de Fuca Plate is subducting beneath British Columbia, Washington, and Oregon.

A Brief History of the Appalachians

Collision and uplift

The Appalachian Chain is an old mountain system. Its internal structures formed during the Paleozoic era, a 330-million-year geologic interval that ended a quarter of a billion years ago. Early in that era, North America was part of a larger landmass called Laurentia. Africa, South America, and several other continents formed a single, giant landmass to the southeast called Gondwanaland. The predecessor of the Atlantic, a sea called the Iapetus Ocean, widened and forced Laurentia away from Gondwanaland and northern Europe. As the continents moved apart, a large carbonate platform built up along what is now the eastern margin of North America.

Then, a change in plate movement forced the Iapetus Ocean to reverse its motion and close. The ocean floor subducted beneath the plates carrying Europe and Gondwanaland, and those continents moved toward Laurentia. As the plates moved forward, they scraped sediments off the ocean floor and accumulated them, along with whatever islands may have been in their path, into wedges which they shoved toward Laurentia.

Northern Europe and the African portion of Gondwanaland eventually collided with the leading edge of Laurentia, and the great wedges of sediment rode up and over the continent's margin. The weight depressed the crust of Laurentia and formed basins and troughs which themselves became filled with sediment as the highlands eroded. The force of the collision, which lasted tens of millions of years, thrusted and folded and heaved rock and sediment into enormous mountains.

Then, once again, the plates reversed direction. South America was left behind, and Europe and Africa moved away from North America. The dance continues today, with the Atlantic filling in in the continents' wake. Both Britain and Northern Europe took remnants of the Appalachians with them, however, and geologists easily identify those pieces today.

On North America, the once great mountains created by those collisions have long since eroded away. The Appalachians we see today—the Great Smokies, the Blue Ridge Mountains, the Valley and Ridge Province, the Hudson Highlands, and most of Newfoundland—are the product not of those earlier, epic collisions, but rather of gentle uplifting and erosion that has occurred more recently—within the past 70 million years or so. But the internal structures of these easternmost mountains, the parts buried and hidden, originated long ago when Europe and Africa rammed North America.

Dance of the Continents

As a consequence of plate tectonics, the world's geography has changed dramatically over the past 2.5 billion years. Continents have migrated around the globe; oceans have opened and closed; entire mountain ranges as big as the Himalayas have risen and eroded away. In an attempt to document these transformations of the earth's crust, geologists have proposed a number of different plate reconstructions, based mostly on magnetic and fossil data preserved in the rock formations of continents. Although some debate still lingers about the positions of certain continents at specific times, most agree on the overall changes during the last 250 million years. Geologists still disagree, however, on where continents moved prior to this period. The reconstructions shown here represent one of the more current theories of how North America has moved relative to the other continents over the past 750 million years.

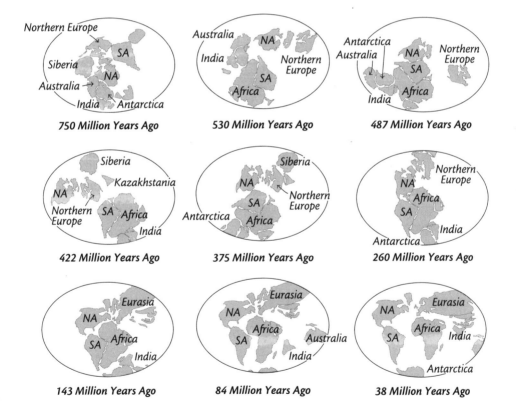

750 Million Years Ago
530 Million Years Ago
487 Million Years Ago
422 Million Years Ago
375 Million Years Ago
260 Million Years Ago
143 Million Years Ago
84 Million Years Ago
38 Million Years Ago

Significant Moments in the History of Life on Earth

Plate tectonic specialists aren't the only ones interested in paleogeography. Many paleontologists believe significant moments in the history of life on earth may have been triggered by the coming together and rifting apart of continents.

They theorize, for example, that fundamental changes in the climate and atmosphere occurred when all the continents converged to create a single supercontinent at the close of the Precambrian, some 500 to 700 million years ago. The creation of this giant landmass would have affected the patterns of atmospheric and ocean circulation, and might have triggered several global ice ages, including the most extensive one known.

The ice ages, in turn, changed sea levels and had a major effect on life on earth. The fossil record indicates that the assembly of the supercontinent coincides with a dramatic increase in photosynthesizing organisms in the oceans and the appearance of the first complex, multicellular creatures.

The movement of plates has continued to influence evolution in important ways—by periodically isolating continents like Australia, for example, or through the formation of land bridges, such as the one that once existed between North America and Asia. Recent research suggests a link between rapid spreading of the sea floor and the diversification of flowering plants during the early and middle Cretaceous.

The Migration of North America

Slip-sliding away

As the saying goes, nothing in the world lasts, save eternal change. North America is moving away from Europe and Africa at a rate of about an inch a year. Tracking the movement over the past 180 million years, we see that the continent once straddled the equator. It first drifted northwest. About 60 million years ago, its trajectory changed to the west-southwest, bringing it to its present position. North America continues on that same path today.

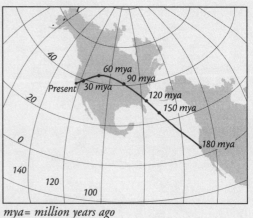

mya= million years ago

Exotic Terranes in North America

As lithospheric plates glide over the earth's surface, islands and microcontinents riding on ocean plates occasionally collide with continents. The islands and microcontinents, composed of relatively light rock, are not subducted beneath the continent, but thrust against or pushed on top of it. These new additions to the continent are called exotic terranes (or, sometimes, suspect or displaced terranes). Over hundreds of millions of years, North America has encountered and added many of them. Geologists have identified over two hundred along the western margin of the continent alone, for example. A much smaller number exist on the east side, in the Appalachian region. These foreign fragments are usually readily identified by geologists because they show evidence of abrupt contacts with their surroundings and contain unique rock types and fossils. Among the most common rocks that make up exotic terranes are volcanic materials, ocean sediments, and ocean crust.

Exotic terranes complicate the study of geology in the west enormously. The overview is relatively simple, however. Most of the terranes attached themselves during the Mesozoic Era, the period from 245 to 65 million years ago, when a series of lithospheric plates collided with and subducted beneath the continent.

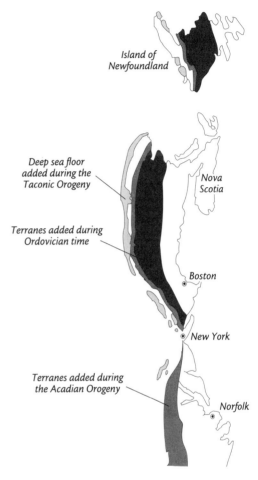

Exotic terranes of eastern North America

Exotic Terranes of the West

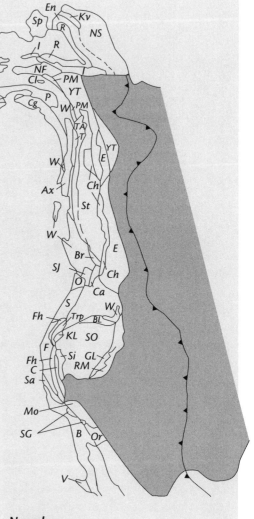

Alaska

Ax	Alexander
Cg	Chugach and Prince William
Cl	Chuitna
En	Endicott
G	Goodnews
I	Innoko
Kv	Kagvick
NF	Nixon Fork
NS	North Slope
P	Peninsular
PM	Pingston and McKinley
R	Ruby
Sp	Seaward Peninsula
T	Taku
TA	Tracy Arm
W	Wrangellia
YT	Yukon-Tanana

Canada

Ch	Cache Creek
St	Stikine
BR	Bridge River
E	Eastern Assemblages

Washington, Oregon, and California

Ca	Northern Cascades
SJ	San Juan
O	Olympic
S	Siletzia
BL	Blue Mountains
Trp	Western Triassic and Paleozoic of the Klamath Mountains
KL	Klamath Mountains
Fh	Foothills Belt
F	Franciscan and Great Valley
C	Calaveras
Si	Northern Sierra
SG	San Gabriel
Mo	Mohave
Sa	Salina
Or	Orocopia

Nevada

SO	Sonomia
RM	Roberts Mountains
GL	Golconda

Mexico

B	Baja
V	Vizcaino

EARTHQUAKES AND RIFTS

MOST, BUT NOT ALL, EARTHQUAKE ACTIVity is associated with tectonic plate boundaries. Along the ocean ridges, earthquake activity occurs at shallow depths within the lithosphere as the oceanic plates are rifted apart. Because the lithosphere is thin and weak in these zones, the stress is not prolonged enough to cause large quakes. Shallow and generally small earthquakes also occur along the faults that join segments of a spreading ridge. When these faults pass through continental lithosphere, as in the case of the San Andreas Fault, the friction is so great that enormous strains build up, strains that are released in the form of large earthquakes. The shaking usually occurs along only a part of the fault, though, during any single quake. During the 1906 San Francisco quake, only the northern end of the San Andreas Fault ruptured.

Where oceanic and continental plates collide, the oceanic plate subducts beneath the continental. Along the coasts of Washington and Oregon, for example, the Juan

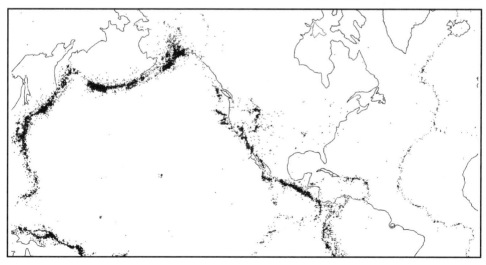

Centers of earthquake activity on and around the North American Plate over a ten-year period

de Fuca Plate is being pushed beneath the North American Plate. Earthquakes in these zones can happen at any depth down to 350 to 450 miles. The largest earthquakes occur at subduction zones.

Some earthquakes are centered far from plate boundaries. These may be related to volcanic activity, as in Hawaii, but more commonly they simply reflect the adjustment of a plate to the forces of plate tectonics, usually along existing faults or ancient rifts. The New Madrid earthquakes that shook the center of North America during the nineteenth century occurred along an ancient rift, a zone of weakness in the plate.

Measuring Earthquakes

Richter and Moment-Magnitude

The Richter Scale was developed in 1935 as a way to measure the relative size of earthquakes. It estimates magnitude by measuring the amplitude of seismic or ground waves recorded on a seismograph. Because amplitude decreases with distance from the epicenter, the scale is adjusted to a standard distance from the location of the quake. It expresses magnitude in whole numbers and decimal fractions. A magnitude 5.3, for instance, might be computed for a moderate earthquake, while a strong quake might be rated at 6.3. The basis of the scale is logarithmic; each whole number increase in magnitude represents a tenfold increase in amplitude. Each whole number step in the scale corresponds to an increase of about thirty-one times the energy released by the earthquake.

Earthquakes with magnitudes of about 2 or less on the Richter Scale are usually called microearthquakes—too weak to be felt by people and are generally recorded only on local seismographs. Events of about 4.5 or greater—there are several thousand of these annually—are strong enough to be recorded by sensitive seismographs all over the world. Great earthquakes, such as the 1964 Good Friday earthquake in Alaska, register magnitudes of 8 or higher.

Although the Richter Scale is familiar to many North Americans, most seismologists no longer use it. They have instead adopted the Moment-Magnitude Scale, which was devised as a more precise measure of great earthquakes. Moment-magnitude is a number proportional to the slip on the fault times the area of the fault surface that slips. It is a better measure of the total energy released by a quake. The moment can be estimated

EARTHQUAKE MAGNITUDE

Magnitude	Description
3–3.9	Minor
4–4.9	Light
5–5.9	Moderate
6–6.9	Strong
7–7.9	Major
8 or more	Great

from seismograms and is then converted into a number similar to other earthquake magnitudes by a standard formula. One advantage of this scale is that it provides an estimate of earthquake size valid for even great earthquakes.

Modified Mercalli Intensity

Magnitude scales like Richter and Moment-Magnitude are not used to describe the damage caused by earthquakes. An earthquake in a densely populated area, for example, which results in many deaths and

MODIFIED MERCALLI EARTHQUAKE INTENSITY

Level	Description
I	Not felt, except by a very few under especially favorable conditions.
II	Felt only by a few persons at rest, especially on upper floors of buildings.
III	Felt quite noticeably by persons indoors, especially on upper floors of buildings. Many people do not recognize it as an earthquake. Standing motor cars may rock slightly. Vibrations are similar to the passing of a truck.
IV	Felt indoors by many, outdoors by few during the day. At night, some awakened. Dishes, windows, doors disturbed; walls make cracking sounds. After, many report the quake felt like a heavy truck had struck a building. Standing motor cars rocked noticeably.
V	Felt by nearly everyone; many awakened. Some dishes, windows broken. Unstable objects overturned. Pendulum clocks may stop.
VI	Felt by all, many frightened. Some heavy furniture moved; a few instances of fallen plaster. Damage slight.
VII	Damage negligible in buildings of good design and construction; slight to moderate damage in well-built ordinary structures; considerable damage in poorly built or badly designed structures; some chimneys broken.
VIII	Damage slight in specially designed structures; considerable damage in ordinary substantial buildings, with partial collapse. Damage great in poorly built structures. Fall of chimneys, factory stacks, columns, monuments, walls. Heavy furniture overturned.
IX	Damage considerable in specially designed structures; well-designed frame structures thrown out of plumb. Damage great in substantial buildings, with partial collapse. Buildings shifted off foundations.
X	Some well-built wooden structures destroyed; most masonry and frame structures with foundations destroyed. Rails bent.
XI	Few if any masonry structures remain standing. Bridges destroyed. Rails bent greatly.
XII	Damage total. Lines of sight and level are distorted. Objects thrown into the air.

a good deal of damage may have the same magnitude as a shock in a remote area that does no damage. Hence, seismologists have developed other scales, called intensity scales, to measure how much damage an earthquake does at a specific location.

An intensity scale consists of a series of effects—the awakening of people, the movement of furniture, damage to chimneys, and so on. Many intensity scales have been developed over the last several hundred years, but the one currently used in the U.S. is the Modified Mercalli (MM) Intensity Scale. Composed of twelve increasing levels of intensity that range from imperceptible shaking to catastrophic destruction, the scale uses Roman numerals to represent an arbitrary ranking based on observed effects. The lower numbers of the scale generally relate to the manner in which the earthquake is felt by people, while the

higher numbers relate to observed structural damage. After a widely felt earthquake, seismologists mail questionnaires requesting information on the intensity of the quake to postmasters in the disturbed area. They assign an intensity value based on the results of this canvass and information furnished by other sources.

Major Quakes

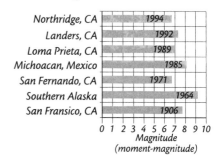

Magnitude
(moment-magnitude)

A Juan de Fuca Shake-up

When it comes to West Coast earthquakes, most people think of California, but researchers recently discovered evidence that the Juan de Fuca Plate, the small lithospheric plate that is colliding with and diving beneath the coast of British Columbia, Washington, and Oregon, may be snagged and storing up energy—the same kind of deep, earth-rattling energy that produced the catastrophic 1964 Alaska earthquake. They warn that Vancouver, Seattle, Tacoma, and Portland—cities not built to withstand strong earthquakes—may experience one of the most devastating quakes of the century.

Scientists have known for a long time that the Juan de Fuca Plate is subducting beneath the North American Plate. The boundary between the two plates is now recognized as the largest active fault in North America outside Alaska. Until recently, geologists assumed that, in the absence of any big earthquakes since Europeans arrived some 200 years ago, the subduction zone was benign—or, of a type that doesn't generate large earthquakes. Most believed the Cascadia subduction zone—the 620-mile-long boundary between the Juan de Fuca and North American Plates—was slipping smoothly, in a manner similar to the subduction zone that lies between the Philippine and Pacific Plates in the western Pacific, where there is no history of big earthquakes.

But a few years ago, researchers found evidence that at least six giant earthquakes have occurred in the Pacific Northwest within the last several thousand years. The evidence—buried trees and estuaries, tsunami-deposited sediments, and Native American stories of a village vanishing at the head of Pachena Bay on the west coast of Vancouver Island—suggests that periodically massive earthquakes have caused portions of the coast to suddenly drop or rise by as much as 5 feet. Using carbon-14 dating techniques, scientists have determined that big quakes hit the area as often as once every three hundred years, although sometimes a thousand years may pass between rumbles. They think the last big earthquake struck around 1700 with a magnitude of 9 or greater, and they believe it caused a large tsunami that devastated parts of the Japanese coastline on January 27, 1700.

Another team of geologists has used laser devices to show that the subducting Juan de Fuca Plate is squeezing the margin of North America, compressing it like someone pushing his or her heels against the edge of a large, heavy piece of carpet. The pressure is narrowing Puget Sound—Olympic National Park creeps a little closer to Seattle every year. Even more significant, the force is lifting the entire coast—by several millimeters a year. Both phenomena suggest that the sinking Juan de Fuca Plate has hung up on the North American Plate. Because the forces pulling the Juan de Fuca Plate into the mantle are still at work, pressures will continue to build until the plates slip. And when they do, North America will rebound, vibrating the Pacific Northwest like a drum skin.

Unfortunately, no one can yet predict the timing of such an event. It could occur anytime during the next several hundred years. In the meantime, seismologists are urging Northwest coastal communities to modify their building codes to provide better protection against great earthquakes (magnitude 8 and larger). In response, earthquake design standards in Oregon and Washington have toughened, and many existing structures have been reinforced. So far, hundreds of millions of dollars have been invested in these measures. Canada is also revising its National Building Code. These measures are only prudent when one considers the damage done by the magnitude 7 quake that hit Kobe, Japan. That city, which had a relatively high level of earthquake preparedness, lost over 5,500 lives and suffered more than $100 billion in damage.

While the possibility of a major quake has scientists concerned, flurries of small quakes and the January 1998 eruption of a 4,500-foot-high underwater volcano along the Juan de Fuca ridge have them excited. The caldera sits 300 miles west of the Oregon coast, atop the mid-ocean ridge separating the Pacific and Juan de Fuca Plates. The eruption and the accompanying low-magnitude earthquakes—as many as one hundred per hour—are evidence of new crust being formed along the ridge. They provide scientists with yet another reason to study the Juan de Fuca Plate.

The Next Big One in Northern California

When will the next major earthquake, like the devastating 1906 San Francisco quake, strike northern California? Seismologists, insurance companies, and most northern California residents would love to know. The 1906 quake, one of the worst of the century, killed more than 3,000 people and caused roughly $400 million in damage (in 1906 dollars). With the growth that has occurred in northern California over the past ninety years, an earthquake today of that magnitude could kill tens of thousands of people and destroy hundreds of billions of dollars in property. According to the U.S. Geological Survey (USGS), it could be the worst natural disaster in the nation's history.

Estimated at 7.7 on the Moment-Magnitude Scale, the 1906 earthquake occurred along the San Andreas Fault where the Pacific Plate meets the North American Plate. As the plates move past each other, strain builds along the fault until, periodically, something gives, and a portion of the Pacific Plate surges northwest against the North American Plate. In 1906, a 270-mile-long segment lurched 21 feet in just a few seconds.

To predict the odds of another big quake occurring in the near future, scientists are looking at the seismic history of the region to determine the periodicity of major earthquakes. In one technique, they dig trenches across the San Andreas Fault in search of soil layers with evidence of catastrophic disturbance. By dating the charcoal found in the layers, they have determined that the last big earthquake occurred about three hundred years ago. Faults similar to the San Andreas in China and Japan, where accurate earthquake records have been kept for centuries, show a similar pattern. The data suggests we may have another two hundred years before the next big earthquake strikes. But such predictions are imprecise at best, and other data suggests a major earthquake could occur sooner.

In the seventy years prior to the 1906 quake, strong earthquakes (magnitude 6 to 6.9) occurred every 4.5 years on average. After strain on the fault had been relieved in 1906, the region experienced almost seventy-five years of tectonic quiescence; only one earthquake with a magnitude greater than 6 hit the Bay Area during that time. But the period of relative quiet has apparently ended. Between 1979 and 1984, three earthquakes with magnitudes of about 6 occurred, and in 1989, the Loma Prieta quake, magnitude 7, struck. Many seismologists believe these earthquakes are evidence that the strain on the San Andreas Fault is building again, and we are experiencing a period of seismic activity similar to that preceding the 1906 earthquake. Another big rupture may be on the way. In 1990, scientists used this and other information to estimate a 67 percent chance of one or more earthquakes of magnitude 7 or larger in the Bay Area before the year 2020. If they are right, most of northern California's residents may live to see exactly what a 1906-size earthquake will mean for a modern, densely populated San Francisco.

The "Stable" Interior

The interaction of tectonic plates causes most earthquakes, which is why geologists rely on earthquake zones to delineate plate boundaries. Until recently, those geologists who study the present-day faulting and deformation of the earth's crust attended little to the interior of North America. The middle part of the continent is thousands of miles from the nearest plate boundary and has proved remarkably stable for hundreds of millions of years.

But recorded history shows that the central and eastern parts of the continent have experienced large earthquakes, and although these intra- or midplate earthquakes are infrequent, they can be damaging, even more so than similar-sized events on the West Coast. Energy from large earthquakes carries farther in the rigid rock of the central and eastern parts of the continent than it does along the West Coast where the rock is younger and more heterogeneous. For example, the San Francisco, California, earthquake of 1906 (magnitude 7.7) was barely felt in central Nevada, some 350 miles away, whereas the New Madrid, Missouri, quake of December 1811 (estimated at magnitude 8.0) rang church bells in Boston, 1,000 miles distant.

Geologists still don't understand the processes that cause most of these midplate earthquakes. The interplay between stresses and ancient faults is complex, and the historical record is brief. Most of the quakes, however, appear to be associated with large faults and other tectonic features like the ancient rift underlying the New Madrid seismic zone.

Perhaps the most spectacular of midplate quakes occurred in the winter of 1811–12 when three great earthquakes—the largest to occur in the conterminous U.S. during the last two hundred years—rattled the central Mississippi Valley. By winter's end, few houses within 250 miles of the Mississippi River town of New Madrid remained undamaged. Survivors reported a tremendous roar and gaping cracks in the earth's surface. The ground rolled in visible waves, and large blocks of it sank or rose. Damage was reported as far away as Charleston and Washington, D.C.

The quakes had special meaning for both the Shawnee and Creek Indian tribes. According to their histories, the Shawnee chief, Tecumseh, was traveling south in 1811 from his village of Tippecanoe on the Wabash River in an attempt to recruit supporters. At a town of Creek Indians near the present-day site of Montgomery, Alabama, he declared that the Creek would know he was sent by God because, after arriving in Detroit, he would stamp his foot on the ground and shake down all their houses. After Tecumseh left, the Creeks counted the days, and on the morning they expected him to arrive in Detroit, the earth shook and houses fell; the first of the New Madrid quakes had hit.

Geologists believe that even though these earthquakes occurred far from the nearest plate boundary, they were still caused by plate movement. The strain produced by shifts in the position of the North American Plate reactivated an ancient fault, one that had developed along a failed rift where the earth's crust had thinned and weakened. And because the plate is still moving, the chance of a large to great earthquake reoccurring in the New Madrid seismic zone is considered high. Scientists estimate the probability that a strong to major quake, one in the range of magnitude 6 or 7, will occur within the next fifty years is greater than 90 percent, and they warn that the consequences could be devastating because the region is no longer sparsely populated.

MIDPLATE QUAKES

Location	Year	Magnitude	Map #
La Malbaie, Queb.	1534	6.67	1
La Malbaie, Queb.	1663	6.67	2
St. Lawr. Riv. Val.	1732	6.12	3
Cape Ann, MA.	1755	6.33	4
New Madrid, MO	1811	8.20	5
New Madrid, MO	1811	?	6
New Madrid, MO	1812	8.09	7
New Madrid, MO	1812	8.30	8
northeast Arkansas	1843	6.37	9
La Malbaie, Queb.	1860	6.08	10
La Malbaie, Queb.	1870	6.55	11
Charleston, SC	1886	7.56	12
Carleston, MO	1895	6.79	13
La Malbaie, Queb.	1925	6.86	14
Grand Banks, Can.	1929	7.38	15
NE Baffin Isl., Can.	1933	7.70	16
Timiskaming, Ont.	1935	6.35	17
NE Baffin Isl., Can.	1963	6.11	18
Svedrup Basin, Arctic	1972	6.28	19
Ungava, Quebec	1989	6.30	20

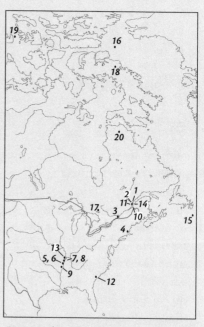

Historical earthquakes of magnitude 6 or greater in the Midplate region of North America

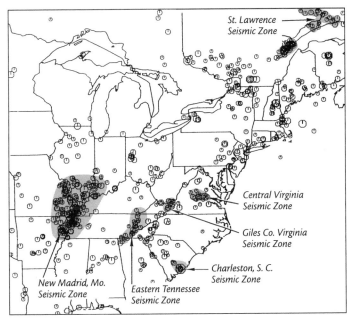

Midplate earthquakes of magnitude 3 or greater, 1568 to 1987

Clues to Prehistoric Quakes

Seismologists estimate that there have been ten strong to major earthquakes in southern Illinois and Indiana over the past 12,000 years. One of the largest, with a magnitude of about 7.5, hammered the area along the Wabash River some 5,000 years ago. An even bigger quake shook the Wabash 7,000 years before that. Major earthquakes also occurred during prehistoric times along the Sangamon, White, and Kaskaskia Rivers.

How do seismologists know about earthquakes that took place so long ago? Evidence comes from a variety of sources, among them something called liquefaction. In liquefaction, severely shaken water-saturated sand behaves like a liquid. During an earthquake, river sands can form a slurry, and as the pressure on the water increases with increased shaking, that slurry can squirt into cracks and erupt on the surface in spouts, or sand blows. Fossilized sand blows and other evidence of liquefaction reveal earthquake history. In Illinois and Indiana, seismologists scouted river banks from canoes and searched exposed sediments for such clues.

In the Wabash River Valley, where many fossilized sand blows were found, seismologists used carbon-14 dating of wood and charcoal from layers of silt and clay both above and below the sand layers to determine when each one formed. Arrowheads, spear points, and pottery collected at the sites also helped date the events.

The size of each earthquake can be estimated by measuring the extent of the disturbance; the area of liquefaction correlates well with the strength of the shaking. Only earthquakes larger than about magnitude 5.5 produce widespread liquefaction.

Earthquake history may predict the chance of future earthquakes and can help in developing design standards for buildings.

Where Three Plates Meet

On June 3, 1932, the largest earthquake recorded in Mexico this century rocked the state of Jalisco. The magnitude 8.2 quake and an aftershock of magnitude 7.8 occurred along the Rivera subduction zone, a major fault where the Rivera Plate descends into the mantle beneath the Jalisco region of the North American Plate. Together the quakes caused widespread casualties and damage.

To better understand plate movement in the region, geologists initiated a project in the mid-1990s to monitor changes occurring along the fault. Because there had been little seismic activity at the Rivera subduction zone since the 1932 event, they believed the subduction fault was locked again and pressure was building. They predicted that another large quake was about to strike. Indeed, on October 9, 1995, another big earthquake (magnitude 7.6) hit Jalisco.

The region is now intensely studied by geologists because it offers a rare opportunity to observe how a continent deforms as two plates (the Rivera and Cocos) moving at different rates slide beneath it. The subducting plates have caused an exceptional amount of faulting in the Jalisco region, much of it along two rift systems—valleys that develop within or between the plates. One trends north, the other angles northwest and extends to the Gulf of California. These two intersect a third, southeast-trending fault, together forming what geologists call a "continental triple junction." The two subducting plates also have caused some volcanic activity. The Jalisco region contains one of the most diverse collections of volcanic rocks on earth, as well as Volcan Colima, North America's most active volcano.

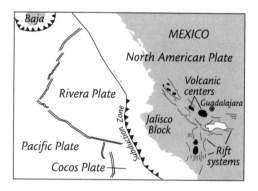

The Jalisco region, where three plates meet

The midcontinent rift zone that almost split the continent

The Rift That Almost Broke North America

Perhaps the greatest disturbance to hit the central part of the continent in the past 1.5 billion years occurred just over a billion years ago, when a great plume of hot mantle material rose beneath Lake Superior. The upwelling stretched the continent enough to initiate a continental rift, a massive zone of faulting and volcanic activity that nearly divided North America in two. The crack followed a giant arc that today can be traced from Kansas north to Lake Superior and then south all the way to Kentucky. Had the rift, which spewed out huge volumes of molten rock, extended itself only slightly farther, it would have reached the margins of the continent and set adrift the eastern third of the U.S., creating another continent. But rifting stopped because North America crashed against another continent along its eastern shore. The pressures caused by that collision canceled further rifting.

Nevertheless, midcontinental rifting left its mark in the form of a great crescent of basalt. This 60-mile-wide, 1,700-mile-long, and 6- to 12-mile-deep scar of iron- and magnesium-rich rock is so dense that it causes a local increase in the earth's gravitational field—in fact, the zone has been labeled the Midcontinental Gravity High. Although most of the basalt is buried deep beneath layers of sediment, part—the Keweenawan basalts—is exposed near the southern border of the Canadian Shield. Little else is visible of the failed rift that almost cracked the continent in two.

Major Rifts of the Continent

Continental rifts are formed by extension and cracking of the lithosphere. They can break a continent into two. Failing that, they create major topographical features—regional domes, uplifts, volcanoes, lava flows, and rift valleys—as well as movements of the earth's surface. A number of failed rifts along the East Coast, like the Newark and Connecticut Grabens, relate to the opening of the Atlantic Ocean. Features associated with failed rifts can affect drainage patterns across enormous areas for millions of years. The ancestral courses of the Mississippi, Rio Grande, and St. Lawrence Rivers all follow developing rifts. Rifts can also cause earthquakes. The ancient New Madrid Rift is responsible for one of the most dangerous earthquake zones in the continent's interior. Evidence suggests that the reactivation of old rift-associated faults caused the great quakes that occurred in this zone in the 1800s.

The 620-mile-long Rio Grande Rift, reaching from central Colorado through New Mexico, is another failed rift. It borders the Basin and Range Province, another area where the crust has been stretched. While similar to a failed rift, the Basin and Range is officially classified as a highly extended terrain. Farther east is the Midcontinent Rift, a fracture that nearly split the continent in half 1 billion years ago. Rifting ceased just before the production of oceanic crust started on a major scale.

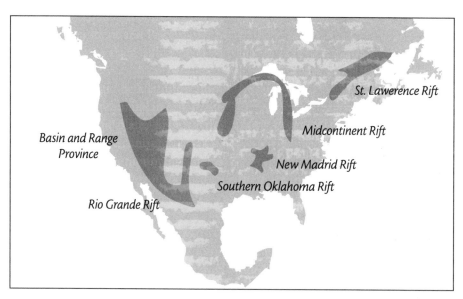

Major rift zones of North America

Volcanoes

Volcanic eruptions can cause rivers of lava, devastating shock waves, blasts of debris, avalanches of hot rock, and blankets of ash. Even more threatening to humans are water disasters associated with erupting volcanoes. Of the over 28,500 volcano-related fatalities that occurred around the world in the 1980s, 80 percent were attributed to debris avalanches and floods caused by heavy rains that struck without warning after an eruption. In North America, large debris avalanches, debris flows, and floods occurred after most of the volcanic eruptions in the Cascades and Alaska.

The first of the two tables that follow is a list of notable eruptions of the twentieth century. The second, more complete, lists North American volcanoes active within the last 2,000 years, older volcanic areas that show signs of unrest, and areas with active geothermal systems. Volcanic fields that have not erupted in the past 10,000 to 50,000 years are not listed.

Notable Eruptions

Volcano	Year	Type	Impact
Novarupta, Alaska	1912	Explosive; dome	Largest eruption of the 20th century; produced 5 cubic miles of volcanic material, equivalent to 230 years of eruption at Kilauea. Pyroclastic flow filled Valley of Ten Thousand Smokes, and as much as 1 foot of ash fell 100 miles away.
Lassen Peak, California	1914–1917	Explosive	Pyroclastic flows, debris flows, and lava flows covered over 6.25 square miles.
Mount St. Helens, Washington	1980–1986	Explosive; dome	Initial debris avalanche and lateral blast on May 18, 1980, removed the upper 1,300 feet of the volcano, killed 57 people, and triggered debris flows that temporarily stopped shipping on the Columbia River and disrupted highways and rail lines. The blast devastated 232 square miles, and destroyed timber valued at several millions of dollars. Measurable amounts of ash fell as far east as North Dakota. Subsequent to May 1980, the volcano produced pyroclastic flows, debris flows, and lava domes.

NOTABLE ERUPTIONS (CONT.)

Volcano	Year	Type	Impact
Augustine Volcano, Alaska	1986	Explosive; dome	Ash plume disrupted air traffic and deposited ash in Anchorage. A dome in the crater led to fear of dome collapse triggering a tsunami along the east shore of Cook Inlet, as happened in 1883.
Redoubt Volcano, Alaska	1989–1990	Explosive; dome	Debris flows caused temporary closing of the Drift River Oil Terminal. A 747 jet aircraft temporarily lost power in all 4 engines when it entered the volcanic ash plume, and it would have crashed had its engines not been started just 4,000 feet above the mountain peaks toward which it was plunging.

NORTH AMERICAN VOLCANOES

Volcano	Eruption Type	# of Erup. (past 200 yrs)	Last Activity	Description
Wrangell, AK	Ash	1?	1902?	Emission of gases and vapors from vents.
Mount Hayes, AK	Ash	0	450?	
Mount Spurr, AK	Ash	1	1953	
Redoubt Volcano, AK	Ash, dome	4	Ongoing	Eruption began December 1989.
Iliamna Volcano, AK	Ash	?	?	
Augustine Volcano, AK	Ash, dome	5	1986	
Katmai Group, AK	Ash, lava			
Mount Mageik		4	1946	
Mount Martin		7	1990	
Novarupta		1	1912	The world's largest 20th-century eruption.
Trident Volcano		1	1964	
Mount Ugashi — Mount Peulik (Ukinrek Maars), AK	Ash	1	1977	Ukinrek Maars formed 0.93 miles south of Becharof Lake, 7.5 miles from Peulik.
Yantarni Volcano — Mount Chiginagak, AK	Ash	2	1971	
Aniakchak Crater, AK	Ash, dome	1 (or 2?)	1931	
Mount Veniaminof, AK	Ash, lava	7	1983–84	

NORTH AMERICAN VOLCANOES (CONT.)

Volcano	Eruption Type	# of Erup. (past 200 yrs)	Last Activity	Description
Mount Emmons — Pavlof Volcano, AK	Ash, lava	30	1987	Pavlof is most frequently active volcano in Alaska.
Mount Dutton, AK	Ash, lava	0	?	
Kiska Volcano, Aleutian Islands, AK	Ash, lava	7	1990	Steam and ash emission.
Little Sitkin Volcano, Aleutian Islands, AK	Ash, lava ?	1?	1900?	
Mount Cerberus (Semisopochnoi), Aleutian Islands, AK	Ash, lava ?	1	1987	Possibly from Sugarloaf, satellite vent on south flank.
Mount Gareloi, Aleutian Islands, AK	Ash, lava	6	1987	
Tanaga Volcano, Aleutian Islands, AK	Ash, lava	1	1914	
Kanaga Volcano, Aleutian Islands, AK	Lava	2	1933	
Great Sitkin Volcano, Aleutian Islands, AK	Ash, dome	6	1974	
Kasatochi Island, Aleutian Islands, AK	?	1	1828	
Korovin Volcano, Aleutian Islands, AK	Ash	7	1951?	
Pyre Peak (Seguam), Aleutian Islands, AK	Ash, lava	5	1977	Eight lava fountains, as high as 300 feet.
Amukta Volcano, Aleutian Islands, AK	Ash, lava	3	1987	
Yunaska Island, Aleutian Islands, AK	Ash	2	1937	Minor ash emission.
Carlisle Volcano, Aleutian Islands, AK	?	1	1987	Probable small steam and ash eruption, though possibly it came from Cleveland.
Mount Cleveland, Aleutian Islands, AK	Ash, lava	10	1987	1945 eruption resulted in only known fatality from Alaska volcanism.
Kagamil Volcano, Aleutian Islands, AK	?	1	1929	
Mount Vsevidof, Aleutian Islands, AK	Ash	1	1957	
Okmok Caldera, Aleutian Islands, AK	Ash, lava	11	1988	

NORTH AMERICAN VOLCANOES (CONT.)

Volcano	Eruption Type	# of Erup. (past 200 yrs)	Last Activity	Description
Bogoslof Volcano, Aleutian Islands, AK	Ash, dome	6	1951	
Makushin Volcano, Aleutian Islands, AK	Ash	7	1980	
Akutan Peak, Aleutian Islands, AK	Ash, lava	21	1988	
Westdahl Peak, Aleutian Islands, AK	Ash, lava	2	1978	
Fisher Dome, Aleutian Islands, AK	Ash	0	1830	
Shishaldin Volcano, Aleutian Islands, AK	Ash, lava	About 18	1987	
Isanotski Peaks, Aleutian Islands, AK	Ash, lava	0	1845	
Mount Baker, WA	Ash, lava	1?	1870	Increased heat output and minor melting of summit glacier in 1975.
Glacier Peak, WA	Ash	> 1?	Before 1800	
Mount Rainier, WA	Ash, lava	1?	1882 (?)	History of massive debris avalanches and debris flows. Occasional shallow seismicity.
Mount Adams, WA	Lava, ash	0	> 3,500 years ago	Debris flows are the most recent events.
Mount St. Helens, WA	Ash, dome, lava	2–3	1980–present	Continuing intermittent activity.
Mount Hood, OR	Ash, dome	2?	1865	Occasional seismic swarms.
Mount Jefferson, OR	Ash, lava	0	> 50,000 years ago	Debris flows in 1934, 1955; young basaltic flows in area.
Three Sisters, OR	Ash, lava	0	950?	Debris flows in this century.
Crater Lake, OR	Ash, lava, dome	0	4,000 years ago	Largest known eruption in Cascade Range. Also there was a catastrophic, caldera-forming eruption 7,000 years ago.
Newberry Crater, OR	Ash, lava	0	600	Latest eruption was obsidian flow.
Medicine Lake, CA	Ash, lava	0	1065	Latest eruption formed Glass Mountain.
Mount Shasta, CA	Ash, dome	1	1786?	Debris flows in this century.

Nᴏʀᴛʜ Aᴍᴇʀɪᴄᴀɴ Vᴏʟᴄᴀɴᴏᴇꜱ (ᴄᴏɴᴛ.)

Volcano	Eruption Type	# of Erup. (past 200 yrs)	Last Activity	Description
Lassen Peak, CA	Ash, dome	1	1914–1917	Lateral blast occurred in last eruption.
Clear Lake, CA	Lava, ash	0	Not known	Geothermal energy and long seismicity suggest "active" status.
Long Valley Caldera, CA	Ash, dome, ashflow	3?	About 1400	Youngest activity represented by nearly simultaneous eruptions of rhyolite at Inyo craters; currently restless.
Coso Peak, CA	Lava, ash, dome	0	About 40,000 years ago	Geothermal energy production and seismic activity suggest "active" status.
San Francisco Field, AZ	Lava	2	1065–1180	Sunset Crater; disrupted Anasazi settlements.
Bandera Field (McCarty's Flow), NM	Lava	1	About 1000	Most voluminous lava within past 1000 years.
Craters of the Moon, ID	Lava	About 1	2,100 years ago	Youngest activity in the Snake River Plain.
Yellowstone Caldera, WY, MT, and ID	Ashflow	0	70,000 years ago	Numerous hydrothermal explosions, geysers, geothermal activity; restlessness shown by seismicity and deformation.
Popocatepetl, Mex.	Ash	4	1997	Earthquakes and explosions mark the start of a new episode of eruptive activity in its deep, bell-shaped crater.
Colima, Mex.	Ash, lava, dome	10 to 15	1976	One of North America's most active volcanoes.
Parícutin Volcano, Mex.	Lava, ash	1	1943 to 1952	Born in a cornfield in 1943. In less than a week the cone was 140 feet high with a quarter-mile-wide crater.
Volcan de las Tres Virgenes, Mex.	Lava	1	Late 1700s	Located in a region not noted for being volcanic. Has erupted a remarkable variety of lava types.

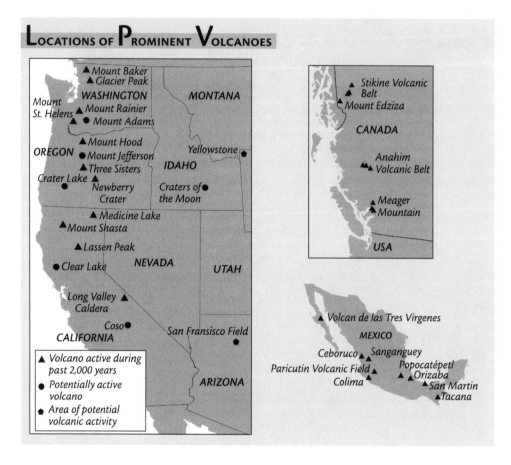

LOCATIONS OF PROMINENT VOLCANOES

▲ Mount Baker
▲ Glacier Peak
WASHINGTON
Mount
St. Helens ▲ Mount Rainier
▲ ● Mount Adams
MONTANA

▲ Mount Hood
OREGON ● Mount Jefferson
▲ Three Sisters
Crater Lake ▲
● Newberry
Crater
Yellowstone
IDAHO
Craters of ●
the Moon

▲ Medicine Lake
▲ Mount Shasta

▲ Lassen Peak

● Clear Lake **NEVADA**
UTAH

Long Valley ▲
Caldera

Coso ●
CALIFORNIA
San Fransisco Field

▲ Volcano active during
past 2,000 years
● Potentially active
volcano
♠ Area of potential
volcanic activity

ARIZONA

▲ Stikine Volcanic
▲ Belt
Mount Edziza

CANADA

Anahim
▲▲ Volcanic Belt

▲ Meager
▲ Mountain

USA

▲ Volcan de las Tres Virgenes

MEXICO

Ceboruco ▲ Sanganguey
Paricutin Volcanic Field ▲
Colima ▲
Popocatépetl
▲ ▲ Orizaba
▲ San Martin
▲ Tacana

Popocatépetl

Popocatépetl, one of Mexico's most famous volcanoes, may be entering a new period of eruptive activity. Although the last major eruption occurred over seventy years ago, recent earthquakes, an increase in sulfur dioxide emissions, and a series of explosions in 1994 and 1997 suggest the volcano is waking.

Popocatépetl, a steep-sided volcanic cone located just 35 miles east of Mexico City, has erupted about thirty times in recorded history, most recently in 1997. It also erupted in 1994, and between 1920 and 1922. Most of the eruptions have been relatively mild, ejecting only steam and ash. American scientists are now working with Mexican scientists to assess hazards for the more than 30 million people living within view of Popocatépetl. Because Popocatépetl is geologically similar to volcanoes in the Cascade Range, the Americans hope the collaboration will help them protect communities in the U.S. from eruptions such as the one at Mount St. Helens in 1980.

Locations of Prominent Volcanoes (cont.)

ALASKA

. Anchorage

Map #	Volcano				
1	Mt. Wrangell				
2	Mt. Spurr				
3	Redoubt Volcano				
4	Iliamna Volcano				
5	Augustine Volcano				
6	Mt. Katmai				
7	Novarupta				
8	Mt. Trident				
9	Mt. Mageik	21	Westdahl Peak	33	Korovin Volcano
10	Mt. Martin	22	Akutan Peak	34	Kasatochi Island Volcano
11	Mt. Peulik	23	Makushin Volcano	35	Great Sitkin Volcano
12	Ukinrek Maars	24	Bogoslof Island Volcano	36	Kanaga Volcano
13	Mt. Chiginagak	25	Okmok Caldera	37	Tanaga Volcano
14	Aniakchak Crater	26	Mt. Vsevidof	38	Mt. Gareloi
15	Mt. Veniaminof	27	Kagamil Island Volcano	39	Mt. Cerberus
16	Pavlof Volcano	28	Carlisle Island Volcano	40	Little Sitkin Caldera
17	Mt. Dutton	29	Mt. Cleveland	41	Segula Peak
18	Isanotski Peaks	30	Yunaska Island Volcano	42	Kiska Volcano
19	Shishaldin Volcano	31	Amukta Island Volcano		
20	Fisher Caldera	32	Seguam Volcano (Pyre Peak)		

The Mount St. Helens Experience

Earthquakes generally precede volcanic eruptions. The first quakes preceding the great Mount St. Helens eruption of 1980 struck on March 20 of that year. Centered directly beneath the mountain, the temblors increased over the next few days and triggered avalanches that closed some recreation areas. Geologists and geophysicists quickly converged on the mountain and warned local authorities that a volcanic eruption was possible. Indeed, on March 27, steam and ash exploded from the summit, the first of several small blasts that occurred during the following two months.

Based on the volcano's past behavior, authorities closed the area to public use. Monitoring indicated that the volcano's north flank was becoming unstable, vulnerable to landslides and large avalanches. But public pressure led the authorities to allow some cabin owners into the area to retrieve belongings. One such trip, scheduled for the morning of May 18, never took place because at 8:30 a.m. an earthquake triggered a massive landslide on the north flank. The quake unleashed a major eruption—a scorching, explosive blast of rock and hot gas, flows of gas-rich volcanic rock, and massive floods of mud and rock that ran down most of the mountain's stream drainages. The explosion tore off the top 1,300 feet of the volcano and leveled everything within a 232-square-mile area. The water-soaked landslide debris generated thick slurries that raced downstream and ultimately stopped shipping on the Columbia River.

The eruption killed fifty-seven people and transformed the mountain's old growth forests into a volcanic wasteland. The explosion also blanketed everything from the eastern half of Washington state to Montana with a thick layer of ash. Tragic as it was, it might have been worse. Had the eruption occurred on a Monday rather than a Sunday, several hundred loggers at work in the affected area would have died in the explosion.

Mount St. Helens before and after the eruption

Yellowstone: A North American Hot Spot

Yellowstone Park is a hot spot, and not just for tourists. In geologic terms, a hot spot is a place where a thermal plume or column of hot rock is rising from the mantle and producing volcanism at the earth's surface. The geysers and volcanoes that have been active in Yellowstone for millions of years are evidence of the plume. So are the numerous earthquakes and the dramatic uplifts and subsidences that have occurred in the area. Eventually, the Yellowstone hot spot will store up enough energy to cause

another major earthquake or volcanic eruption.

The prediction is based on how this particular hot spot has behaved in the past. Typically, some of the magma produced accumulates near the base of the North American Plate, where it melts rocks in the earth's lower crust. This melted rock, in turn, rises to a spot near the surface where it forms giant reservoirs of explosive magma. Eventually these reservoirs erupt and spew magma across vast areas. This scenario has happened many times in the past, sometimes on a catastrophic scale. Some of the resulting craters, called calderas, are more than 30 miles across. Because the North American Plate has been moving an inch or so a year southwestward over the hot spot for at least 17 million years, groups of calderas are strung out like beads across parts of Idaho and Wyoming, and lava flows half a mile thick or more blanket large areas.

The most recent caldera-forming eruption occurred about 650,000 years ago in Yellowstone and left a 53-by-28-mile caldera. The eruption disgorged ground-hugging flows of hot volcanic ash, pumice, and gases that surged across more than 3,000 square miles and then solidified to form a massive layer of rock with a volume of 240 cubic miles, enough to cover the entire conterminous U.S. with a layer 5 inches thick. This formation, called the Lava Creek Tuff, is visible in Yellowstone Park at Tuff Cliff along the lower Gibbon River. The same eruption shot a column of volcanic ash and gas into the earth's stratosphere. The ash fell far enough and in quantities large enough that a layer of it is still recognizable in drill cores taken from the floor of the Gulf of Mexico.

The processes responsible for Yellowstone's volcanic eruptions are still at work. Eventually another "bead" will probably join the 300-mile-long string of calderas. In the meantime, thousands of small earthquakes shake the region every year. Most are too small to be noticed, but at least eight quakes of magnitude 6 or greater have oc-

curred during recorded history. In addition, the ground surface near the center of the Yellowstone Caldera rose more than 3 feet between 1923 and 1985 and has since subsided about 6 inches. Studies of shorelines near the outlet of Yellowstone Lake show that the caldera's center has risen and fallen three times during the past 10,000 years; the total vertical change during each of these "breaths" was in the neighborhood of 65 feet. All the while, Yellowstone's hydrothermal system released and is still releasing heat energy at an average rate of about 4,500 megawatts.

The current levels of earthquake activity, ground deformation, and hydrothermal energy in Yellowstone, although high by most geologic standards, is probably typical of the long periods between eruptions. And although potentially damaging earthquakes are likely to occur every few decades, as they have in the recent past, nothing indicates that an eruption is imminent.

Migration of the Yellowstone Hot Spot over the last 12.5 million years

GEOLOGIC
HISTORY

ACCORDING TO A THEORY PROPOSED BY geologist Paul Hoffman, North America's first billion years can be divided into four intervals based on a series of major geologic events. The following chronology highlights those events and summarizes the first four chapters in the history of the continent.

2.0 to 1.8 billion years ago

Six already ancient microcontinents drifted together to form a single landmass that included the northern and central regions of North America and parts of Northern Europe. These pieces survive today as the Superior, Wyoming, Nain, Slave, Rae, and Hearne Provinces. As this new continent (known as Laurentia) drifted, it picked up fragments of young continental crust in the form of chains of volcanic islands transported on subducting oceanic plates. The island arcs stuck to Laurentia's western, southern, and southeastern margins. Convection currents in the mantle pushed the plates holding Laurentia and other early continents toward each other.

1.8 to 1.6 billion years ago

Laurentia continued to pick up large amounts of younger crust, including a 745-mile-wide belt known as the Mazatzal Region, which today stretches from southern California to Ohio. Soon after, Laurentia and the earth's other early landmasses collided and joined, forming the earth's first supercontinent.

1.6 to 1.3 billion years ago

Like a blanket of insulation, the supercontinent trapped heat within the mantle. A giant plume of hot rock, called a superswell, rose to the earth's surface. It lifted Laurentia and melted the lower part of the crust. This melted, silica-rich rock then rose to create red granites and rhyolites, rocks that today underlie much of North America.

1.3 to 1.0 billion years ago

The superswell eventually forced the supercontinent to split apart, mostly along its original seams. In the process, a series of basalt dikes formed across northern and central Canada. While the plates carrying the continents reshuffled, a giant rift zone developed in the center of Laurentia. It failed to split the continent apart, but left behind an enormous scar that today forms an arc running from Kansas to Tennessee. As the rift developed, Laurentia smashed into another landmass on its southern and eastern sides. The collision crumpled the continent and pushed up a 3,100-mile-long belt of mountains, a region now known as the Grenville Province.

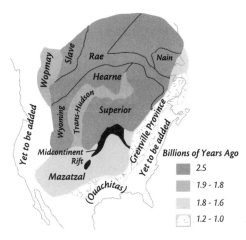

The microcontinents of proto-North America

The Oldest Rock

Geologists are continually searching for the world's oldest rocks to learn at what point the first continents appeared, how extensive they were, and what the basic nature of the earth was during its formative years. The uranium-lead method is one of several radioactive dating methods for measuring age. Uranium decays into lead at a known rate, so that the amount of each isotope contained within relatively stable crystals gauges the rock's age. Rock in the ocean crust is constantly being pulled back into the mantle and recycled, so it is out of the competition; no ocean crust exists that is more than 200 million years old. So geologists scour continents for the most ancient stones.

As continents wandered the globe over the past few billion years, their rock was mangled, buried, and transformed. These alterations complicate dating. In recent years, though, geologists have developed techniques that have yielded new information about the age of the oldest parts of the crust.

So far, the oldest rock identified is a block of metamorphic rock known as the Acasta gneiss that lies southeast of Great Bear Lake in the Northwest Territories of Canada. Estimated to be about 3.96 billion years old, the Acasta gneiss is considered the oldest known intact piece of the earth's crust, although rocks just slightly younger have been found in Greenland, Labrador, Western Australia, and Antarctica.

Based on these findings, it appears that the blocks of crust that would ultimately become the heart of North America formed within a few hundred million years of the earth's formation. Soon after, they were joined by large volumes of relatively light material that separated from the mantle and rose to the earth's surface. The fragments grew into continents that expanded rapidly for another 1.3 billion years. Since then, North America has added only bits and pieces of continents and island arcs to its margins.

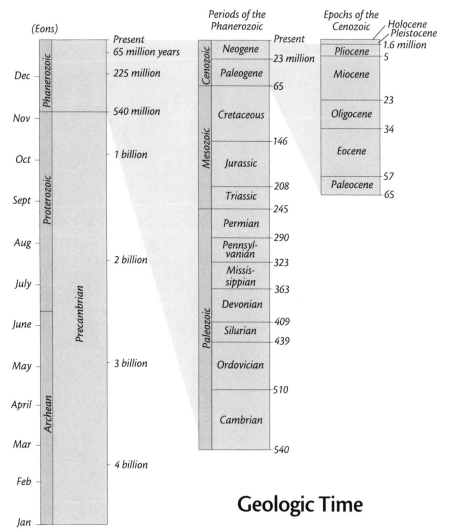

Geologic Time

This geologic time scale, developed before the age of radioactive dating but still in use, is based on major units of sedimentary rock and their fossils. The names have been derived, in most cases, from the places where the fossils were found. The twelve months of the year have been added to show how long each geologic eon would take if the entire history of the earth were compressed into a single year.

A Brief History of the Continent

The Precambrian

The Precambrian is an informal designation for the first 4 billion years of the earth's history. Four billion years is 90 percent of geologic time, so the interval encompasses many important events. It was during the Precambrian, for instance, that the crust formed, that the atmosphere developed, that continents came into being, and that life originated. Most exposed Precambrian rocks in North America are part of the Canadian Shield, although they can also be found in the cores of mountain ranges and in the bottoms of deep canyons like the Grand Canyon. Geologists have divided the Precambrian into two intervals: the Archean and the Proterozoic eons.

Archean Eon
(4.6 to 2.5 billion years ago)

During this, the first interval of earth's history, the earth underwent great change. The core, mantle, and crust came into being, although the crust was thinner then than now. Small continents formed, and hundreds of volcanic arcs produced enormous volumes of dark igneous rock that, after eroding, formed thick deposits of sediment in shallow basins.

The earth was hotter during the Archean because of an abundance of radioactive elements, most of which have now decayed. The changing atmosphere was primarily water vapor, hydrogen, hydrogen chloride, carbon monoxide, and nitrogen. There was little oxygen until life developed.

The first bacteria appeared. They were simple, single-celled organisms or prokaryotes that lacked nuclei and other internal structures. But they thrived in oxygen-free environments and across a broad range of temperatures. One group, the cyanobacteria, left behind fossil structures called stromatolites.

Proterozoic Eon
(2.5 billion to 540 million years ago)

Conditions around the world stabilized. The earth cooled and modern plate tectonic processes began. Larger continents formed as landmasses (protocontinents) joined with each other and with island arcs. Sediments collected in shallow seas, and modern mountains rose. The Wopmay Orogen, for example, formed along the margin of a young continent about 2 billion years ago; geologists still find evidence of this early mountain range just west of Hudson Bay. Several major episodes of glaciation occurred, including one that affected most of the globe. The atmosphere underwent major changes—oxygen levels increased. Life evolved from single-celled, prokaryotic organisms into single-celled organisms with nuclei called eukaryotes and eventually into multicellular plants and animals.

North America, Greenland, Scotland, and part of modern-day Siberia formed a single landmass called Laurentia that added other terranes throughout the eon. A major episode of continental rifting almost split the continent in two, but halted when

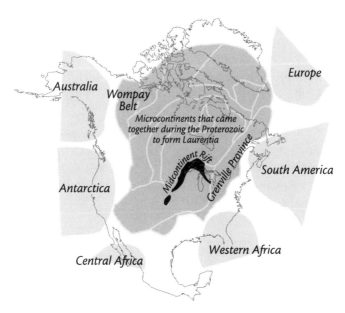

North America about 900 million years ago, during the Proterozoic Eon

Life Takes a Great Leap Forward...

Thanks to a failure in digestion

Paleontologists believe life on earth has been around for 3.5 to 3.9 billion years, making it about as old as the oldest known rocks. But it took a long time—from 1.5 to 2 billion years—for those early life forms to evolve beyond the prokaryotic stage (simple, single-celled organisms without chromosomes, nuclei, or other internal structures). The leap from prokaryote to eukaryote (organisms with nuclei, organelles, and DNA arranged into discrete chromosomes) was one of the most significant biological events ever to occur because it enabled life on earth to diversify into the many complex forms we see today.

How did it happen? The most widely accepted hypothesis is that one prokaryote engulfed another but failed to digest it. Entrapped, but still alive, the swallowed cell became a permanent part of the one that engulfed it, changing over time into what, today, we call mitochondria. Mitochondria, possessing their own DNA, are the power-houses of cells because they produce energy by breaking down complex carbon compounds. It is thought that the first single-celled plants evolved the same way—when an animal-like eukaryote swallowed a blue-green algae (cyanobacteria) cell. The blue-green algae cell with its chlorophyll, the pigment responsible for photosynthesis, became a functioning part of the cell that engulfed it. Today, we call it a chloroplast. The combination eventually evolved into flowers, trees, and other higher plants.

the eastern margin of Laurentia collided with another large landmass, a collision that formed a long belt of terrane known today as the Grenville Orogenic Belt. Collisions with other continents occurred as well; Laurentia ended up near the center of a supercontinent. Failed rifts in the western part of proto-North America produced enormous basins that filled with sediments. Finally, a massive episode of rifting expelled Laurentia from its place within the supercontinent.

The Paleozoic Era

Spanning the interval from 540 to 245 million years ago, the Paleozoic, or "Era of Ancient Life" as it is sometimes called, encompassed an evolutionary explosion. Throughout the 4 billion years of the Precambrian, life remained at the prokaryotic level, but during just the first few million years of the Paleozoic, virtually all of the major designs of animal life appeared. The era, which began with a blossoming of invertebrate species, saw the development of the first fishes, land animals, land plants, amphibians, and reptiles as well as several mass extinctions. North America experienced major episodes of mountain build-

ing and, near the end of the era, became part of a second supercontinent, this one called Pangea. Descriptions of each of the seven periods within the Paleozoic era follow.

Cambrian
(540 to 510 million years ago)

Although the land and freshwater streams and lakes were barren, the oceans teemed with life. Stromatolites abounded, and small animals with shells evolved from the worms and jellyfish-like creatures that dominated the Proterozoic. These and other soft-bodied organisms evolved into larger animals. Many, like the trilobites, brachiopods, and mollusks, had shells or hard outer skeletons, although worms and other soft-bodied forms were still common, especially in deeper waters. Jawless fish evolved. Every several million years throughout this period, the climate changed, causing many species to disappear.

Sea levels rose progressively. Laurentia, having just rifted from a supercontinent, lay near the equator. Encroaching oceans gradually flooded it and other continents. Silica-rich sediments accumulated along its

The First Creature to Behold the Earth

The Cambrian seas swarmed with trilobites—flat-bodied arthropods that fed mostly on the ocean bottom not unlike today's horseshoe crabs. Although some may have been planktonic and some were almost certainly predaceous, most grazed the bottom of the sea. And so it was probably there, roughly 530 million years ago, that the earth's first eye looked out at its surroundings—from the head of a trilobite, the oldest creatures known to have had eyes. The eye was compound, similar to that of a modern-day insect.

margin (the portion that remained above sea level). In shallow water, beyond these deposits, carbonate platforms built up. The continental interior was mostly flat except for low hills along the Transcontinental Arch.

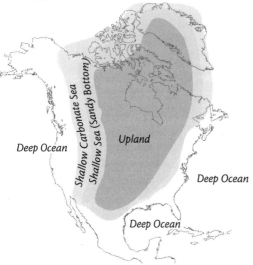

North America about 540 million years ago, during the Cambrian

The Ordovician
(510 to 439 million years ago)

The last mass extinction of the Cambrian ushered in the Ordovician and another evolutionary explosion. Trilobites declined, but new species of organisms expanded, among them snails, bivalve mollusks (clams, mussels, oysters, scallops), brachiopods (lamp shells), primitive corals, sponges, nautiluses, sea urchins, starfish, several new reef-building animals, and small, free-floating creatures called graptolites. While about 150 families evolved during the Cambrian period, over 400 new families originated during the Ordovician. In addition to marine species, the first land plants appeared. Near the end of the period, stromatolites declined, an ice age lowered sea levels, and one of the greatest mass extinctions of all time occurred.

The southern part of Laurentia (the central-interior part of the U.S.) was inundated throughout much of the Ordovician. The Iapetus (proto-Atlantic) Ocean narrowed, and northern Europe moved closer to Laurentia. A colliding island arc or microcontinent pushed up mountains and lifted and crumpled the shelf along the eastern margin of the continent, an event known as the Taconic Orogeny. Rain and wind wore away the mountains and deposited a thick wedge of sediment along the continent's edge.

North America about 440 million years ago, during the late Ordovician

Silurian
(439 to 409 million years ago)

Sea level remained high during most of the Silurian, and a broad shallow sea covered almost all of Laurentia. New species filled the empty niches created by the Ordovician mass extinction. Large reef communities flourished, the first jawed fish appeared, and both fish and bivalve mollusks moved into fresh water. The first animals— millipedes, springtails, mites, and possibly insects—invaded the land. Early land plants colonized new habitats and developed vascular tissues. Inland, on the eastern side of the continent, great barrier reefs built up along the edge of several large basins—the Michigan, Ohio, and Appalachian. The reefs grew large enough to restrict the inflow of water. The rate of evaporation in these new, reef-formed basins exceeded the rate of replenishment, and so thick deposits of salt and gypsum formed. Sea level dropped sharply during the latter part of the Silurian as the continents clustered. Baltica rammed Laurentia, and the

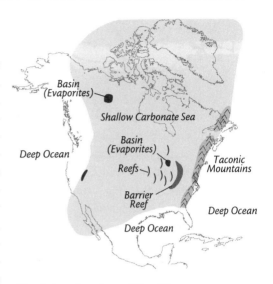

North America about 425 million years ago, during the middle Silurian

collision initiated the pulse of Appalachian-region mountain building known as the Acadian Orogeny.

Devonian
(409 to 363 million years ago)

In the Devonian period, fish developed quickly. Primitive sharks, bony fish, lungfish, and lobe-finned fish evolved from heavily armored fish called placoderms. Primitive amphibians developed from lobe-finned fish. Organic reefs of coral, sponge, calcareous algae, and other organisms flourished. Large barrier reefs grew in southern and western Alberta. Seedless vascular plants appeared, and land plants covered most of the continent. Near the end of the Devonian, forests spread, some with large trees. Early insects, spiders, snails, and amphibians populated these timbered areas. Global cooling at the end of the Devonian caused the disappearance of many marine

The First Creature to Walk on Land

There is tremendous controversy over which group of organisms first tread on land. The fossil evidence is sparse. Early on, paleontologists had settled on scorpions, but they now believe early scorpions were aquatic. Today's leading candidate is the millipede, a creature that would have left more than a few prints in the mud. Springtails, mites, insects, and what appear to be primitive spiders followed.

species. The cooling hit certain reef and phytoplankton communities and placoderms especially hard. At the same time, seas dropped.

Throughout the early part of the Devonian, much of Laurentia was above sea level, and erosion sculpted its surface. The northern part of the Iapetus Ocean closed when Baltica attached to Laurentia and achieved a new larger continent, christened Laurussia. The Acadian Orogeny intensified and developed into the greatest mountain-building episode ever to occur in the Appalachian region. Immense volumes of sediment eroded off the mountains and accumulated to the west. The orogeny also created the Appalachian Province, which extended across much of

North America about 370 million years ago, during the late Devonian

proto-North America. Meanwhile, the northern edge of Laurussia plowed into an island arc or small continent. The resultant uplifting and thrusting (the Ellesmerian Orogeny) became the Franklin Mountain Belt. When the western edge of the continent rammed into a volcanic arc, the force raised mountains from southern Nevada to Idaho—an event known as the Antler Orogeny.

Mississippian
(363 to 323 million years ago)

The continents were tightly clustered during the Mississippian. Sea levels rose, and a shallow, carbonate-rich sea, the last of its kind, spread across Laurussia. Crinoids—animals that attached to the sea floor—captured food as it floated by. Reefs were smaller than during the Devonian but widespread. Faster, more mobile species like sharks and ray-finned bony fish replaced heavily armored swimming animals like placoderms. Debris from marine animals formed limestone deposits over most of the continent. On land, vegetation resembled that of the latter part of the Devonian with the addition of new spore-bearing plants. Different amphibians appeared, some species 20 feet long. As the Mississippian period ended, the seas dropped, and many species disappeared, especially marine organisms. Throughout the period, Laurussia gradually tilted up in the east, and the land above sea level was subject to erosion. The Antler and Franklin mountains eroded significantly.

North America about 340 million years ago, during the middle Mississippian

Pennsylvanian
(323 to 290 million years ago)

Sea level repeatedly rose and fell due to advances and retreats of the glaciers covering the polar region of Gondwanaland, the supercontinent encompassing Africa, South America, India, Australia, and Antarctica. Shorelines migrated back and forth across Laurussia. Gymnosperms—plants with unenclosed or naked seeds—appeared. Spore- and seed-bearing trees colonized low, swampy areas in dense forests. The plants died and accumulated, their remains destined to become massive coal deposits. Insects evolved a new type of wing, one that could be folded over the body. Freshwater fish and mollusks diversified. The first reptiles appeared on the scene. Meanwhile, the Tethys, the sea separating Laurussia and Gondwanaland, vanished as the two landmasses came together. The Alleghenian Orogeny—an event involving massive folding, faulting, and uplifting—resulted. The mountain building extended the Appalachian chain farther to the southwest and thrust up the Ouachita Mountain Belt, which stretched across Oklahoma, Texas, Louisiana, and Mississippi. North and west of these mountains, uplifts and basins formed, the uplifts known today as the Ancestral Rocky Mountains.

A Few Big Bugs...
And lots of small ones

Descriptions of this period often depict enormous dragonflies. Indeed, one genus had wingspans of over 2 feet, but almost all of the insects of the Pennsylvanian and Permian periods were the size of today's insects. Many would have looked familiar to us, for it was during the latter part of the Paleozoic that grasshoppers, locusts, and crickets made their first appearances, along with cockroaches. Judging by the fossil record, the latter group appears to have been at least as abundant 290 million years ago as they are today. Beetles also appeared on the scene about this time, as did mayflies, lacewings, and the primitive ancestors of modern flies and butterflies. Other invertebrates that evolved during the period include centipedes and a 6-foot-long, giant millipede that lived in the warm coal swamps of what is now Pennsylvania.

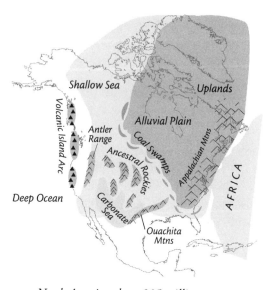

North America about 305 million years ago, during the middle Pennsylvanian

Over the course of the Permian, the climate dried. Vegetation communities shifted, and dune deposits accumulated. Basins dried up, leaving behind large deposits of salt and other evaporites. A microcontinent collided with the western edge of the continent and fattened and crumpled the crust of North America (the Sonoma Orogeny). As the Permian came to a close, the earth cooled significantly and seas dropped. The changes destroyed many species in perhaps the greatest biological calamity in the history of the earth. Eighty percent of both marine and terrestrial species disappeared.

Permian
(290 to 245 million years ago)

Siberia joined to eastern Europe, almost completing the assembly of Pangea, the supercontinent composed of all the earth's continents. Pangea, so large it stretched almost from one pole to the other, drifted north. Seas, restricted to the west, covered less of the continent. On land, forests of gymnosperms dominated. Reptiles diversified and replaced amphibians in many habitats by way of adaptations like the amniote egg (an egg with a yolk and a hard outer shell), a more advanced jaw structure, and greater speed and agility. Mammal-like reptiles appeared, including a warm-blooded group called the therapsids, known for their powerful jaws, complex teeth, and advanced limbs.

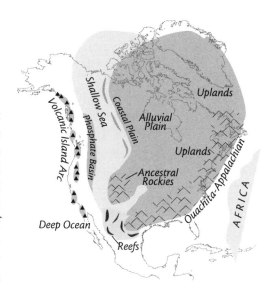

North America about 268 million years ago, during the middle Permian

The Mesozoic Era

The Mesozoic, or Era of Middle Life, spanned a 180-million-year interval that extended from 245 to 65 million years ago. Though slow to recover at first, the earth's biota, devastated at the end of the Permian, ultimately blossomed during the Mesozoic. Mollusks, fish, and reptiles diversified. Large, predatory marine reptiles dominated the oceans. On land, dinosaurs took center stage. Birds appeared for the first time, as did mammals. Flowering plants evolved to dominate terrestrial vegetation. The continents, a single landmass at the beginning of the era, gradually rifted apart. As North America moved west, mountain-building activity shifted from its eastern margin to its western side. Periodic mass extinctions continued, the most significant occurring at the end of the era when a large extraterrestrial object struck the earth.

Triassic
(245 to 208 million years ago)

Early in the Triassic period, the assembly of Pangea was complete. Mollusks recovered from the Permian extinction and diversified, and modern reef-building corals thrived. Large reptiles joined fish as the dominant marine predators. The first crocodiles lurked in rivers and estuaries. The supercontinent Pangea had not fractured yet, so immense areas lay far from the ocean, many of them quite arid. The dominant trees were gymnosperms, with ferns among the most common understory plants. Thecodonts, a group of reptiles, differentiated into the first dinosaurs. Mammals also evolved from reptiles. The mammals, however, remained small, about the size of domestic cats. Late in the Trias-

sic period, the first flying vertebrates appeared in the form of pterosaurs. Frogs and turtles appeared on the scene. The period ended with many species disappearing. Though not as heavy as the extinction that closed the Permian, the end-of-the-Triassic event wiped out 20 percent of all marine families and many marine reptiles, mammal-like reptiles, and large amphibians.

The Sonoma Orogeny, which had added a large microcontinent to the western margin of the continent, ceased. After a period with little tectonic activity, the western edge of North America encountered another subduction zone and experienced yet another major pulse of mountain building. In the east, erosion almost leveled the Appalachian Mountains, which were located near the center of Pangea. As the Triassic ebbed, the North American Plate rifted away from Pangea. In the Ap-

North America about 215 million years ago, during the late Triassic

palachian region, block faulting from rifting created a series of long, narrow basins and ranges.

Jurassic
(208 to 146 million years ago)

Crabs and lobsters gained a foothold and added new forms. The oceans also saw an expansion of bivalve mollusks (clams, mussels, oysters, and scallops), snails, sea urchins, and large reef-building corals. Fish developed modern traits like overlapping scales, bony skeletons, symmetrical tails, more advanced jaws and teeth, and swim bladders. Sharks, too, took on modern shark traits. On land, the forests consisted mostly of cycads (primitive seed plants with columnlike trunks and feathery leaves), although cycadlike trees, conifers (plants with cones and needles), and ginkgoes (deciduous trees with small fan-shaped leaves) were also common. Dinosaurs underwent rapid diversification, filling niches that had been opened by the late Triassic extinction. The first birds crossed the skies. Another moderately heavy mass extinction occurred at the end of the Jurassic.

Throughout the period, Pangea continued fragmenting. Africa and South America separated from the North American Plate. The Gulf of Mexico formed along a rift zone. As rifting there progressed, seawater periodically filled basins and evaporated, leaving behind thick deposits of salt known today as the Louann Salt Deposits. Evaporite deposits of salt also accumulated in rifts off the eastern coast of Canada. On the western margin of

North America, a massive wedge of metamorphosed deep-water sediments and volcanic rocks known as the Franciscan and Great Valley Terranes pushed against what is now California. Granite and other igneous rocks also accumulated in California in the Sierra Nevada region (the Nevadan Orogeny). To the north, North America collided with a long, narrow microcontinent that stretched from Washington to Alaska. As sea level rose during mid- and late-Jurassic times, the western interior of the continent flooded several times. The last and largest of the floods, the Sundance Sea, reached from the coast to the Dakotas and from southern Saskatchewan south to New Mexico. At the end of the period, uplifting on the West Coast expelled this sea.

North America about 155 million years ago, during the late Jurassic

A Hot-Blooded Debate

At present, we don't know if dinosaurs were endotherms (animals with a core temperature maintained by a high metabolic rate) or ectotherms (animals whose core temperature varies proportionally with the ambient temperature). The two premises support divergent views of how these prehistoric giants behaved and lived.

Evidence seems to support endothermy. For example, dinosaur bones possess haversian systems, which allow for the transfer of calcium and phosphorous through the tissues. Haversian systems are present in mammals but absent in most reptiles. Also, it appears from fossil finds that dinosaurs thrived in subpolar latitudes, in regions with climates far beyond the tolerance range of existing reptiles. Had dinosaurs been ectotherms, they probably wouldn't have lived in these colder areas.

An interpretation follows of how the two modes of temperature regulation would have affected dinosaur ecology, physiology, and anatomy.

Trait	Warm-Blooded Dinosaurs	Cold-Blooded Dinosaurs
Posture and Gait	Upright posture with limbs that move like those of mammals.	A more horizontal posture with limbs resembling those of crocodiles more than mammals.
Blood Pressure and Heart	High blood pressure and a 4-chambered heart.	Low blood pressure with a 3-chambered heart.
Activity Levels	Similar to that of modern mammals.	Intermittently sluggish when cold, active when warm.
Predator-Prey Ratios	Predators with high food demands requiring large numbers of prey species (that dinosaur predator-prey relations were similar to those of modern mammals suggests endothermy).	Require less food; fewer prey species.

Cretaceous
(146 to 65 million years ago)

The seas were high during most of the Cretaceous. Early in the period, temperatures increased around the world. (The breakup of Pangea would have triggered tremendous volcanic activity, which would have released greenhouse gases such as carbon dioxide.) Ocean plankton blossomed and left behind large chalk deposits. Teleost fishes, the group that dominate today's marine and freshwater environments, made their appearance. On land, the first flowering plants, or angiosperms—plants that develop from seeds enclosed within an ovary—evolved. Pro-

North America about 85 million years ago, during the late Cretaceous

liferating species rapidly, they spread to dominate the vegetation. A coevolutionary relationship emerged between flowers and insects—many insects evolved to feed on the nectar produced by flowering plants and the plants evolved devices like fragrance and color to attract insects. Dinosaurs held their dominance over the larger animals. Modern frogs, salamanders, turtles, and lizards flourished during this period, and the first snakes appeared. Late in the period, temperatures dropped.

The Cretaceous began with the continents grouped relatively close together, but as Pangea rifted apart, new, smaller oceans and seas formed between the landmasses. Spreading along the Mid-Atlantic Rift between North America and Africa, the North Atlantic Ocean widened. The rift eventually split into two branches, forcing Greenland and Eurasia to separate from North America. Along the western margin of the continent, subduction continued, but the angle of the subducting plate decreased. Because of the change, the upwelling of molten rock that had been occurring near the coast moved farther inland (the Sevier Orogeny). Along the west coast of Canada, another microcontinent tagged onto North America. Seas rose, and a narrow sea, known as the Cretaceous Interior Seaway, flooded the continent from the Gulf of Mexico to the Arctic Ocean. As the Cretaceous period came to a close, a new episode of mountain building (the Laramide Orogeny) started in the west.

The Cretaceous ended abruptly with the extermination of many species of plants and animals, including the dinosaurs. Many scientists believe these organisms disappeared after a massive extraterrestrial body struck the earth.

Modern Plants with Cretaceous Relatives

Some of our most familiar flowering plants have descended from the Cretaceous with little change. Among them are sumacs and poison ivy (*Rhus*), birches (*Betula*), sassafras, magnolia, palms (*Palmoxyon*), oaks (*Quercus*), sycamores (*Platanus*), apples (*Pyrus*), poplars (*Populus*), breadfruits (*Artocarpus*), figs (*Ficus*), elms (*Ulmophyllum*), and cinnamons (*Cinnamonmeides*).

The Cenozoic Era

The Cenozoic Era, or Era of Modern Life, began 65 million years ago and continues today. At the beginning of the era, mammals no longer faced competition or predation from dinosaurs. They filled the niches vacated by dinosaurs and quickly came to dominate the earth. Thus, the Cenozoic bears the informal designation "The Age of Mammals." Modern snakes and frogs, songbirds, whales, seals, and primates appeared. Mountain building continued along the western margin of North America, and uplifts created the Rocky Mountains. In the most recent part of the era—the last 3 million years—glaciers sculpted surface features across the northern part of the continent. Humans appeared and became a major force in biological and environmental change.

Paleogene
(65 to 23 million years ago)

The disappearance of so many species at the end of the Cretaceous opened a variety of marine niches. Organisms like bottom-dwelling mollusks and teleost fishes swiftly dominated the oceans. Carnivorous mammals took to the sea and evolved into whales. Penguins emerged, as did walruses, seals, and sea lions. Flowering plants continued to develop new forms. The first grasses appeared and quickly expanded their range. Many modern forms of insects also evolved. New forms of mammals appeared. At the beginning of the Paleogene, mammals, as a group, were small and showed little variance, but by the end of the period, most of the modern types were present—ungulates, elephants, rodents, rabbits, bats, dogs, cats, weasels, and primates. Birds had not yet fully diversified. Among the existing species, an 8-foot-high, flightless predator called diatryma stalked the land. It had a massive body, sharp claws, and a tremendously large beak designed for ripping and tearing meat.

During the Paleogene, the earth's poles cooled. Antarctica's new ice cap caused seas to drop worldwide. Cold, dense seawater surrounding Antarctica sunk to the ocean bottom and flowed northward creating, for the first time, the psychrosphere, a relatively thick, cool layer of water that presently occupies the bottom of the ocean. As a result, climates cooled and dried, leading to the disappearance of many species. Forests declined, but grasslands spread. Greenland

North America about 50 million years ago, during the middle Paleogene

and North America no longer moved apart, although the Atlantic continued to widen. To the west, a bridge of land connecting Alaska to Siberia was above sea level, and animals and plants migrated freely between the two continents. The Laramide Orogeny came to a halt, and erosion leveled much of the mountain terrain in the west.

Neogene
(23 million years ago to the present)
Climates grew cooler, drier, and more seasonal. Grasses and herbaceous plants, thriving under these new conditions, spread at the expense of forests. Snakes, frogs, toads, songbirds, rats, and mice benefited from the changes and spread to fill new niches.

Where Have All the Giant Mammals Gone?

North America was a different place 12,000 years ago; all sorts of spectacular, big creatures, now extinct, walked the land. Why they disappeared remains a mystery, although three theories prevail: (1) the climate warmed, and the animals could not adjust; (2) humans arrived on the continent for the first time and hunted the animals to extinction; and (3) both factors contributed. A recent study of mammoth and mastodon tusks suggests the second explanation is the most likely. Tusks record details of an animal's life, especially its diet and reproductive history. Microscopic examination of the fossilized tusks indicates both species were eating well at the time of death, an unlikely condition if climate change eliminated habitat. Mammoths and mastodons were not the only species to die off at the end of the ice age. North America lost more species than any other continent. The following table lists the megafauna that became extinct between 12,000 and 11,000 years ago.

Extinct Worldwide Between 12,000 and 11,000 Years Ago	
Mammoths	Mastodons
Saber-toothed cats	Glyptodonts (armadillo-like animals)
Giant short-faced bears	Ground sloths
Giant beavers	Dire wolves
Giant broad-horned bison	American lions and cheetahs

Disappeared from North America but Continued Elsewhere	
Horses	Yaks
Camels	Peccaries
Tapirs	Capybaras
Spectacled bears	Asiatic antelopes

Cloven-hoofed ungulates, elephants, pigs, and whales also increased. The first hyenas and bears appeared, and members of the dog and cat families evolved into their present forms. From primitive primates came many species of monkeys and apes, including humans. With the western mountains mostly eroded away, the crust rebounded, raising the modern Rockies and the Colorado Plateau. The Sierra Nevada Range rose. Lavas poured across the Columbia River region, and the modern Appalachians took shape. Beginning late in the period, the global climate began to fluctuate between cool and warm. During the cool periods, glaciers spread across large areas of the Northern Hemisphere, and during warmer periods, they contracted. The Great Lakes formed along the southern margin of the receding glaciers.

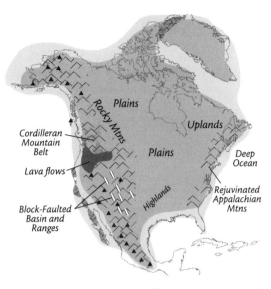

North America about 18 million years ago, during the early Neogene

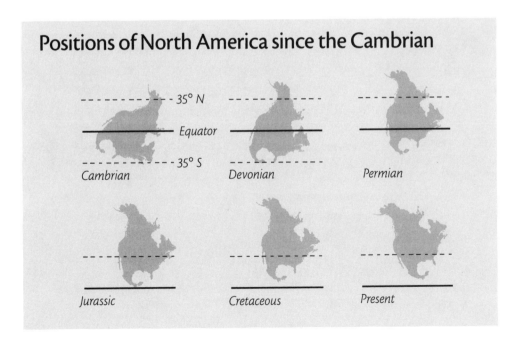

Positions of North America since the Cambrian

The Modern Ice Age

The most consequential events of the Neogene started between 3 and 2.5 million years ago when the climate of the world became intermittently cold. Near the end of the Pliocene and throughout the Pleistocene, North America and the rest of the Northern Hemisphere saw a series of major glaciations, each followed by a relatively warm interglacial period. During each episode of glaciation, 6 million square miles of ice covered as much as a third of the continent. Three times more ice than exists today lay atop the oceans and continents of the world. Glacial ice locked up so much fresh water that sea level dropped some 390 feet; most of the world's continental shelves lay exposed.

In North America, glaciers picked up, transported, and deposited debris such as boulders, sand, and mud. They left behind enormous deposits of glacial till. The glaciers scoured bedrock across vast areas, sculpted mountains, and gouged valleys into wide U shapes. Their massive weight depressed the earth's crust; Hudson Bay is an ice-age depression that has not completely rebounded. Like mammoth bulldozers, glaciers scooped out broad, shallow basins such as those now occupied by the Great Lakes. Plant and animal com-

TRADITIONAL PLEISTOCENE CHRONOLOGY

Glacial Stage	Substage (Stadial)	Onset (yrs ago)
Wisconsinan Glacial		100,000
	Greatlaken Advance	10,000 to 11,500
	Twocreekan Interstadial	11,800 to 12,500
	Woodfordian Advance	12,500 to 22,000
	Farmdalian Interstadial	22,000 to 28,000
	Altonian Advance	30,000 to over 40,000
Sanamonian Interglacial		250,000 ± 50,000
Illinoian Glacial		?
	Jubileean or Buffalo Heart Advance	?
	Monican Advance	?
	Liman Advance	?400,000
Yarmouthian Interglacial		?600,000
Kansan Glacial		1,000,000 ± 100,000
Aftonian Interglacial		?
Nebraskan Glacial		2,000,000 ± 500,000

munities migrated south with each surge of ice and then north again as the ice receded during each interglacial period.

A Revised Chronology

The most recent glacial advance, the Wisconsinan, occurred between 35,000 and 10,000 years ago and obscured those that preceded it. Until recently, we knew relatively little about pre-Wisconsinan glacial intervals, and scientists had developed only an incomplete chronology (see Traditional Chronology, opposite).

Recent work suggests that the Wisconsinan Glacial alone involved multiple glacial advances and retreats separated by as few as 10,000 years; that deposits attributed to each of the major glacials (such as the Kansan and Nebraskan) actually represent an extended series of both major and minor glaciations that in some cases overlap; and that the various lobes of continental ice sheets didn't necessarily expand and contract at the same rate because of variations in local conditions. Hence, the traditional chronology and its nomenclature has been revised in favor of a more flexible system (see Revised Chronology, below).

The Wisconsinan Glacial Interval covered more of North America with ice than most of the other glacial intervals of the Pleistocene or late Pliocene. A single, vast ice sheet called the Laurentide blan-

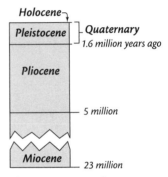

The Neogene Period

Revised Chronology	
Name and Climate Trend	***Time*** *(yrs ago)*

Late Wisconsinan
  Major advance at 18,000 to 20,000 years ago
  Minor advances at 15,000, 12,500, and 11,000 years ago
  No substantial temperate periods
	10,000 to 22,000

Middle Wisconsinan
  Moderate advance at about 33,000 years ago
  Mostly cool-temperate at other times
	22,000 to ?55,000

Early Wisconsinan
  Major advance roughly 55,000 to 65,000 years ago
  Minor advance roughly 75,000 years ago
  Cool-temperate substages 65,000 to 75,000 years ago
	?55,000 to ?75,000

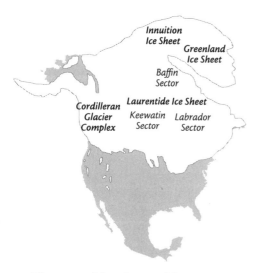

The extent of the advance of the main ice sheets of the last ice age

keted everything east of the Rocky Mountains, from the Arctic Archipelago to latitude 39° N in the Mississippi River Valley. At times connected to the Greenland Ice Cap, the Laurentide Ice Sheet grew outward from two distinct centers: one east of Hudson Bay in Nouveau, Quebec-Labrador, the other west of Hudson Bay in the District of Keewatin, Northwest Territories. At the same time, much of the western part of the continent also lay under glacial ice—the Cordilleran Glacier Complex, encompassing two series of mountain glaciers: one in the Rockies, the other in the Cascades and Sierras. As the Cordilleran formed, mountain glaciers coalesced into ice fields and ice fields into an ice sheet that covered the mountain ranges and spilled into valleys and basins and out onto the plains. Only the highest peaks and a few scattered lowlands stood

above the ice. Whether the Laurentide Ice Sheet and the Cordilleran Glacier Complex met somewhere just east of the Rockies or whether an ice-free corridor separated the two is still unresolved.

The Really Great Lakes

Immense meltwater lakes originated in the Wisconsinan Glacial Interval. The Great Lakes and other large North American lakes—Lake Athabaska, Great Slave Lake, and Great Bear Lake—are remnants of spectacularly large ice-age lakes formed by meltwater. Lake Agassiz occupied some 193,000 square miles of Minnesota, Ontario, and the Dakotas around 12,500 years ago. That's an area about the size of the Yukon Territory. Lake Ojibway-Barlow inundated a good deal of eastern Ontario and western Quebec a few thousand years later. The largest North American lake of all, Lake McConnell, extended across 9 degrees of latitude in northwestern Canada.

The glaciers of the Pleistocene also created big lakes by periodically damming rivers. One such lake, Glacial Lake Missoula, pooled behind an ice dam on the Clark Fork River in northern Idaho. Although it occupied only 1,000 square miles, modest by Pleistocene standards, Glacial Lake Missoula fashioned some of the continent's most remarkable terrain. The lake had only one outlet, so when the ice dam broke, as it did periodically, the entire lake drained in a single outburst. The catastrophic flooding shaped giant ripple marks, deposited huge gravel bars and deltas, and scoured a remarkable area south and west of Spokane called the Channeled Scablands, a region replete with gigantic dry waterfalls, channels, and stream-cut valleys.

How Much Colder Was It?

Paleontologists examined plankton fossils to reconstruct the climate during the Wisconsinan Glacial Interval. The analyses show north-south temperature gradients more extreme than today. The temperature in the northern part of the continental interior may have averaged 18°F lower than today, while at the equator it was about 9°F lower. Some areas that were desert both before and after the Pleistocene became wet during glacial intervals. The now arid Great Basin, for example, received huge amounts of rainfall during glacial intervals and contained enormous, internally drained lakes as a result. The largest was Lake Bonneville; it was salty during interglacial periods. The Great Salt Lake is a remnant of this former giant, which matched Lake Michigan in size. Lake Lahontan, about half as large, lay to the east, in Nevada.

About 18,000 years ago, the Wisconsinan Glaciation peaked, although the last glacial advances in southern Canada and the northern U.S. occurred as recently as 10,000 years ago. By 9,900 years ago, the ice sheets had receded from the lower 48, and most of southern Canada was ice-free by 8,000 years ago. The continental crust, depressed about 1,400 feet by the weight of glacial ice about 1 mile thick, has since rebounded at variable rates with many areas still rising. The Great Lakes region is currently tilting downward to the north (the southern section is rising faster than the northern).

The Reason for the Chill

The cause of Pleistocene glaciation is unresolved, although there are several hypothesis. Scientists generally agree that the earth experienced a gradual though erratic cooling from the Cretaceous to the Pliocene. But late in the Pliocene, the cooling trend accelerated, triggering an ice age. Some have speculated that late-Pliocene cooling reflected a drop in greenhouse gases in the atmosphere. Others believe that solar energy dropped or that the uplifting of mountain ranges in the Cordilleran Mountain Belt changed the climate. The latter theory holds that already-existing alpine glaciers expanded as the mountains lifted. As the glaciers expanded, they reflected more sunlight. That brought on further cooling, which in turn caused the glaciers to grow larger, and so on. Perhaps the most widely accepted theory on Pleistocene glaciation is that the formation of the Isthmus of Panama about 3.5 million years ago strengthened the Gulf Stream. That, in turn, increased snowfall in the Arctic, which enlarged the ice cap. The reasons for glacial oscillations (glacials separated by interglacials) is also a matter of debate, although most scientists believe they were caused by changes in the earth's axis tilt, which altered the amount of solar radiation received at different latitudes on the earth.

A Brief History of the Cordilleran Mountain Belt

The Cordilleran Region, the young mountainous zone that parallels the western margin of the continent, includes a number of major mountain systems and plateaus: the Rocky Mountains, the Basin and Range Province, the Colorado Plateau, the Columbia Plateau, the Interior Mountains and Plateaus, and the Pacific Coast Mountain System. The Rockies are a diverse region; they alone extend from the Bering Sea to Santa Fe, New Mexico, and comprise over 100 individually named ranges. Similarly, the Pacific Coast Mountain System stretches from the northern part of the Alaska Range to the U.S.–Mexico border and includes all of the mountains and plains adjacent to the Pacific Ocean. Between these two great systems lies an equally diverse province, the Interior Mountains and Plateaus, with climates that range from subtropical to arctic.

Whereas geologic details differ from range to range, all are similar in origin: the subduction of ocean plates beneath the western margin of the continent created, for the most part, all the mountain systems of the Cordilleran. A brief geologic history of the belt follows.

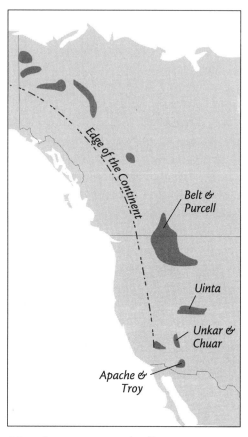

Major basins 800 to 900 million years ago

1.4 billion to 850 million years ago
Failed rifts from northern Canada to southern Arizona produced basins that filled over hundreds of millions of years with enormous volumes of sediment. The largest of these accumulated sediments is known today as the Belt Supergroup.

600 million years ago
The western margin of North America resided east of its present position. For the next several hundred million years, it lay unaffected by large-scale tectonic processes

like rifting, subduction, and transform faulting. A vast platform of sediment accumulated offshore.

390 to 360 million years ago

In an episode of mountain building known as the Antler Orogeny, an ocean plate carrying a group of islands called the Klamath Arc converged on the western margin of the continent. As the continent's crust slid beneath the volcanic base of the arc, the islands and a thick layer of deep-sea deposits slid atop the continent. The thrusting of these "exotic terranes" across Nevada represents the first significant episode of mountain building in the Cordilleran region of North America. Evidence of it persists as the Roberts Mountains Thrust of central Nevada.

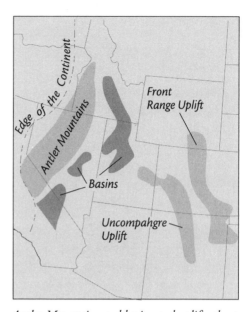

Antler Mountains and basins and uplifts about 300 million years ago

323 to 290 million years ago

Shallow seas flooded large portions of western North America. Basins and uplifts developed in what are now Colorado, Utah, Nevada, and New Mexico. The two highest uplifts, the Front Range and the Uncompahgre of the Ancestral Rocky Mountains, had peaks rising a mile or two above the surrounding sea. The uplifts were leveled by erosion long ago, but rocks from the roots or base of these mountains are still evident where rivers like the Gunnison have cut deep gorges.

A second mountain-building episode, a replicate of the Antler Orogeny, occurred when a volcanic island arc slammed into the continent in the vicinity of Nevada. (At that time, the northwestern part of Nevada was at the edge of the continent.) The event, known as the Sonoma Orogeny, welded marine sediments and a large island or microcontinent called Sonomia to North America's western margin. Northern Nevada, northern California, and southeastern Oregon all comprise part of this massive exotic terrane.

220 to 97 million years ago

After a brief, uneventful period, mountain building resumed. The main episode, known as the Nevadan Orogeny, was analogous to what is happening today in the Andes of South America: large volumes of molten mantle material rose from just above a subducting ocean plate and added themselves to the crust of the continent. Volcanoes developed, and these added

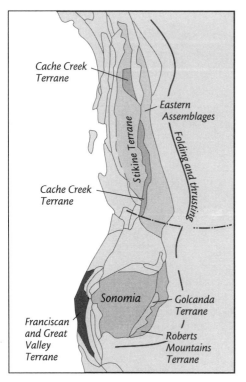

Exotic terranes 150 million years ago

more material to the continent's surface. The ocean plate diving beneath the western edge of North America pushed a wedge of deep ocean sediments against it. The compression caused by the addition of these sediments, the Franciscan and Great Valley Terranes, produced uplifts in the Sierra Nevada Region.

To the north, at about the same time, another large landmass joined with the western margin of North America. Actually a composite of smaller microcontinents known today as the Eastern Assemblages and the Cache Creek and Stikine Terranes, this long, narrow landmass stretches from northern Washington to Alaska. As during

the addition of earlier exotic terranes, the melding of this composite with North America compressed and buckled the crust and generated folding and thrusting far inland.

97 to 68 million years ago
Ocean plates continued to dive under the continent, generating volcanoes and intrusions of huge volumes of igneous rock. A change had taken place, however, in where this activity was surfacing. In the northern U.S., the zone of melting in the mantle caused by the sinking plate had migrated away from the coast, deep into Nevada and Idaho. The change occurred because the angle at which the ocean plate was subducting had decreased; the plate now had to travel farther before it was deep enough to cause melting. The change also pushed the fold and thrust belt to the east. This was the Sevier Orogeny. Meanwhile, farther north, in what is now Canada, another microcontinent attached itself to the exotic terranes added previously.

68 to 23 million years ago
Igneous activity (volcanoes and massive intrusions of igneous rock) and the fold and thrust belt now extended in a broad belt through Canada and into the U.S. It stopped in southern Montana but picked up again in New Mexico and continued all the way to Mexico. The central part of the western U.S., from the West Coast to the Colorado Plateau, was oddly quiet. The region just to the east, however, experienced major uplifting because the subducting plate slid beneath the continent at an ever-

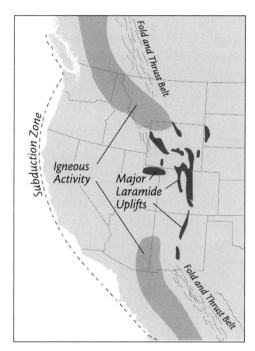

Laramide uplifts and other mountain-building zones, 40 million years ago

diminishing angle. Most of the uplifting occurred in the region that would later become the central and southern Rockies, although the most eastern rise formed the Black Hills of South Dakota. The entire mountain-building episode—the uplifts, the igneous activity, and the fold and thrust belt to the north and south—is known as the Laramide Orogeny. Most of these uplifts would be all but leveled by erosion before the modern Rockies appeared.

23 to 5 million years ago

Magma rising from the mantle wedge overlying the sinking ocean plate generated volcanoes in the Cascade Range. Faulting, also associated with the descending plate, raised

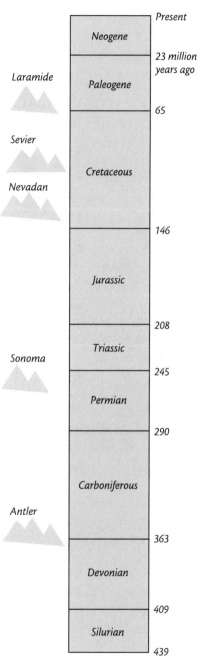

Major mountain-building episodes of the Cordilleran Region

parts of the Coast Ranges of California. Volcanism began to shape the Basin and Range Province, and enormous volumes of basalt flowed across the Columbia Plateau. During the same period, a tremendous uplift changed a broad area that included the Rocky Mountains, the Colorado Plateau, and the Basin and Range Province. The continental crust simply bobbed upward in response to the leveling of the Laramide uplifts by erosion.

5 million years ago to recent

Continued volcanic activity in Washington, Oregon, and Idaho extended the Columbia Plateau eastward and formed new peaks in the Cascades. Many of today's most famous volcanoes are among them. In California, the Sierra Nevada was thrust up. Deformation associated with faulting in the San Andreas zone continued to build the Coast Ranges, while movement of the San Andreas Fault carried a slice of the coast of southern California northward some 60 miles. Movement along that fault zone bore consequences inland. It stretched the crust in the Basin and Range Province. The shearing force created the north-south-trending valleys and intervening ridges we see today. Meanwhile, the Rocky Mountains and the Colorado Plateau underwent yet another dramatic pulse of uplifting; some areas gained as much as 1 to 2 miles in elevation. As the mountains and plateaus rose, major rivers cut through them and created deep canyons—most of the Grand Canyon, for example. Finally, about 2.5 million years ago, the climate cooled. Ice sheets and glaciers spread across many of the mountain ranges of the Cordilleran Region and sculpted them into their present form.

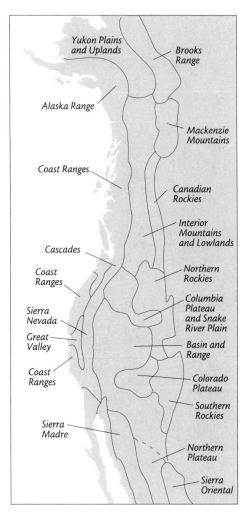

Major physiographic provinces of the Cordilleran Mountain Belt at present

Fossils

The Record of Early Life

The oldest known intact solid rock yet discovered on the earth is the 3.96-billion-year-old Acasta gneiss, a small outcrop of metamorphic rock southeast of Great Bear Lake in the Northwest Territories. The oldest known fossils in North America are about 1 billion years younger.

These, and all but the youngest Precambrian fossils, are the remains of single-celled organisms.

In contrast to preserved traces, multicellular body fossils—the remains of the actual organisms—are known only from rocks younger than 800 million years old. Some of the oldest fossils are listed below.

THE CONTINENT'S OLDEST FOSSILS

Age (in millions of yrs)	Rock Unit and Locality	Description
2700 (±?)	Soudan Iron Formation, MN	Microspheres, filaments, hydrocarbons
2600 (+200,–100)	Steeprock Group, ON	Stromatolites
2000 (+200,–100)	Gunflint Iron Formation, ON	Microspheres, filaments, bacilliform structures, irregular microforms, tubular and branching filaments, stromatolites, hydrocarbons; apparent blue-green algae, bacteria, other prokaryotes
1800 (+400,–50)	Belcher Group, Hudson Bay, Canada	Filaments, microspheres, tubular branching forms, large double-walled spheroids; apparent filamentous blue-green algae, bacteria, other prokaryotes
1300 (±100)	Beck Springs Dolomite, Southern CA	Blue-green filamentous and coccoidal algae, large spheres, eukaryotes in mitosis, chlorophyta, chrysophyta, other eukaryotes
1300 (±100)	Newland Limestone, Belt Supergroup, MT	Filamentous blue-green algae, large microspheres; possible eukaryotic algae
800 (±50)	Worldwide	First appearance of metazoans

IMPORTANT DINOSAUR ASSEMBLAGES

Assemblage	Description
Morrison Formation, western U.S. from MT to NM	Perhaps best known of world's dinosaur collections. Has filled many museum displays with the sauropods Apatosaurus ("Brontosaurus"), Camarosaurus, Diplodocus, and Brachiosaurus; the carnosaurs Allosaurus (Antrodemus) and Ceratosaurus; the ornithopod Camptosaurus; and the stegosaur Stegosaurus.
Trinity Group, Glen Rose, TX	Contains no important skeletons at all but numerous preserved tracks from a variety of dinosaurs. Shows herding behavior in giant sauropods, and predation on sauropods by carnosaurs (converging tracks); gives the general impression that dinosaurs were at least locally and temporally common.
Maestrichtian Laramie/ Lance/Hell Creek/Old Man/Belly River/Judith River formations in MT, WY, and southern Alberta	Remains of the following dinosaurs are abundant: carnosaurs Albertosaurus and Tyrannosaurus; hadrosaurs Edmontosaurus, Kritosaurus, Saurolophus, Parasaurolophus, Anatosaurus, and Lambeosaurus; coelurosaur Ornithomimus (Struthiomimus); ceratopsians Triceratops, Anchiceratops, and Styracosaurus; and the ankylosaur Euoplocephalus. Many other less common genera are also known from the Laramie equivalents.
Other Sites	Dinosaur fossils have been found at many other North American sites including Upper Triassic red beds in Nova Scotia, New Jersey, and Connecticut; Lower Jurassic coastal plain deposits in Massachusetts, New Jersey, and Connecticut; Lower Jurassic strata in Arizona; Lower Cretaceous strata in Wyoming, South Dakota, and British Columbia; and Upper Cretaceous strata from a very wide area. The latter assemblages include marine (coastal plain) strata in New Jersey, North Carolina, Delaware, Alabama, Mississippi and Georgia; and nonmarine or interior-seaway strata in New Mexico, Colorado, Kansas, and other states adjacent to the Laramie and equivalent outcrop.

Fossils of Pleistocene Predators

The Pleistocene is famous for its big mammals and large herds of grazers, species such as the mammoths, mastodons, giant beavers, broad-horned bison, ground sloths, antelope, deer, horses, camels, and yaks. Big cats, bears, and packs of dire wolves preyed on this bounty. The giant short-faced bear (*Arctodus simus*) was the most powerful

Locations of giant short-faced bear (circles) and saber-toothed cat (triangles) fossil remains

predator in North America at the time. Large but short bodied, surprisingly light, and unusually long legged, this species was built for running and was probably faster than today's grizzly bear (which can cover 180 feet in 3 seconds). With a broad muzzle and a short face, this animal may have resembled a cat. It spent at least part of each year in caves. The species was probably hunted by Paleo-Indians and may have been a threat to them as well. It became extinct for unknown reasons about 12,600 years ago. On the map above, circles mark the locations of its fossil remains. None

have been found in Florida, but Pleistocene Florida had many bears of other species.

Another of the most powerful Pleistocene predators, the saber-toothed cat (*Smilodon fatalis*) grew as large as today's African lion. On the map, triangles represent finds of its fossil remains. Saber-toothed cats hunted big animals which they stabbed in the neck or belly with their long canines, teeth that extended below their chins. The fossil record suggests they also killed dire wolves and other saber-toothed cats—skulls from both species have been found with saber holes in them. Cuts and markings on saber-toothed cat bones suggest that Paleo-Indians killed them on occasion. The species became extinct about 8,000 to 9,000 years ago.

Part Two
WATER
AND SOIL

Part Two Water and Soil

WATERS

ENERGY FROM THE SUN MOVES WATER from the oceans to the land. A combination of solar energy and gravity returns it to the oceans. What does not evaporate or remain below ground flows in rivers. In this hydrologic cycle, the atmosphere is the workhorse. At any point in time, overland flow represents a fraction of the water moving above us; scientists estimate that in North America, almost six times more water is carried in the air than in the continent's rivers.

The Arctic, Atlantic, and Pacific Oceans receive runoff from North America's rivers, as shown below. The darker shading represents closed basins, those without streams leaving them.

Three oceans receive North America's runoff.

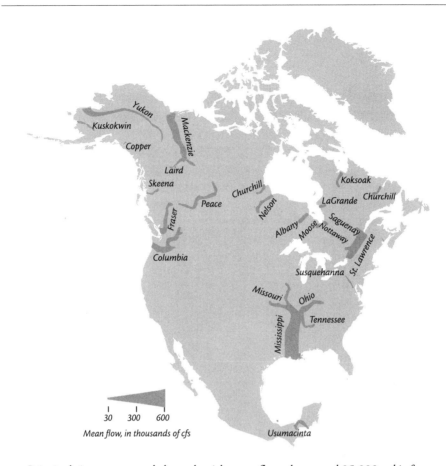

Principal river systems and channels with mean flows that exceed 35,000 cubic feet per second (cfs)

LARGEST RIVERS

Name	Drainage Area (mi²)	Avg. Discharge (in cfs)	Worldwide Rank
Mississippi	1,244	611,000	7
St. Lawrence	498	500,000	11
Mackenzie	697	280,000	17
Columbia	258	256,000	19
Yukon	360	180,000	24
Fraser	92	113,000	32
Nelson	414	80,000	37

Runoff

Differences in precipitation, temperature, and topography across North America translate into differences in runoff—from under a sixteenth of an inch in parts of central Mexico and the West to over 13 feet along the northern Pacific Coast. High temperatures increase water loss. In basins where evapotranspiration exceeds precipitation, runoff is near zero. Runoff within the Great Basin Province never reaches an ocean. It terminates in lakes, sinks, and playas, where it evaporates.

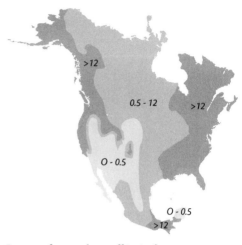

Ranges of annual runoff in inches

Ups and Downs: Variations in River Flows

Year-to-year variations in river flows depend on precipitation, temperature, wind, solar radiation, and vegetation. Usually, streams in regions with abundant precipitation vary the least, while those draining deserts vary the most. Abundant groundwater, reservoirs, or lakes can alter this relation, however. The map shows the variability in annual flow for major streams in North America. Each number, a statistical measure of variation called the coefficient of variation, is expressed as a percentage and ranges from 0 for no variation to over 100 for extreme variation.

Variation in annual flows can be expressed as coefficients of variation (here given as percentages). Zero equals none; 100 and above means extreme variation is the rule.

Muddy Waters: The Load Carried by Major Rivers

This map estimates the amount of sediment delivered annually to coastal deltas, estuaries, and continental shelves prior to European settlement. Most of the sediment came from the western half of the continent; the eastern half is underlain by the erosion-resistant Canadian Shield and has smaller drainage basins, lower topography, and large lakes, all of which limit sediment in rivers.

In all but one or two cases, the amount of sediment delivered to the coasts has decreased or remained the same over the last 300 years, as the chart below shows. In spite of all the agriculture, mining, logging, and building activities that have taken place, sediment loads have decreased because the hundreds of major dams constructed over the last century have served as sediment traps. Reduced streamflows, for example on the Colorado River, have also cut sediment loads. The Columbia River is one of the exceptions to this continentwide trend.

Immediately after the 1980 Mount St. Helens eruption, the Columbia deposited an estimated 260 percent more sediment into the Pacific than it typically did in the years prior to European settlement.

Estimated suspended sediment discharge in millions of metric tons per year before the year 1500

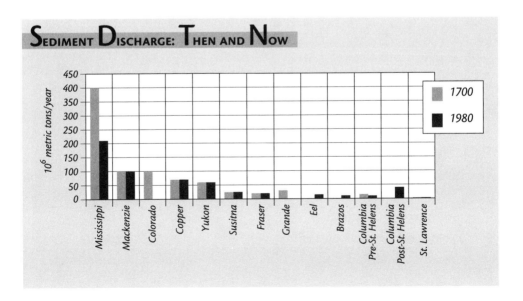

Pre-European vs. Modern Flows

The table below describes how streamflows have changed over the past several hundred years. It compares natural or pre-European flows with current flows for the streams and rivers leaving the continent's thirty-six hydrologic regions (data are unavailable for Mexico). Flows in most areas are between 90 and 100 percent of those in the past. The eleven regions below 90 percent are mostly in the semiarid west and include South Saskatchewan (82 percent), California (68 percent), Missouri (73 percent), Great Basin (59 percent), Upper Colorado (68 percent), Churchill (48 percent), Rio Grande (41 percent), and Lower Colorado (8 percent). A few regions—the Great Lakes; the Assiniboine-Red-Winnipeg, Canada and Souris, Rainy Red, U.S.; and the Lower Saskatchewan–Nelson, Canada—now exceed natural flows; they receive water from adjacent basins through canals.

Hydrologic regions north of Mexico

STREAMFLOWS: NATURAL VS. CURRENT

Map #	Region	Current Outflow (cfs)	Natural Outflow (cfs)	Current/ Natural (%)
1	N. Atl., U.S. + St. John-St. Croix, Can.	147,800	148,789	99
2	Mid-Atlantic, U.S.	122,030	125,703	97
3	S. Atl.-Gulf Coast, U.S.	352,435	361,083	98
4	Great Lakes, U.S. (inflows)	112,430	117,196	96
4	Great Lakes, Canada (inflows)	108,265	103,323	105
5	Ohio, U.S.	275,728	279,611	99
6	Tennessee, U.S.	63,080	63,716	99
7	Upper Mississippi, U.S.	186,985	216,989	86
8	Mississippi, U.S.	662,370	715,001	93
9	Missouri, U.S. + Missouri, Canada	71,306	97,886	73
10	Arkansas-White-Red, U.S.	94,815	106,005	89

Streamflows: Natural vs. Current (cont.)

Map #	Region	Current Outflow (cfs)	Natural Outflow (cfs)	Current/ Natural (%)
11	Texas Gulf, U.S.	43,136	51,220	84
12	Rio Grande, U.S.	3,388	8,190	41
13	Upper Colorado, U.S.	15,320	22,450	68
14	Colorado, U.S.	2,470	29,122	8
15	Great Basin, U.S.	9,107	15,320	59
16	Pac. NW, U.S. + Okanagan, Columbia, Can.	481,245	500,907	96
17	California, U.S.	78,083	114,830	68
18	Alaska, U.S. + Yukon, Can.	1,597,254	1,597,325	100
19	Pacific Coastal, Can.	578,567	575,037	101
20	Fraser Lwr. Mainland, Can.	140,211	144,059	97
21	Peace-Athabasca, Can.	102,475	102,652	100
22	Mackenzie, Can.	361,472	361,648	100
23	Arctic Coast Isl., Can.	361,860	361,860	100
24	N. Saskatchewan, Can.	8,260	8,436	98
25	S. Saskatchewan, Can.	8,436	10,304	82
26	Assiniboine-Red-Winnipeg, Can. + Souris, Rainy Red, U.S.	40,595	38,583	105
27	Lower Saskatchewan-Nelson, Can.	146,177	122,738	119
28	Churchill, Can.	24,745	51,290	48
29	Keewatin, Can.	136,823	136,823	100
30	Northern Ontario, Can.	211,563	220,236	96
31	Northern Quebec, Can.	594,099	594,099	100
32	Ottawa, Can.	70,247	70,317	100
33	St. Lawrence, Can.	366,485	367,650	100
34	North Shore-Gaspe, Can.	307,321	307,357	100
35	Maritime Coastal, Can.	108,760	108,830	100
36	Newfoundland-Labrador, Can.	309,300	329,137	94

Lakes and Wetlands

North America has many lakes, especially in the lower Arctic, the Canadian Shield, the Atlantic provinces of Canada, the northeastern and north-central regions of the U.S., and Florida. Forty-eight percent of the world's largest lakes are in North America, most lying on the Canadian Shield. Lakes comprise 8 percent of Canada's surface area, while another 18 percent is wetland—bog, fen, swamp, marsh, muskeg, or slough. Only 4 percent of the U.S. is wetland.

Lake regions of North America

LAKE REGIONS

Region	Description
Arctic	Lakes and wetlands in the Arctic are underlain by permafrost. Covered with snow and an average of 6 feet of ice for up to 10 months of the year, they recharge between May and July, mostly with snowmelt. The permanently frozen soil prevents water from moving into or out of the groundwater. Little evaporation occurs.
Subarctic	The Subarctic lies in the zone of discontinuous permafrost; most lakes connect to the groundwater through thaw zones, which are melted areas of permafrost. Large lakes like Great Bear and Great Slave probably have no permafrost beneath them. Most recharge arrives during spring snowmelt, although autumn rains provide some water. Evaporation occurs over 5 to 7 months.
Canadian Shield (temperate latitudes)	This forested region, scoured by glaciers during the last ice age, encompasses many lakes and wetlands, most occupying depressions gouged by glaciers. In winter, thick ice covers the lakes. Runoff from snowmelt between March and May is a major source of water. A few lakes receive input from groundwater. Evaporation occurs over 7 months of the year and accounts for considerable water loss.
Great Lakes	Though the Great Lakes drain a relatively small area, they occupy 94,000 square miles of North America, enough to influence the continent's climate. They cause heavy snowfalls in areas to the east, for example. Precipitation over the lakes themselves ranges from about 25 to 47 inches per year. Annual losses to evaporation range from 23 inches in the south to about 18 inches in the north. Water travels through the lakes from Lakes Superior and Michigan to the St. Lawrence River at the outlet of Lake Ontario. There, an average of 2.5 million cubic feet per second discharges.
Mountainous Regions	Most lakes occur in mountain river valleys and depressions. Snowmelt, precipitation, and glacial runoff originating at higher elevations flow into streams that feed lakes and wetlands at low elevations. Little water is lost to evaporation.
Glacial Terrain	Lakes and wetlands, common in this region, lie mostly in glacial moraines, on outwash plains, or in kettle holes (hollows formed when glacial drift surrounded chunks of ice left behind by retreating glaciers). Many are not part of a drainage network.
Riverine Lakes and Wetlands	Lakes and wetlands dot the floodplains of large rivers. Many floodplains are almost entirely wetland. Snowpacks in distant mountains control streamflows, which in turn influence lake and wetland levels. Snowmelt in the headwaters of the Missouri River in Montana, for example, raises lakes and wetlands along the Mississippi River in the southern U.S.

LAKE REGIONS (CONT.)

Region	Description
Desert Lakes	Found mostly in the Basin and Range Province, desert lakes are often large; most are internally drained (no surface water flows out of them). Little precipitation falls, and minimal input comes from groundwater. Most inflow comes from streams originating in surrounding mountains. Evaporation accounts for most water lost.
Sinkhole Lakes	Sinkhole lakes occur in many places but are most common in Florida. They form in limestone terrains with high water tables, usually above the limestone in depressions in surface sediments created by the collapse of limestone chambers below. Streamflow, precipitation, evaporation, and groundwater affect the water balance. A special kind of sinkhole lake occurs in the Yucatan Peninsula. These cenotes, as they are called, lie in the limestone and are directly connected to and influenced by groundwater.

MAJOR LAKES

North America has four of the world's ten largest lakes and almost half (122) of the lakes greater than 195 square miles in area. Most lie on the lake-rich Canadian Shield.

Name	Location	Area (mi²)	Name	Location	Area (mi²)
Superior	Canada-U.S.	31,700	Netilling	Canada	2,100
Huron	Canada-U.S.	24,500	Winnipegosis	Canada	2,000
Michigan	U.S.	22,400	Nipigon	Canada	1,900
Great Bear	Canada	12,100	Manitoba	Canada	1,800
Great Slave	Canada	11,000	Lake of the Woods	Canada	1,544
Erie	Canada-U.S.	9,900	Dubawnt	Canada	1,478
Winnipeg	Canada	9,400	Iliamna	U.S.	1,000
Ontario	Canada-U.S.	7,400	Great Salt	U.S.	965–2,400
Athabaska	Canada	3,000	Chapala	Mexico	421
Reindeer	Canada	2,500			

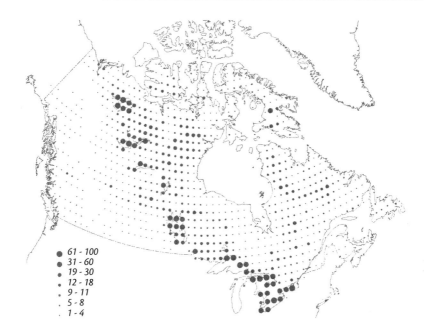

Percentage of large lakes in Canada per 3,900 square miles of land

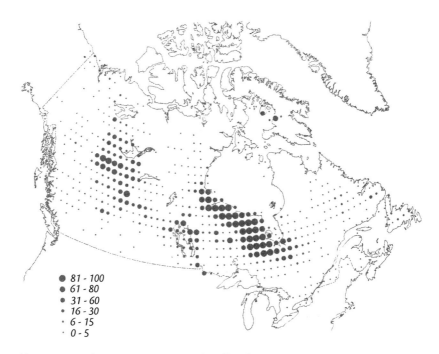

Percentage of bogs in Canada per 3,900 square miles of land

THE GREAT LAKES

Name	Volume (mi³)	Surface Area (mi²)	Drainage Area (mi²)	Shoreline Length (mi)	Outlet
Superior	2,900	31,700	49,300	2,726	St. Marys River to Lake Huron
Michigan	1,180	22,400	45,600	1,638	Straits of Mackinac to Lake Huron
Huron	850	24,500	51,700	3,827	St. Clair River to Lake St. Clair
Erie	116	9,900	22,720	871	Niagara River and Falls to Lake Ontario
Ontario	393	7,400	23,400	712	St. Lawrence River to Atlantic

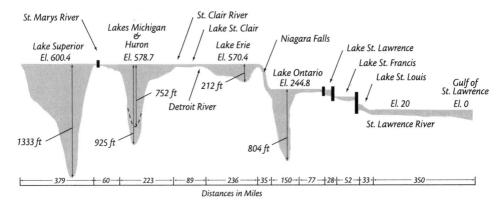

This profile of the Great Lakes–St. Lawrence River drainage system shows average lake elevations.

Closed Lakes

Closed or internally drained lakes have no outlets. Because they are located in topographic sinks, the surrounding groundwater moves toward them, although streams originating in mountains bring the bulk of the water. Evaporation accounts for all of the water lost. Most closed lakes have high salinity levels. The table below gives evaporation rates, salinities, and other key facts about the continent's major closed lakes.

MAJOR CLOSED LAKES

Name	Drainage Area (mi²)	Evaporation (ft/yr) gross	net	Salinity date	ppm	Mean Depth (ft)	Lake Area (mi²)
Devils Lake, ND	3,000	2.5	1.2	1899	8,470	13	45
				1923	15,210	10	26
				1948	25,000	4.5	14
				1952	8,680	10	20
Basin Lake, SK	105	2.25	1.0	1938–41	11,900	20	16
Quill Lakes, SK	2,700	2.0	0.8	1938–41	25,000	10	230
Redberry Lake, SK	120	2.25	1.0	1938–41	14,000	43	27
Great Salt Lake, UT	21,000	3.3	2.7	1877	138,000	18	2,200
				1932	276,000	13	1,300
Sevier Lake, UT	16,000	3.7	3.2	1872	86,400	8	188
Pyramid Lake, NV	2,650	4.2	3.7	1882	3,486	167	200
Walker Lake, NV	3,500	4.2	3.8	1882	2,500	120	110
Mono Lake, CA	600	4.1	3.3	1882	51,170	61	85
Elsinore Lake, CA	717	4.5	3.2	1949	8,880	5	5
Owens Lake, CA	2,900	5.5	5.0	1876	60,000	24	105
				1905	213,700	11	76
Omak Lake, WA	100	3.2	2.2	?	5,704	50	5.5
Lake Abert, OR	900	3.5	2.5	1902	76,000	5	50
				1912	30,000	?	?
				1956–59	20,000	10	60
Summer Lake, OR	330	3.5	2.5	1901	36,000	3	30
				1912	18,000	?	?
Harney Lake, OR	5,300	3.3	2.5	1912	22,380	4.8	47

GROUNDWATER REGIONS

Region	Hydrogeologic Situation	Recharge Rate (inches/yr)	Well Yield (ft³/min)
1. Western Mountain Ranges	Mountains with thin soils over fractured rocks of Precambrian to Cenozoic age alternating with valleys underlain by stream and glacial deposits of Pleistocene age.	0.1–2	2–35
2. Columbia Lava Plateau	Low mountains and plains atop stream deposits and thin soils over thick lava flows mixed with unconsolidated deposits. The lava flows and sediments range in age from Miocene to Holocene.	0.2–10	30–6,400
3. Colorado Plateau and Wyoming Basin	A region of canyons, cliffs, and plains underlain by thin sediments over gently sloping sedimentary rocks of Paleozoic to Cenozoic age.	0.1–2	2–70
4. Central Valley and Pacific Coast Ranges	Broad, relatively flat valleys over thick stream deposits bordered along the coast by low mountains composed of semiconsolidated sedimentary rocks and volcanic deposits of Mesozoic and Cenozoic age.	0.4–4	20–700
5. Great Basin	Alternating wide, relatively flat-floored basins atop thick stream deposits and short mountain ranges composed of igneous and sedimentary rocks of Paleozoic and Mesozoic age and volcanic rocks of Cenozoic age.	0.2–2	20–350
6. Coastal Alluvial Basins	Relatively flat valleys over thick stream deposits separated by mountain ranges composed of metamorphic and sedimentary rocks of Mesozoic age and volcanic rocks of Cenozoic age.	0.2–2	20–350
7. Central Alluvial Basins	Relatively flat valleys underlain by thick stream deposits separated by long, broken mountain ranges composed, in part, of sedimentary rocks of Paleozoic and Mesozoic age and volcanic rocks of Cenozoic age.	0.2–2	20–350
8. Sierra Madre Occidental	A relatively high, broken region with a thin layer of weathered rock over volcanic rocks of Cenozoic age.	0.4–4	20–700
9. Sierra Madre Oriental	A relatively high area of mountain ranges and valleys atop a thin layer of weathered rock over sedimentary rocks of Mesozoic age.	0.2–2	20–350

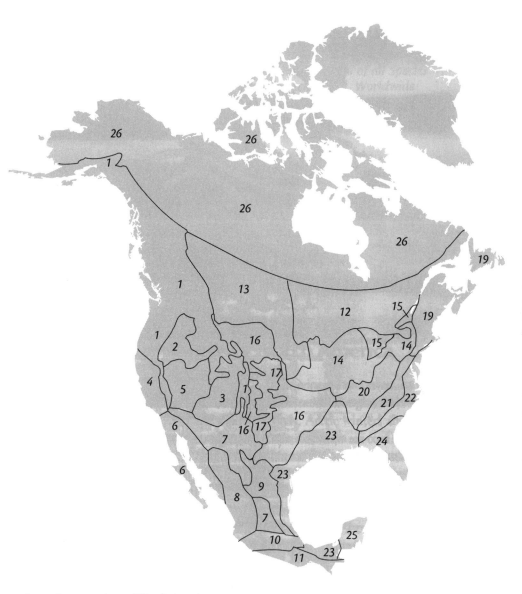

Groundwater regions of North America

GROUNDWATER REGIONS (CONT.)

Region	Hydrogeologic Situation	Recharge Rate (inches/yr)	Well Yield (ft³/min)
10. Faja Volcanica Trans–Mexicana	A high, mountainous area atop a thin surface layer which rests atop a sequence of volcanic rocks of Cenozoic age.	0.4–4	20–700
11. Sierra Madre Del Sur	A steep, mountainous area atop a thin surface layer over metamorphic rocks of Precambrian and Paleozoic age, sedimentary rocks of Mesozoic age, and volcanic rocks of Mesozoic and Cenozoic age.	0.4–4	3.5–350
12. Precambrian Shield	A hilly terrain underlain by glacial deposits over folded to flat-lying metamorphic rocks of Precambrian age. Along the southwest side of James Bay, the bedrock consists of relatively flat-lying consolidated sedimentary rocks mostly of Paleozoic age. They overlap the metamorphic rocks of the Precambrian Shield.	0.4–12	3.5–35
13. Western Glaciated Plains	Hills and relatively unbroken plains underlain by glacial deposits over relatively flat-lying consolidated sedimentary rocks of Mesozoic and Cenozoic age.	0.2–8	7–70
14. Central Glaciated Plains	An area of diverse topography, ranging from the plains of Iowa to the Catskill Mountains of New York, over glacial deposits on flat-lying consolidated sedimentary rocks of Paleozoic age.	0.2–12	7–70
15. St. Lawrence Lowlands	A hilly area atop glacial deposits over flat-lying consolidated sedimentary rocks of Paleozoic age.	0.2–12	7–70
16. Central Non-glaciated Plains	Unbroken plains underlain by a thin surface layer over flat-lying consolidated sedimentary rocks of Paleozoic to Cenozoic age. Includes the Black Hills, where metamorphic rocks of Precambrian age are exposed in a dome structure, surrounded by the upturned, truncated edges of the sedimentary rock layers.	0.2–12	14–350
17. High Plains	A relatively unbroken, eastward-sloping tableland underlain by thick stream deposits over consolidated sedimentary rocks of Paleozoic to Cenozoic age.	0.04–6	14– 350

GROUNDWATER REGIONS (CONT.)

Region	Hydrogeologic Situation	Recharge Rate (inches/yr)	Well Yield (ft³/min)
18. Alluvial Valleys	Thick deposits of sand and gravel, in places interbedded with silt and clay of Pleistocene and Holocene age, beneath floodplains and terraces of streams.	2–20	14–700
19. Northeastern Appalachians	Hilly to mountainous area atop glacial deposits over folded metamorphic rocks of Paleozoic age with intrusions of igneous rock.	1–12	3.5–70
20. Appalachian Plateaus and Valley and Ridge	Hilly to mountainous area atop a thin surface layer over flat and folded consolidated sedimentary rocks of Paleozoic age. The folded rocks of the Valley and Ridge Province differ somewhat in their water-bearing characteristics from the flat rocks of the Appalachian plateaus, but not enough to warrant including them in a separate region.	1–12	3.5–35
21. Piedmont and Blue Ridge	Hilly to mountainous area underlain by a thick surface layer over folded metamorphic rocks of Paleozoic age with intrusions of igneous rocks. Includes basins containing rocks of early Mesozoic age.	1–12	3.5–35
22. Atlantic and Eastern Gulf Coastal Plain	A relatively unbroken, low-lying plain above sand, silt, and clay that thicken toward the east and south. Of Mesozoic and Cenozoic age, the coastal plain deposits overlie igneous rocks.	2–20	18–700
23. Gulf of Mexico Coastal Plain	A relatively unbroken, low-lying plain over sand, silt, and clay of Mesozoic and Cenozoic age that thicken toward the coast.	2–20	18–700
24. Southeastern Coastal Plain	A relatively low-lying area underlain by thick layers of sand and clay over semiconsolidated limestone of Cenozoic age.	1–20	180 –1,800
25. Yucatan Peninsula	A flat, low-lying area atop a thin surface layer over semiconsolidated carbonate rocks of Cenozoic age.	0.8–8	18–180
26. Permafrost Region	A diverse area ranging from the highest mountains in North America eastward across the tundra plains of northern Canada. Commonly underlain by unconsolidated deposits partly of glacial origin, which rest on igneous, metamorphic, and sedimentary rocks of Precambrian to Cenozoic age.	0.2–4	0.4–70

Snow and Ice

A large volume of water falls as snow over North America. The area covered by seasonal snows fluctuates between 1.2 and 7 million square miles, about 14 to 84 percent of the continent's surface. The continent also has a substantial blanket of gla-cial ice—with Greenland included, glaciers cover about 10 percent of the continent; without, they cover 2 percent. Still, the amount of water stored in that 2 percent exceeds the combined volume of all the lakes and reservoirs on the continent.

Major Snow and Ice Masses

Snow or Ice Mass	Area (thousands of mi²)	Volume (thousands of mi³)
Seasonal Snow (average annual coverage)	4,173	
Glaciers & Ice Caps (excluding Greenland)	139	12
Greenland Ice Sheet	651	658

Snow Regions

Region	Characteristics of Snow and Snowpack
Great Plains and Canadian Prairies	This is a flat region with thin, dry, loose snowpacks. Winds blow snows into swales and gullies and cause a significant proportion of the crystals to evaporate. Snows average only 2 to 6 inches of water equivalent but contribute important soil moisture in the spring and insulate plants in the winter.
Cascade Range (Oregon, Washington, and British Columbia)	Snowpacks in the Cascades are thick (from 33 to 94 feet deep at some higher elevations on the west slopes), wet (with more than 195 inches of water equivalent), and relatively warm (rarely dropping much below the freezing point). Because the snowpack is dense, heavy, and made up of coarse crystals, avalanches are common. Evaporation is negligible.
Rocky Mountains	Snowpacks are of moderate thickness; they are relatively cold and extremely variable. Thick snowpacks characterize high elevations. Winds cause some evaporation and tend to concentrate the snow in cornices, valleys, and forest openings. Dry, powdery snowfalls soon compact and become dense. Avalanches are common.

SNOW REGIONS (CONT.)

Region	Characteristics of Snow and Snowpack
Southeastern Canada and Northeastern U.S.	The character of snow ranges between that of the Great Plains and the Rockies. The amount of snow increases with elevation, especially downwind of the Great Lakes. Acid precipitation is a problem. Acid accumulates within the snowpack and then runs off at concentrated levels.
Arctic	The snowpack lasts 9 to 10 months each year. It is shaped in places by winds that build cornices and cause drifting along riverbanks and gullies. Snows may be hard on top, but remain loose beneath, like those of the Canadian Prairie.

The long-term probability (in percent) that an area will have snow cover on January 31 of any given year

The Glaciers of North America

The amount of water stored in the glaciers of the world is equal to all the precipitation that falls over the entire globe for a period of 60 years. Ten percent of North America lies beneath ice, the same percentage as the world at large, but most of North America's ice rests atop Greenland. Second in size only to the ice cap that blankets Antarctica, the Greenland Ice Sheet contains 7 percent of the earth's fresh water. It averages over a mile deep and is twice that thick in places. Other glaciers cover an additional 31,000 square miles of the island.

Excluding Greenland, only 2 percent of North America lies beneath glaciers. Most of that ice is in the Rockies, the Interior Mountains and Plateaus, and the Pacific Rim and Coast ranges. The Chugach, Wrangell, and St. Elias Ranges of Alaska and the Yukon Territory harbor enormous ice fields and glaciers that, combined, cover 19,500 square miles. The greatest single glacier in North America south of the Arctic Islands and Greenland, the Bering Glacier, lies in the Chugach Mountains. It is over 125 miles long and caps approximately 2,260 square miles. The Seward-Malaspina Glacier, also massive, blankets some 2,030 square miles of the St. Elias Range. Many of the glaciers in the St. Elias Mountains are advancing or stable, but in the Alaska Range, to the north, most are receding.

In the Coast Ranges, ice fields and glaciers stretch from southern Alaska to Washington. As recently as the 1960s, many were advancing, but now most are in retreat. South, from southern Washington to north-

The areas with glaciers in the western part of the continent

ern California, only the highest peaks shelter glaciers. The Sierra Nevada Range has a few, as does Mexico on its highest volcanoes.

To the east of the Coast Ranges, a number of small mountain glaciers reside in the Selwyn and Mackenzie Mountains of the Yukon and Northwest Territories. The Canadian Rocky Mountains preserve many small glaciers and some small ice fields. Together, they cover over 100 square miles.

South of Canada, only small cirque glaciers remain in most of the Rocky Mountains. The Wind River Range of

Wyoming receives large amounts of snow and persistent winds, conditions that build large snow drifts and preserve valley glaciers, ice-cap-like glaciers, and large cirque glaciers. Between the Rockies and the Coast Ranges, the Interior Mountains and Plateaus (the Wallowa, Salmon River, and Wasatch ranges) hold perennial snowfields.

The Canadian Arctic islands carry about 42,000 square miles of ice, most of it on Ellesmere, Devon, and Axel Heiberg Islands. The accumulation, the largest in the world outside of the Greenland and Antarctic Ice Sheets, dates to the Laurentide Ice Sheet of 100,000 years ago. Ice cores from these islands and Greenland provide information about ice-age temperatures, precipitation, and levels of greenhouse gases, and atmospheric, cosmic, and volcanic fallout during the ice age.

AREAS OF GLACIAL ICE

Region	Area of Glaciers (mi²)
Greenland (not including the Greenland Ice Sheet)	31,200
Queen Elizabeth Islands	42,354
Baffin and Bylot Islands, Labrador	16,380
Brooks Range, Kigluaik Mountains	273
Alaska Range; Talkeetna, Kilbuk Mountains	5,811
Aleutian Islands, Alaska Peninsula	858
Coastal Mountains, Kenai Peninsula to 52° N	34,476
Mackenzie, Selwyn, Rocky Mountains north of 55° N	351
Coast Mountains south of 55° N	5,460
Cascades, Olympics, Rocky Mountains south of 55° N; Selkirks (Canada); Northern Rocky Mountains	1,560
Middle and Southern Rocky Mountains, Sierra Nevada	39
Mexico	4
Total	**138,840**

Waterworld

Because the climate has warmed, most mountain glaciers have retreated since the latter part of the nineteenth century. The melting has added 4 inches of depth to the world's oceans. How much would the seas rise if all the ice melted? The present volume of the earth's ice, if melted, would cause a 260-foot rise. From those times when glacial ice is at a maximum (an ice-age epoch) to when it reaches its minimum (an interglacial epoch), seas can rise approximately 660 feet. The geologic record is replete with such rises and falls. During the last glacial peak, about 20,000 years ago, oceans lay 390 feet lower than today. During a warmer climatic interval, 125,000 years ago, they were 20 feet above today's level. And 3 million years ago, they had climbed 60 to 140 feet above that. Such changes influence the evolution and distribution of fauna and flora by exposing or inundating land bridges and islands.

Glaciers on Mount Rainier

Appreciated for its year-round cap of snow and ice and its size, Mount Rainier is one of the most scenic peaks in North America. Glaciers and perennial snowfields cover about 36 square miles of the peak. Although they seem unchanging, the glaciers are one of Rainier's most dynamic features. Flowing downhill as thick, slow-moving rivers of ice, they sculpt rock, feed rivers with torrents of meltwater, and grow and shrink in response to climate changes.

The Nisqually Glacier, for example, creeps down Rainier at a rate of about 29 inches a day during the month of May and slightly faster in summer when higher temperatures generate more lubricating meltwater.

Although the ice within a glacier constantly flows downhill, the position of an individual glacier's snout, or terminus, moves uphill and downhill in response to the climate. If summer melt exceeds winter snows, the glacier shrinks, and the terminus recedes. When the opposite occurs, the glacier grows, and the terminus advances. The fluctuations, which take years to notice, reflect long-term climate changes.

Geologists determine how large glaciers were in the past by mapping the outline of deposits and by measuring the distance between older and younger forests and between forests and pioneering vegetation. The evidence reveals that Rainier's glaciers have fluctuated dramatically through time. At the height of the last ice age (25,000 to 15,000 years ago), ice covered most of Mount Rainier National Park. Glaciers extended to the edge of Puget Sound Basin. After the ice age, they shrank until the sixteenth century, when the climate cooled slightly. Between 1500 and 1850, many of the glaciers on Rainier advanced farther downhill than at any point since the last ice age. Then the climate warmed, and the glaciers receded. The trend continued until 1950. Over that 100-year period, Mount Rainier's glaciers lost about one-quarter of their length.

Beginning in 1950 and continuing through the early 1980s, temperatures cooled, and the major glaciers advanced once more. High snowfalls, especially during the 1960s and 1970s fed the Carbon, Cowlitz, Emmons, and Nisqually Glaciers. The trend reversed again in the early 1980s as drier conditions prevailed. Since then, most of the glaciers on Mount Rainier have thinned and retreated.

Permafrost: Below Freezing but Not Necessarily Frozen

Permafrost, any ground that stays below 32°F for two or more consecutive years, forms where the mean annual air temperature is below 32°F—that includes about 50 percent of Canada, 85 percent of Alaska, and alpine areas of the Rockies and Pacific Coast mountain ranges. Permafrost need not be frozen, however. Some coarse gravels and rocky soils remain below 32°F without freezing because they lack water. In other situations, water is present but remains liquid because it contains dissolved minerals that depress the freezing point below 32°F. Ice is usually present and often makes up 80 to 99 percent of the permafrost's total volume. In the southern part of the permafrost zone, where the annual temperature of the atmosphere averages 18°F, the permafrost layer is relatively thin and patchy. In the north, however, permafrost can be over 1,600 feet thick and stretch across vast areas. Throughout the Arctic, permafrost and the annual cycle of freezing and thawing spawn surface features—terraces and steps, raised and depressed circles and stripes, polygons, earth hummocks, ice-cored hills known as pingos, and small ice mounds called palsas.

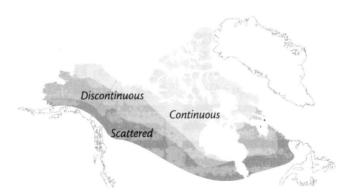

The permafrost zone

Soils

A BRIDGE BETWEEN PLANTS AND ROCK, soil links the living and nonliving parts of the environment. It also serves as the medium through which almost all of the continent's waters pass. Formed over geologic time and influenced by climate, vegetation, and rock, soils vary in their material, structure, chemistry, depth, and layering. Scientists classify them like other parts of the natural environment, although soil taxonomy is more general than that used for plants and animals. The system includes the following ranks: *Order, Suborder, Great Group, Subgroup, Family, and Series.*

The U.S. alone has ten orders that divide into roughly 10,500 series. North America as a whole has many more; the continent encompasses nearly every major soil category in the world. The major orders for North America north of Mexico follow. The names are those employed by soil scientists in the U.S; Canadian equivalents are also given, too.

Soil Orders

Soil Order	Description
1. Alfisols	Comparatively fertile, alfisols have a pale surface horizon and a clay-rich B-horizon. They form in many climates, but are most common in humid and semihumid regions beneath deciduous forests and on prairies, calcareous glacial drifts, and windblown deposits. Equivalent Canadian soil order: luvisolic, some gleysolic and solonetzic.
2. Aridisols	As the name implies, these soils occur in dry or desert areas. Usually found west of longitude 100° W, they support sparse plant life. Surface horizons have little organic matter. Light in color, these horizons have high accumulations of calcium carbonate or mineral salts that inhibit plant growth. Generally equivalent to the solonetzic Canadian soil order.
3. Entisols	These are young and undeveloped soils. They occur under almost any climatic condition and on almost all parent materials. Typically, they lack a B- and E-horizon. The A-horizon sits atop a C-horizon. The C-horizon rests directly on bedrock (see the diagram on soil horizons that follows). Entisols have stabilized enough, however, to support vegetation. Equivalent to regosolic and sometimes gleysolic soils in the Canadian taxonomy.

SOILS OF TEMPERATE NORTH AMERICA

1. Alfisols
2. Aridisols
3. Entisols
4. Histosols
5. Inceptisols
6. Mollisols
7. Spodosols
8. Ultisols
9. Vertisols
10. Soils of mountain areas
11. Glacier or ice cap

SOIL ORDERS (CONT.)

Soil Order	Description
4. Histosols	Unlike other soils, histosols contain mostly organic matter. Commonly called bog, moor, or peat, they can develop anywhere water stands for most of the year. They exist from the tropics to polar regions, although histosols are most extensive on the bog-rich Canadian Shield and in the Northwest Territories. The equivalent Canadian soil orders are called organic soils.
5. Inceptisols	These immature soils can occur almost anywhere. They tend to lack well-developed B- and E-horizons and generally resemble parent materials. Comprising diverse soils, scientists consider inceptisols intermediate between entisols and more mature soils. Generally equivalent to the Canadian soil orders brunisolic and some gleysolic and podzolic.
6. Mollisols	Fertile, dark soils rich in humus, mollisols develop beneath the shortgrass and tallgrass prairies, between the humid east and the arid west. Calcium salts accumulate in lower horizons where they sometimes form nodules. Generally equivalent to chernozemic, some brunisolic, gleysolic, and solonetzic Canadian soil orders.
7. Spodosols	While these acidic soils, characteristic of cool, humid coniferous forests, are scattered throughout the Atlantic Coastal Plain and high mountain areas, they are most extensive around the Great Lakes, in the northeastern U.S., and in eastern Canada. With parent material of quartzite sand, they have a profile of ashy gray sand over dark sandy loam. The A-horizon tends to be infertile because of leaching. The B-horizon is high in iron and aluminum. The generally equivalent Canadian soil order is podzolic.
8. Ultisols	Found mostly in the southeast, in unglaciated areas that receive high amounts of precipitation, these soils are the most weathered of all mid-latitude North American soils. Deep soils, reddish or mahogany in color (unless poorly drained, in which case they tend toward yellow or gray), ultisols have a clay-rich subsurface like alfisols but are more acidic and less fertile. There is no equivalent Canadian soil order.
9. Vertisols	Vertisols, at least 20 inches deep, contain 30 percent clay in all their horizons. During the dry season, they crack in polygonal patterns. Some extend 3 feet or more in depth. Material collects in the cracks and acts as wedges forcing lower soil horizons to the surface. Limited in North America, vertisols form over alkaline parent materials, mostly in east-central and south-eastern Texas, west-central Alabama, and east-central Mississippi. The closest Canadian soil order is chernozemic.
Oxisols	Found on ancient landscapes in the humid tropics, these deeply weathered soils contain a horizon of hydrated oxides of iron and/or aluminum and clay. They are not mapped, and there is no equivalent Canadian soil order.

Soil Horizons

Soil layers or horizons develop in response to weathering and the accumulation of organic matter. Each has a unique texture, color, structure, chemistry, and community of organisms. The number of horizons and their characteristics indicate the age of the soil and the environment in which it formed.

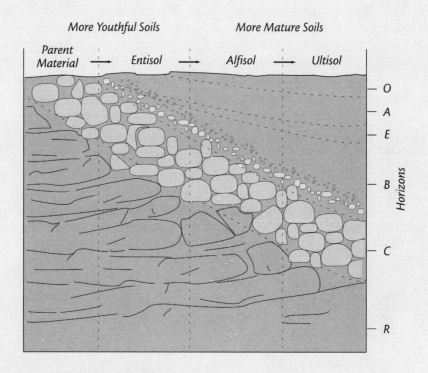

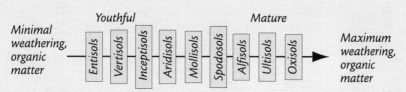

Part Three
ATMOSPHERE
AND CLIMATE

Part Three Atmosphere and Climate

ATMOSPHERE AND SUN

METEOROLOGISTS DIVIDE THE ATMO-sphere into four zones. The lowest, the troposphere, is where weather occurs and where three-quarters of the atmosphere (by weight) concentrates. Temperatures decrease about 3.5°F for every 1,000 feet of ascent, a trend known as the lapse rate. In the tropics, the troposphere is 11 miles high, in polar regions it is about 5 miles high.

The stratosphere rests atop the troposphere. Clouds only occasionally reach this zone, and the air mixes little. Temperatures at the bottom part of the stratosphere remain constant, but in the middle and upper regions, they increase sharply with elevation. Ozone, which accumulates there, absorbs ultraviolet radiation from the sun and warms the air.

In the mesosphere, the next zone, temperatures decrease at higher altitudes. They bottom out at -137°F approximately 55 miles above the earth's surface. Above the mesosphere is the uppermost layer, the thermosphere, where the temperature trend again reverses, and the atmosphere gains heat with elevation. Though temperatures reach as high as 2,300°F, the air at such high elevations is too thin to hold much heat. Temperatures at this altitude are not equivalent to those at the earth's surface, because objects gain little warmth.

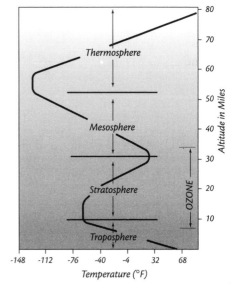

The four layers of the atmosphere

What's in the Air?

Our atmosphere is mostly nitrogen and oxygen. Atmospheric nitrogen, the most abundant gas, is relatively inert and not directly available to plants. Certain common bacteria, however, have access to it and, in a process called nitrogen fixation, convert nitrogen gas into organic molecules that plants can use. Oxygen, the second most abundant gas, is involved in many processes—respiration, the weathering of rocks, combustion, and the decomposition of organic materials. While nitrogen, oxygen, and a third element, argon, make up 99.96 percent of the atmosphere by volume, they have little or no affect on our weather. With carbon dioxide, only about three-hundredth's of a percent by volume, it's a different story. Carbon dioxide absorbs energy radiating outward from the earth and traps heat within the atmosphere. The percentage of carbon dioxide in the air has increased for more than a century and has warmed the earth. Water vapor also influences weather—it affects humidity, storms, precipitation, and temperature, for example. Ozone, considered a pollutant at lower levels, forms a protective filter in the upper atmosphere that shields the earth from ultraviolet radiation. Without this shield, most life on earth would not survive.

MOLECULAR MAKEUP

Molecule	Percent by Volume
Gas	
N_2	78.084
O_2	20.946
Ar	0.934
CO_2	0.034 (varies)
Ne	0.00182
H	0.000524
CH_4	0.00015
O_3	0.00006
H_2	0.00005
H_2O	0–4
Pollutant	
CO	0.00002
O_3	0.000004
SO_2	0.000001
NO_2	0.000001
Dust	0.00001

Continental Albedos

The fraction or percentage of solar radiation reflected from a surface is measured in albedos. Albedos for the same kind of surface will vary from place to place depending on the amount of cloud cover and pollution and the angle of the sun's rays. Controlling for these variables, the albedo for fresh snow is 80 to 85 percent; for grass 20 to 25 percent; for dry earth, 15 to 25 percent; and for forest 5 to 10 percent. The albedo for the earth as a whole is around 30 percent. A generalized albedo map follows.

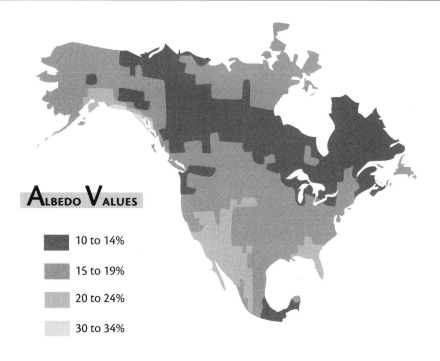

ALBEDO VALUES

- 10 to 14%
- 15 to 19%
- 20 to 24%
- 30 to 34%

TIMES BETWEEN SUNRISE AND SUNSET

Latitude	Summer Solstice June 21–22 (hours: min)	Winter Solstice Dec 21–22 (hours: min)	Equinoxes Mar 21–22 & Sept 22–23 (hours: min)
90° N (North Pole)	24:00 (6-month-long day)	00:00	12:00
80° N (Ellesmere Island)	24:00 (4-month-long day)	00:00	12:00
70° N (Disko, Greenland)	24:00 (2-month-long day)	00:00	12:00
66.5° N (Arctic Circle)	24:00	00:00	12:00
60° N (Lake Athabaska)	18:27	05:33	12:00
50° N (Winnipeg, Manitoba)	16:18	07:42	12:00
40° N (Indianapolis, Indiana)	14:52	09:08	12:00
30° N (New Orleans, Louisiana)	13:56	10:04	12:00
20° N (Mexico City)	13:12	10:48	12:00

Solstice and Equinox

The official beginning of summer, the summer solstice, falls on June 21 or 22, when the earth's axis in the Northern Hemisphere tilts 23.5° toward the sun. At that angle, the sun's vertical rays strike 23.5° N latitude (the Tropic of Cancer), and the North Pole is at the point of maximum inclination toward the sun. On this day, North America experiences the longest period of daylight and the highest noon sun.

Conditions reverse during the winter solstice. On December 21 or 22, the beginning of winter, the North Pole reaches the point of maximum inclination away from the sun. The sun attains its lowest angle, and the Northern Hemisphere receives the least amount of daylight.

Equinoxes, the official beginnings of fall and spring, fall halfway between the solstices, when the vertical rays of the sun strike the equator. During an equinox, every place on the earth has 12 hours of daylight and 12 hours of darkness.

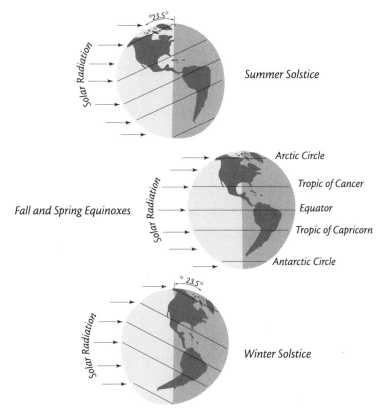

Angle of the sun during summer and winter solstices and fall and spring equinoxes

CLIMATE

A BALANCE EXISTS BETWEEN THE AMOUNT of solar radiation the earth receives and the amount of energy radiating from the planet. Without this balance, or heat budget, the earth would become colder or warmer. Ultimately, life would cease. The earth's temperature has fluctuated many times since the Precambrian era for various reasons, all having to do with shifts in the heat budget. Every change affected life on earth; the major swings destroyed many species.

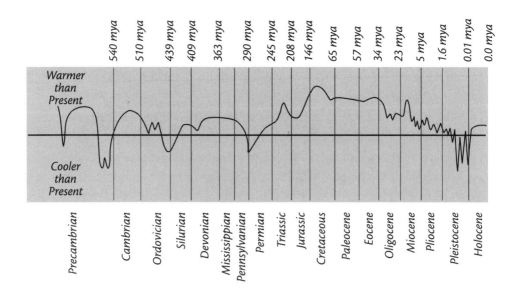

Estimated changes in global temperatures from the Precambrian to the present

The Flow of Air

The sun drives the most basic pattern of circulation in the lower atmosphere. Air warmed in the tropics rises and moves toward the poles, where it displaces cold air, which moves back toward the equator. This very simple pattern would prevail but for the earth's rotation and the tilt of its axis, which give the flow of air both a vertical and horizontal structure. The vertical structure consists of three large cells: the tropical Hadley, the midlatitude Ferrel, and a weak and erratic Polar Cell. The horizontal structure, which operates close to the earth's surface, includes the tropical Trade Winds, the midlatitude westerlies, and the polar easterlies.

In the tropical zone, from the equator to between 20° and 35° N latitude, the Hadley Cell moves warm air poleward. As air rises at the equator, cumulus clouds form, and precipitation falls. The air, depleted of moisture, then flows aloft until it reaches the latitude of Baja California, where it sinks back to the surface of the earth and splits, part rushing back toward the equator, part flowing north toward the pole. For centuries, the zone where the Hadley Cell subsides has been called the Horse Latitudes because winds there are mostly vertical and have often stranded large sailing ships. Sailors, low on feed and water, threw their horses overboard. The Coriolis force, generated by the earth's rotation, causes winds in the Northern Hemisphere to deflect to the right. Air flowing southward from the Horse Latitudes moves dependably from the northeast to the southwest, a horizontal flow known as the Trade Winds.

In the midlatitudes, between 30° and 60° N, the Ferrel Cell operates, moving air in a manner opposite that of the Hadley: the air aloft flowing south, the air at the surface north, toward the pole. Here, the Coriolis force deflects the surface flow to the east, and the winds are known as the Prevailing Westerlies (wind direction is defined as the direction *from* which the wind

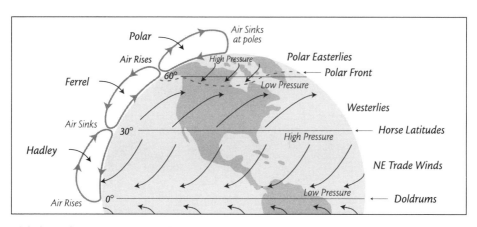

Global circulation patterns over the Northern Hemisphere

blows). Disrupted by both low and high pressure systems, westerlies are less reliable than Trade Winds. Still, they force most of the weather over North America to move from west to east.

The three-cell model of global circulation suggests an easterly flow aloft at mid-latitudes (in the upper half of the Ferrel Cell) because of the Coriolis force. But a westerly flow prevails, because temperature differences create a pressure gradient that stretches from the equator to the poles. The difference in pressure, when combined with the Coriolis force, generates westerly winds at just about all latitudes except the equator and the pole.

Above 60° north latitude, the Polar Cell moves the air aloft toward the pole, and the air at the surface toward the equator. The surface flow is easterly because of the Coriolis force. The polar front occurs where the cold, polar easterlies encounter the warmer westerlies. The front migrates

between 30° and 70° north latitude and generates storms and most of the precipitation received across a wide swath of North America.

Temperatures vary considerably over continent-sized landmasses, especially during winter, and the mix of continents and oceans disrupts the global flow of air. Whereas the three-cell model predicts four discrete belts of high and low pressure—a low at the equator, a subtropical high between 20° and 35° N, a subpolar low between 50° and 60° N, and a polar high at the top—the Northern Hemisphere actually has a group of semipermanent pressure cells that change with the seasons.

These two maps, one for January and one for July, depict a better approximation of the pressure patterns over North America during the winter and summer. The numbers represent average surface pressures, the arrows average wind directions. The cells of low and high pressure mediate the short-

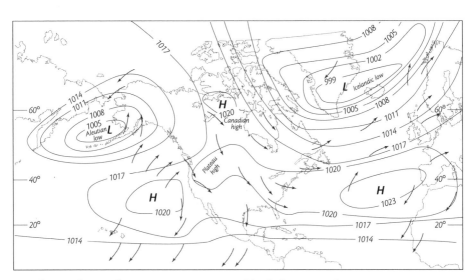

Circulation of air and average air pressures over North America in January

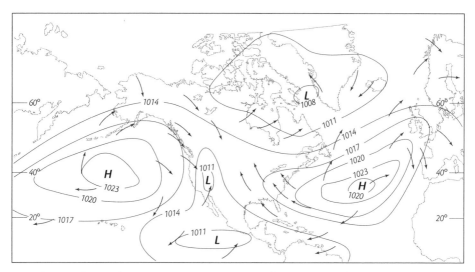

Circulation of air and average air pressures over North America in July

term changes in humidity, temperature, and precipitation that we call "the weather." The lows, or cyclones, generally coincide with stormy conditions and account for most of the precipitation the continent receives. The highs bring fair weather.

Three high pressure systems directly affect North America in January: the Canadian High in the far north and two subtropical highs—one over the eastern Pacific and one over the eastern Atlantic. A portion of the Eastern Atlantic High, known as the Plateau High, extends as far as the western U.S. Strong circulation above the continent increases the size of the Plateau High. To the north, mild, moist Pacific air rushes inland and moves rapidly across the northern U.S., usually dropping some precipitation on the West Coast. At other times, the Canadian High dominates and extends a wedge of high pressure

into the southwest. The Plateau High weakens or disappears; little surface air flows from west to east across the continent. Two lows—the Aleutian and the Icelandic—dominate circulation over the oceans; a large number of storms moving eastward across the globe converge in these two areas. Low pressure does not extend across most of North America because the continent is too cold.

In the summer, North America warms, and a low pressure cell forms over the southwestern U.S. Meanwhile, the two subtropical highs over the Pacific and Atlantic, which are broken by the low pressure cell, become strong enough to dominate circulation over the oceans. They send air flowing over the continent. The high pressure center above the Atlantic Ocean, for example, causes a stream of warm, moist air to flow inland from the Gulf of Mexico.

El Niño

According to meteorologists, no place on earth is indifferent to the air and ocean currents of the tropical Pacific. In 1982 and 1983, for example, *El Niño*, the periodic warming of the tropical Pacific, brought North America one of the warmest winters and wettest springs on record. The *El Niño* of 1997 and 1998, set new records for winter warmth and wetness.

Coastal Peru is a desert, but the Pacific Ocean there abounds with life, thanks to a cold, plankton-rich upwelling that flows north. During an *El Niño*, a south-flowing current moderates the otherwise low surface temperatures. For centuries, locals called this current *El Niño* (the child Jesus) because it arrives around Christmastime. Every three to ten years, however, the current warms and penetrates farther south and deeper into the central Pacific. During these years, *El Niño* brings unusual amounts of precipitation to western South America and causes unusual weather just about everywhere else around the globe. Now, the name *El Niño* describes these periodic episodes of ocean warming, when the warm south-flowing current is at its maximum and affects circulation throughout the entire ocean basin. Meteorologists use the term *La Niña* (the girl) to refer to more normal years.

Changes in atmospheric circulation over the Pacific precede an *El Niño*. During most years, a high pressure center resides over the eastern Pacific near South America, and low pressure dominates the region of the Pacific near Indonesia. Because air flows from a region of high pressure to one of low pressure, the Pacific Trade Winds blow to the west, toward Indonesia. Warm surface water builds up in that part of the Pacific and seas there rise. Meanwhile, in the eastern Pacific, cold water wells up from the ocean bottom as the sea level drops. During *El Niño*, this situation reverses. Barometric pressure drops in the east and rises in the west, and the normal pressure gradient weakens or flips. Pacific Trade Winds reverse direction, blowing toward South America. Warm surface water follows. The eastern Pacific warms, and the ocean rises. Scientists call the shift in atmospheric pressure that seems to trigger *El Niño* the Southern Oscillation, but they do not know its causes.

When the Southern Oscillation occurs, higher barometric pressure over the tropical Pacific and Indian Oceans initiates changes in rainfall patterns and winds worldwide. Monsoons sometimes fail and cause drought. In the eastern tropical Pacific, near South America, warmer ocean temperatures heat the overlying air and force warm, wet conditions inland. The heat feeds the tropical jet stream, which generates storms and precipitation across the Western Hemisphere. During *El Niño* years, North America has warmer, wetter winters and soggier springs.

The intervening *La Niña* is not totally benign. Some meteorologists blame intense *La Niña* conditions for the North American drought of 1988.

El Niño and North America's Weather

North America generally receives its strongest *El Niño* impacts during the winter and early spring. The most noticeable change in the weather is much-higher-than-normal winter rainfall for the southern United States. However, important changes can occur much earlier in the year. The persistence of abnormally warm ocean waters off the West Coast, for example, may bring marine species from the Baja Peninsula to the Pacific Northwest. This happened during the record-breaking 1997–98 *El Niño* event. Another early impact may be reduced tropical storm and hurricane activity across the eastern seaboard and Gulf Coast of the United States. In 1997, for example, only one system (Danny) entered the country.

In the future, *El Niño* will likely contribute to record warm temperatures in North America. The very strong *El Niño*-Southern Oscillation episode in 1997 and 1998 was a major factor causing the record high global temperatures in 1997, according to the World Meteorological Organization. During that year, temperatures averaged well above normal over Alaska and the West Coast of North America. A region-by-region summary follows.

Western Canada and the Northwest

Typically, this region experiences less precipitation and warmer-than-normal temperatures during *El Niño* winters.

Ohio Valley States

This area can expect drier-than-normal conditions from January to March.

Southern Alaska

El Niño normally contributes to warmer-than-normal temperatures in the winter season in southern Alaska.

California

Abnormally wet weather is expected across the state during an *El Niño*, with excessive snowfall over the Sierra Nevadas and other ranges. These conditions result from an overall southward shift in winter storms from the Pacific Northwest to the latitude of central California. Between July 1, 1997, and mid-February of 1998, for example, San Francisco received over 34 inches of rain. It normally receives around 20 inches a year.

Southwestern United States

This region can expect enhanced winter rainfall at lower elevations and increased snowfall at higher elevations. The chances of winter drought are significantly reduced across the region during an *El Niño* event.

Northern Tier of the United States

This area can expect warmer-than-normal winter conditions.

Central Plains and Texas

This area often receives above-normal precipitation in the fall preceding an *El Niño*. During the *El Niño* winter of 1997 and 1998, heavy rains flooded parts of Texas.

Southeastern United States

Storms tend to be more vigorous in the Gulf of Mexico and along the southeast

Years of Strong to Moderate El Niños

1911-19	1920-29	1930-39	1940-49	1950-59	1960-69	1970-79	1980-89	1990-97
1911	1925	1939	1941	1951	1965	1972	1982	1991
1912	1926			1953	1969	1976	1986	1997
1914	1929			1957				
1918				1958				
1919								

coast of the United States during *El Niño* years. This results in wetter-than-normal conditions from October to March, with cooler-than-normal temperatures throughout the Gulf Coast States. During February of 1998, severe *El Niño*-driven storms hit in and around Orlando, Florida. They brought tornadoes that killed over fifty people and injured more than two hundred. Associated wind gusts were estimated at 248 miles per hour. Authorities described the disaster as the worst day of tornadoes ever to hit central Florida. Earlier, in late December of 1997, another record-breaking *El Niño*-associated storm dumped up to 9.75 inches of snow in the southeastern U.S. Parts of Louisiana recorded unusual December snow that year, as well.

Disease and Climate
Button Up That Overcoat

Scientists now suspect that climate has a major effect on human diseases. New research has linked specific outbreaks of Lyme disease, hantavirus, malaria, cholera, Ebola, and even the plague of fourteenth century Europe, to changes in the weather.

For example, *El Niño* may have triggered the 1991–92 outbreak of cholera in Central and South America, the 1993 eruption of hantavirus in southwestern North America, and the major outbreaks of malaria that have occurred in the Western Hemisphere over the last thirty years. The hantavirus cases coincided with the year *El Niño* broke a six-year drought in the southwest. The drought had suppressed populations of deer mouse predators. Deer mice carry the hantavirus disease and can transmit it to humans. *El Niño* brought rain, vegetation rebounded, and the mouse population soared. Because of their large numbers, deer mice came into more frequent contact with humans. The disease spread. Some authorities now attribute the Black Death of the Middle Ages to a similar sequence of climate-triggered events.

As climates change worldwide, scientists warn that global warming will allow subtropical and tropical diseases to migrate north. Warmer temperatures can shorten disease gestation times, increase the food and lifespan of disease-carrying organisms, and allow infections to spread to previously uninfected species. Health researchers utilize weather satellites and radar, climate-change models, and global weather-data networks to monitor potential disease outbreaks. Buttoning up that overcoat may help prevent a cold, but if the climate warms as predicted, colds may be the least of our worries.

Air Masses and Their Source Regions

Air masses—immense pools of air that generate much of North America's weather—form in predictable areas called source regions. The source region determines the characteristics of an air mass—how wet, dry, hot, or cold it will be. As the air migrates, it carries those characteristics with it, bringing weather, good or bad, to a large part of the continent.

Meteorologists classify air masses according to the latitude of the source region and the humidity of the air. Latitude, which affects only temperature, has four categories: polar (P), arctic (A), tropical (T), and equatorial (E). (The terms *polar* and *arctic* can be confusing; here, polar refers to air masses that originate at latitudes between 45° and 66° N and that are cold; arctic designates frigid air that originates even farther north.) Continents and oceans determine the humidity: the continents generate continental air masses (c) that are dry; the oceans, maritime air masses (m) that are humid. The air masses that influence North America the most are:

cA	continental arctic
cP	continental polar
cT	continental tropic
mP	maritime polar
mT	maritime tropic

Sometimes meteorologists add other letters, a lowercase "k" for cold and a "w" for warm, to describe the temperature of the air mass relative to the air at the surface. A continental polar air mass moving over warmer surface air is designated cPk. A "u" indicates unstable conditions.

Air masses change as they move across continents, so designations can be misleading. As polar maritime air moves across the Rockies, it loses moisture and gains heat, so that by the time it reaches the plains, it is warm and dry; meteorologists refer to it as *modified* mP air.

Arctic air masses (cA) carry the most frigid temperatures to North America. As they move south, they bring clear skies, low humidity, and high pressure. And because they encounter no significant obstacles like mountains, they can affect every midwestern and eastern state in the U.S., including Florida, during the winter months. In summer, arctic air generally reaches only as far south as mid-Canada. Polar air masses, which are more common than arctic air masses, are not as cold because they form over Canada and the Gulf of Alaska. But they are as dry. In winter, they, too, move rapidly across the Great Plains and can travel all the way to Mexico without warming much.

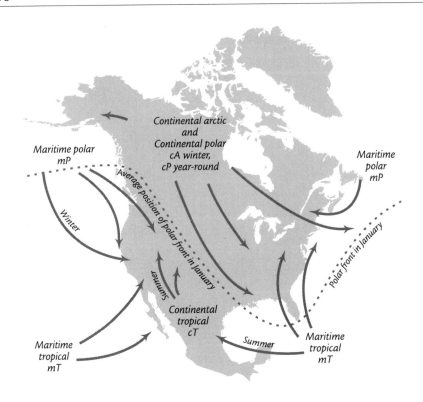

North American air masses and their source regions

In summer, only the extreme southern part of the continent sees tropical air masses. In winter, however, tropical air can reach the Canadian border. Sometimes during the winter, tropical air masses form between California and Hawaii. Drifting eastward, they affect weather on the West Coast.

When an air mass moves from its source region, it encounters an adjacent air mass with different properties. Meteorologists refer to the zone between the two as a front—the line where contrast between temperature, humidity, and wind direction is often considerable. The cold front, the most common type in North America, can generate squalls, tornadoes, and strong winds, especially during the transitional months between winter and spring and between summer and fall. Warm fronts are common during winter and cause fog and precipitation as they move north into Canada. Stationary fronts, which generate weather similar to cold and warm fronts, occur when the leading edge of an air mass fails to displace the air ahead of it. An occluded front forms when a fast-moving cold front catches a slower warm front. Clouds and rain or snow are usually more extensive along occluded fronts.

Air Masses and Source Regions

Air Mass	Source Region	Characteristics	Associated Weather
cA	Arctic Basin and Greenland Ice Cap	Bitterly cold and very dry in winter. Stable.	Cold waves in winter.
cP	Interior Canada and Alaska	Very cold and dry in winter. Cold and dry in summer. Stable entire year.	a. Cold waves in winter. b. Modified to cPk in winter over Great Lakes. It brings heavy, wet snow to leeward shores.
mP	North Pacific	Mild (cool) and humid entire year. Unstable in winter. Stable in summer.	a. Low clouds and showers in winter. b. Heavy orographic precipitation on windward side of western mountains in winter.
mP	Northwestern Atlantic	Cold and humid in winter. Cool and humid in summer. Unstable in winter. Stable in summer.	a. Occasional "northeaster" in winter. b. Occasional periods of clear, cool weather in summer.
cT	Northern interior Mexico and southwestern U.S. (summer only)	Hot and dry. Unstable.	a. Hot, dry, and clear, rarely influencing areas outside of source region. b. Occasional drought to southern Great Plains.
mT	Gulf of Mexico, Caribbean Sea, western Atlantic	Warm and humid entire year. Unstable entire year.	a. In winter, it usually becomes mTw moving northward and brings occasional widespread precipitation or fog. b. In summer, hot and humid conditions, frequent cumulus development and showers or thunderstorms.
mT	Subtropical Pacific	Warm and humid entire year. Stable entire year.	a. In winter, it brings fog, drizzle, and occasional moderate precipitation to northwestern Mexico and the southwestern U.S. b. In summer, this air mass occasionally reaches the western U.S. and is a source of moisture for infrequent convectional thunderstorms.

What the Wind Tells Us
Using Wind to Determine Pressure Centers

Wind moves from an area of high pressure into an area of low pressure; its strength is proportional to the pressure difference. A deepening low pressure system advancing across the midlatitudes in winter will usually generate strong winds in advance; the lower the pressure, the greater the likelihood of gales.

Because of the Coriolis effect, winds in the Northern Hemisphere blow inward and counterclockwise around a low pressure center. Winds associated with a high pressure system blow slightly outward from the center, clockwise. To determine the location of pressure centers, stand with your back to the wind; the pressure to your left will always be lower. The opposite holds true south of the equator.

The Polar Front and the Jet Stream

The most important weather phenomenon at midlatitudes in North America is the polar front, where polar and tropical air masses converge. The zone of the polar front, which extends between 45° and 55° N, receives more precipitation than areas to the north and south because the competing air masses generate frequent storms and sharp temperature contrasts. It might be 70°F along the Gulf Coast, for example, and near freezing 100 miles to the north.

The steep temperature gradients found along fronts, especially during winter, give rise to high winds aloft. The winds, called jet streams, range from 50 to 250 knots (58 to 287 mph). Narrow, meandering rivers of fast-moving air, they move in an undulating wavelike pattern 30,000 to 35,000 feet above the earth. The polar jet stream, the predominant high-altitude wind crossing the middle latitudes of North America, flows just north of the polar front. To the north of it, cold air dominates; to the south, warmer air. Whereas the jet stream generally moves west to east, it meanders freely, sometimes flowing almost due north or south. Strongest in the winter, the polar jet stream influences the weather of North America by supplying energy to surface storms and by directing their paths. In summer, the polar jet stream migrates north and carries with it severe thunderstorms and tornado activity.

A second, almost permanent jet stream influences the southern half of the U.S. Subtropical, it travels globally between 20° and 30° north latitude, and while its winds are considered strong over the U.S., this more southern jet stream attains its highest speeds off the coast of Asia.

Average position of the polar jet stream in summer and winter

Major North American Climates

A mixture of factors determines climate: latitude, the distribution of land and water, prevailing winds, mountain ranges, ocean currents, and pressure systems. Latitude, for example, governs the length of the day and the angle of the sun, factors which in turn affect the amount of solar radiation received and, therefore, the temperature. The distribution of land and water also affects temperature. Land heats and cools faster than water and experiences higher maximum and lower minimum temperatures. Areas influenced by oceans generally have milder climates than those in the middle of continents. Marine cli-

mates also have different seasonal precipitation patterns. Prevailing winds determine whether an area will have a marine or continental climate. Much of the Atlantic Coast, on the lee side of North America, has a continental climate, while the Pacific Coast, on the windward side, has a maritime climate. Mountains can block the flow of maritime air and, through a process called orographic lifting, force air masses to drop their moisture on windward slopes, leaving the leeward sides dry. Ocean currents, both warm and cool, also affect climates. And pressure systems, generated by global circulation patterns and the earth's

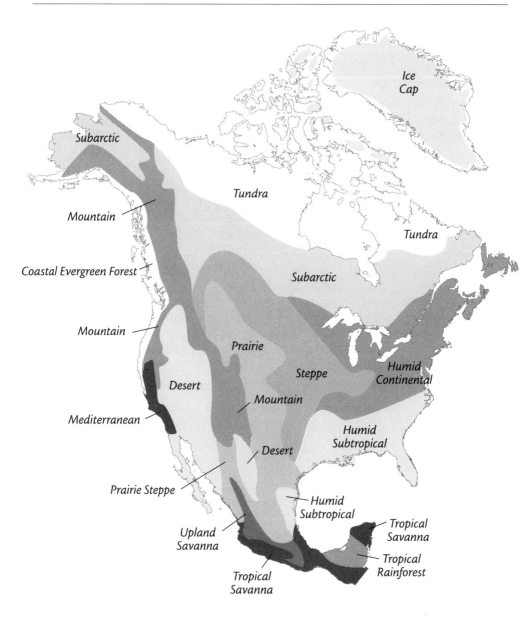

Climates of North America

rotation, influence the distribution of storms and precipitation. All these factors and more contribute to North America's climate, a complex mix that ranges from frigid cold in Greenland to sultry heat in the Florida tropics and from damp in the rain-soaked mountains of coastal British Columbia to arid in the deserts of northern Mexico.

Wladimir Köppen developed the Köppen Classification System, one of the simplest and most widely used methods of classifying climates. Köppen believed natural plant communities reflect climate, especially temperature and precipitation patterns, so he defined climatic regions based on the distribution of plant communities. Descriptions of North American climatic regions follow.

Ice Cap

Permanent ice sheets over water and land define this northern climate. Bitterly cold temperatures dominate; the annual mean ranges from -20° to -5°F. Winters are dark almost 24 hours a day. Even though summer days are long, summers are cool because the sun remains low in the sky, and the ice reflects 80 percent of all solar radiation. Temperature inversions, common in the region, foster strong winds and blizzardlike conditions. Most of the Ice Cap Region receives under 10 inches of moisture a year, the majority falling during the summer months.

Tundra

Only low shrubs, sedges, grasses, mosses, and lichens grow in the Tundra Region. Trees are mostly absent; scattered clumps of stunted spruce hide in sheltered depressions. Subsoils are frozen year-round; during the warmest months, surface soils may thaw 3 feet down. Most of the Tundra Region has a continental climate characterized by long, severe winters; short, cool summers; and great annual temperature differences. July temperatures average between 41° and 50°F, February's between 5° and -22°F (although they can drop as low as -60°F). Precipitation is meager and comes mostly in the form of light, steady summer drizzles; thunderstorms rarely occur. Winter snows tend to be fine, light, and dry.

Warmed by the North Atlantic Drift, the southern coast of Greenland enjoys a milder, maritime climate with relatively warm winters; February temperatures average 20°F. Southern Greenland receives almost eight times the precipitation that most locations in the Tundra Region receive.

A tundra climate also occurs at high elevations in the western Cordillera as far south as Mexico.

Subarctic

Dominated by a vast forest of few species of trees—spruce, fir, larch, birch, poplar, and alder—the Subarctic Region is cold in the winter and warm in the summer. January temperatures average below 10°F, but temperatures frequently drop to as low as -60°F. Winter minimums are among the lowest recorded on the continent outside of Greenland; the severe cold is a result of high pressure cells that often settle over the region. Although any month can see frost, summertime temperatures average above 50°F and can reach 100°F. Nowhere else in North America is the annual temperature range as great. For instance, in Dawson, Canada, the difference between the mean temperature of the coldest month, January, and that of the warmest month, July, is 82°F.

The source region for dry continental-polar air masses, the Subarctic itself receives little precipitation. Winter, the driest season, sees only fast-moving fronts that drop meager amounts of dry snow. The east is an exception, however. Quebec and Labrador receive five times as much snow (195 inches) and have twice as many snow days (100) as western locations. As a whole, the region averages 20 inches of precipitation a year, two-thirds of which arrives in summer during long, steady rains. Thunderstorms occur five to ten days each year.

Humid Continental

The Humid Continental Region nourishes a richer forest community than the Subarctic; still, winter temperatures average below freezing four months or more of the year. Means range from 0° to 15°F in the Great Lakes–St. Lawrence Region to 30°F in New York City, which is under the influence of maritime air. Large temperature shifts happen quickly in winter because a steep north-south temperature gradient crosses the region. Summer temperatures are more uniform and are often above 70°F. Most precipitation falls in summer. Annual means range from 25 to 40 inches. The East Coast and southern reaches, influenced by flows of maritime air, are wetter. Thunderstorms occur thirty days a year.

Humid Subtropical

The Humid Subtropical Region encompasses the southeastern U.S., where over two hundred deciduous and coniferous tree species thrive, thanks to mild winters and hot, tropical summers. Frosts are common during winter in the more northern latitudes, although monthly means stay well above freezing. Farther south, frosts are rare, and winter temperatures are warm much of the time. January means in southern Florida range between 64° and 68°F, and the growing season is 350 days long.

In the summer, daytime temperatures range from 60° to 100°F. The yearly precipitation average for almost all locations exceeds 40 inches; the Gulf Coast receives in the range of 50 to 60 inches. As maritime air masses move inland, they heat up and become increasingly unstable; thunderstorms ensue. Fifty to one hundred thunderstorm days a year soak the region in the summer, bringing most of the precipitation. Tropical cyclones, some of which develop into hurricanes, also peak in the summer and account for about 15 percent of the precipitation along the Gulf and Atlantic coasts.

Prairie-Steppe, or Grassland

A continental climate with four well-defined seasons dominates this region, which is located in the heart of North America. Encompassing the tallgrass prairie in the east, the shortgrass prairie or steppe in the west, and the mixed-grass prairie in between, the region is dry for two primary reasons: it is situated in the center of the continent, and mountain ranges to the west block moist Pacific air masses. In winter, cold, dry continental air dominates. Cold fronts can cause temperatures to plummet—from the low 50s to below 0°F in a matter of hours. Continental air masses encountering low pressure systems often generate blizzard conditions—winds in excess of 15 to 20 miles per hour and snow. January temperatures in northern latitudes average around -5°F but sometimes drop to -50°F. By contrast, summer temperatures are hot. The July mean in Alberta reaches 65°F; in North Dakota, 70°F; and in Kansas, above 80°F. During July and August, in central portions of the region, daytime temperatures stay above 90°F more than half the time, and in Texas, the thermometer registers above 90° more than 80 percent of the time. West winds often blow during hot spells. Heating up as they descend from the Rockies and cross the plains, they contribute to droughts.

Between 20 and 35 inches of precipitation a year falls on the tallgrass prairie, which extends from central Illinois to the 100th meridian. Only 10 to 20 inches water the western shortgrass prairie. Around three-quarters of the moisture that falls on the prairie arrives between April and September, much of it during thunderstorms brought by warm, moist air masses moving in from the Gulf of Mexico or tropical regions of the Atlantic. Tornadoes are common during the roughly forty thunderstorm days a year.

Winter moisture falls mostly as fine, light snow brought by air originating over the northern Pacific. Winter chinooks—strong, warm winds off the Rockies—blow between January and March, with gusts reaching speeds exceeding 80 mph. In a matter of hours, they often raise the temperature by tens of degrees, melt snow, and desiccate plant life.

Mountain

A diverse terrain with a complicated climatic pattern unique to North America, the Western Cordillera includes the Rocky Mountains, the Interior Mountains and Plateaus, the Colorado Plateau, and the Pacific Rim and Coast ranges. The dramatic relief within and between ranges accounts for the complexity. As elevation increases, temperatures decrease. Colorado Springs, for example, is 6,000 feet above sea level and has a mean annual temperature of 48°F. The mean for Pikes Peak, just 9 miles to the west but 8,100 feet higher is only 19°F. Atmospheric moisture also decreases with increasing elevation. However, wind speed, the intensity of solar radiation, and the proportion of precipitation that falls as snow increases as the land gains in elevation.

As moist, mild, maritime air rises to move across the mountains, it cools, and the moisture it holds condenses. Clouds form and precipitation falls on the windward side of the ranges. In the rain shadow, the leeward slopes receive little moisture. Sixty-six inches of moisture fall on Startup, Washington, on the windward side of the Cascades. Ephrata, Washington, on the leeward side, receives only 7.3 inches. Most precipitation falls during the winter as snow. The Cascades, which receive among the heaviest snows, get up to 580 inches between November and June. Elsewhere along the West Coast, means range from 300 to 400 inches, although Mount Rainier has recorded annual snowfalls of near 1,000 inches.

On summer days, the air along mountain slopes warms more than the air on the valley floor. This differential generates upslope winds called valley breezes. During winter nights, mountain slopes lose heat quickly, and winds called mountain breezes blow downhill.

Desert

Technically, what most people refer to as desert in North America—the Mojave, the Chihuahuan, the Sonoran—are not true deserts. Most years they receive too much rain—more than 4.7 inches a year, the cutoff point for a true desert—although areas within each fit the definition. North America's dry terrains are officially classified as semideserts with semiarid climates. Here, however, they will be referred to as deserts.

All of North America's desert climates are characterized by meager and erratic precipitation exceeded by evaporation. The continent's arid landscapes include midlatitude upland deserts in the Rockies and more western ranges; tropical deserts in northern Mexico and on the southern fringes of California, Arizona, and New Mexico; and a West Coast tropical desert in Baja California.

Cloudless skies dominate. During the summer, deserts receive more than 80 percent of the sunshine possible. In winter, those at lower latitudes receive more than 70 percent. The figure is lower, about 50 percent, for midlatitude deserts, because winter storms from the northern Pacific bring cloudy skies. All that sunshine, combined with humidities of 10 percent or lower, generate high temperatures and high levels of evaporation. The temperature regime for an average August day at Yuma, Arizona, typical of tropical deserts, starts

MAJOR DESERTS AND NEAR DESERTS

Great Sandy Desert in central Oregon

Desert of southeastern Washington and northern Oregon

Bighorn and Bridger Basins of Wyoming

Great Basin, extending from southeastern Oregon to southern Nevada

Colorado Plateau of Colorado, Utah, Arizona, and New Mexico

Mojave Desert, northeast of Los Angeles

Death Valley, along California's border with Nevada

Coachella Valley, southeast of Los Angeles

Imperial Valley, extending from southernmost California into northern Mexico

Sonoran and Chihuahuan Deserts of Arizona, New Mexico, and northern Mexico

at 78°F at dawn and reaches 111°F by mid-afternoon. Dry soils can reach 150°F and atmospheric humidity generally hovers between 8 and 10 percent. Famous for extreme temperatures, Greenland Ranch in Death Valley has a July mean of 100°F and a record of 134°F. Yuma averages 95°F but has reached 120°F. Midlatitude deserts tend to be cooler: at Redmond, Oregon, the July mean is 66°F. Desert temperatures drop quickly at night when cloudless skies and low levels of humidity allow terrestrial radiation to dissipate. Low-latitude deserts endure the greatest daily temperature ranges on the continent.

Precipitation, 10 inches or less in most North American deserts, is unreliable. In midlatitude and California deserts, most moisture arrives during winter, whereas in middle latitude deserts in the eastern part of the region, such as the Bighorn Basin, the bulk of the precipitation falls during the summer. Precipitation patterns in tropical deserts are more erratic and difficult to characterize.

Coastal Evergreen Forest

Fifty to 100 miles wide, the Coastal Evergreen Forest Region runs along the western, or windward, edge of North America from the Cooke Inlet of Alaska to San Francisco Bay. Influenced primarily by moist maritime air from the North Pacific, the region is famous for mild temperatures, heavy precipitation, and humidity—conditions that support dense, damp, coniferous forests of spruce, hemlock, and alder in the north and Douglas fir and redwood in the south. In Alaska, at places like Sitka

and Yakutat, the winter mean temperature ranges from 28° to 32°F. Eureka, California, averages a balmy 46°F. On rare occasions, frigid continental air pours over the mountains from the east and causes temperatures to drop. But, usually, coastal ranges protect the region from cold, dry continental air. During the summer, temperatures are cool. Along the coast from Alaska to California, the monthly mean in June, July, and August hovers around 55°F. Means inland vary from 58° to 66°F.

The region is one of the wettest in North America because coastal ranges force moist Pacific air masses to rise and drop their moisture; precipitation totals are almost twice as high as they would be if there were no mountains. Average annual precipitation is around 80 inches; however, many areas receive from 100 to almost 200 inches. Less moisture falls during the summer months when a subtropical high in the eastern Pacific migrates northward. Although too weak to bring long periods of fair weather, the high pressure cell reduces rainfall.

Mediterranean

Dominated by chaparral and scrubby live oak trees, the Mediterranean Region, stretching from north of Redding, California, into Baja California, is a transition zone between the rain-soaked evergreen forests to the north and the deserts to the south. A subtropical high pressure cell over the Pacific Ocean enforces mostly clear skies and warm to hot temperatures in the region all summer. The moderating influence of the ocean and the cold California

Current ensures that the coast stays cooler, cloudier, and more humid than inland areas. The average daily high in July in San Francisco, located on the coast, is 65°F. Inland, at Sacramento, it is 80°F. Winters are mild and, about a third of the time, without clouds. January temperatures in the north average above 35°F but drop to as low as 18°F on clear nights. In the south, the January mean is above 40°F.

Most precipitation arrives during the winter. Means range between 16 and 32 inches, although most sites see considerable variation around the mean. Red Bluff, California, for instance, records a mean of 25 inches of precipitation a year but has received as little as 10 and as much as 68. Areas in the north see a longer rainy season and more moisture: San Francisco, which receives 95 percent of its precipitation between October and April, gets just under 20 inches. Los Angeles, with a rainy season two months shorter, receives 15 inches a year. Snow rarely falls, except in the mountains. Thunderstorms, unusual outside of the mountains, occur on only three to five days a year. Fog and clouds are common along the coast.

Tropical Rainforest
Half an acre of tropical rainforest fosters as many species of trees as the entire southeastern portion of the U.S. Tall, broadleaved, and luxuriant, the forests are green year-round. Every month of the year, temperatures average above 77°F, and abundant rain falls. The regularity of warmth and moisture—the absence of extreme temperatures—nurtures the rich and diverse plant communities. In the Tropical Rainforest Region, days are all about the same length regardless of the season, so the amount of solar radiation remains constant. Surprisingly, the temperature range over a 24-hour period is two to five times greater than the range between monthly means. Precipitation is high; some areas receive more than 190 inches a year.

Tropical Savanna
The Tropical Savanna Region is made up of grasslands with scattered deciduous trees. Although the region has only a slightly lower mean annual temperature than the Tropical Rainforest Region, and an annual temperature range only slightly greater, the savanna gets less rainfall during a pronounced winter dry season. And unlike the rainforest, the Tropical Savanna has a warm season in spring.

During the dry season, which is longest in the north, drought conditions prevail; a high pressure system brings stable, fair conditions all winter long. Trees lose their leaves and grasses turn brown. After the spring equinox, however, the high pressure cell shifts to the north. Moisture conditions become similar to those of the rainforest. But because rains fall only during the summer, the savanna receives about 50 inches of precipitation a year—one-quarter of what the rainforest gets.

Evidence of a Changing Climate
A Record in Rock Cast Across the Ocean Bottom

Radical temperature shifts during the last glacial period may explain debris scattered across the ocean floor. During major cold intervals, which occurred every 7,000 to 10,000 years, the Laurentide Ice Sheet (the vast ice sheet that covered much of Canada) apparently surged forward into the Hudson Strait, where it calved thousands of icebergs that clogged the North Atlantic. Between the surges, which occurred every 2,000 to 3,000 years, minor cold episodes caused a different lobe of the ice sheet to pulse forward and discharge ice into the Gulf of St. Lawrence. Both events left behind signatures on the ocean bottom: trails of pulverized carbonate rocks from the Hudson Strait region and red hematite from the Gulf of St. Lawrence.

Scientists do not know the cause of the temperature swings. Some attribute them to shifts in ocean currents, others to cyclic variations in solar output. In either case, the findings have prompted researchers to take a closer look at more recent portions of the Greenland ice cores, those representing the modern period—the Holocene, which began 11,000 years ago. It has long been assumed that the Holocene has experienced a relatively stable climate, but ice cores are revealing that temperatures in the Northern Hemisphere have shifted between cold and balmy every 2,600 years or so. We know from the record left by glaciers that the most recent period of global cooling, The Little Ice Age, started about 1400 and continued until 1850. The ice cores also describe another major bout of cooling between 6,100 and 5,000 years ago and two less intense cool periods from 3,100 to 2,400 years ago and from 8,800 to 7,800 years ago. Scientists do not know where we are in the cycle or what the effects of global warming caused by greenhouse gases will be, only that the climate equation is more complex than they once thought.

Think the Weather Is Capricious Now?

Locals just about everywhere recite the old adage: "Tired of the weather? Stick around for a few minutes, and it'll change." But research in Greenland suggests North America's present climate is stable compared to the climate of 20,000 years ago.

To learn about past climates, scientists measure oxygen isotopes from ice cores drilled nearly 2 miles deep into the ice of central Greenland. The cores reach ice that formed over 110,000 years ago; they provide an estimate of the weather for each year since. The thickness of an annual ice layer tells how much snow fell. The ratio of different oxygen isotopes in the layer supplies estimates for the temperature at the time, and the amount of dust and sea salt provides clues to the degree of aridity and windiness.

Twenty thousand years ago, during the height of the last glacial maximum, a stormy climate and turbulent atmosphere prevailed. Vast ice sheets and colder northern oceans sustained a steep thermal gradient between the equator and the pole, a gradient that gave rise to an energetic atmosphere. The turbulence generated severe storms with extreme temperatures and winds. Annual snowfall accumulations varied by a factor of two or three, dust deposits by a factor of 100. So, to see truly erratic weather, just stick around until the next ice age.

TEMPERATURE, PRECIPITATION, AND STORMS

THE TWO MAPS BELOW DISPLAY MEAN sea-level temperatures for January and July, the coldest and warmest months in the Northern Hemisphere. Sea-level temperatures eliminate differences related to elevation. The maps reveal a poleward temperature decrease. The ability of solar radiation to heat the earth's surface and atmosphere depends on the angle of the sun and the length of daylight, both functions of latitude. The maps also reveal the effects of the seasonal latitudinal shift in the posi- tion of the vertical rays of the sun that strike the earth. The annual temperature range, the difference between January and July temperatures, increases with latitude. No- tice, too, how temperatures fluctuate over land where there is little water to moder- ate temperatures. The coldest and hottest temperatures occur on the continent, and the isotherms are closer over North America than either the Atlantic or Pacific, meaning as one travels north, temperatures drop faster over land than sea.

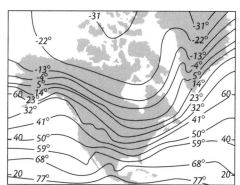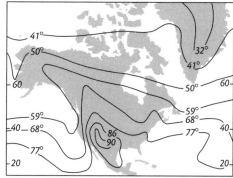

Mean sea-level temperatures (°F) for January (left) and July (right) for latitudes above 20° N

RECORD TEMPERATURES

Record	Temp (° F)	Place	Date
Lowest temperature in North America	-87	Northice, Greenland	January 9, 1954
Lowest temperature in North America outside of Greenland	-81	Snag, Yukon Ter.	February 3, 1947
Lowest monthly mean temperature excl. Greenland	-54	Eureka, NW Ter.	February 1979
Highest temperature in Western Hemisphere	134	Death Valley, CA	July 10, 1913
Hottest average summer	98	Death Valley, CA	1941–1971
Largest 24-hour temperature fall in U.S.	100	Browning, MT	January 23–24, 1916
Largest 2-minute temperature rise	49	Spearfish, SD	January 22, 1943

The Sway of the Sea

The sea exerts a moderating influence on temperatures at coastal sites, as shown by the monthly temperature averages for two North American cities: Vancouver, British Columbia, by the sea and Winnipeg, Manitoba, inland. Both cities are at about the same latitude, but Winnipeg has colder winters and slightly warmer summers.

Oceans provide less influence where prevailing winds blow from the land toward the ocean, which explains why the coast of Northern California has cooler summers and warmer winters than the coast of New York. On the windward side of the continent, mountains can block the moderating effect of oceans. Areas east of the Coast Ranges of British Columbia and Washington, for instance, tend to have a more continental climate.

Ocean currents also affect climates. The warm current sweeping the southeast-

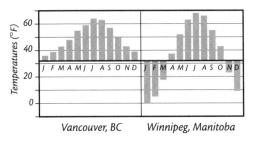

Monthly temperature averages of two cities, one near the sea, the other inland

ern margin of the continent originates in the tropical region as the Equatorial Current. Flowing through the Caribbean Sea and the Gulf of Mexico into the North Atlantic, it becomes known as the Gulf Stream and brings warm, rainy weather to the subtropical portion of eastern North America. At Cape Hatteras, the Gulf Stream, leaving the coast, encounters the cold Labrador Current. The sharp temperature gradient there often generates dense fog. North of Cape Hatteras, the Labrador Current brings cool summer temperatures. Labrador itself is bathed by a polar current originating in Baffin Bay.

Along the West Coast, the cool California Current flows toward the equator from the vicinity of the Oregon-California border and carries cool winds to the coast. The Mediterranean climate there is known for its dry summers. To the north, the warm Alaska or North Pacific Current moves poleward and contributes to a maritime climate: cool summers, warm winters, and abundant precipitation.

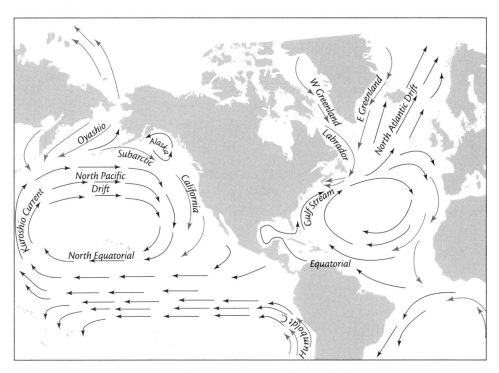

Major ocean currents affecting North America are shown here with the dark arrows indicating a warm current, the lighter arrows a cool current.

Precipitation Patterns

The map below of mean annual precipitation shows that the wettest regions of the continent are generally associated with the Polar Front, where polar and tropical air masses converge. Except for southern Mexico, precipitation tapers off both north and south of this zone. Seasonal patterns are as follows: the subtropics are mostly dry all year; the Mediterranean Region has rainy winters and dry summers; the temperate latitudes receive some precipitation in every season, but most of their moisture falls during the summer months; polar regions receive meager amounts of moisture throughout the year.

Mean annual precipitation across the continent

RECORD PRECIPITATION

Record	Amount (inches)	Place	Date
Greatest average yearly precipitation in North America	256	Henderson Lake, BC	14-year period
Lowest average yearly precipitation in North America	1.2	Bataques, Mexico	14-year period
Possibly world's greatest 24-hour rainfall on flat terrain	43	Alvin, TX	July 25–26, 1979
World's greatest 42-minute rainfall	12	Holt, MO	June 22, 1947
World's greatest 1-minute rainfall	1.23	Unionville, MD	July 4, 1956
Greatest snowfall in one season in North America	1,122	Rainier Paradise, WA	1971–1972
Greatest 24-hour snowfall in North America	76	Silver Lake, CO	April 14–15, 1921
Greatest snowfall in one storm in North America	189	Mt Shasta, CA	Feb. 13–19, 1959
Greatest depth of snow on the ground in North America	451	Tamarack, CA	March 11, 1911
Largest hailstone in U.S.	17.5 (circum)	Coffeyville, KS	Sept. 3, 1970

Major Droughts of the Last One Hundred Years

All parts of North America experience droughts. Similarly, all parts of the continent experience protracted periods of higher-than-normal wetness.

An analysis of tree rings, old lake levels, and precipitation records indicates that most of the western U.S. endured a severe drought between 1830 and 1850. Precipitation data show that droughts also struck the plains in 1889, 1890, 1894, 1901, 1910, and 1917.

One analysis describes thirty-eight one-year droughts between 1881 and 1934 in the eastern and southeastern parts of the U.S. and twenty-eight droughts over the same period in the semiarid states. Included among the latter is the well-known Dust Bowl drought of the 1930s, one of the longest, most severe, and most widespread dry spells to hit North America in modern times.

Severe drought struck again from 1942 to 1956 across most of southern California, Arizona, New Mexico, and west Texas. Precipitation dropped to less than 85 percent of normal for more than eight years. The southern half of the U.S. experienced dry weather from 1952 to 1956, and the most severe period of dryness to hit the eastern U.S. and adjacent Canada occurred from 1961 to 1966.

One of the worst short droughts in North America over the last fifty years occurred from 1976 to 1977. During that spell, the combined flow of the "big five" rivers—the Mississippi, Columbia, St. Lawrence, Ohio, and Missouri—dropped to below normal for six consecutive months, and much of the continent experienced record low precipitation and streamflows for over a year. Groundwater levels reached record lows across large areas, and irrigators and municipalities pumped reservoirs dry. Another serious drought in 1988 saw record low flows on many major rivers. Drought struck again in the southwest in 1996. Reservoir contents sank to record low levels, and temperatures soared. Corpus Christi, Texas, for example, tied their record high temperature three days in a row during the summer of 1996.

The first two columns of the table that follows represent the area of the Great Plains region characterized by drought in a given year, the third and forth columns, the area that was unusually wet.

The numbers suggest that drought (or wetness) on the Great Plains rarely lasts for two or more consecutive years and

WET AND DRY YEARS

Dry Year	Area of Drought	Wet Year	Area of Wetness
1901	69%	1902	42%
1904	44	1905	40
1910	71	1908	40
1913	57	1915	73
1917	53	1923	40
1924	56	1927	62
1929	51	1935	40
1930	51	1941	61
1931	71	1942	77
1934	87	1951	47
1936	67	1957	61
1937	48	1965	67
1939	48	1968	45
1943	43	1973	44
1949	40	1978	47
1952	54		
1954	44		
1956	59		

that, generally, droughts and wet periods do not extend across large areas. Most dry and wet years affected less than 60 percent of the region. Data for the Great Lakes and Midwest regions describe a similar pattern. The 1980s, however, broke these trends on the plains—much of the region experienced severe droughts early in the decade.

Scientists search for long-term cycles in rainfall. Some believe rainfall in the Great Plains and Great Lakes regions follows a twenty- or twenty-two-year cycle (twenty-two years is the sunspot cycle). But recent work reveals some irregularity—a 15- to 25-year periodicity. One researcher concluded that although several weak cycles in the 2- to 6-year range occur in the Great Plains, droughts are not periodic.

Recent studies on the western half of the continent suggest that droughts and floods reflect an 18.6-year periodicity— that the cycle of droughts in the western U.S. and Mexico and of floods in western Canada occur in phase with the period of the lunar nodal tide. In spite of the correlation, predictions of when or where the next drought will strike generally fail. All we can say for certain is that long and short dry spells will continue to be a regular part of the continent's climate.

Winter Storm Tracks

Although storms follow many paths, most parallel the polar jet stream. Consequently, they tend to converge on the northeastern states where they dump much of their moisture. Farther west, storms are more spread out; winters are drier.

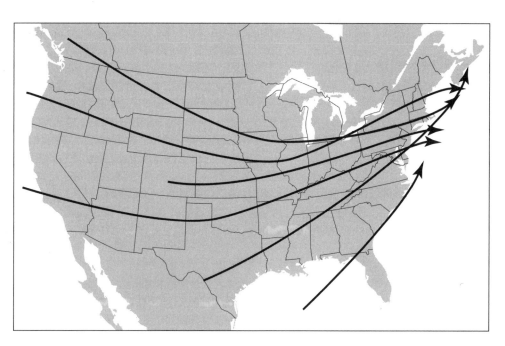

Typical winter storm tracks across the U.S.

RECORD THUNDERSTORMS

Record	Number (Days)	Place	Date
Highest frequency of days with thunderstorms in U.S.	100 per year average	Tampa International Airport, Florida	1934

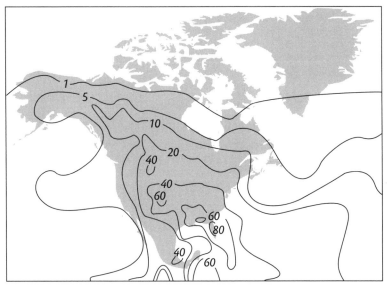

Number of annual thunderstorm days across North America

RECORD WINDS

Record (excluding tornadoes)	Speed (mph)	Place	Date
Highest surface wind speed (peak gust) in world	231	Mount Washington, NH	April 12, 1934
Highest surface wind speed (peak gust) in Greenland	207	Thule, Greenland	March 8, 1972
Highest surface wind speed (5-minute speed) in world	188	Mount Washington, NH	April 12, 1934
Highest mean for 24 hours	128	Mount Washington, NH	April 11–12, 1934
Highest mean for a month	70	Mount Washington, NH	February 1939

Tornadoes: The Basics

Less than 1 percent of the hundred-thousand-plus thunderstorms that form over the U.S. each year produce tornadoes. In spring, when cold, dry continental polar air encounters moist, warm tropical air from the Gulf of Mexico, conditions are ripe for tornado formation, especially when the temperature contrast between the two air masses is great. The exact mechanism of formation remains unknown, but most tornadoes form when strong updrafts of a thunderstorm mix with horizontal winds in the lower atmosphere.

 Tornado Facts

North America sees an average 770 tornadoes a year, although some years have as few as 450 and others have as many as 1,200.

Most tornadoes occur between April and June, the fewest between December and January.

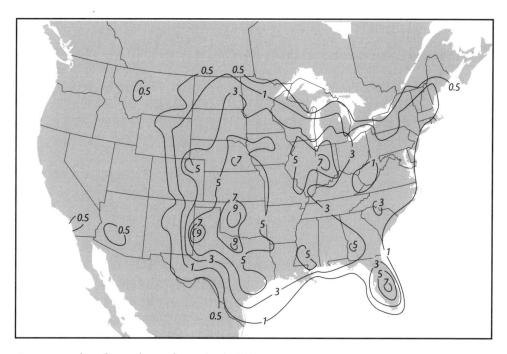

Average number of tornadoes each year in the U.S.

Tornado Facts (cont.)

The worst single tornado on record, the Great Tri-State Tornado of 1923, traveled 219 ground miles and killed 695 people.

The worst outbreak of tornadoes occurred on April 3 and 4, 1974. Residents of the southeast reported 147 tornadoes in two days, storms that took 335 lives.

While the average tornado has a diameter of between 500 and 2,000 feet and travels about 16 miles, over half are under 300 feet in diameter and travel under half a mile.

Winds range from 90 miles per hour in a short-lived, low-intensity storm to 275 miles per hour in a severe one. Sixty-three percent of all tornadoes are classified as weak (they have winds under 111 miles per hour). Only 2 percent of tornadoes are classified as violent (their winds exceed 206 miles per hour).

The center of maximum tornado activity migrates as warm, moist air masses from the Gulf penetrate deeper into the heart of the U.S. In February, when the season begins, most tornadoes form over the central Gulf states, but by March, the center of activity moves to the southeastern Atlantic states and by May and June, to the southern plains, northern plains, and the Great Lakes region.

Tornadoes are classified according to the Fujita Intensity Scale (F-scale) shown below, which is based on the worst damage caused by a storm.

Class	Wind Speed (mph)	Damage
F0	< 70	Light
F1	70–112	Moderate
F2	113–157	Considerable
F3	158–206	Severe
F4	207–260	Devastating
F5	> 260	Incredible

Hurricanes

The greatest storms experienced by North Americans are hurricanes—storms that average 370 miles across with winds that reach speeds of over 185 miles per hour. Hurricanes begin over the ocean as tropical disturbances. Until their winds exceed 37 miles an hour, they are called tropical depressions. When wind speeds are between 38 and 71 miles an hour, they are labeled tropical storms. Storms with winds exceeding 71 miles an hour are hurricanes.

Hurricanes form within the Trade Wind Belt, between latitudes 5° and 20° N, in a region where water temperatures remain above 81°F. As storms mature, they move west with the Trade Winds and turn north when they encounter the western edge of the subtropical high.

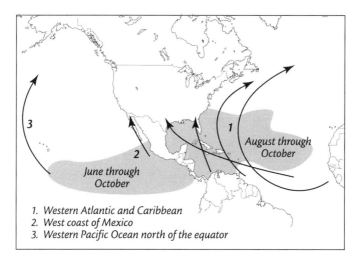

Regions of hurricane genesis around North America

Part Four
PLANTS

Part Four Plants

NUMBERS AND DISTRIBUTION

LARGELY TEMPERATE, NORTH AMERICA north of Mexico lacks the diversity of continents that are mostly tropical. Mexico alone, with both subtropical and tropical regions, has more indigenous flowering plant families than all of the rest of North America combined—some 235 altogether. The data in the chart below were compiled in such a way that Mexico is included with Central America rather than North America. Still, with 312 indigenous families, temperate North America's plant life is more diverse than that of the former Soviet Union, Europe, and New Zealand.

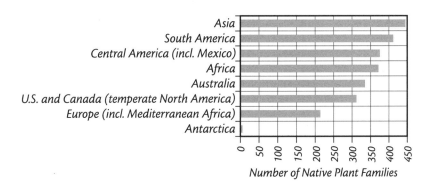

Number of Native Plant Families

Number of native plant families by continental region

The floristic richness of states and provinces as measured by the number of native plant families

Floristic Provinces

Name	General Description	Number of Species
Circumboreal Region Arctic Province	Treeless, mostly tundra grading into polar desert to the north, the Arctic lacks endemic families and has relatively few species. Many species occur throughout the polar regions of both the Eastern and Western Hemispheres. Endemic species number under 100. Because of Pleistocene glaciation, the present floristic communities of the Arctic are only a few thousand years old. Individual species, however, may be ancient.	The only complete flora of the Arctic region lists 70 vascular plant families, 230 genera, and 892 species.
Canadian Province	Dominated by coniferous forests and dotted with lakes and *Sphagnum* bogs, the Canadian Province has only about 25 endemic species. Many of the plants are also found in boreal regions of Eurasia or are closely related to species found there. Because of Pleistocene glaciations, plant communities formed quite recently.	No complete flora of the province exists. The province hosts in the range of 1,600 species.
North American– **Atlantic Region** Appalachian Province	Prior to European settlement, this province was mostly a vast forest comprised of maple, buckeye, birch, hickory, beech, tuliptree, magnolia, cherry, oak, basswood, and a number of conifer species. Many of the genera also occur in eastern Asia. Many of the genera in the southern part of the province are found in western North America. Because of the pattern of Pleistocene glaciations and coastal plain inundations, the Appalachian Province includes many endemic species.	The province has an estimated 5,500 to 6,000 species.
Atlantic and Gulf Coastal Plains Province	Because of frequent fires and excessively or poorly drained and sandy soils, this floristically rich province is dominated by pine. Bald cypress and various broad-leaved hardwoods are found in swampy areas. Several hundred endemic species, several endemic genera, and one endemic family grow here. Because of Pleistocene flooding, vegetation communities are young with elements recruited from neighboring provinces. Many of the plants on the southern coastal plain are also found in the highlands of Mexico.	We have no comprehensive floristic treatment of the province, but some local counts provide one measure of diversity: the coastal plain of southern New Jersey supports 1,373 species; the Delmarva Peninsula, 2,111; southwestern Georgia, 1,750; and central Florida, 2,197.

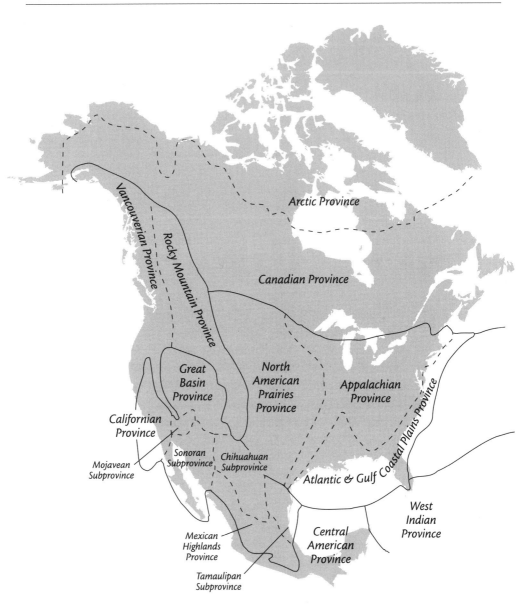

The floristic provinces of North America

Floristic Provinces (cont.)

Name	General Description	Number of Species
North American Prairies Province	This vast grassland of prairie and plain has been maintained, to a large extent, by fire. The province probably has fewer than 50 endemic species. Because of Pleistocene glaciations, vegetation in northern portions of the province is recent.	The Great Plains in the U.S. shelters 3,067 species.
Rocky Mountain Region Vancouverian Province	The province is dominated by conifers but has more broad-leaved species than other northwest provinces. The coastal slopes on the north end support a wet and tall temperate rainforest. Redwoods grow on seaward slopes to the south. The province has roughly 500 to 600 endemic or near-endemic species.	It is estimated the province supports 3,000 to 3,500 species of indigenous vascular plants.
Rocky Mountain Province	Because of continental glaciation, the vegetation of the northern (Canadian) part of the province is recent, relatively poor in species, and low in endemic species. Many species are also found in the boreal and polar areas of Eurasia. Flora is richer and endemism higher in the U.S. portion of the province. Forty species are endemic to special habitats and another 50 to the southern Rocky Mountains. The province, dominated by conifers, has an eastern deciduous forest element, circumpolar and circumboreal elements, and a southwestern desert-steppe element.	The province probably has from 4,000 to 4,500 species.
Madrean Region Great Basin Province	In this province, most of which lies above 4,250 feet in elevation, north-south-trending mountain ranges separate internally drained valleys or basins. The vegetation, shaped by aridity and cold winters, is mostly sagebrush, shadscale, greasewood, and grasses. On higher slopes, pinyons and junipers are common. The province shares elements of the neighboring Rocky Mountain, desert, and steppe provinces. Endemic species number between 500 and 700.	The province has about 3,000 species.

FLORISTIC PROVINCES (CONT.)

Name	General Description	Number of Species
California Province	Floristically rich, this province has many native species and many endemic species; about 50 genera and some 2,000 species are found only in the California Province. In its natural state, the California Province encompassed a huge variety of diverse vegetation types including prairies, savannas, woodlands, mixed evergreen and evergreen forests, vernal pools, alpine tundra, and sage scrub. Many elements of the California Province derive from adjacent provinces. The part of the province with a Mediterranean climate shares 100 species with parts of Chile that have a Mediterranean climate. Its flora is similar as well to that of the Mediterranean region of southern Europe and north Africa.	About 4,000 species grow in this province.
Sonoran Province	This arid province is divided into four subprovinces. The Mojavean is diverse in topography and climate. It has 21 distinct plant communities. At least 107 species are endemic. The Sonoran subprovince, lower and hotter than the Mojave, has more rain in summer and less frost in winter, a more subtropical climate. It is characterized by woodlands of small-leaved trees and tree-like cacti. About a quarter of the species (670) are endemic. The Chihuahuan subprovince, characterized by creosote bushes and various yuccas, is cooler than the Sonoran and has more frost in winter. About 545 species are endemic. The Tamaulipan subprovince is not as dry as other subprovinces and supports thornscrub and mesquite-grassland.	Some 1,899 species live in the Mojavean subprovince. An estimated 2,700 species grow in the Sonoran subprovince. The Chihuahuan subprovince has 3,233 species.
Caribbean Region West Indian Province	The North American part of this province includes only the southern third of Florida and the Florida Keys. It is dominated by West Indian genera, tropical families, palms, mangroves, and the like. In southern Florida, about 61 percent of the plants are considered tropical. In the entire province, about 50 percent of the species are endemic.	No complete flora of the North American part of this province has been completed, but the three southernmost counties of Florida are home for an estimated 1,647 species.

NUMBER OF PLANT SPECIES IN MEXICO

Group	Estimated Number of Species	% of all Species Worldwide
All Plants	29,000–34,0000	11–12.7
Orchids (Orchidaceae)	935	5.3
Cacti (Cactaceae)	900	54.5
Legumes (Leguminosae)	1,706	10.4
Conifers (Coniferophyta)	80	14.5
Ferns (Pteridophyta)	900–1,000	8.3
Mosses (Bryophyta)	2,000	12.0

The Vegetation Regions of North America

Arctic

Occupying 1.56 million square miles or about 20 percent of the continent, the Arctic is a treeless area that supports evergreen and deciduous shrubs, cushionlike and matlike herbs, grasses, sedges, mosses, and lichens—plants adapted to cold temperatures, winter desiccation, ice abrasion, regular summer drought, and strong, gale-force winds. Arctic winters are long, frigid, and dark; summers are cool and nightless. Soils are poorly developed and, except for a thin surface layer, are frozen year-round. Cold air holds little moisture, so precipitation is

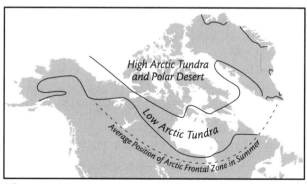

The Arctic Region

scarce. Still, melting snow and poor drainage leave surface soils saturated in the early part of the growing season.

Before the last ice age, forests blanketed the Arctic; then, during the ice age, glaciers scoured the land of all its vegetation. So, present communities are not more than a few thousand years old. They have had less time to evolve than those of other North American vegetation types. Most of the plants now growing in the Arctic probably derived from species in the mountainous parts of central Asia; fewer have come from the Rockies to the south.

Adaptive Strategy in the Arctic

The Arctic challenges plants with its short growing season, continuous darkness in winter, low intensity sunlight in summer, permafrost, nutrient-poor soils, aridity, ice abrasion, dry winds, and scarcity of pollinating insects. Arctic plants grow in ways similar to temperate species, except they photosynthesize at lower temperatures, grow faster, and respond to different environmental cues. Adaptations include:

• The ability to start in spring with an explosion of growth. Growth begins when bud temperatures reach 32°F for just a few hours a day. Many plants grow under the snow. Some species produce flowers within a day or two of spring thaw; they rely on sugars stored the previous summer and they winter with leaf and flower buds in an advanced state of development.

• The ability to photosynthesize at temperatures as low as 32°F. In addition, Arctic plants grow best at lower temperatures, and their roots are less temperature sensitive. In Arctic species, rates of mitochondrial activity, shoot respiration, and phosphate absorption are higher. Maximum rates of photosynthesis match those of temperate plants.

• The ability to control water loss more efficiently than temperate species. Arctic plant leaves (small, entire, firm-textured, or hairy) and growth forms (short, cushionlike, or mat-forming) limit desiccation. The growth forms also keep the plants close to the ground where Arctic air is the warmest.

• The ability of the leaves and roots of some species to function for two years or more, which means the plants need fewer nutrients. Others relocate nutrients to underground organs and to the bases of shoots before their leaves drop.

• The ability of mosses and lichens, common throughout the Arctic, to grow during any season; in other words, growth occurs whenever conditions are favorable.

• The ability of most perennials to reproduce both vegetatively and by seed. Members of the rose, sunflower, and other families produce flowers and seeds asexually, an advantage with scarce insect pollinators. Few annuals live in the Arctic.

Vascular plant diversity, abundance, height, and percent cover (the percentage of the ground covered by plant growth) generally decrease with latitude, while lichen and moss diversity, abundance, and percent cover increase. About 700 species of plants grow in the Arctic in two vegetative zones or formations. The Low Arctic Zone is characterized by almost 100 percent plant cover and moist to wet soils, especially in the spring, when water from melting snow collects atop slow-thawing soils.

The High Arctic Zone, comprised of the polar desert and polar semidesert, lies mostly in the northeast part of the Northwest Territories and northern Greenland. Dry soils limit plant cover to less than 5 percent. Most of the vegetation hugs meltwater channels and other damp areas. The short growing season and arid conditions limit productivity.

Boreal Forest or Taiga

Mostly spruce and fir, the boreal forest, the largest vegetative type in North America, comprises over a quarter of the continent. In the south, the taiga begins where winters last longer than six months and the growing season is under 120 days. In the north, the taiga surrenders to tundra where the winters last longer than eight months, and the growing season is under ninety days. Neither boundary is easily defined, however. In the southeast, the boreal forest fades into mixed deciduous forests and in the southwest into the coniferous forests of the Rockies. The northern boundary, known as treeline, is more sharply defined but still irregular. Sheltered valleys can harbor fingers of trees that extend more than 200 miles into the tundra. Likewise, tundra on exposed ridges can reach deep into the forest.

Spruce, fir, larch, and pine dominate this forest community, although hardy deciduous trees like alder, birch, poplar, and aspen thrive, too. Scattered throughout are meadows, shrubfields, and bogs. Cool summers and cold winters limit diversity; only the Arctic has fewer species. Frost can descend any month and, oddly, winter temperatures are frequently lower in the Boreal Forest Region than in the Arctic, which is warmed by maritime air. Annual precipitation ranges between 12 and 35 inches, most falling during the summer.

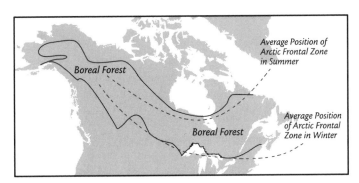

The Boreal Region

Many areas appear wetter, however, because during the cool summers evaporation rates are low. As in the Arctic, glaciers scoured this region during the ice age, and the present plant communities have occupied it for only 3,000 to 6,000 years.

Soils in upland areas are typically acidic and relatively infertile. The region falls within the zone of discontinuous permafrost, and the presence or absence of frozen subsoils affects the pattern of vegetation. Plants with deep taproots, like jack and white pine, cannot grow where permafrost is near the surface. Shallow-rooted species like black spruce and larch occupy those sites. Because of the harsh conditions, conifers generally grow only 50 feet high and form dense stands everywhere except on dry sites in the far north.

Large fires burn regularly, and many species have adapted to fire. Some spruces and pines, for instance, release seeds in response to the heat generated by wildfires. Similarly, aspen and birch sprout from root crowns after fire has killed their trunks. Fires encourage plant diversity and make openings used by wildlife. Many boreal species would disappear without fire.

Three formations constitute upland portions of the boreal forest. The largest and most southern of these, the closed-canopy forest, is dominated by black spruce or white spruce in the overstory and feathermoss beneath. White spruce and balsam fir communities thrive in the east,

With a Little Help from Their Friends

What's a tree without its fungi? Unhealthy, if it's growing in the boreal forest where most species establish mutually beneficial relations with fungi. The mycelia of the fungi, a network of fine white threads, attach to and form sheaths around the roots of both trees and shrubs, each species of fungus bonding to a specific host species or group of species. The fungus helps the host plant absorb nutrients like nitrogen and phosphorous while protecting it against disease. The tree or shrub meanwhile provides carbohydrates to the fungus.

Coral-root orchids and certain members of the wintergreen or heath family also tap specific hosts. Lacking chlorophyll, orchids and wintergreen plants obtain all their nutrition from trees via the fungi. Radioactive carbon compounds injected into trees show up in nearby coral-root orchids and wintergreen plants. Similarly, radioactive phosphorous injected into the orchids ends up in neighboring trees. The fungi benefit because the orchids supply them with organic nutrients and growth-stimulating compounds.

Trees have other friends, too. The feathermosses found in the spruce-moss community hold moisture in the soil. Like a mulch, they protect the trees against periodic droughts. Mosses also absorb mineral nutrients directly from the rain. As they die and decay, they release the nutrients into the soil in a form available to trees and shrubs and their fungi. The trees in turn provide shade for the mosses.

black spruce in the west. More productive and diverse, the eastern closed-canopy forests support an understory of shrubs, herbs, and moss.

The second largest formation, a lichen woodland, lies to the north. It is also dominated by an overstory of black or white spruce, but the trees are more scattered. Six-inch-tall reindeer lichens carpet the woodland floor. The third formation, the forest-tundra ecotone, lies on the northern edge of the lichen woodland and represents a transition zone between taiga and tundra. South of the treeline, the formation is half forest or woodland, half tundra. North of the treeline, tundra surrounds widely scattered clumps of dwarfed trees.

All three formations host shrubfields of green alder, dwarf birch, and willow. Shrub communities are stable in the north but grow only in wet or recently burned areas in the south, sites eventually taken over by conifers. Bogs—communities of black spruce, shrubs, and herbs growing in wet peat—dot much of the Boreal Forest Region.

Eastern Deciduous Forest

Occupying 11 percent of the continent, the Eastern Deciduous Forest Region extends from the Canadian-U.S. border to southern Georgia, and from the western edge of the Great Lakes to the East Coast in the north and the Coastal Plain in the south. Beyond the northern boundary, the growing season is too short for deciduous trees to produce enough sugar to compensate for the cost of producing new leaves each spring, a problem evergreens do not face. Beyond the western boundary, seasonal

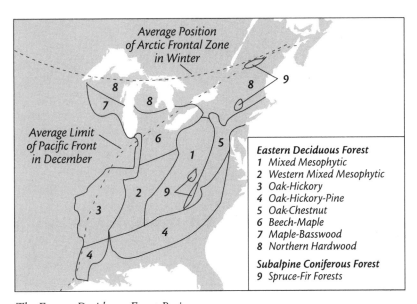

The Eastern Deciduous Forest Region

water deficits favor grasslands over forest, though the amount of precipitation necessary to support trees varies. For instance, in the north, where evaporation rates are low, eastern deciduous forests need only about 23 inches of moisture a year. In the south, where it is hotter, trees require 35 to 40 inches.

In the northern part of the region, the growing season is under 150 days, the mean annual temperature is only 48°F, and mean annual precipitation is 27 inches. In the southeast, the growing season is over 280 days long, the mean annual temperature is about 66°F, and annual precipitation is over 78 inches in places.

Although the range of climates across the region nurtures a mixture of forest types, some generalizations can be made. Oak, maple, beech, and basswood are common throughout, as are white pine and eastern hemlock. Most of the forests have five layers: a dense, 80- to 100-foot-high overstory of mature trees with trunk diameters as large as 3.5 to 5 feet; a more open subcanopy of immature and mature trees with low-stature species like flowering dogwood and redbud; a complex, three- to

Good-bye to a Tree
An introduced disease changed the forest

Once, the American chestnut claimed a third of the canopy in segments of the Eastern Deciduous Forest. From Maine to Wisconsin in the north to Mississippi and Alabama in the south, the tree prospered, growing up to 33 feet in circumference. People benefited from the chestnut's bounty: they gathered and sold its nuts, fed them to their hogs, and enjoyed the wildlife dependent on the tree. The wood made up a quarter of all the hardwood cut in the southern Appalachians.

Then the blight hit. Around 1904, importers of Asian chestnuts brought in a fungus native to China. The disease, known as the chestnut blight, destroys the phloem or food-transporting layer in the trunks of American chestnuts; Asian varieties are immune. Carried by birds, insects, and wind, the fungal spores spread throughout the east and killed almost half the native chestnuts in the northeast by 1920. Twenty years later, most chestnuts in western and southern portions of the forest had succumbed. Today almost none survive, although shoots continue to form on the still-living roots of destroyed trees. Soon after sprouting, these shoots are also taken by the blight. Meanwhile, chestnut oaks, red oaks, and red maples have filled the openings left by the giants. But unlike the chestnut, which produced prolific crops each year, oaks produce acorns intermittently.

Foresters have initiated breeding programs to hybridize the American chestnut with Chinese trees immune to the blight and have discovered a hypovirulent strain of the disease that spreads through wild trees; it hybridizes with and weakens the more lethal strain. Perhaps this American giant will return to reoccupy the important place it once did in the eastern forest.

four-tiered understory with one or two layers of shrubs; a layer of mostly perennial herbs; and a mat of mosses and lichens.

The Eastern Deciduous Forest is often subdivided into eight associations, which are described in the table below.

Eastern Deciduous Forest Associations

Name	General Description	Dominant Trees
Mixed Mesophytic	At the center of the province, this association has the greatest species diversity (any one of 33 different tree species may dominate any particular stand). Soils tend to be moist, well-drained, and fertile. Rainfall is reliable (mesophytic means growing in a moist environment). This association is best developed in the Cumberland Mountains.	American beech, tuliptree, several basswoods, sugar maple, sweet buckeye, red oak, white oak, and eastern hemlock (sweet buckeye and white basswood are best indicators). Oak dominates on upper slopes, oak-pine on poorer sites. American chestnut was a dominant species until the chestnut blight epidemic.
Western Mesophytic	Intermediate between the mixed mesophytic and the drier oak-hickory, this association is a transition zone supporting a mosaic of stands. Species diversity is almost as great as in the mixed mesophytic.	In the east, dominant species are similar to that of the mixed-mesophytic association. In the west, various oak and hickory species predominate. The gradient is a reflection of decreasing rainfall from east to west
Oak-Hickory and Oak-Hickory-Pine	Oak-hickory is the most widespread of all the associations. The size and density of trees decrease westward with declining rainfall. In the north and south, these associations grade into savanna. The greatest diversity occurs in central Arkansas. Regionally, soils are infertile and porous.	Mature stands dominated by oaks. White, red, and black oaks are widespread. Burr oak is dominant in the west, post oak and blackjack oak in the south. Hickories (bitternut, mockernut, red, and shagbark) are secondary in importance. Pine sometimes dominates in the east and south (oak-hickory-pine association), often occupying sites disturbed by fire or humans.
Oak-Chestnut	Since the introduction of the chestnut blight in 1906, this association has lost its dominant species and has undergone radical change.	Once dominated by American chestnut and various oaks and hickories, the oak-chestnut now supports chestnut oak, red oak, several other oaks, and hickories. Pitch pine invades burned or cut areas. Azaleas and rhododendrons tend to dominate the understory.

EASTERN DECIDUOUS FOREST ASSOCIATIONS (CONT.)

Name	General Description	Dominant Trees
Beech-Maple and Maple-Basswood	These associations are found only on glaciated terrain and are best developed on moist and well-drained soils. Young associations, they evolved from species migrating north after the Wisconsin glaciation.	American beech (in the canopy) and sugar maple (in the understory) are plentiful. American elm, ashes, and red maple are also common, especially in wet areas. Oaks and hickories are common on drier sites. American basswood replaces American beech west of Lake Michigan (maple-basswood association).
Northern Hardwood	Transitional between the deciduous and boreal forests, this association is defined by soil and fire. Over-cutting and associated slash-fires retarded white pine regeneration. Many sites supported giant white pines before European settlement but now grow hardwoods.	On fertile sites undisturbed by fire, sugar maple, American beech, American basswood, eastern hemlock, birch, and quaking aspen are dominant. On sandy, dry soils and sites disturbed by fire, white pine, red pine, and jack pine are more common. Other common species include red maple, yellow birch, larch, black spruce, white spruce, and red spruce.

High Elevation Appalachian Ecosystems

Deciduous forests cannot survive the harsh winters and short growing seasons of the Appalachian's upper elevations. Subalpine-coniferous forests and tundra claim these islands of high mountains from New England to southwestern North Carolina. In Vermont and New Hampshire, subalpine communities begin at 2,500 feet, while in the Great Smokies to the south, they begin at 5,500 feet. In the lower subalpine zone, red spruce is predominant. Birch, mountain ash, blueberries, pin cherry, and viburnum flourish, especially on sites disturbed by fire or insects. A double canopy develops, a 40- to 90-foot-high overstory shading a 14- to 40-foot-high subcanopy. Fir trees—balsam fir in the north and Fraser fir in the south—increase with elevation until they form pure stands. In the northern part of the region above 6,200 feet, fir ultimately gives way to alpine tundra.

More than two-thirds of the plants in the Appalachian tundra also grow in the Arctic. Like the subalpine coniferous forests, the tundra communities are relicts of the last ice age when glaciers reached as far south as 40° north latitude.

Southeastern Coastal Plain

The southeastern 3 percent of the continent has unique soils, topography, climate, and fire histories that favor a mix of communities—grasslands, savannas, shrublands, pine woodlands, evergreen hardwood forests, moist deciduous forests, coastal vegetation, and freshwater swamps. While pine-dominated forests reign on upland sites, wetlands dominate low-lying areas. The western boundary of the region, the line separating the Piedmont Plateau from the Coastal Plain, marks not only a shift in soils and geology but a change in climate. Humid and subtropical, the region is a transition between the moist deciduous forest and the wet tropics. To the south, broad-leaved evergreen trees—with tropical affinities like gumbo-limbo, pigeon-plum, strangler figs, and mahogany—thrive because, as in the tropics, winters

A cypress savanna

on the Southeastern Coastal Plain are warm and dry, and summers are hot and wet.

The longest growing season north of Mexico (350 days) is found along the coast and in the south. Rainfall peaks there, too. Lightning fires are common, and fire-adapted species are prevalent. More lightning storms hit the Coastal Plain than anywhere else on the continent. The same is true for hurricanes and severe convectional storms with their forest-leveling winds.

The plain has the greatest diversity of wetland communities anywhere in North America; 15 percent is classified wetland.

The Southeastern Coastal Plain can be broken into five formations, descriptions of which follow.

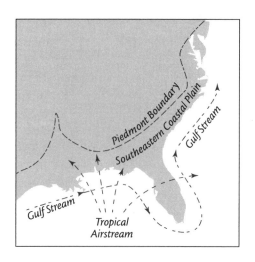

The Southeastern Coastal Plains Region

SOUTHEASTERN COASTAL PLAIN FORMATIONS

Name	General Description	Dominant Species
Upload pine forests		
Northern pine barrens	Limited to the coastal plain north of Delaware Bay, the pine barrens experience frequent fires. The canopy reaches its greatest height and density on coarse-textured soils.	Pitch pine, shortleaf pine, post oak, and blackjack oak. Similar in species composition to the ridgetop pitch pine forests of the southern Appalachians.
Dry sand communities (includes sandhill pine forest, pine scrub, and mesic forest communities)	Found throughout the southern part of the Coastal Plain, these communities are arid in spite of abundant rainfall; their coarse-textured sands hold little water. Frequent fires of low intensity race through the sandhill pine forest every 3 to 6 years. Less frequent but more intense, fires scorch the pine scrub communities every 30 to 60 years.	Longleaf pine in the overstory, blackgum, persimmon, and wiregrass in the understory in the sandhill pine forest. Sand pine in the overstory, saw and scrub palmetto, scrub live oaks, and some rosemary in the understory of sand pine scrub communities. In moist pine flatwood and savanna communities, the overstory is longleaf pine, slash pine, loblolly pine, and/or pond pine.
Upland hardwood communities	Generally, these are sites where fire has been excluded and hardwoods have succeeded pines.	Live oak in the overstory and American holly, various scrub oaks, saw palmetto, and lyonia in the understory on dry sites in Florida and along the Gulf. Moist, fertile sites in the same region are dominated by evergreen magnolia, American beech, various oaks, sweet gum, and loblolly pine. On moist, fertile soils in the Carolinas, fire exclusion leads to an overstory of hickory, American beech, white oak, and laurel oak.
Alluvial wetlands (wetlands associated with streams and rivers)	Characteristics vary. Botanists classify communities based on how often they flood. Types include: (1) permanent watercourses, (2) river swamp forests, (3) lower hardwood swamp forests, (4) forests of backwaters and flats, and (5) transitions to uplands.	The dominants by type are: (1) duckweed, water fern, various submerged aquatics, and alligator weed and water hyacinth (the latter two are exotics); (2) bald cypress and pond cypress, water and swamp tupelo, and eastern white cedar; (3) overcup oak and water hickory; (4) laurel oak, willow oak, American elm, green ash, and sweetgum; (5) baslet oak, cherry bark oak, water oak, live oak, hickory, and spruce pine.

SOUTHEASTERN COASTAL PLAIN FORMATIONS (CONT.)

Name	General Description	Dominant Species
Paludal (or nonalluvial) wetlands (wetlands associated with rainfall and groundwater flow)	Characteristics vary. Major types include: (1) prairie or grass-dominated, (2) shrub-dominated (pocosins), (3) Atlantic white cedar swamp forests, (4) bayheads (bay forests or baygalls), and (5) wet hammocks (cypress domes or cypress heads).	The dominants by type are: (1) sedges and rushes; (2) *Sphagnum*, pond pine, feterbrush, titi, and zenobia; (3) Atlantic white cedar; (4) sweet bay, red bay, loblolly bay; and (5) bald cypress, pond cypress, Spanish moss, resurrection fern.
Tropical hardwood forests (hammocks)	Tropical communities thrive only at the south end of Florida where soils are fertile and well drained and where fires burn infrequently. Communities are generally limited in size.	Live oak and various broad-leaved evergreen species associated with tropical climates.

Patterns of Change in Southeastern Wetlands

Plant communities change over time. The plants that occupy a site immediately after a fire or flood alter it by creating shade, holding moisture, and building soils. These modifications allow other species to establish, and a new community forms. But it, too, alters the site as it matures, ultimately creating conditions—such as heavy shade—that are unfavorable for its own reproduction. Different species—species able to reproduce under these new conditions—move in. The process continues like this until a disturbance—a flood, fire, logging operation, or strong wind—sets it back, or until a relatively stable community is reached: one that can reproduce and perpetuate itself on the site indefinitely. The process, called succession, is not always neat and predictable. Change, however, is an inevitable part of every plant community.

In the southeast, small stands of bald cypress and pond cypress grow in wetland areas known locally as cypress domes. In the areas that remain permanently flooded, cypress remains dominant, and the community is stable, at least until a severe fire sweeps through. But when nutrients are added to the system, as happens during a major flood, broad-leaved deciduous species like oak, pop ash, and red maple overtake cypress. On the other hand, when cypress domes dry out, broad-leaved evergreen species like sweet bay, red bay, and loblolly bay take over.

Cypress requires areas that are permanently inundated, yet cypress seeds will not germinate in flooded soils. How does the tree become established? One theory suggests that seedlings sprout in openings during periods of drought, a circumstance that occurs after fires of low to moderate intensity. Fire also helps maintain cypress, because the species can withstand light fires better than its competitors. In fact, without low- to moderate-intensity fires, many cypress domes would be replaced by bayhead forests. Severe fires, however, pose a threat. When the surface layer of peat burns, as happens in an especially intense fire, recovery is slow because there is little seed and because severely charred cypress trees produce few, if any, root sprouts. In the past, logging and the draining of wetlands created conditions that favored severe fires, and the practices devastated cypress stands. Most of the stands logged and set ablaze by humans over the last fifty years show no signs of recovery. The diagram below shows patterns of succession in the Okefenokee Swamp.

Cypress establish themselves in other ways, however. On a grass-sedge wetland, chunks of peat occasionally break loose from the bottom and float to the surface of the swamp. Although free floating, these new "dry" habitats are colonized by a handful of shrub species. The shrubs send down roots that bind and stabilize the peat. More peat accumulates. Before long, cypress trees begin to sprout from seed. These islands are called "houses" in the southeast.

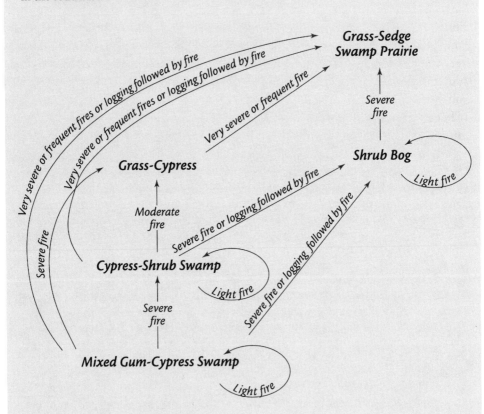

Patterns of succession in the Okefenokee

Grasslands

Second only to the Boreal Forest Region in area, the Grassland Region occupies just under a quarter of the continent. While there are large islands of grasslands outside of the Great Plains, such as in California and the Inland Empire of the Pacific Northwest, the lion's share of the Grassland Region lies in the relatively dry center of the continent, in a broad belt that stretches from central Saskatchewan to Mexico. To the east, the prairies start in eastern Indiana, at the point where precipitation grows too meager to support trees. In the west, it ends where the Great Plains meet the Rockies, or where the climate is too dry and hot for grassland, and desert scrub takes over.

In general, grasslands occur where the annual precipitation is between 10 and 24 inches, and where definite dry and wet seasons rule. Except in certain moist types of grassland, such as the tallgrass prairie, evaporation exceeds precipitation. Most grasslands experience an annual moisture deficit of about 12 inches a year; only deserts have a lower ratio. And although weather is unpredictable from year to year, summers tend to be hot and windy, and winters cold.

Fires—both lightning- and human-lit—play a big part in maintaining grasslands. Grasslands have few barriers, so fires, when pushed by wind, sweep across vast areas quickly—one midwestern blaze covered 125 miles in a single day. Most fires kill the woody plants and leave the nonwoody species—the grasses and wildflowers—invigorated. The flames release nutrients, remove the dead growth of pre-

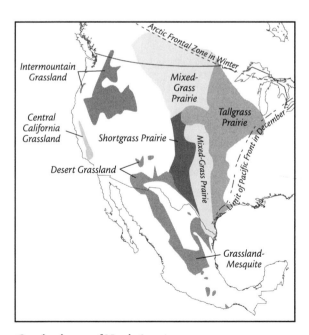

Grassland types of North America

vious years, and blacken the soil (blackened soils absorb more solar radiation, so that the plants get an earlier start the following spring). The exception is the shortgrass prairie, where fire appears to be detrimental to many species, at least in modern times. Before European settlement, when burrowing animals and bison tilled soils, fire may have played a beneficial role.

Generally, grasslands support two layers of nonwoody, herbaceous plants. Grasses, grasslike plants like sedges and rushes, and wildflowers—chiefly members of the sunflower and pea families—dominate most

GRASSLAND TYPES

Name	General Description	Dominant Native Species
Tallgrass prairie	Often called the true prairie, tallgrass once carpeted the eastern third of the Great Plains, from southern Manitoba to Texas. It formed a belt narrow in the north and south and broad in the prairie peninsula of Illinois. The tallgrass is a mixture of sod-forming grasses (those that produce rhizomes or underground stems) and bunchgrasses (single plants that have many shoots forming dense clumps); the flowering parts of most grow to 6 feet, with foliage reaching from 16 inches to over 3 feet. In good years, big bluestem can grow to 12 feet. Most of the tallgrass prairie is now under cultivation for corn and soybeans.	Mostly long-lived perennials. In lowland areas with ample moisture: big bluestem, Indian grass, switchgrass, Canada wild rye. Prairie cordgrass thrives in wet areas, while little bluestem, needlegrass, prairie dropseed, side-oats grama, and Junegrass occupy dry sites.
Mixed-grass steppe	The mixed-grass steppe forms a belt stretching from mid-Alberta to Mexico with eastern and western boundaries that migrate with precipitation patterns. A series of wetter years favors mid-sized grasses and tallgrasses and pushes the boundary farther west; dry years favor the shortgrasses and shift it east. The mixed-grass steppe, a transition that includes a mixture of both tallgrass and shortgrass plants, hosts more species than the tallgrass prairie or the shortgrass steppe. Plants form an open canopy that reaches 4 feet high. Beneath it is a second, dense, foot-high canopy.	Tallgrasses and midgrasses include little bluestem and needle-and-thread grass, side-oats grama, and wheatgrass. The dominant shortgrasses are blue grama, hairy grama, and buffalo-grass.
Shortgrass steppe	In the rain shadow of the Rockies, the shortgrass steppe extends from southeastern Wyoming to south Texas. A narrow band also runs through Mexico, along the base of the Sierra Madre from Chihuahua to Jalisco. Grasses are 8 to 19 inches high and drought tolerant. Moisture is limited; by midsummer many grasses go dormant. In Mexico, bare ground exceeds 50%.	Buffalo-grass and blue grama, needle-and-thread grass, wire grass, Junegrass, and western wheatgrass.

GRASSLAND TYPES (CONT.)

Name	General Description	Dominant Native Species
Desert grassland	Desert grasslands blanket plateaus above 3,300 feet along the edge of the Sonoran and Chihuahuan Deserts. Situated between desert and pinyon-juniper woodlands, low-stature bunchgrasses once dominated desert grasslands, but desert shrubs, favored by human disturbance, are now the most common plants.	Among the grasses: grama grasses, tobasa grasses, and wire grasses. Shrubs include mesquite, creosote bush, and acacias. Yuccas and prickly pear cacti are also common.
Intermountain grasslands	Found in eastern Washington and Oregon, northeastern California, northern Nevada, and central and southern Idaho, this is the grassland of the Columbia Basin and Palouse regions. Moisture is limiting here, and most plants stop growing by midsummer. Downy chess, an introduced annual grass, and sagebrush have increased because of human activities and now dominate. Large regions of the type are now considered shrub-steppe grassland.	Dominant grasses are red threeawn, downy wheatgrass, giant wild rye, Idaho fescue, prairie Junegrass, bluestem wheatgrass, various bluegrasses, bluebunch wheatgrass, squirreltail, dropseed, and needlegrass. Dwarf sagebrush, stiff sagebrush, and big sagebrush are also common.
California grasslands	These grasslands, which once occupied about one-sixth of California (mostly the Central Valley), evolved separately from other grasslands and under different climatic conditions. Native communities no longer exist, however. Nonnative annuals have replaced indigenous species. Two hundred years ago, cool-season bunchgrasses of moderate height made up about 50% of California grasslands. Native annual grasses and both annual and perennial forbs also prospered. Most communities resembled the mixed-grass steppe of the central plains.	Originally, purple needlegrass dominated, but now introduced annuals are more common, among them wild oats, mouse barley, brome grasses, and fescues.

areas. Shrubs and trees thrive along stream courses, and in hollows, ravines, and other protected places. Although the wildflowers, also known as forbs, outnumber the grasses by a factor of three or four, grasses produce most of the biomass. Rather than adding new growth onto the ends of shoots, grasses grow from a point at or beneath the soil surface. They can cope more easily with wind, drought, grazing, trampling, and fire.

The region is diverse, encompassing some 7,500 species, although on local sites only four or five species of grass may domi-

Dealing with Drought: Plants of the Prairie

Prairie and steppe plants have devised some ingenious ways of dealing with drought. Most have a high root-to-shoot ratio; two-thirds of their biomass is, in fact, underground. Placed end to end, the roots and root hairs feeding a square foot of tallgrass prairie would stretch more than two miles. Such networks suggest intense below-ground competition. But just as the aboveground portions of plants divide into layers, so do the roots of plants on the prairie. Some species send roots only into the upper soil, others grow roots much deeper. The roots of big bluestem, for example, reach deeper than 6 feet. Grassland plants also tend to keep their reproductive structures—bulbs, corms, tubers, rhizomes—underground, where they are less likely to desiccate when it is hot and dry.

Narrow leaves represent another adaptation. Heat is less of a problem for grasses and grasslike plants because thin leaves cool easily. In addition, many prairie plants have fine hairs on their leaves that shade the leaf surface. Others wilt: their leaves curl inward during hot periods to reduce the area exposed to the sun and to cut down on water lost through transpiration. Still others, like milkweed, reduce water loss by producing a thick latex sap.

Many grassland species grow their leaves in arrangements that collect and channel rainwater toward the stem and root system. The plants also time their growth cycle around the seasonal pattern of precipitation, sprouting and reaching peak productivity during spring and early summer, the cool moist season. They are dormant during the hot, arid part of the summer. Some can remain dormant for extended periods.

nate. As a rule of thumb, the number of species of all plants on the Great Plains increases as moisture increases and as the topography becomes more diverse. Whereas flat, semiarid terrain might support fifty species, a similar moist site will sport two hundred. Sites with a subhumid climate and broken terrain might harbor four hundred species. In areas only slightly disturbed by humans, the bulk of the plants are perennials; only one out of every twenty is an annual. Where grazing, fire exclusion, farming, or weeds have altered the site, annuals rule.

The major divisions of the Grassland Region are the tallgrass prairie, and the mixed-grass and the shortgrass steppes of the central plains; the desert grasslands of the southwestern U.S. and Mexico; the California grasslands; and the Palouse Prairie in the intermountain part of British Columbia and the northwestern U.S.

Desert Scrub

Located entirely in the southwest U.S. and Mexico, and mostly within the Basin and Range physiographic region, North America's deserts can be classified in two ways. The first is based on the type of precipitation received. Warm deserts, such as the Mojave, Chihuahuan, and Sonoran, receive their moisture in the form of rain; cold deserts get the bulk of theirs as snow. The only cold desert in North America

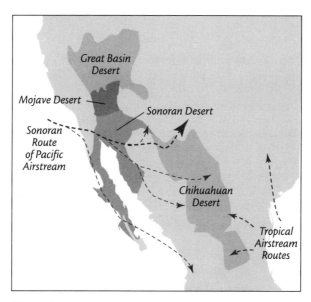

Major deserts

south of the Arctic is the Great Basin, and it makes up 32 percent of the Desert Scrub Region. The second classification scheme is based on the schedule of precipitation, which relates to the east-west location of the desert. In the Great Basin, Mojave, and Sonoran Deserts in the east, precipitation peaks in the summer. In the Chihuahuan Desert in the west, it peaks in the winter. The timing of precipitation influences the type of vegetation.

Generally, North American deserts lie at elevations below 5,600 feet. They receive less than 15 to 16 inches of precipitation a year in unpredictable patterns. They experience long periods without rain each year,

low precipitation-to-evaporation ratios, and high water-budget deficits (23 to 35 inches a year for the cold desert and 78 to 117 inches a year for the warm). During the summer, all North American deserts endure hot days and cool nights. All experience frequent drying winds. Desert-scrub vegetation predominates—two layers of mostly low-growing, widely spaced evergreen and drought-resistant deciduous shrubs; a layer of mostly annual herbs; a surface layer of algae and fungi; and, in some cases, an uppermost layer of very widely spaced trees or plants with treelike growth forms. Sand dunes often intersperse vegetation.

MAJOR DESERTS

Name	General Description	Dominant Species
Chihuahuan	At 177,000 square miles, this is the largest and easternmost of all North American deserts. A warm, temperate desert, the Chihuahuan extends from southern New Mexico in the U.S. to San Luis Potosí in Mexico but is centered around the Mexican state of Chihuahua. Elevations of most areas range between 3,600 and 4,920 feet, although in the south, some sites exceed 6,500 feet. Cooler and moister than other warm deserts, the yearly mean temperature is 65° F, and precipitation ranges from 6 to 16 inches a year, over three-fourths of which falls in the summer. Bedrock is limestone. Dunes are common; soils are heavy, hard, and saline. Plant cover exceeds 20%.	Considerable plant diversity characterizes the Chihuahuan Desert. Dominant plants include tarbush, lechuguilla, acacias, creosote bush, ocotillo, mesquite, indigo bushes, Mormon or Mexican teas, red barberry, chittam wood, desert willows, yellow trumpet flower, crucifixion thorn, agaves, numerous cacti, and yuccas.
Sonoran	The Sonoran Desert, 107,250 square miles, is the only subtropical desert in North America. Known as the warmest of the warm deserts, in part because it lies below 2,000 feet, the Sonoran suffers hot summers. Many days reach above 105° F. Winter frosts are rare. A nearly permanent high pressure system ensures that the Sonoran remains dry. Annual rainfall peaks in the winter on the west side of the desert, which receives from near 0 to 2 inches a year. Wetter, the east side averages 12 inches a year and experiences a more biseasonal precipitation pattern; rains fall in both winter and summer. The Sonoran supports more species, especially of cacti, than the other deserts. Plant cover ranges from 25 to 50%.	Bur sage and creosote bush dominate lowland regions. Higher elevations are more diverse and include blue palo verde and foothill palo verde, saguaro and many other cacti, desert ironwood, elephant tree, agaves, ocotillo, desert cotton, desert olive, desert broom, canyon ragweed, bur sages, and yuccas.
Mojave	At only 54,600 square miles, the Mojave is the smallest of the deserts and represents a transition between the Great Basin and Sonoran. Elevations lie between 2,000 and 3,900 feet. Precipitation, variable, peaks in late winter, and ranges from between 1.5 inches in the east to 10.7 inches in the west. Summer temperatures average between 86 and 104° F. Cacti are uncommon in this desert and are of mostly low stature. Low-growing, widely spaced perennial shrubs dominate. One-quarter of all the plants are endemic varieties, species found only in the Mojave desert.	Three-fourths of the region is dominated by creosote bush and bur sage. Other species include sagebrush Mojave yucca, Joshua tree, Parry saltbrush, desert crucifixion thorn, Death Valley sage, Mojave sage, indigo bushes, spiny senna, horse brush, and Mormon tea. Diversity is intermediate.
Great Basin	The Great Basin is North America's only desert south of the Arctic that receives most of its precipitation as snow. Second in size at 159,500 square miles, this coolest of the deserts lies at an altitude of between 3,900 and 5,250 feet. Winter temperatures seldom rise above freezing, and frosts can occur on any summer night. In the rain shadow of the Sierra Nevada and the Cascade Mountains, this desert receives between 4 and 12 inches a year, about 40% falling in summer. The rainy season is winter–spring. Few species grow here.	The Great Basin has the fewest species of plants of the four deserts. Sagebrush dominates, except on hot, dry, alkaline soils where shadscale reigns. Other species include rabbit-brush, spiny hopsage, winter fat, greasewood, saltbush, bitterbrush, and horse-brush.

And the Desert Bloomed (at Night)

Where do cacti grow? In the desert, of course, but only if the desert isn't too arid. Cacti do not do well, or do not grow at all, in extreme deserts. No cacti, for example, survive in the center of Death Valley. There is not enough rain. Like other plants, cacti need rain to replenish the water they lose to transpiration, and rain brings blossoms.

And what extraordinary blossoms they are. Cacti flower physiology varies considerably from that of other plants. For instance, flowers do not wilt until their cells exhaust the proteins within their stamens and petaloids (the cactus equivalent of petals). The flowers of other plants wilt when their cells deplete the supply of carbohydrates. And unlike other flowers, cacti blossoms last only from one to a few days for most species. Some are night blooming: their large, wonderfully fragrant, pale white and yellow flowers open only after the sun goes down and wilt a few hours after sunup the next day. Pollinated by nocturnal creatures like moths and bats, they depend on fragrance rather than color to attract pollinators. The Queen-of-the-Night cactus of the east coast of Mexico is one such night-bloomer. The sepals and petaloids unfold so quickly that one can watch them move. To see the flower open during daylight hours, some enthusiasts keep the plant (with flowers that are ready to open) in twenty-four hours of darkness, then watch it open in the light.

Mediterranean and Madrean Scrublands and Woodlands

The Mediterranean area extends from southern Oregon to northern Baja California and has a climate similar to that of the Mediterranean region of Europe: cool, wet winters and hot, dry summers; between 8 and 39 inches of precipitation a year, 65 percent of which falls between November and April; unpredictable rainfall; and little frost (only about 3 percent of the hours each year have frost). In addition to the normal seasonal drought, the Mediterranean Region experiences occasional winter dry spells and periodic extreme droughts. The Madrean Region extends from central Arizona into southern New Mexico and southwestern Texas, and along the Sierra Madre Occidental into southern Durango. Like the Mediterranean, it

enjoys a warm, temperate climate and a seasonal drought but receives more summer rain—three times more—than California

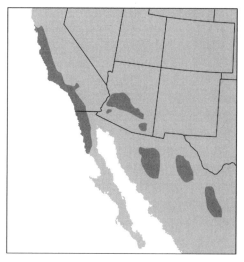

Mediterranean and Madrean scrublands and woodlands

gets. The Mexican part of the Madrean Region is of special interest to botanists because it hosts some 150 native species of oak.

Together, the Madrean and Mediterranean Regions encompass distinct plant communities, among them a mixed evergreen forest, an oak woodland and savanna, grasslands, and chaparral. The mixed evergreen forest gets the most rain. A transition zone between the lower oak woodlands and the higher coniferous forest, it supports many species and is dense and lush with low-growing to medium-tall trees and both broad-leaved evergreens and conifers. The

tallest conifers—mostly ponderosa pine, Douglas fir, and Coulter pine—reach heights of 100 to 200 feet and are scattered. The broad-leaved species form a shorter but denser canopy that includes canyon live oak, big-leaf maple, and bay, as well as Pacific madrone, black oak, and golden chinquapin, among others. In Mexico, there are more pine trees and a greater number of species.

Mixed in among fingers and pockets of savanna, grassland, and chaparral, the oak woodland of the Mediterranean Region lies just below the mixed evergreen

The Distribution of Communities

Many factors—elevation, topography, soils, fire frequency, moisture—affect where an individual plant species can live and where specific communities occur. Any given mountain terrain in the Mediterranean Region, for example, will support a mosaic of species and communities, as this schematic shows.

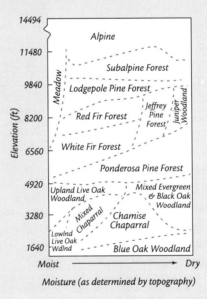

Moisture (as determined by topography)

type. Warmer and receiving 8 to 11 inches less rainfall a year than the mixed evergreen forest, this oak zone develops more open, 15- to 50-foot-high canopies dominated by blue oak. Coast live oak, interior live oak, Engelmann oak, Oregon white oak, black oak, valley oak, and digger pine also thrive. The understory, mostly herbs, includes the same species common in California grasslands. The Madrean oak woodlands support more shrubs, vines, and epiphytes (nonparasitic plants that grow on other plants) than the Mediterranean, as well as an assortment of white and black oaks.

Three- to 9-foot-tall shrubs comprise the chaparral, a type of dense scrub or brushland that burns every twenty-five to seventy-five years. Most species resprout from their roots after burning. Botanists divide the chaparral into three subtypes: the Californian and Madrean chaparrals and the southern coastal scrub.

Californian chaparral grows from southern Oregon to Baja and is dominated by chamise in the south and manzanitas and ceanothus in the north. Silk-tassel bush, scrub oak, barberries, California styrax, foothill ash, mountain mahoganies, and redberry predominate among the fifty-plus shrub species. Inland, the Madrean chaparral extends from northern New Mexico and Arizona and west Texas to northern Mexico with many of the same genera—scrub oaks, manzanitas, ceanothus, and redberry—although species vary. Despite its name, the southern coastal scrub type is not on the coast but inland. More open than other chaparrals, its shrubs

are drought deciduous rather than evergreen, and are soft gray in color. Coastal sagebrush and herb understories dominate.

Pacific Coast Coniferous Forest

Pacific Coast forests accumulate more biomass than any other forest in the world, tropical rainforests included. Rainfall and mild temperatures nurture this high level of productivity. Located on the windward side of the continent, this 40- to 75-mile-wide band of the coast runs 1,300 miles in length. With a maritime climate, the region gets wet winters and mild, comparatively dry, though cloudy, summers. Four-

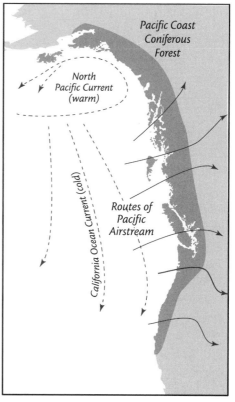

Pacific Coast Forest Region

fifths of the precipitation (30 to 115 inches or more a year) arrives between October 1 and April 1. It rarely freezes hard; temperatures seldom drop below 5°F.

Moist, temperate climates generally produce hardwood forests, but in the northwest, conifers outnumber hardwoods by 1,000 to 1, largely because mild temperatures allow up to 70 percent of the annual net photosynthesis to occur outside of summer. Conifers with year-round foliage have an advantage. Douglas fir, western hemlock, western red cedar, sitka spruce, and coast redwood dominate. Stands are dense and canopy trees often grow 250 feet high, their trunks reaching diameters of over 6 feet. Though many of the species are sensitive to fire, the forests here burn infrequently. Every several hundred years, a blaze may occur. Net annual productivity ranges from 1500 to more than 2500 grams per square meter (g/m²).

The region is divided into three forest types. In Alaska, western hemlock reigns in the canopy, although Alaska cedar, Sitka spruce, and mountain hemlock thrive, too. Dogwood, bramble, and huckleberry stock the understory. The central part of the region, also dominated by western hemlock, supports other species such as Sitka spruce, Douglas fir, Pacific silver fir, grand fir, western red cedar, and Pacific yew. The southern end of the region, in California, nourishes a community in which coast redwood has dominion over species such as grand fir, tan oak, Douglas fir, and mountain hemlock. Fire maintains coastal redwood stands. The species evolved with and resists both fire and flood.

Big, Old Trees

Pacific Coast forests are unique in that they are dominated by conifers that live long and grow large. Nurtured by the wet maritime climate, this region generally escapes large, catastrophic fires. When Europeans arrived, the average age of the dominant overstory species was between 400 to 1,200 years. Since 1850, logging has taken about 90 percent of those ancient trees. The chart shows the typical ages and sizes Pacific Coast conifers once attained on good sites.

Species	Age (yr)	Diameter (in)	Height (ft)
Pacific silver fir	400+	35–45	150–180
White fir	300+	40–60	130–180
Grand fir	300+	30–50	130–195
Subalpine fir	250+	20–25	80–115
Red fir	300+	40–50	130–165
Noble fir	400+	40–60	150–230
Port Oxford cedar	500+	50–70	195
Alaska cedar	1000+	40–60	100–130
Western larch	700+	55	165
Incense cedar	500+	35–45	150
Engelmann spruce	400+	40	150–165
Sitka spruce	500+	70–90	230–245
Lodgepole pine	250+	20	80–115
Sugar pine	400+	40–50	150–180
White pine	400+	45	195
Ponderosa pine	600+	30–50	100–195
Douglas fir	750+	60–85	230–260
Coast redwood	1250+	60–150	245–330
Western redcedar	1000+	60–115	200+
Western hemlock	400+	35–45	165–215
Mtn. hemlock	500+	30–40	115

Western Montane Coniferous Forest

Forests blanket most of this long, narrow, mountainous region, which extends from the Yukon to central Mexico. Its mountain ranges include the Rockies, the Sierras, the Cascades, the Coast Ranges, and the Transverse and Peninsular Ranges. The dominant species vary from north to south, but two trees, ponderosa pine and Douglas fir, stand out.

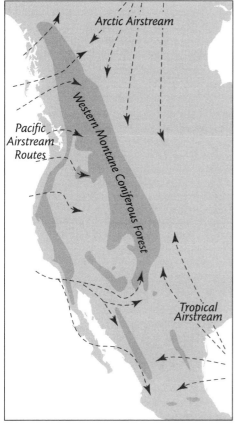

The Western Montane Coniferous Forest Region

Elevation shapes plant communities. Moving up, precipitation increases and temperature decreases. As little as 10 to 25 inches of precipitation a year falls on the lowest forests, savannas, and open woodlands of ponderosa pine, which are maintained by fire. But from 70 to 100 inches a year water higher elevations, slopes with dense and diverse forests of spruce and fir that burn only once every two or three hundred years. Cold temperatures and heavy snowpacks that linger into the summer discourage diversity in the highest zone. Near treeline, where growing conditions are harsh, the canopy opens again. While elevational zones are somewhat predictable, they vary locally depending on slope, aspect, soils, and disturbance patterns. In narrow valleys, for example, cold air flows downhill in the evening and may invert vegetation patterns somewhat.

Fire also plays a part in determining the character and structure of plant communities. Fire races through the understory of some stands, such as the low elevation savannas, every five to ten years. In others— mid- to high-elevation moist forests, for example—fires burn more intensely and consume the canopy as well as the understory, but visit only once every four to five hundred years. Insects and disease, blowdown from windstorms, and avalanches take their tolls. Under natural conditions, these disturbances fashion a mosaic of stands with different species and ages.

Botanists split the region into four subregions.

WESTERN CONIFEROUS FOREST SUBREGIONS

Name	General Description	Dominant Species
Rocky Mountain Forests		
Far North	This subregion intergrades with the Boreal Forest. Many understory species occur in both; trees easily hybridize with their adjacent counterparts. Species are few.	White spruce on lower to mid-elevation slopes and Engelmann spruce and subalpine fir at higher elevations.
North	Pacific maritime air masses strongly influence species on the western slopes. Understory species are the same as those found in Pacific Coast forests.	Ponderosa pine-Rocky Mountain juniper woodlands at lower elevations (mountain mahogany, sagebrush, and bitterbrush in the understory). Grand fir, Douglas fir, western redcedar, and western hemlock at mid-elevations. Subalpine fir, Engelmann spruce, whitebark pine, and subalpine larch at high elevations.
South	Little Pacific air reaches this region; warm, dry continental air dominates. Summer heat and aridity influence species composition.	Low to high elevations support pinyon pine and juniper; ponderosa pine; Douglas fir, white fir, and blue spruce; lodgepole pine; subalpine fir, Engelmann spruce, and bristlecone pine.
Madrean	A complex, diverse region that, unlike other Rocky Mountain regions, receives most of its precipitation in summer.	From low to high elevations: either pinyon-juniper (north) or pine-oak woodlands (south); ponderosa pine; Douglas fir, white pine, and limber pine; Engelmann spruce, subalpine fir, bristlecone pine, and limber pine.
Pacific Northwest Montane Forests	These species-rich forests blanket the ranges that rise above West Coast rainforests. They are wet on the western slopes and dry on the eastern, and the number of species reflects moisture differences.	On western slopes: Pacific silver fir, mountain hemlock, western hemlock, subalpine fir, noble fir, western white pine, Douglas fir, and Alaska cedar. On eastern slopes: juniper-sagebrush savanna, ponderosa pine, Douglas fir, subalpine fir, and mountain hemlock.
Montane Forests of Alta and Baja California	The northern portion of the subregion extends from the southern Cascades to the Sierra Nevada, an area that encompasses low-elevation forests dependent on frequent, low intensity ground fires. The southern portion includes the Transverse and Peninsular Ranges.	The northern portion: at lower elevations, white fir, California incense-cedar, sugar pine, ponderosa pine, and Douglas fir; at upper elevations, California red fir; and at high elevations, an open woodland of whitebark pine, foxtail pine, Sierra lodgepole, limber pine, white pine, and mountain hemlock.

WESTERN CONIFEROUS FOREST SUBREGIONS (CONT.)

Name	General Description	Dominant Species
Montane Forests of Alta and Baja California (cont.)		The southern portion: at lower elevations, Jeffrey pine and ponderosa pine; at mid-elevations, open stands of white fir, California incense-cedar, sugar pine, Jefferey pine, and western juniper; at higher elevations, lodgepole and limber pine.
Intermountain Region Montane Forest	A region of dry island mountain ranges sandwiched between the Rocky Mountains and the Cascade-Sierra Ranges, the Intermountain forests include one of the largest vegetation types in North America, the pinyon-juniper woodlands. They also incorporate some of the Great Basin bristlecone pines, individuals of which are over 4,000 years old.	Utah juniper and single-leaf pinyon at low to mid-elevations; above that, white fir, then limber pine and Great Basin bristlecone pine.

Methuselah: The Oldest of the Old

Methuselah, the oldest of the Great Basin bristlecone pines, was already 2,600 years old the day Christ was born. The tree grows high in California's White Mountains in a grove of other ancient trees, many 4,000 years old or older. A few decades ago, the oldest bristlecone grew in the Snake Range of eastern Nevada. That tree was over 5,000 years old when a graduate student studying bristlecones sawed it down in 1964.

Great Basin bristlecone pines decay slowly after they die, especially in the White Mountains. Trees that died thousands of years ago still stand. The trunks of trees that fell thousands of years ago still lie on the ground because their pitch-heavy wood decays slowly in the cold, dry mountain environment. Scientists match up the rings of these dead trees with those of living trees to construct a master tree-ring chronology reaching back 9,000 years. Bristlecone is especially sensitive to variations in moisture and temperature. Thus the chronology records climate change.

In the White Mountains of California, bristlecones grow in infertile dolomitic soils on arid, cold northern aspects at elevations above 9,500 feet. The oldest trees, those over 4,000 years, are above 10,000 feet. The sites are so harsh that the trees grow very slowly, often requiring 200 to 250 years to add an inch in diameter. One dwarf tree, only 3 inches thick and 3 feet tall, is 700 years old. Such slow growth produces highly lignified, decay-resistant cells. The harsh conditions account, at least in part, for the bristlecone's longevity. Trees on more moderate sites grow faster but develop heartrot and die at a relatively young age.

Sherman: The Biggest of the Big

In addition to ancient trees, California grows big trees. The giant sequoia is the most massive, and the largest sequoia is the famous 3,000-year-old "General Sherman" tree in Sequoia National Park on the west slope of the Sierras. General Sherman's diameter at breast height (d.b.h.) measures 26.75 feet, and its height is 272 feet. For comparison, the largest bristlecone, 1,500 years old, has a d.b.h. of 12.5 feet and a height of 47 feet. The climate, soils, and fire history of the west slope of the Sierras seem ideal for conifers. Many midslope species—white fir, coastal Douglas fir, sugar pine, ponderosa pine, and Jeffrey pine—surpass 6 feet in diameter and 200 feet in height. Higher-elevation species also do well. Record trees from the upper parts of the Sierras follow.

Species	Diameter (d.b.h.)	Height
Mountain hemlock	7.5	113
California red fir	8.5	180
Foxtail pine	8.3	71
Lodgepole pine	6.8	91
Sierra juniper	13.5	87

Tropical and Subtropical Forests

A warm, wet climate and a multitude of species distinguish this region, which encompasses tropical communities in southern and central Mexico and subtropical communities in central and northern Mexico and southern Florida. Mangrove swamps, thorn forests, cloud forests, subtropical deciduous forests, tropical evergreen forests, and tropical rainforests comprise the major vegetation types.

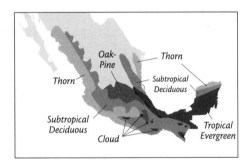

Forests of the Tropical and Subtropical Regions

Tropical areas lack strong temperature-based seasons; daily temperature fluctuations exceed the difference between the means of the coolest and warmest months. Year-round, temperatures are high, and abundant rain falls, the quantity always exceeding evaporation rates. Tropical rainforests are structurally complex and harbor more species than any other vegetation community in the world. The subtropical area, less diverse, enjoys a more seasonal climate, especially as measured by rainfall. The subtropics also suffer more storms and hurricanes. Major vegetation types follow.

TROPICAL AND SUBTROPICAL FOREST VEGETATION TYPES

Name	General Description	Dominant Species
Mangrove swamps	Mangrove swamps occur on both sides of the Florida peninsula south of 29° N latitude, in Mexico in lagoons and estuaries along the Gulf Coast south of the tropic of Cancer, on the Pacific Coast south of Sonora and Tiburón Island, and in Baja along the Gulf of California south of Santa Rosalía. Red mangrove swamps, havens for fish and mollusks, are nearly impenetrable to humans and other predators. Inland, black mangrove and white mangrove communities flourish.	Red, white, black, and button mangrove.
Thorn forests	Relatively dry, low-stature forests (only up to about 20 feet high) of shrubs and small trees. Thorn forests occur in long strips parallel to and near both coasts of Mexico. These communities are dominated by spiny members of the legume or bean family, species that have expanded due to harsh land use practices.	Acacias, including the sweet, boat-thorn, hat thorn, bullhorn, and flat-thorn acacias; lotebush; and morning-glory tree.
Cloud forests	Oak-pine forests are continuously shrouded in clouds; in this high-humidity environment, epiphytes (plants that grow on trees) thrive.	Many of the tree species are the same as or closely related to those of the temperate eastern deciduous forest, among them sweetgum and blackgum. Epiphytic species of begonias, bromeliads, orchids, pepperomias, ferns, and mosses are also common.
Subtropical deciduous forests	These forests are found mostly on the eastern and western foothills of the Mexican Plateau, a frostless zone with a prolonged winter dry season. The trees, shorter than those of tropical forests, reach a maximum height of about 100 feet. During the summers, these forests are dense, hot, and humid; in winter, they are nearly leafless and much drier and cooler.	Variation makes it difficult to list dominant species. The trumpet tree and the morning-glory tree are common in some areas as are springbells, lysiloma, and yellowsilk shellseed.
Tropical evergreen forests	This zone has been logged heavily but once blanketed large expanses of the Chiapas lowlands and the southern Yucatan. The shorter dry season favors evergreens and larger trees; most grow 75 to 150 feet high. Diversity is high.	Many species are "dominant," too many to list. But common and noteworthy trees include mahogany, cedro, cecropia, strangler figs, ramon, chicozapote, and mamey.
Tropical rainforests	True tropical rainforest is found only in a few valleys in southern Chiapas where there is no limiting dry season and where trees grow 225 feet high or higher. Species are many.	Tropical rainforests have many of the same species as the tropical evergreen forests except that rainforest trees are much larger.

Coastal Salt Marshes

Salt marshes—lowlands periodically flooded by rising and falling ocean tides—are harsh places for plants because salts accumulate in soils, tides and currents constantly shift sediments, ice shears off plant stems, salinities are continuously changing, and floods leave little oxygen for plants.

Coastal marshes occur all around the perimeter of the continent from Barrow, Alaska, south, although they concentrate in Georgia, South Carolina, and Gulf Coast states where estuaries or barrier islands and spits provide protection from tides. Together, southeastern marshes host roughly 350 species of plants. Pacific Coast marshes, with steeper shorelines, higher sea energies, and fewer sheltered areas average about 80 species. Marshes bordering

Pacific Coast marsh reeds

Coastal salt marshes of North America

Hudson Bay and the Arctic support only two dozen. Some salt marsh plants, such as orache, seashore saltgrass, pickleweed, cordgrass, and seaside arrow-grass occur around the continent.

Salt marshes show a distinct gradation of vegetation, a zonation dictated by wave energy, salinity, and flood frequency. Usu-ally, two zones are present. The narrow low marsh zone (3 to 30 feet wide) extends from mean sea level to mean high water and floods regularly—once or twice daily. The high marsh zone is potentially thousands of feet wide and floods only once a month at most.

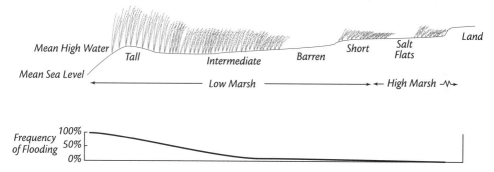

Plant zones in a coastal marsh of southeastern North America

PRODUCTIVITY OF SELECTED VEGETATION TYPES

Vegetation Type	Productivity (g/m²/yr)
Arctic Wet Tundra	150–200
Low Arctic Shrub Habitats	250–400
High Arctic	5–30
Taiga (infertile, dry sites)	480
Taiga (moist, fertile sites)	1,280
Northern Eastern Deciduous Forest	1,200–1,500
Southern Eastern Deciduous Forest (fertile sites)	2,500
Grasslands (most diverse sites)	500–1,000
Grasslands (least diverse sites)	50
Deserts	under 70
Western Montane Coniferous Forest	600–1,100
Coastal Marshes	300–2,000

NATURAL HISTORY

To simplify communication about plants and to aid in understanding kin relationships, the science of plant taxonomy names and groups plants into categories. Plants generally bear both common and scientific names, but common names can vary from one locale to another, and the same common name often describes two or more species. People have christened at least half a dozen trees and bushes with the common name wild cherry, for example. On the other hand, each scientific appellation is unique, a genus name followed by a species name. The genus describes a group of structurally related species and the species describes a group of closely related individuals capable of interbreeding and nearly identical in form, in genetic identity, and in their relations to the environment. Taxonomists distinguish varieties, as well—subdivisions of species based on minor variations in inherited characteristics, differences too subtle to warrant classifying populations as distinct species.

The scientific name for coneflower, a purple-flowering, sunflower-like species native to the dry, open prairies and plains of North America, is *Echinacea pallida*. The generic or genus name, *Echinacea*, is Greek for hedgehog or sea urchin and describes the bracts of the plant. The specific name is *pallida*. (Generic names are always capitalized; specific names are not.) The complete classification for this plant is:

Kingdom—Plantae
Division—Anthophyta (flowering plants)
Class—Dicotyledones (plants having two seed leaves)
Order—Asterales
Family—Compositae (the daisy family)
Genus—*Echinacea*
Species—*Echinacea pallida* (coneflower)
Variety—*Echinacea pallida* var. *angustifolia* (Great Plains variety)

The Creation of a New Species

A recent study of two species of monkey-flower suggests that only a few mutations can create a new species. *Mimulus cardinalis* and *M. lewisii*, when crossed in a green-house, produce fertile offspring. The two do not hybridize in nature, however, because they attract different pollinators. *M. cardinalis* bears bright red-orange flowers, a color that draws hummingbirds but that looks black to bees. Hummingbirds probe the flower's long, tubular corolla; the stigmas and anthers are positioned to receive pollen from and deposit pollen on the bird's head. The large amount of dilute nectar produced by the plant attracts hummingbirds.

The flowers of *M. lewisii*, on the other hand, are designed for bees. They possess bee-sized landing platforms, bee-attracting nectar guides (pink and yellow in color), low quantities of highly concentrated nec-

Mimulus lewisii *is built to attract bees.*

tar, and anthers and stigmas enclosed so that only bees and other insect legs might touch them. The differences ensure pollinator fidelity and perpetuate the separation of the two plants.

The difference in blossom development depends on only a few genes. Most evolutionary biologists once believed dozens of mutations separated such similar species. But this research shows that a few mutations are all that is needed to create a new species, if those mutations prevent the two populations from interbreeding.

Fire-Dependent Plant Communities

Many North American plant communities evolved with fire. Some burned every five to ten years, others every two hundred years. But after thousands of years of periodic blazes, communities adapted; some now depend on wildfires to recycle nutrients, reduce dead plant matter, stimulate growth, or lower insect and disease populations. By altering natural fire frequencies over the last fifty to one hundred years, modern North Americans altered both the structure and composition of grasslands and forests. On prairies, for instance, where

fire has been kept at bay, fire-dependent species have all but disappeared. The change has long-term consequences for other prairie species because many of the plants lost supported bacteria capable of converting atmospheric nitrogen into a form useful to plants.

The status of some of these fire-adapted communities follows.

Western Juniper Woodlands

Juniper woodlands now cover 42 million acres within the Intermountain Region.

Before Europeans arrived, juniper wood-lands occupied a much smaller area and were more savanna-like or confined to rocky outcrops where fire seldom reached. By the late 1800s, fire suppression had transformed those savannas into wood-lands, enabling juniper to move into new habitats. The government relocated Indians who were responsible for many of the fires prior to European settlement. Also, cows and sheep grazed down grasses and shrubs that served as fuel for the fires.

Juniper woodland communities

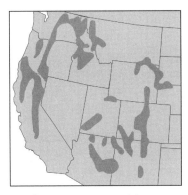

Ponderosa pine communities

Sagebrush-Grass

Fire frequencies are increasing in these communities, which now cover about 112 million acres. Between 1960 and 1969, for example, 1,344 wildfires burned 663,000 acres of sagebrush steppe. Between 1980 and 1989, 2,334 fires burned 1,316,000 acres. The fires, combined with heavy graz-ing pressure, have favored nonnative Eu-ropean annual grasses like cheatgrass and medusahead at the expense of native pe-rennials. Exotic species now dominate the sagebrush steppe.

Ponderosa Pine Forests

Ponderosa pine forests, which blanket 40 million acres in the western U.S., seldom see fires anymore, whereas before Europe-ans arrived, fires swept through their un-derstories every seven to fifteen years. The low intensity blazes cleaned out the brush and competing trees and created open, parklike stands of ancient ponderosa pine. In fire's absence, thickets of Douglas fir have taken over. Epidemics of insects and disease plague the trees, which are now sus-ceptible to severe fires.

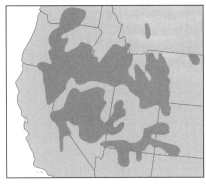

Sagebrush-steppe communities

Lodgepole Pine Forests

Historically, lodgepole pine grew in a mosaic of many different-aged stands, few over fifty to sixty years old. Today, after a century of fire suppression, the mosaic is gone, and stands over one hundred years old dominate. One-hundred-year-old lodgepole pines are extremely susceptible to insect and disease epidemics. As trees across these large areas die from insects and disease, they fuel unnaturally large and severe fires that damage soils and threaten wildlife.

Southern Pinelands

Southern pine forests of longleaf, slash, loblolly, and shortleaf pine blanket 193 million acres in the south. Historically, low intensity ground fires consumed 10 to 30 percent of the understory annually. Now, fires burn less frequently and at a different time of the year (fall and winter instead of spring and summer). Species have changed, and some have disappeared entirely from the forest.

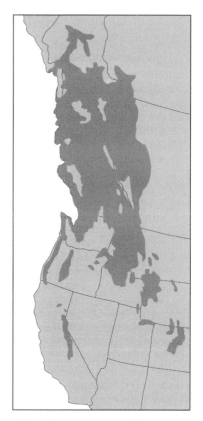

Lodgepole pine communities

Natives That Did Not Evolve in North America

Not all of the plants native to North America originated on the continent. Many immigrated from far-flung places, transported by migrating birds and animals, ocean currents, and winds. One of the dominant plants of arid North America, creosote bush, evolved in Patagonia. Similarly, the plant known in North America as crucifixion thorn originated in Bolivia. Mesquite also has South American roots. The migration went both ways, of course,

and a portion of South America's flora evolved in North America. Interestingly, some North American plants with links to South America, genera such as *Menodora*, *Lycium*, and *Nicotiana*, have close relatives in South Africa. The connection reminds us that Africa and South America once formed a single continent.

Before the last ice age, water covered most of southern Florida. Now the lower third of the peninsula is populated with tropical Caribbean species from the Bahamas, Cuba, other West Indian islands, and tropical Mexico, most transported by hurricanes, birds, and the Gulf Stream.

Eurasia also has a floristic connection with North America. Many species found in the polar and boreal regions of Canada and Alaska and the alpine mountain regions of Canada and the U.S. grow in similar climatic regions of Europe and Asia. They migrated from one continent to the other via the ancient land bridges. (During the latter part of the Paleocene, about 57 million years ago, two land bridges linked North America to Europe: one from Greenland to Scotland, the other from Greenland to Spitzbergen. Two million years ago, during the Pleistocene, the Beringian land bridge connected North America and Asia.) It is likely, too, that some plants sprouted from seeds blown across frozen polar seas.

Other Eurasian connections exist south of the polar and boreal regions of North America. Big sagebrush, a characteristic shrub of the western U.S., is Asian in origin, and the closest relatives of some plants found in the southeastern U.S. live in China. No one knows for sure how those plants arrived.

The Mediterranean and Southeast Asian regions also share a significant number of North American plants. A few species and genera—like crowberry, mare's-tail, and primrose—are bipolar; they exist at both ends of the globe and nowhere in between. Birds like the Arctic tern, it is assumed, carried their seeds from one polar region to the other.

Since the time of Columbus, humans have brought plants from all over the world to North America. Before European-Americans set foot in California, its flora included around 5,900 species. Today it hosts over 6,900. Continentwide, one-sixth of plant species are nonnative, introduced either purposely or accidentally by humans. An ironic example is tumbleweed, that symbol of the Old West; it was introduced from Russia in the 1870s.

Weeds: An Enemy of Diversity

Botanists estimate that North America supports around 2,000 species of weeds. About 60 percent of those are alien species, plants introduced to North America from other places since the time of Columbus. Because introduced weeds tend to displace native plants, they threaten the variety of North America's plant communities.

What is a weed? There is no precise definition, but most plants called weeds possess the ability to inhabit and thrive in disturbed areas—often places affected by the activities of humans. Most weeds can also germinate in a variety of environments. They have internal rather than external factors that control their germination, and they produce seeds that remain viable for long periods. Most have short life cycles and rapid growth rates, and dedicate considerable energy to reproduction. Many weeds produce seeds as long as growing conditions permit and possess adaptations for both short- and long-range dispersal. Most weeds are capable of self-pollination and can be cross-pollinated by wind and a variety of insects and other animals. Most produce a large number of seeds under fa-vorable conditions and some seeds even under adverse conditions. Perennial weeds tend to have the ability to reproduce vegetatively (which means they do not have to rely on seeds) or to regenerate from fragments; they are brittle and not easily pulled from the ground.

European brooklime, an alien species, demonstrates a typical pattern of invasion: a weed, often a European or Asian species, enters a seaport and then expands its range until it occupies much of the continent.

Plants That Run and Hide

Life doesn't get much simpler than single-celled algae, at least that's the conventional wisdom. But certain kinds of algae possess at least one trick that multicellular plants haven't yet developed: the ability to flee grazers.

A daphnia

While studying the role that fish play in lakes, researchers purposely killed off all the daphnia or water fleas in several lakes in Michigan. Shortly thereafter, the population of a certain kind of algae, a group called the flagellates, increased dramatically in number. Flagellates, eaten by daphnia, propel themselves with a whiplike tail or flagella. Upon closer examination, the researchers discovered that reproduction could not account for the sudden increase in the flagellate algae population. The algae came out of the mud on the bottom of the lakes. Perplexed, the scientists brought samples into the lab. In their tanks, the flagellates swam throughout the water column; that is, until the scientists placed a daphnia or two in with them. The algae, sensing the predator, immediately propelled themselves into the mud at the bottom of the tank, safely out of the reach of the daphnia. When the researchers removed the daphnia, the algae streamed back into the water column where they could once again photosynthesize.

One of the researchers, Lars-Anders Hansson, thinks the algae are prompted by chemicals released into the water by daphnia. He suspects other single-celled organisms may be equally sophisticated when it comes to sensing predators. As one of the team members remarked, "We should never underestimate the cell."

IN FOCUS: FIRE MOSS

Distribution

Fire moss (*Ceratodon purpureus*), also known as purple horn-toothed moss, grows in every province, territory, and state in Canada, the U.S., and Mexico.

Description

Sporting short, hairlike leaves and half-inch to three-inch-long stems, fire moss forms carpetlike tufts or cushions. It is a dioecious species, which means it produces male and female parts on separate plants. Fire moss depends on wind for spore dispersal, although it also reproduces vegetatively through threadlike growths.

Life History

Preferring low levels of competition and abundant light, fire moss pioneers disturbed sites. High-severity fires that expose bare mineral soil and rock provide ideal conditions for spore germination. The plant's ability to rapidly colonize these kinds of sites helps prevent soil erosion and promotes the accumulation of organic matter, which favors insects, other invertebrates, and eventually higher plants.

As soils build and other plants gain a roothold, they crowd out fire moss, although in some areas, such as the black spruce-lichen woodlands of Alaska and Canada, the plant can dominate for twenty years following a catastrophic fire. On these sites, fire moss increases, even after shrubs move onto the site. Only as the shrubs grow dense does fire moss surrender.

Because fire moss can tolerate higher pollution levels than other moss species, it is common in urban and industrial settings, along highways, and on the tailings and refuse associated with coal and heavy-metal mining activities. Although small in stature and modest in appearance, this little pioneer carries out one of the most important roles on the continent: that of restoring disturbed areas.

The Green Carnivores

Deficient in nitrogen and other essential elements, acidic, boggy soils in North America are poor habitats for most plants. Some species, however, have evolved mechanisms to take advantage of these conditions. Among the strategies employed is one we don't often associate with green things—luring, trapping, and consuming members of the animal kingdom. Plant predators employ both passive and active traps to capture their quarry, and they digest them with some of the same acids and enzymes animals use.

Trumpet pitchers are among the plants sporting passive schemes, those that do not involve movement. Luring insects with nectar and color, they trap their prey in a pitfall. Flies, bees, and ants follow a nectar

The trumpet pitcher

trail to a waxy, slippery surface where they lose their footing and plummet down a trumpetlike tube. A lining of stiff, down-pointing hairs prevents their escape. At the bottom lies a liquid saturated with enzymes and acids that dissolves the victim. Liquefied into a juice of proteins, starches, and fats, the insect is then absorbed by cells at the base of the tube. Though effective against most insects, pitcher plant enzymes are impotent against the larvae of a certain mosquito, which thrives in the traps. Trumpet pitchers possess large appetites—a single plant consumes thousands of creatures in its lifetime.

Eight species of trumpet pitcher (genus *Sarracenia*) grow in North America, mostly in the southeastern part of the U.S. They include the yellow, white, and sweet trumpet plants, and the green, pale, hooded, parrot, and purple pitcher plants. The purple pitcher, which ranges into the Arctic, is the only species found as far north as Canada.

The cobra lily (genus *Darlingtonia*) traps insects in the forests of western Oregon and northern California. This species also employs a pitfall but lacks its own enzymes and acids and relies on bacteria to digest prey. The bacteria, brought in by the insects themselves, secrete a nitrogen-rich solution easily absorbed by the plant.

Butterworts and sundews use active traps. Butterwort leaves smell like fungus, which may be what attracts their prey—tiny flies, springtails, and small crawling insects. Ensnared by sticky secretions, the creatures squirm, stimulating the plant to ooze a mucilage containing acids and enzymes. The plant's leaves then roll inward, bringing the insect into closer contact with the enzymes. Of the continent's butterwort species (all fall within the genus *Pinguicula*), six grow in the southeast, several in Mexico, and one throughout most of Canada and portions of the northern U.S.

Sundews belong to the genus *Drosera* and are best known for their gland-tipped tentacles that wrap around prey. At the top of each is a red, egg-shaped gland that secretes a sticky mucilage charged with enzymes and acids. These glands also absorb the juices of dissolved victims. Most sundews in North America overwinter in the form of a green, resting bud called a hibernaculum. Although the roots beneath the bud die, they anchor the bud through the winter. In the spring, new roots sprout as the bud opens and sends up shoots. Among this group is the round-leafed sundew, the love-nest sundew, the great sundew, and the thread-leaf sundew. An evergreen species, the pink sundew is found along the Gulf Coast from Virginia to eastern Texas.

Although a member of the sundew family, the Venus fly trap operates a differ-

A sundew with its gland-tipped tentacles

ent kind of snare, essentially a spring trap. Perhaps the most familiar of all North American carnivorous plants, the Venus fly trap has leaves like a jawed trap. Trigger hairs in the center cause the leaves to snap shut. The two lobes of the trap are coated with tiny glands, some of which secrete nectar, others that exude digestive enzymes. The species is near extinction, in part because its range and habitat requirements are so narrow. The plant is found only in a corner of coastal North and South Carolina on damp sandy soils with small amounts of peat. Attempts to introduce it elsewhere have failed.

Bladderworts, mostly aquatic plants of the genus *Utricularia,* possess the most sophisticated traps. Their many small, transparent, oval bladders capture primarily single-celled protozoans, rotifers, and daphnia, although the largest bladders catch mosquito larvae and fish fry. Supported by stems and stolons, bladderworts lack roots.

There are roughly 250 species of bladderworts, the traps of which all function similarly. Each bladder holds a partial vacuum sealed by a trap door. Prey, guided to the vicinity of the door by structures called antennae, release the door by touching sensitive hairs. The vacuum sucks the door inward. Water rushes in, pulling the victim along. The bladder filled, the door then springs back, with the prey inside. The entire process lasts a fifteenth of a second. Immediately, certain glands within the bladder secrete enzymes and acids; others pump water out to recreate the vacuum and reset the trap. Terrestrial species function in a similar way, their bladders located in soils wet enough to support an aquatic fauna.

Surprisingly, the seeds of some plants can consume animals. Shepherd's purse, a weed of European origin, has invaded all of temperate North America. With little stored food, the seeds are armed instead with a mucilage that is sticky when wet—a tanglefoot that ensnares small organisms. An enzyme contained in the mucilage dissolves the creature. The nutrients accumulate around the seed to feed the seedling after germination.

Some fungi are also carnivores. The hyphae of an aquatic species, for example, attract rotifers—small aquatic organisms that feed on algae and detritus. As the rotifer bites the end of the fungal hypha, the hypha swells. The rotifer, with fungus swollen within its mouth, can't detach and eventually dies. The hypha continues to grow through the rotifer's body, where it sends out branches to feed on the carcass.

Quaking Aspen: The Tree with the Most "Mosts"

States and provinces throughout North America designate official trees and flowers—plants that represent that part of the world. If North Americans were to declare an official tree, they might choose quaking aspen (*Populus tremuloides*). It is the continent's most widely distributed tree and one of its most colorful. It is also the most genetically diverse plant ever studied, and it counts among its number not only the world's most massive individual organism, but also the oldest organism known.

Ranging from central Mexico to northern Alaska and spanning the continent from west to east, aspen flourishes in a remarkable diversity of habitats; no other tree succeeds in as many distinct plant communities. Quaking aspen also crosses a surprising range of elevations, from sea level to treeline. Because temperature affects it less than moisture, aspen thrives where the thermometer dips to -70°F and grows where temperatures top 105°F. In experiments, the tree has survived temperatures as low as -314°F.

In this enormous range of growing conditions, aspen takes on a variety of growth forms. Under ideal conditions, an aspen tree might send its perfectly straight trunk 100 feet into the air. Seeds from that same tree planted at treeline in the Rocky Mountains might reach 2 or 3 feet in height, their trunks severely twisted. One can find countless variations in between.

The ability of aspen to reproduce asexually, through suckering, gives rise to two other extreme attributes: the tree's abil-

Aspen leaves

ity to reach enormous dimensions and its longevity. Root suckering is the process whereby an individual aspen stem sends out lateral roots that sprout new stems. Although the new stems grow to look like separate trees, they belong to a single genetic individual. Remove the soil from the roots of these clones, and one finds all the stems connected. They are like vertical branches. The largest single clone discovered takes in 106 acres in the Wasatch Mountains of south-central Utah. Comprising roughly 47,000 stems, it weighs an estimated 13.2 million pounds. The most massive living organism known, it is larger by far than the "humongous fungus" of Michigan or the largest of the giant sequoias in California. Named *Pando* (Latin for 'I Spread'), the clone is estimated to be 1 million years old. Age, in such a case, can only be guessed through indirect means; no one knows for sure how old it is. Many aspen clones are thought to be at least 10,000 years old. (These clonal ages refer to the age of the genome; actual physical tissue doesn't survive that long.) Other long-lived North American clonal species include bracken fern, red fescue, sheep fescue, and velvet grass. Their clones may be over 1,000 years old. Creosote bush and huckleberry may live in clones over 11,000 years old.

DNA analysis reveals that aspen claims yet another "most." It is the most genetically variable plant yet studied. The average amount of protein variation in plants is about 50 percent. Aspen has a score in excess of 90 percent. Genetic variation increases with the amount of environmental variation experienced by the species, its population size, and the size of the geographic range. Aspen ranks high in all.

 ## A Few Aspen Facts

Quaking aspen is also called trembling aspen. Its generic name, *Populus*, derived either from the ancient Roman expression *arbor populi*, which translates as "the people's tree," or the Greek verb *papaillo*, which means to shake or tremble. The Irish called aspen "the shaking tree"; the Welsh, "the tree of the woman's tongue"; the Onondaga Indians, "noisy leaf."

Individual clones of aspen are either male or female. Male clones dominate in dry climates, female clones in wet ones. In some places, the trees at lower elevations are mostly female, while those higher up are almost entirely male.

An old female stem may produce as many as 54 million seeds. In the arid west, however, seeds rarely make new trees. Many scientists believe widespread quaking aspen establishment from seeds has not occurred in the western U.S. for over 10,000 years because the climate is too arid. In the more humid New England states, new aspen trees commonly start from seeds.

A young aspen can grow 3 or 4 feet in a single summer. Females grow faster than males.

The density of new shoots in a clone can exceed 400,000 per acre.

Aspen catkins

In Focus: Northern Floodplain Forests

Distribution

Northern floodplain forests border rivers and streams in Canada from eastern Alberta to Manitoba and in the U.S. from eastern Montana to Minnesota, south to eastern Colorado and northern Oklahoma. Elm-ash-cottonwood forests, similar to those on northern floodplains, blanket the lower terraces and floodplains of the Mississippi, Missouri, Platte, Kansas, and Ohio Rivers and reach as far south as southern Illinois, southern Indiana, and Kentucky.

Description

Northern floodplains nourish low to tall broadleaf deciduous forests of eastern cottonwood, black willow, and American elm, with the cottonwoods often occurring in pure or nearly pure stands. Among the other species present are boxelder, red maple, silver maple, river birch, American bittersweet, hackberry, slippery elm, virgin's bower, white ash, green ash, honey locust, black walnut, Virginia creeper, eastern poison ivy, various willows, sycamore in the south, and plains cottonwood in the west.

Wildlife

Northern floodplain forests are complex communities that provide some of the most important wildlife habitat on the continent, particularly for birds. One hundred forty-two species nest along the Platte River in Nebraska, for example. Floodplain forests also provide key habitats for reptiles, amphibians, and mammals. One-third of the wildlife species or subspecies listed as threatened or endangered by the U.S. Fish and Wildlife Service use these forests.

Relations

On the Great Plains, moisture and fire limit the floodplain forest, which requires moist, sheltered sites on the bottoms and lower slopes of draws. Prior to 1855, woody vegetation in the Great Plains survived almost exclusively along or near rivers and streams, a zone seldom charred by prairie fires. Floodplain forests help regulate river water levels, flow rates and directions, bank stabilities, and evapotranspiration. Flood damage increases when they are destroyed.

Status

Northern floodplain forests once covered over 17 million acres but today occupy under 700,000. Stream channelization, timber harvesting, grazing, and residential developments have reduced acres. In a few areas, however, where dams and irrigators cut streamflows, these forests have increased.

Asymmetry Can Be Costly for Flowers

Appearances count. Even minor imperfections in flowers—one petal being slightly smaller than others, for example—has major implications for flowering plants; reproductive success is at stake.

Just how picky can an insect be? Pretty darn picky, say evolutionary biologists Anders P. Møller and Mats Eriksson. Not only are nectar-drinking bees, butterflies, beetles, and flies capable of perceiving subtle differences in flower symmetry, but they consistently avoid blossoms marred by any imperfections.

Are these insects after truth and beauty or are pollinators able to glean valuable information about a flower from its symmetry? To find out, Møller and Eriksson correlated nectar production with symmetry in individual plants and discovered that, as a rule, symmetrical blooms produce more nectar. They also learned that bigger blossoms are generally more perfect than smaller ones. For the insects that make their living drinking nectar, beauty (in this case symmetry) conveys a potent message.

Because symmetrical flowers are favored by insects, they are pollinated more often than asymmetrical flowers, and the pollen they receive tends to come from other similarly endowed flowers. Selection, then, favors symmetry—the blossoms that, to our eyes, may seem the most perfect and beautiful.

To determine if other factors might operate against flower imperfections, Møller took pollen from both asymmetrical and symmetrical blossoms (he chose fireweed plants) and artificially pollinated the symmetrical blooms on other plants. The pollen from symmetrical flowers consistently produced more seed. Again symmetry wins, although in this case Møller is not yet sure why. Suffice it to say that for plants, asymmetry is a problem, which is probably the reason so many flowers appear so nearly perfect.

What a Little Rust Can Do (or How to Place an Ecosystem in Peril)

Nurserymen inadvertently introduced white pine blister rust to North America in 1910. The disease, which attacks white pines, quickly spread because none of the continent's white pines had evolved defenses against it. The rust enters the pines through the breathing pores or stomata on their needles and travels to the vascular tissue of the stems where it grows, disrupting each tree's ability to transport water and nutrients. The trees die or, at a minimum, fail to reproduce. The fungus then migrates to its alternate host, a currant or gooseberry bush, before returning to infect another pine. Since its introduction, this rust has killed 90 percent of the whitebark pine stands infected.

Whitebark pine, a white pine adapted to cold, dry conditions, populates mid- to high-elevation forests of the northern Rocky Mountains and North Cascades and Sierra Nevada ranges. The first to colonize burns and other disturbed areas, this species traps snow, shades snowbanks, and provides wind- and sun-breaks for other less hardy species. Over time, they turn high-elevation meadows into forests. In addition, over forty species of wildlife use or depend on the nuts from these trees, a list that includes grouse, ravens, jays, woodpeckers, sapsuckers, chickadees, nuthatches, crossbills, grosbeaks, finches, mice, voles, chipmunks, squirrels, black bears, and grizzly bears.

Thus, the loss of whitebark pine has altered forest succession patterns and re-duced the number and kind of animals living at high elevations. Trees are no longer recolonizing harsh sites after fires. The loss has also set back the recovery of endangered grizzly bears in the region. Streamflows have changed because the trees no longer shade snowpacks.

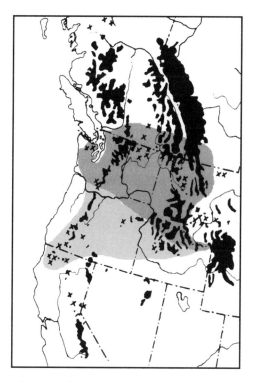

The natural distribution of whitebark pine (in black) and the extent of infection with the microfungi white pine blister rust (in gray). Dark gray represents a 51 to 100 percent infection rate, light gray, a 20 to 50 percent rate. Rates are not known for either Canada or the southern part of the U.S.

Honey Bees against the Natives

Honey bees are not native to North America, though their prevalence might lead one to believe otherwise. Leaving almost no place on the continent untouched, they number in the billions. Introduced to the New World at Jamestown, Virginia, in 1621, the European honey bee now seems as indigenous as the native plants it visits.

The honey bee, an import from Europe, threatens native plants and pollinators.

On the surface, the introduction might seem beneficial. Honey bees provide us with honey and pollinate our crops and many native plants. Aside from the occasional sting, it seems they do only good. But like most exotic species, this one has some hefty costs associated with it, most of which have gone unnoticed until recently.

According to Gary Nabhan and Steve Buchmann, authors of *The Forgotten Pollinators* (Island Press, 1996), honey bees displace native pollinators—other bees, wasps, ants, butterflies, moths, bats, hummingbirds—and this harms native plants.

Because honey bees are better at scouting the locations of flower patches and are able to communicate what they learn to the rest of the hive, they are more efficient exploiters of nectar and pollen. They can harvest most of what's available before native pollinators have a chance. Honey bees are also more flexible; they feed on many kinds of flowers. So when a housing development takes most of the native plants in an area, a hive simply alters its foraging patterns, taking nectar from other plants, native and nonnative. Meanwhile, the indigenous pollinators, generally specific to certain species or groups of plants, are unable to adapt and may disappear entirely from areas when faced with competition for reduced native floras.

Hard-working, efficient, adaptable—these qualities should make honey bees excellent pollinators, in which case the loss of the indigenous pollinators would have little impact on native species. But native bees are better at the actual act of pollinating than honey bees, in part because honey bees pack their pollen with nectar and saliva. Pollen treated in this manner is often rendered inviable, or at a minimum, it is harder to rub off on the female parts of other flowers. A honey bee, for example, needs to visit a wild squash or gourd flower at least two and a half times more often than a native squash or carpenter bee to achieve the same degree of pollination. Native bees tend to visit individual blossoms more often than honey bees and at more optimal times; that is, when plants are most likely to be successfully pollinated. They are also better at transferring pollen and more discriminating in the flowers they visit—less likely to deposit pollen from one species on the stigma of another. For a plant in danger of extinction, every pollen grain counts.

Although we know a great deal about honey bees, we know little about native pollinators. Nabhan and Buchmann report that for a typical region of the U.S., we know the indigenous pollinators for only one of every fifteen endangered plants. This begs the question: How can we protect the plant if we don't know who or what is responsible for propagating it? More distressing, honey bees are not the native pollinators' only problem. Pesticides and habitat fragmentation caused by human developments pose threats, as does fire suppression.

Now, honey bees are in trouble, thanks to two nonnative parasites—the tracheal mite, which bores holes in the bee's windpipe, and the *Varroa* mite, which sucks juices from outside the bee's body. The mites have destroyed 70 percent of the wild stock and have cut the total number of colonies by 50 percent from what it was fifty years ago. Half of the loss has occurred in just the last five years. Scientists now warn of a "pollination crisis" that could cripple North American agriculture and further threaten native plants that—thanks to the honey bees—can no longer depend on native pollinators.

Nabhan, Buchmann, and other scientists conclude a major investment is needed to recruit native pollinators to replace the disappearing honey bees. They also argue for beefed-up national programs to protect habitat, not only for native plants but also for the creatures that pollinate them. They suggest farmers plant lands retired under the conservation reserve program with forage attractive to native pollinators.

Plants Remember Their Enemies

When it comes to defending themselves, plants employ some of the same mechanisms animals do.

A caterpillar bites a leaf. The plant senses the attack and begins producing potent chemical deterrents. Scientists have known for a long time that many plants are able to temporarily produce chemicals to discourage grazers. Now researchers studying tobacco plants have demonstrated that these defenses operate much like those of mammals under siege. The parts of a plant that are injured use an immunelike response; that is, the chewed-on leaves signal for help from other parts of the plant, usually the roots. A caterpillar munching a tobacco leaf triggers the leaf to produce a chemical messenger called jasmonic acid. The acid, transported to the roots, prompts the production of nicotine. Nicotine, toxic to many insects, is then shuttled back to the leaf in concentrations high enough to discourage the feeding caterpillar. Once attacked by an insect or mammal, the leaves of coyote tobacco, a native of dry, open areas of western North America, accumulate the same amount of nicotine in their leaves as is found in one hundred unfiltered Camel cigarettes.

Even more remarkable, the plants seem to learn from the experience of being attacked. The second time around with a pest, they mount a more speedy defense, much the way an animal's immune system remembers exposure to certain pathogens. Whereas, during a first attack, a plant might require several days to accumulate nicotine, it needs only one day in a second attack. Two days can save plenty for a plant being stripped of its foliage by a hungry hoard of caterpillars or mammals.

IN FOCUS: THE BLUESTEM PRAIRIE

Distribution
Bluestem prairie blankets portions of Manitoba, North and South Dakota, Minnesota, Iowa, Nebraska, Kansas, and Oklahoma.

Description
Occasional plateaus, glacial moraines, ravines, stream courses, and potholes break up this mostly flat or gently rolling terrain. Grasses, like big bluestem, little bluestem, switchgrass, and Indiangrass, grow dense and tall and mingle with abundant forbs. Little bluestem reigns on uplands—where soils are driest—and once made up 50 percent of the plant cover there. Big bluestem claims the lowland prairie with its moister soils. Before agriculture, the grass comprised about 80 percent of the cover on the lowland prairie.

Wildlife Use
Today, pronghorn antelope, white-tailed deer, foxes, ground squirrels, prairie dogs, pocket gophers, mice, voles, badger, skunks, waterfowl, grouse, and northern bobwhite live on the prairie. Until the 1800s, great herds of bison roamed the prairie with such predators as grizzly bears and wolves.

Relations
Once, large and frequent fires seared the prairie. Scientists still do not know how frequently they burned. Native Americans regularly lit fires over huge expanses to drive game animals. Lightning fires, perhaps several per decade, raged across tens of thousands of acres at a time. Grasslands can ignite whenever soils are dry, even in midsummer when foliage is still green. Fires devour the dead growth of previous years and encourage stronger and heavier new growth.

Status
The bluestem prairie once occupied 166 million acres of the continent, but now only a few small remnant stands remain, the largest in Kansas and Oklahoma.

How Much Prairie?

Type	Historic (acres)	Current (acres)	Decline (%)	Currently protected (%)*
Tallgrass				
Manitoba	1,481,500	750	99.9	N/A
Illinois	21,975,300	2,300	99.9	<0.01
Indiana	6,913,600	1,000	99.9	<0.01
Iowa	30,864,200	30,000	99.9	<0.01
Kansas	17,037,000	2,963,000	82.6	N/A
Minnesota	18,024,700	75,000	99.9	<1.0
Missouri	14,074,000	75,000	99.9	<1.0
Nebraska	15,061,750	303,700	98.0	<1.0
North Dakota	2,963,000	3,000	99.9	N/A
Oklahoma	12,839,500	N/A	N/A	N/A
South Dakota	7,407,400	1,108,650	85.0	N/A
Texas	17,777,800	1,777,800	90.0	N/A
Wisconsin	2,397,500	9,900	99.9	N/A
Mixed Grass				
Alberta	21,481,500	8,395,000	61.0	<0.01
Manitoba	1,481,500	750	99.9	<0.01
Saskatchewan	33,086,400	6,172,850	81.3	<0.01
Nebraska	19,012,350	4,691,400	77.1	N/A
North Dakota	34,321,000	9,629,600	71.9	N/A
Oklahoma	6,173,000	N/A	N/A	N/A
South Dakota	3,950,600	N/A	N/A	N/A
Texas	34,814,800	24,197,500	30.0	N/A
Shortgrass				
Saskatchewan	14,567,900	2,074,100	85.8	N/A
Oklahoma	3,209,900	N/A	N/A	N/A
South Dakota	442,000	N/A	N/A	N/A
Texas	19,259,250	3,950,600	80.0	N/A
Wyoming	7,407,400	5,926,000	20.0	N/A

*N/A means data not available

The Garden on a Lizard's Forehead

Plants grow in some strange places. One of the strangest has to be the forehead of a 14-inch-long lizard. Of epizoics, the plants that live on the bodies of animals, only a handful are known to science: an algae that resides on the hair of sloths; lichens that live on the backs of giant tortoises; and algae, lichens, and mosses that thrive atop weevils. All live in tropical latitudes. Recently, near Chiapas, Mexico, researchers discovered an entire community—a liverwort and five species of algae—occupying the head of a slow-moving lizard, a species that ranges from lowland rainforests in Veracruz, Mexico, to northern Columbia.

Olive brown and green with black-and-white-speckled legs and tail, the *Corythphanes* lizard resembles a dry branch coated with lichens. Camouflaged, the lizard remains motionless for hours, even when approached by humans.

This lizard's forehead seems an easy place for plants to start, as far as foreheads go. Because it is concave, it readily catches and holds rain. And because the lizard spends so much time sitting motionless, spores have time to attach and germinate. The high humidity and relatively constant temperature of the rainforest are important ambient factors. Once established, the plants probably aid the lizard by adding camouflage, like foliage festooned atop a soldier's helmet.

The discovery marks the first time any kind of plant with stems and roots (the liverwort) has been found growing on a vertebrate. To date, all the other known epizoic species residing on vertebrates are either algae or lichen.

Squirt Gun Plants and Surgeon Beetles

Nature is full of examples of predator-prey ploys and counterploys, and not all are restricted to the animal kingdom. Some plants mount clever defenses, their adversaries countering with equally creative responses. One such chess game is waged in the Zaptitlán basin of the Tehuacán Valley in central Mexico.

Bursera plants, members of the frankincense family long used for incense, are chock-full of a half-dozen or more potent chemicals known as terpenes. Designed to repel would-be grazers, the terpenes taste foul and can be toxic to animals. They circulate through stems and leaves of the plants in a network of resin canals. Many plants use terpenes to ward off pests, but one species of *Bursera*, *B. schlechtendalii*, evolved two novel strategies. An unwitting deer, for example, that bites off a leaf, gets a face full of terpenes. Upon losing a leaf, this *Bursera* instantly fires off a three- to four-second syringelike spray of chemicals. Researchers plucking leaves to photograph this "squirt gun" effect had their hands and camera lenses coated with the sticky substance. They observed that whereas other species adjacent had been heavily grazed by cattle and goats, the *Burseras* went untouched.

The plant is capable of a different response when the target is too small to be hit with a narrow stream. Insects chewing leaves suffer what researchers describe as a "highly fluid front" of terpenes, a foglike spray of chemical that saturates more than half of both of the leaf's surfaces. The researchers labeled this the "rapid-bath" response. When hit with a rapid-bath, *Chrysomelid* beetle larvae, relatives of the Colorado potato beetle and the plant's chief predator, attempt to clean themselves, then abandon the leaf.

Not to be outwitted, the beetles have developed a way to neutralize the "guns" of the *Burseras*. They mount a sneak attack, a surgical strike that neutralizes the plant's spraying mechanism. When a larva arrives on a new leaf, it positions itself along the midrib, head facing the leaf stalk near the base. The larva carefully gnaws the tissue near the midrib, a zone where biting does not trigger a response from the plant. The beetle larva takes up to ninety minutes to sever the leaf's resin canals while preserving the midrib itself. The leaf is neutralized, and the larva goes on to consume the entire leaf in ten to twenty minutes, a fraction of the time required to disarm the spraying mechanism.

Researchers speculate that the beetle larvae, although successful at avoiding the *Bursera's* defense, incur some costs. For example, the surgery likely increases the larvae's chances of being eaten by a bird or lizard, and because the larvae waste so much feeding time disarming leaves, the onset of pupation is probably delayed. *Bursera* leaves must be worth the price.

Meanwhile, both plant and beetle evolve. If today's *Burseras* are employing squirt guns, and *Chrysomelid* beetles surgery, what's next?

Fen, Bog, Marsh, or Swamp?

Names can be confusing, especially wetland names. One person's marsh is another's swamp. To a certain extent, wetland designations vary with locale. A few definitions follow.

Fens and bogs are two of the least understood designations. Both are peat-storing wetlands; peat is an accumulation of partially decomposed plant matter, mosses of the genus *Sphagnum* in particular. Peat collects in fens and bogs because plant growth exceeds decomposition. The difference between these two types of wetland depends on the amount of nutrition available for plants and the acidity of the water. Fens, fed by mineral-rich ground water or surface water, are the most fertile and tend to be high in calcium. They support a comparatively diverse community of plants—anywhere from twenty to seventy species is typical. Most fen plants are grasslike;

sedges often predominate. The pH of fens spans a broad range. A pH of 7 is neutral. Anything under that is acidic, anything above is alkaline. Mineral-poor fens are on the acid side with pHs in the range of 4 to 6; those richer in mineral nutrients are closer to neutral pHs of 6 to 7.5.

Bogs lie above the water table on top of peat and acquire all their mineral nutrients from precipitation—rain or snow or fog. More acidic than fens, their pH ranges between 3 and 4. Bogs are mineral-poor and acidic; few plants find them suitable habitats. A *Sphagnum* bog supports around fifteen species—mostly *Sphagnum* mosses but also heath shrubs. As bogs mature, trees such as black spruce encroach.

Marshes and wet meadows do not accumulate much peat and experience fluctuating water levels. Their soils are oxygenated, their pHs, neutral. Decomposition is more rapid then in a fen or bog. Mineral rich and productive, marshes stand in water for at least part of the year, often during spring floods. Most support communities dominated by grasses and sedges. Sedge meadows are similar but drier.

Swamps are wooded wetlands. Moving water with pHs in the neutral or slightly alkaline range aerate soils that are mineral rich and productive—good conditions for some species of trees. In the southern Great Lakes region, swamps host overstory communities of red maple, black ash, yellow birch, or pin oak, tamarack, and shrubs. To the north, they sustain tamarack or white cedar communities scattered with balsam fir, white spruce, black spruce, and yellow birch.

Exchanging Pollen in Water

Long ago, some flowering plants that had evolved on land invaded the water. In this new environment, they faced a problem: how to exchange pollen among themselves. On land, they relied on wind and animals, but pollen dispersal in water is less predictable; the pollen is much less likely to reach its intended target. Scientists estimate that pollination in water is several thousand times less efficient than in air. Erratic currents and tides capable of inundating plants or leaving them high and dry complicate the challenge. The difficulties account for the scarcity of water-pollinated plants; a handful exist worldwide.

During World War II, a mathematician, B. O. Koopman, developed what has become known as "search theory" to improve the U.S. Navy's chances of finding enemy submarines. He demonstrated that if a search vehicle moves randomly on the water, the probability of finding an object increases dramatically when the path of the vehicle widens. For ships, this meant that even a modest increase in the range of their radar improved results spectacularly. Recently, botanists discovered that water-pollinated plants employ the same principle when they send out pollen grains in search of stigmas. Some, like *Phyllospadix*, a surfgrass that grows along the northern California coast, have evolved long, sticky, noodle-shaped pollen that clumps together into rafts that float on the surface of the water. The clumping yields a wider search path.

Pollination in this species and in others also occurs underwater. But beneath the water, rules change—Koopman's equation does not apply in three dimensions. Experiments using supercomputers show that the most efficient search vehicles beneath the surface are elliptical in shape rather than spherical, a design natural selection isolated millions of years ago. Pollen used by underwater-pollinating plants forms strands. The sticky pollen noodles, that on the surface form snowflakelike rafts, clump in linear bundles beneath the surface.

Other adaptations of water-pollinated plants include stigmas with broad target areas shaped to make contact with pollen. Another is dioecism—the separation of male and female flowers onto distinct plants. Dioecism, more common among water-pollinated plants than terrestrial species, improves the chance of cross-pollination and prevents inbreeding in aquatic settings.

In Focus: The Conifer Bog

Distribution

Conifer bogs are scattered throughout Canada (especially from the maritime provinces west to Quebec and Ontario) and the northern U.S. as far south as New Jersey, Ohio, and the Great Lake states. The peatlands of the Glacial Lake Agassiz area of Minnesota are the largest unbroken tracts of bog terrain in the northern U.S.

Description

Conifer bogs are dense to open, low to medium-tall forests of conifers and deciduous trees rooted in peat. They fall into three categories: dwarf-shrub bogs comprised of scattered tamarack or black spruce trees with an understory of mostly dwarf evergreen heath shrubs; tall-shrub-thicket bogs dominated by deciduous-heath shrubs beneath a canopy of black spruce, tamarack, and red maple; and forest bogs of black spruce and dwarf-heath shrubs. The waters of all conifer bogs are acidic and nutrient poor. Moss and lichen flora may be rich, but higher plant diversity is usually quite low.

Wildlife

None of the animal species that occur in conifer bogs occur there exclusively, but birds such as spruce grouse, yellow-bellied flycatchers, palm warblers, Connecticut warblers, northern waterthrushes, and Lincoln's sparrows reach their highest densities in bog habitats. Dozens of other bird species frequent bogs, including such threatened and rare types as the sharp-tailed sparrow, sora, short-eared owl, greater sandhill crane, and great gray owl. Most of the large mammals of the region spend little time in peatlands. Exceptions include moose, white-tailed deer, and black bears.

For black bears, bogs provide escape cover and an abundance of succulent food, especially in the spring when bears emerge from their dens. In winter, wolves frequent white cedar stands because deer winter in them. Moose find bogs good summer habitat. In Canada, woodland caribou sometimes feed in bogs. Porcupine, southern and northern bog lemmings, and various shrews and mice spend much of their lives in bog habitats, as do wood, green, and northern leopard frogs and blue-spotted and four-toed salamanders.

Relations

Conifer bogs develop in lakes if woollyfruit sedge is present. The sedge forms rhizomes that grow out into the water. The rhizomes develop into a floating mat that *Sphagnum* mosses and heath shrubs invade, and the sedge mat eventually grows deep enough to reach the lake bottom. Eventually, trees colonize the community. Bogs also form through a process called paludification, the drowning or submergence of upland habitats—the result, for example, of a beaver dam. Regional paludification is the widespread expansion of peatlands through the elevation of the water table. The rising water suffocates the roots of upland plants, and peat accumulates. Peat encourages the process by retaining water and impeding drainage. Conifer bogs shelter rare plants such as ram's-head lady-slipper and several sundews. Human developments have destroyed and fragmented many conifer bogs.

Medicine from a Tree

Plants once provided half of the medicines that doctors prescribe today. The list includes one of the most promising group of cancer drugs yet discovered—the taxoids, based on the taxol molecule first obtained from the bark of Pacific yew trees.

Yew is a 15- to 25-foot-high, slow growing conifer that thrives beneath old growth canopies in the Pacific Northwest. Able to reproduce vegetatively, yew forms dense copses along heavily forested streams from Alaska to San Francisco and as far east as Montana. The foliage is similar to that of coastal redwood—sprays of needles that are deep yellow green on top and pale green beneath. The flowers, with male and female borne on separate trees, produce bright red, pea-sized, berrylike fruit favored by birds. The bark, thin and purple, flakes off in long, wavy scales. The wood is bright orange to rose red and is heavy, hard, strong, and elastic. Tribal groups made bows from it, as well as harpoons, canoe paddles, war clubs, and eating utensils. The genus name, *Taxus*, derives from the Greek *taxon*, which means bow; Europeans, too, made bows from the European species of yew, *T. baccata*.

American Indian tribes—groups like the Quinault, Multnomah, Tlingit, and Nez Perce—knew the bark was a potent medicine. They applied extractions of it as a disinfectant. Women drank a yew tea to induce abortions. Their medicine men and women administered compresses of the bark to halt skin cancer. Aware of the tribal uses, the U.S. Department of Agriculture tested the bark's pharmaceutical potential in 1962. Other researchers discovered yew extractions could kill leukemia cells. By 1967, they had isolated the active ingredient, taxol. Taxol blocked cell division in a way unknown before. Succeeding where other treatments had failed, taxol exceeded all expectations. However, a single gram of the drug, about half the amount needed for a treatment, required all the bark growing on a hundred-year-old tree. Pacific yew trees, found in the already beleaguered old growth forests of the Pacific Northwest, could not supply enough taxol.

Chemists working in as many as thirty different research groups set out to synthesize the drug. After ten years, a group working in France succeeded. They started with a substance similar to taxol, obtained from the needles of European yew trees. (Unlike the bark of Pacific yew, the needles of European yew can be harvested without killing the trees.) They then attached the molecule derived from the needles to a simpler compound synthesized in the laboratory. Concurrently, groups working in the U.S. developed other methods of making taxol and similar compounds effective as tumor fighters. In 1994, the U.S. Food and Drug Administration approved one of the semisynthetic forms of the drug. Women with advanced ovarian cancer who received the drug lived an average of fourteen months longer than those receiving other therapies. People with drug-resistant breast cancer also improved, and taxol shows promise against colon, lung, prostate, and pancreatic cancers and leukemia. Researchers continue to tinker with the taxol molecule.

NATIVE PLANTS OF COMMERCIAL VALUE

Native peoples employed an enormous number of plants for a variety of purposes. Ethnographers estimate that over 170 species served as food, 52 provided beverages, and over 400 yielded medicines or other products. Many crops produced around the world today descended from species used by native peoples. Some of these follow.

Plant	Commercial Uses
Sunflower	The sunflower genus *Helianthus* contains 49 species and 19 subspecies, all native to North America. American Indians originally domesticated the sunflower and the Jerusalem artichoke, both of which are today cultivated for food. Wild-species sunflowers remain potential sources of genes for enhancing insect and disease resistance, salt tolerance, protein content, and fatty acid concentration in the domestic sunflower, an enormously important crop in many regions of the world.
Barley	Some hybrids occur naturally; others can be obtained only through controlled crosses. Some hybrids hold promise for increasing salt and drought tolerance of crops.
Proso Millet	Many wild species of this group have commercial potential.
Grass Crops	Many forage crops (forage grasses and forage legumes) and turf grasses are native to temperate regions of the continent. They are used for hay, pasturing, soiling, and silage and are often sown along with legumes. Several species of forage and turf grasses, members of the family Triticeae, represent genetic resources for cereal crop-breeding programs.
Plum and Cherry	Thirty species of *Prunus*, two-thirds of which are plums, are native to the U.S. Many of the Japanese-type plums grown all over the world have genetic contributions from North American species. Beneficial traits found in the North American species include winter hardiness, earliness, disease resistance, and desirable fruit characteristics. Most cherry-breeding programs employ native-American species.

NATIVE PLANTS OF COMMERCIAL VALUE (CONT.)

Plant	Commercial Uses
Grape	Worldwide, grape cultivation depends on grape rootstocks developed from native North American species, plants with resistance to the *Phylloxera* insect. Most American *Vitis* species are tolerant to *Phylloxera*, which devastated European vineyards in the 1800s. Genes for resistance to powdery mildew are also found only in American species of *Vitis*. Other examples of useful traits in native American species include drought resistance, salt tolerance, and crown-gall and nematode resistance.
Strawberry	The cultivated strawberry is a hybrid of two species, both native to the U.S. The genetic base of strawberry cultivars is quite narrow. Most introductions in North America derived from a small population. Wild species carry many traits such as resistance to heat and drought, frost tolerance, salinity tolerance, and higher photosynthetic rates, attributes that might enhance domestic varieties.
Raspberry and Blackberry	The North American red raspberry is part of the ancestry of most red raspberry cultivars grown in both northern Europe and North America. Another native species, the black raspberry, is an important fruit crop in North America that contributed useful traits to the improvement of the red raspberry. Purple raspberries are hybrids of red and black raspberries and are grown in some northeastern states in the U.S. Several blackberry species are also native to North America. The genetic base for the world's leading cultivars of red and black raspberry and blackberry is extremely narrow; North American species offer genetic diversity and resistance to major fungal pathogens and insect pests.
Blueberry	The blueberry has been domesticated only since the early twentieth century, and most of the crop harvested in Canada descends directly from native wild stands. Cultivated blueberries derive from a subgenus of *Vaccinium*, with 24 species, all native. The primary species of cultivated highbush blueberry is produced in Canada and 17 states in the U.S. The most important commercially harvested lowbush blueberries are from managed native stands in Maine and Quebec and the maritime provinces of Canada. Rabbit-eye blueberries are commercially produced in the southeastern U.S.
Cranberry	The cultivated cranberry derived from a native eastern North American species. Although it grows in 21 states in the U.S., most of the commercially cultivated clones descended directly from wild populations in Massachusetts and Wisconsin. The full range of the wild cranberry has not been completely surveyed and evaluated for genetic diversity.
Currant and Gooseberry	Many species of currants and their relatives occur in temperate North America. Some of the useful characters found in the native species include resistance to mildew, leafspot, and other fungal pathogens, drought resistance, fruit size, aphid resistance, and spinelessness.
Pawpaw	The pawpaw is native to the U.S. Most pawpaws consumed in the U.S. are gathered in the wild or from trees in home gardens. Only about 20 cultivars are commercially available; many of the early ones have been lost. Pawpaw could be an important fruit crop with improved traits in yield, fruit set, and the number of seeds.
Other Fruits	Other native fruit crops of importance include saskatoon or serviceberry, chokecherry, and wild rose.

NATIVE PLANTS OF COMMERCIAL VALUE (CONT.)

Plant	Commercial Uses
Pecan	Pecan grows along the Mississippi River and its tributaries from Illinois and Iowa to the Gulf of Mexico. The most continuous groves occur in Texas and Oklahoma. Pecan is the most valuable native U.S. nut crop and the most important nut crop in Mexico. Useful traits present in native populations include disease and insect resistances and climatic and soil adaptations.
Walnut	Six species of walnut are native to the U.S. One, the American black walnut, is the most valuable hardwood produced in the U.S. Black walnut is prized for furniture and gunstocks, and the nuts are used in candies, baked goods, and ice cream. Nuts of the butternut are harvested to a lesser degree. Most of the English walnuts grown in California are grafted onto rootstocks of hybrids of native species.
Wild Rice	Three species of wild rice are native to the U.S., but only the one native to the Great Lakes region is harvested for food. The plant has been a staple crop since prehistoric times. Prior to about 1950, all harvested wild rice came from natural stands; however, since then, cultivation has picked up dramatically. The development of shatter-resistant cultivars has improved yields.
Medicinal Plants	Hundreds of species native to North America possess medicinal properties. Noteworthy examples include buckthorn, or cascara sagrada, which is native to the northwestern U.S. and has bark used throughout the world as a cathartic; the roots of ginseng, native to the eastern U.S. and harvested in such large quantities that wild plants are declining; rattlesnake weed, a nonspecific immune system stimulant used in many pharmaceutical preparations; goldenseal, one of the best-selling herbs, used to treat inflamed membranes of the mouth, throat, digestive system, and uterus and for jaundice, bronchitis, and gonorrhea; the American mandrake mayapple, applied to treat testicular and small-cell lung cancers; bloodroot, used commercially as a plaque-inhibiting agent in toothpaste, mouthwashes, and rinses; white willow, used as a source of salicylic acid, a precursor to aspirin; and Pacific yew, a major source of taxol, a chemical effective against melanoma, mammary, and ovarian cancer. Other medicinal and health food crops include evening primrose and false gromwell. Horseradish is grown for the condiment market and for peroxidase production.
New Crops	Several native plant species being investigated for potential as crops include jojoba, an evergreen shrub native to the Sonoran Desert in southern Arizona and California, the seeds of which contain a unique oil used for cosmetics, lubricants, detergents, and other products; Lesquerella spp. the seed oil of which is high in a hydroxy fatty acid similar to imported castor oil and has potential for use in adhesives, lubricants, plasticizers, pharmaceutical and medical products, waxes and polishes, soaps, inks, detergents, and cosmetics; buffalo gourd, which grows in the southwest and has food and nonfood uses; guayule, native to Texas, with bark that is a good source of natural rubber; Grindelia camporum, native to California and a source of resin used in inks and adhesives and as a substitute for pine rosin; milkweeds, from which the floss of the seed pods is used as batting for comforters, sleeping bags, and arctic apparel; and Cuphea viscosissima, native to the southeastern and eastern U.S. and a source of industrial seed oils used in soaps, detergents, lubricants, and other products.

FUNGI

NO ONE KNOWS HOW MANY SPECIES OF fungi are in North America. Where fungi are well studied, the ratio of vascular plants to fungi is about 6 to 1, suggesting that the U.S. alone may have 120,000 species.

Microfungi—the molds, mildews, rusts, and smuts—are the most diverse group and also the least understood. Mycologists have described only about 5 to 10 percent of the species. Worldwide, that amounts to about 200,000 species, out of an estimated 1 to 1.5 million. Estimates put the number of microfungi species *known* in the U.S. at 29,000, a fraction of the species that actually occur.

Macrofungi—the mushrooms, morels, puffballs, bracket fungi, and cup fungi— are more familiar to the average person. No checklists of North American mushrooms or comprehensive regional treatments exist. Mycologists base their best estimates of diversity on comparisons with western Europe, where more than 3,000 species are reported. Most scientists believe North America hosts far more species. More than twice as many species of *Lactarius, Amanita,* and *Clitocybe* are reported from the continental U.S. than from western Europe, for example. Mycologists estimate between 5,000 and 10,000 species of macrofungi live in the U.S. alone.

Boletus *mushrooms*

Fungi: Closer to Plants or Animals?

Most people consider mushrooms and other members of the kingdom Fungi (molds and lichens) to be more closely related to plants than to animals. Mushrooms rest plantlike on soil, anchored by a mass of rootlike threads called mycelium. Although fungi lack chlorophyll and make their living by breaking down organic matter, they are wanting when it comes to characteristics we associate with animals—mobility, a nervous system, complex sense organs, a gut, and so on.

Nevertheless, genetic studies reveal fungi as near relatives of animals. A new discovery adds weight to this theory. A researcher investigating the microfungus *Microbotryum violaceum*, which lives on the anthers of flowering plants, discovered that tiny hairlike tubes that coat the cells of this and many other fungi are built from collagen, a protein heretofore associated only with the animal kingdom. Collagen is one of the fundamental proteins employed by animals to hold together skin, bones, muscles, tendons, and internal organs. Proteins shared with animals but not plants indicate that fungi are more closely related to animals than plants.

Fungi and Plants: It's a Love-Hate Relationship

On the love side, fungi send out vast networks of tiny threads called mycelia, which secrete enzymes that break down organic matter—dead wood and leaves. The process releases nutrients needed for plant growth. Without fungi, much of the organic debris produced by forests and other plant communities would fail to rot, and the nutrients plants require would be locked up. Fungi are more than decomposers, however. Some, such as *Boletes*, *Amanitas*, and *Russulas*, form mutually beneficial associations with trees and shrubs, the mycelia of the fungus growing veil-like sheaths around and through the rootlets of plants. In this association, called mycorrhizae, the fungus delivers water, nitrogen, and phosphorus. The latter are nutrients essential for plant growth and are otherwise difficult to obtain in the quantities needed. In exchange, trees and shrubs supply the fungus with carbohydrates. Enough of North America's trees depend on this kind of association that if mycorrhizal fungi disappeared tomorrow, the forests would collapse.

The flip side is that not all fungi are beneficial to plants. Many species can kill or injure plants. Endemic fungal pathogens, always present in forests but at low levels, hinder individual or small stands of trees and play a necessary role in the way natural plant communities function. At endemic levels, fungi such as heartrot, rootrot, butt rot, and canker fungi create openings in the forest canopy that provide opportunities for other tree species and thus promote diversity. Such is the case in the Cascades of Oregon where root-rot kills older hemlocks. The openings allow Pacific silver fir, a species that is less susceptible to the disease but that requires light, to increase. Fungus-killed trees supplying food and shelter also contribute to insect, mammal, and bird diversity. Sapsuckers, for example, excavate holes in aspen trees infected with the heartrot fungus, holes later used by swallows and other cavity-nesting birds and by some small mammals.

Epidemics, on the other hand, can wreak havoc with plant communities. Native plants cannot defend themselves against some exotic or introduced fungi. The fungus that causes chestnut blight, a disease introduced from Asia in 1904, killed most of the continent's American chestnut trees, a species that was widespread across eastern North America a century ago. Similarly, white pine blister rust has all but wiped out two of the west's most common tree species, western white pine and whitebark pine.

Sometimes native fungi reach epidemic levels, generally after a major human disturbance. Airborne spores of a root-rot fungus infect the stumps of a number of conifer species in northern forests. Moving through roots of cut trees, root-rot can infect adjacent living trees. In areas that have been selectively logged, the fungus often takes more trees than the logging operation.

Truffles Anyone?

When most Americans think of truffles, they picture fancy European restaurants serving up expensive dishes of exotic mushrooms rooted out by trained pigs. Few realize that North America also grows truffles, mushrooms that are not only good to eat but that play a vital ecological role. Truffles (*Ascomycetes*) and the similar-appearing false truffles (*Basidiomycetes*) determine, perhaps more than any other organism, the structure and function of many of the continent's forest communities. Like other fungi, they provide nutrients to trees. In exchange they receive carbohydrates. The technical term for this mutually beneficial association is mycorrhizal symbiosis. It is an obligate relation; neither truffle nor tree could survive without the other. One of the problems in reforesting large areas of the southwest is identifying fungi suitable for inoculation of tree seedlings.

Although truffles and false truffles are of major ecological importance, little is known about their distribution. A recent survey of the Great Basin, an area of 275,000 square miles that includes most of Nevada and parts of California, Idaho, Utah, Wyoming, and Oregon, produced 1,119 collections of truffles and false truffles. Prior to the survey, none had been reported from the area. The survey turned up new endemic species, expanded the known geographic ranges of others, and found evidence that some truffle species have probably disappeared from the region.

Ecologists warn that unless we increase our knowledge of truffles, we run the risk of losing or degrading plant communities. That, in turn, would threaten the birds, mammals, and insects dependent on them.

A chanterelle

Part Five
INVERTEBRATES

Part Five Invertebrates

NUMBERS AND DISTRIBUTION

PERHAPS 255,000 SPECIES OF PLANTS, 1.6 million species of fungi, 4,600 species of mammals, 9,000 species of birds, and 18,800 species of fish populate the earth. We have no such number for invertebrates. We don't even know how many species of insects there are. A good estimate for insects puts the number in the neighborhood of the tens of millions—perhaps as many as 30 to 50 million. Biologists have described about three-quarters of a million insects, an average of 3,500 each year since 1758, the year Linnaeus originated our modern system of nomenclature. Two of every five living organisms described so far are insects; about 40 percent of those are beetles.

Because of their sheer numbers, insects are thought to possess the highest biomass of all land animals. The ant population alone at any moment probably exceeds 10 million billion individuals. If one adds other invertebrates, the numbers become astronomical. An ordinary acre of temperate meadow supports an estimated 666 million individual mites, 248 million springtails, 18 million beetles, and another 135 million or so aphids, bristletails, and other miscellaneous arthropods.

Forty percent of all known insects are beetles.

North America north of Mexico probably hosts just under 90,000 insect species in thirty-four orders. Of the described species, 23,701 are beetles; 19,562 are flies; 17,777 are ants, bees, or wasps; and 11,300 are butterflies or moths (Mexico alone supports an estimated 25,000 butterflies and moths). And insects represent but one type of invertebrate. Within a typical acre of land and water, there are likely hundreds of non-insect species that together make up a lacework of builders, gatherers, collectors, predators, and grazers. Most of these go unnoticed.

We understand little about the behavior, communication, and function of most of these creatures. Some metamorphose into several distinct life stages. For example, some insects transform from egg to larva to pupa to winged adult. Others, such as some aquatic invertebrates, skip pupal stages; their larvae (nymphs or naiads) grow larger by molting. Biologists possess information on some aspect of the early stages of only about a tenth of the described species.

Found in all types of climates, invertebrates are hardy, surviving all sorts of extreme natural conditions. Nevertheless, unnatural disturbances such as siltation, acid rain, excessive nutrients, or contamination by toxic substances take their toll on populations.

Butterfly Numbers: Go Figure

How many butterflies reside in temperate North America? In his book *The Butterflies of North America*, James A. Scott figures it this way: Around 700 species live north of Mexico, each with a range of about 117,000 square miles. On average, every 2.5 acres of a species range supports one adult butterfly of that species per generation (about 256 butterflies per square mile). And butterflies lay eggs twice a year on average. Multiplying 700 x 117,000 x 256 x 2 gives an estimate of 42 billion butterflies. Scott then goes on to figure the number of butterfly eggs laid each year by calculating that half of those 42 billion butterflies are females, and each female lays about 100 eggs. That adds up to over 2 trillion eggs—like grains of sand on the beach, a quantity too large to imagine.

The Real Multitudes

Entomologists take some pride in the diversity of insects, but zoologists who study even smaller creatures are quick to counter that every insect probably has at least one or two parasitic nematodes, protozoans, bacteria, and viruses specialized to its type. The number of species invisible to the eye could be five times greater than the total number of insects.

Insects by Vegetation Types

Vegetation Type	Description
Arctic	Few insect species reside in the Arctic, a treeless zone of permafrost covered by snow much of the year. But the species that do occur there usually occur in large numbers, mosquitoes and biting flies, for example. The Arctic also supports a modest array of other insects, among them a few dozen species of butterflies, most with biennial life cycles.
Boreal or Taiga	The northern coniferous forests, comprised mostly of spruce, fir, and pine, have a limited insect fauna. The most common types include mosquitoes, black flies, butterflies, wood-boring beetles, needle-feeding moth caterpillars, plant-eating wasp caterpillars, and parasitic wasps.
Deciduous Forests	This zone, encompassing a broad range of climates and forest types, hosts a large variety of insects: moths and butterflies, flies, aphids, cicadas, ants, termites, and beetles are among the most common.
Grasslands	The grasshopper, with over a thousand species, is the grassland's best-known insect. But the prairie is also home to a modest diversity of other insects such as harvester ants, armyworms, leafhoppers, and butterflies and moths. A few dozen species of butterfly grace the prairie.
Desert, Scrub, Chaparral, and Thorn Scrub	This arid zone shelters many insect species in spite of the fact that water is scarce. Almost all groups are represented. The order Hymenoptera (bees and wasps) is a good example. In the Sonoran Desert alone, there are over 1,500 species of native bees, more bee species than anywhere else on earth.
Western Montane and Pacific Coast Coniferous Forests	Similar to the coniferous forest of the boreal region, this zone, because of its limited flora, has a relatively sparse insect fauna. Even the temperate rainforests support few species. Higher mountains may harbor endemic species, many of which are closely related to Arctic species. Scavenging rock-crawlers (inch-long, cylindrical, wingless insects that live beneath rocks and logs at the edges of high-elevation glaciers) are among the more unique and rare species found on mountaintops. Butterflies are often abundant in alpine meadows.
Tropical Rainforests	Because of the diversity of plant life, tropical rainforests flaunt the greatest number of insect species. Ants, bees, wasps, and beetles thrive in surprising numbers. A single tree might harbor as many as 50 species of ants and 125 species of beetles.
Inland Waters	Aquatic insects, many of which are aquatic for only a part of their life, include a number of the continent's most common insects. Dragonflies, mayflies, caddisflies, stoneflies, and dobsonflies are among the better-known orders, but aquatic insects also include true bugs (such as water boatmen) and larvae of crickets (pygmy molecrickets), moths (pyralid), beetles, and flies.
Oceans	There are few marine insects. The only truly marine species belong to the subfamily Halobatinae, the water striders. One species of this group, the Pacific pelagic water strider, hunts off the coast of California. Other species (some 1,400 known) from a handful of different orders (beetle, fly, true bug, caddisfly, and thrip) live in and near saltwater habitats but only at intertidal zones.

Insect Families and Species Numbers

Too many numbers can be numbing; nevertheless it is interesting to look at frequency values in order to get a sense of relative abundance. The chart below provides that perspective for North American insects north of Mexico. It shows, for example, that we have described twice as many grasshoppers and crickets as dragonflies and damselflies. Similarly, we know eleven species of butterfly and twenty-three species of beetle for every species of grasshopper.

Entomologists estimate that Mexico hosts in the neighborhood of 25,000 species of butterflies, moths, and skippers and some 2,000 species of bees. We have no good estimates for the number of other insect species in Mexico. The climate and vegetation, however, suggest abundance.

FAMILY AND SPECIES NUMBERS NORTH OF MEXICO

Name	Families	Species
Non-Insect Hexapods		
Springtails and Allies	7	677
Proturans	3	20
Entotrophs	4	64
Insects		
Bristletails	2	20
Silverfish	3	18
Mayflies	17	611
Dragonflies and Damselflies	11	407
Stoneflies	9	465
Grasshoppers, Katydids, and Crickets	11	1,080
Earwigs	5	20
Mantids and Cockroaches	6	69
Termites	4	44
Biting Lice	8	943
Sucking Lice	9	56
Bugs	40	3,587
Cicadas, Hoppers, Whiteflies, Aphids, and Scale Insects	38	6,359
Dobsonflies, Lacewings, Antlions, and Allies	15	349
Beetles, Weevils, and Stylopids	113	23,701
Wasps, Ants, and Bees	70	17,777
Caddisflies	18	1,261
Moths, Skippers, and Butterflies	75	11,300
Flies and Keds	108	19,562
Fleas	7	325

The Non-Insect Hexapods

Springtail with tail released

Springtails, proturans, and two-pronged bristletails are not insects because their mouth parts are enclosed within a cavity and because most move their antennae with muscles, traits insects lack. Also, whereas 99.9 percent of insects belong to a class in which the adults have wings (although they may be lost in some groups), none of the springtails, proturans, or two-pronged bristletails sports wings.

Springtails, named for their spring-loaded, forked tail, range in size from one- to two-tenths of an inch. They live on damp soils, pools of water, or snow and feed on bacteria, pollen, fungi, algae, decomposing organic material, and plants. Often abundant, as many as 2,000 will dwell in a quart of healthy soil. Sometimes they are so dense they color snowfields gray or black. Some springtail species build elaborate tiny chambers out of their own dung during droughts.

Proturans, under a tenth of an inch long, live in soil and feed with sucking mouth parts on fungi. Little is known about their biology despite their widespread numbers.

Two-pronged bristletails, also widespread, live beneath logs and rocks. Most reach only three-tenths of an inch in length, although some species grow to be almost 2 inches long. Most, if not all, are blind. Males deposit their sperm in a stalked packet, which the females find and pick up.

Freshwater Mussels in Trouble

More species of freshwater mussels live in temperate North America than anywhere else on earth, but this record might not last. A recent survey by the American Fisheries Society found that 7 percent of North American mussel species or subspecies are listed as endangered and presumed extinct. Another 26 percent are classified as endangered, 14.5 percent as threatened, and 24 percent as species of special concern. Of the 297 taxa (281 species and 16 subspecies), 72 percent are in trouble. (By comparison, only 7 percent of the continent's bird and

Seventy-two percent of the continent's mussels are in trouble.

mammal species are imperiled to the same degree.) The culprits are introduced species, habitat loss to dams, channel modifications, dredging, and siltation. Biologists warn that the 23 percent of the species considered stable will likely suffer declines in the near future because the zebra mussel is displacing them. The zebra mussel, an introduced species, is expanding into the large rivers and reservoirs in the southeast, an area with the highest diversity of mussels in the world.

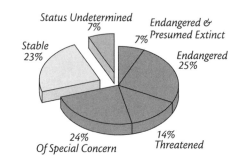

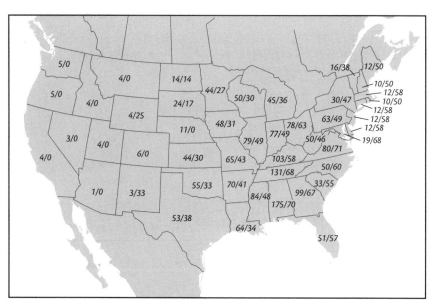

Number of species and subspecies of mussels in each state and the percentage of those classified as endangered

Acacias and Their Standing Armies

ABOUT 100 MILLION YEARS AGO, AS FLOWering plants diversified and spread around the world, the first ants appeared. Some species joined as partners with plants. Over the ages, the two—plant and ant—developed intricate relationships. Ants (*Pseudomyrmex ferruginea*) and acacia trees (any one of five different species) in Mexico provide a good example of that mutuality.

After her mating flight, a queen *Pseudomyrmex* ant searches for an unoccupied acacia thorn to live in—no other site will do. Chewing a hole in the end, she slips inside and begins laying and tending eggs. When the eggs hatch, she rears the brood and then lays another batch. Within six months, her colony has grown to 150 to 200 workers. They patrol the leaves and branches surrounding the queen's thorn, where they clean and defend the foliage and gather food. Their food, protein- and lipid-rich nectar secreted by the extrafloral nectaries and berrylike structures called Beltian bodies, grows on the acacia. Once the Beltian bodies are harvested, nurse workers in the colony break them apart and push the fragments into special food pouches on the thorax of larval ants, pouches not found on any other kind of ant. As the colony increases, the workers venture farther from the thorn and eventually patrol all the leaves and branches of the plant. They attack smaller colonies attempting to establish themselves in other thorns and keep enemies of the acacia—plant-eating insects, deer, cows, and humans—at bay. Eventually, if successful, the colony expands into surrounding acacias.

Ants and acacia thorns

The acacia, with its Beltian bodies, hollow thorns, and extrafloral nectaries, seems specifically adapted to attract and keep *Pseudomyrmex* ants. Indeed, acacias without ants do not survive long. Researchers who robbed a tree of its ant army by clipping its thorns reported that soon a host of creatures assailed the tree. Leaf-footed bugs and treehoppers sucked on shoot tips and new leaves. Scarab and leaf beetles and hungry caterpillars also set upon the leaves, while woodboring beetles girdled the shoots. Mammals browsed freely. And other plants grew close enough to shade the acacia, a sun-loving species. Normally, the ants prune and even remove competing plants. The ant-free acacias were short-lived.

Pseudomyrmex ants and acacias are an example of coevolution—organisms developing special structures (such as Beltian bodies and larval pouches) in response to each other's presence. In this case, the two are so entwined that neither can survive long without the other.

Waste Not, Want Not

Nature can be very efficient. The North American black cherry (*Prunus serotina*) of the Great Lakes region possesses sugar-producing organs called extrafloral nectaries that attract large numbers of ants. But the nectaries produce syrup only during the first three weeks after budbreak, a period that coincides with the hatching of eastern tent caterpillars, a major pest of black cherry trees. During those first three weeks, the caterpillars are small enough to be captured and killed by ants. Once the caterpillars grow too large, the nectaries dry up, the ants do without and move on to other food sources, and the tree diverts its energy toward its own growth.

Desert Ants: Flourishing in the Heat

During an average August day in the Yuma Desert, the air temperature reaches 110°F and the soil temperature reaches 150°F. Death Valley, even more torrid, holds the record for the hottest temperature in the Western Hemisphere—134°F. Still, both deserts support ants. One species, *Messor pergandei*, is legendary among entomologists for its ability to survive heat and extended periods of severe drought—as long as twelve years. Apparently able to survive solely on seed caches stored deep underground, these ants require neither insects nor nectar.

Messor pergandei, the most abundant ant species in Death Valley, has a collective biomass estimated to equal that of the total rodent population of the desert. In the early mornings and evenings, long columns of workers with as many as 17,000 individuals collect and carry seeds back to their nest. There, other workers crack the most nutritious part—the endosperm—into pieces and place them atop the larvae. The larvae consume the pieces and regurgitate a carbohydrate-rich solution, which feeds the workers.

While most of their foraging follows this pattern, *Messor pergandei* workers are flexible. When food is scarce they rely more on individual searching than on systematic searches with their great columns. And they grow less picky, consuming seeds and plant parts they normally ignore. Even during good times, workers rotate their columns around the nest so they are constantly encountering new seed sources. This kind of flexibility, along with their ability to rely entirely on stored seeds, may be the key to this species' ability to thrive in environments too extreme for most insects.

The Caterpillar and the Ant: The Power of Selection

Myrmecophily: plants do it; aphids do it; so do some butterflies. The word, which literally means "the love of ants," refers to the ability of an organism to associate symbiotically with ants. Ants are notoriously pugnacious—on the lookout for intruders and aggressive in their defense of territory and food. So it shouldn't be surprising that some species have developed partnerships with them. Typically these partnerships involve an exchange of food for protection. Aphids, for example, produce honeydew, which the ants eat. The ants reciprocate by guarding the aphids from predators. Ants build shelters for aphids and carry aphids to new food sources. Likewise, certain trees, like acacias, produce sugary or protein-rich foods that draw ants. The ants defend the tree from browsers. The relation between butterflies and ants, while based on the principle of food for protection, involves more elaborate adaptations.

Myrmecophily has evolved in two families of butterflies: the Lycaenidae (the harvesters, hairstreaks, coppers, and blues) and the Riodinidae (the metalmarks). While not all of the species in these two families are myrmecophilous, many are. A typical species is *Thisbe irenea*, a metalmark. Occurring in tropical forests from Mexico to South America, this species' caterpillars employ a combination of tactics that win the favors of ants—tactics that go beyond offers of food. *Thisbe* caterpillars have also evolved organs designed to deceive ants.

Female *Thisbe* butterflies lay eggs on young trees of the genus *Croton*. When the caterpillars hatch, they eat *Croton* foliage and sip secretions from the tree's extrafloral nectaries—glands situated at the base of each leaf. Like other tropical species, *Croton* trees probably found the nectaries useful in attracting ants in that classic barter of food for protection. But the caterpillars have insinuated themselves between ant

Thisbe caterpillars offer ants a rich nectar from nectary organs on their posteriors.

and tree. Not only do the ants allow the caterpillars to feed on the tree's leaves, but the ants serve as bodyguards against predatory wasps that specialize in stinging and carrying off *Thisbe* caterpillars as food for their brood.

Like acacias and aphids, *Thisbe* caterpillars bear an offering that works like a bribe. On their posteriors, they sport their own set of nectary organs that, when stroked, extend like fingers and secrete drops of clear fluid. The ants prefer this caterpillar nectar over the tree's. Unlike the tree's nectar, the fluid secreted by *Thisbe* caterpillars is rich in amino acids and contains almost no sugar. Amino acids are the building blocks of proteins. Meanwhile, the caterpillars feast on leaves or the tree's nectar where, like nursing babies, they fasten their mouths on the extrafloral nectaries.

Moreover, *Thisbe* caterpillars have evolved an organ apparently designed to stimulate the ant's protective instincts. When extended, two gland-tipped tentacles located just behind the caterpillar's head discharge a chemical similar to the ant's own alarm pheromone. It immediately sends the ants into a defensive posture—bodies raised, mandibles open, ab-

domens curled. This counterfeit pheromone may explain why individual ants stay with a caterpillar for a week or more at a time. Seemingly more loyal to the caterpillar than their own colony, these ants neglect colony chores.

Additionally, caterpillars can make the same sounds that the ants make when they call their fellow nest mates. Just behind and extending over the head, *Thisbe* caterpillars bear two rodlike appendages covered with concentric grooves that emit sounds when the caterpillar moves its knobby head in and out. The sounds, traveling through whatever solid substrate the caterpillar is sitting on, vibrate with the same frequency and pulse rate as sounds made by ants when they signal the discovery of foods. (The ants make their sound by tapping specialized organs on their abdomens against the substrate.)

The relation reminds us that symbiosis can involve multiple complex interactions between several species—ant, plant, caterpillar, wasp—and for various ends—territorial defense, food gathering, predation, communication. We may never fully appreciate all the nuances of such a relationship.

In Focus: Mountain Pine Beetle

Mountain pine beetle

Mountain pine beetle distribution

Distribution

The mountain pine beetle, native to western North America, ranges from the Pacific Coast to the Black Hills of South Dakota and from northern British Columbia to northwestern Mexico.

Description

Larvae are white with brown heads; they lack legs. Adults are small, black, typical-looking beetles with shiny, iridescent bodies and heads partially hidden beneath a dorsal plate.

Life History

Mountain pine beetles feed on the inner bark or cambium layer of pine trees. They spend all but a few days of their life beneath bark. Late in the summer, female beetles chew straight, vertical egg galleries through the phloem, where they lay their eggs. Two weeks later, the eggs hatch into larvae which, over the next ten months, eat horizontal tunnels through the phloem. The larvae then pupate, and in July, the pupae metamorphose into beetles. The beetles emerge from the bark but only for one or two days. During that time, some of the females land on uninfested trees.

Their pheromones attract masses of both male and female beetles, which attack the trees, and start the cycle over again.

In a special structure on their heads, mountain pine beetles carry the spores of blue-staining fungi. The fungi spreads throughout the sapwood of infested trees and reduces the flow of pitch. This, combined with the beetle's tunnels, kills pines.

Relations

Because we have excluded fires from many forests for the last ninety years, mountain pine beetles, seldom seen in earlier eras, destroy an ever increasing number of pine stands, especially lodgepole pines. In the 1980s, in the Flathead Valley of Montana, beetles killed over 170,000 acres of lodgepole. The dead trees became a tinderbox; 30,000 acres went up in smoke in 1988.

In beetle epidemics, some forest acres convert to grassland. Mammals like bear, moose, and elk lose hiding and thermal cover but gain forage. Several birds increase in number: woodpeckers, which eat the larvae, for example, and nuthatches, which feed on the adult beetles when they emerge from beneath the bark.

The Rocky Mountain Grasshopper Riddle

Not surprisingly, Rocky Mountain grasshoppers are not what most people think of when they consider the obstacles faced by western pioneers. The species died out over ninety years ago; few people alive today have seen one. But just a century ago, when swarms of grasshoppers stretched from horizon to horizon, the insect ranked as *the* obstacle limiting westward migration, more so than Indians, drought, grizzly bears, wolves, and outlaws.

Rocky Mountain grasshopper

At their worst, Rocky Mountain grasshoppers numbered in the billions. They formed mile-deep clouds that measured over 100,000 square miles in area, dense enough to stop trains. From north-central Alberta to Mexico and from the Pacific Ocean to the Ohio Valley, grasshoppers consumed virtually every scrap of every crop sown, while they left native plants relatively undamaged. They stripped not only the bark and leaves from nearly every tree, but devoured clothing, mosquito netting, leather, dead animals, and wool. Governments paid bounties of one to five dollars per bushel of hoppers. Farmers attempted to trample or plow or flood irrigate the egg beds and applied kerosene and coal oil to swarms.

Then, suddenly and without explanation, the frequency and severity of the swarms declined in the 1880s. They stopped altogether by the early 1890s, and in 1902, entomologists declared the species extinct. What happened? How had an insect so populous and with such a vast range succumbed so suddenly to such

seemingly ineffective control efforts? The disappearance is especially remarkable considering that the Rocky Mountain grasshopper is the only known pest species that humans have completely extinguished in the history of agriculture. Even today, with all of our pesticides and airplanes, we cannot completely eradicate such pests. Ecologists once described the "riddle of the Rocky Mountain grasshopper" as one of the most compelling unsolved ecological mysteries of our time. But now, two researchers, entomologists Jeffrey Lockwood and Larry DeBrey, think they have an answer.

For decades, scientists attempted to explain the extinction by looking at events that occurred over the grasshopper's entire range. For example, they speculated that climate change might have accounted for the loss, but the data showed weather patterns had not changed. Others suggested the loss of Indian culture caused the extinction. For millennia, Indians had burned the grasshopper's habitat, and by the late 1880s, disease, war, starvation, and government relocation policies had decimated tribes. Native burning came to an abrupt halt about the time the grasshopper population declined. Ecologists point out, however, that natural fires continued, and fire-dependent plant communities persisted long after the extinction. Ample grasshopper habitat remained. Was it the loss of the buffalo? Probably not; the normal habitat of bison was different from that occupied by the Rocky Mountain grasshopper, and ecologists find no link between the two species. Cattle numbers increased dramatically during the late 1800s. Had they consumed all the grasshopper's forage? Doubtful; cattle numbers were too small.

Realizing Rocky Mountain grasshoppers concentrated their egg beds in extremely small, mostly riparian areas, Lockwood and DeBrey looked to smaller-scale, more localized effects for an answer. They found at least four human activities that, combined, might well have caused the grasshopper's demise. First, settlers, although few in number, settled in valleys next to rivers, the same areas chosen by the grasshoppers for laying their eggs. Egg beds suffered regular plowing, one of the most effective ways to kill grasshopper eggs. Second, settlers irrigated, another practice lethal to eggs. Third, trappers had virtually wiped out beaver. Without beaver dams, flooding increased dramatically and probably drowned a significant portion of the eggs. Cattle, a fourth factor, are poorly adapted to arid terrain, unlike bison. Like gravid grasshoppers, they concentrated in riparian zones and further degraded habitat, as did trees, alfalfa, and predatory birds—eastern species that followed the settlers west.

Lockwood and DeBrey conclude that it was the combination of these small-scale factors that ruined the species. They argue that ultimately, the railroad, which accelerated settlement, emerged as the greatest factor in the extinction of the Rocky Mountain grasshopper.

Glacial Grasshoppers

The Rocky Mountain grasshopper is extinct, but it can still be seen in the frozen food section of one glacier. Eleven thousand feet high in Montana's Beartooth Mountains, the Grasshopper Glacier preserves millions of the locusts, which appear as dark bands across the ice, swarms caught perhaps by a surprise summer snowstorm. As the ice melts, the carcasses drop to the gravel and stream below, where, on occasion, birds and fish gobble them up.

The Roots of the River

Until recently, river ecologists believed they had described most of the invertebrates living in the rivers of temperate North America. Then limnologist Jack Stanford discovered the complex communities dwelling in the gravels beneath the floodplains. Whereas some of the organisms, such as stoneflies, spend a portion of their lives in this underground world, many of the creatures—primitive worms known as archiannelids, crustaceans called bathynellids, half-inch-long blind shrimplike creatures called amphipods, and an assortment of microorganisms—never come to the surface at all but spend their entire lives deep in the water-saturated gravels under the river. Stanford and other researchers studying a section of one mountain floodplain in Montana discovered over eighty such creatures, about half of them new to science.

The channels of mountain rivers and streams typically alternate between narrow canyons and broad floodplains. In the can-

Stoneflies are at the top of a newly discovered, subterranean food chain.

yons or narrows, the bedrock converges on the river and constrains its flow. In the floodplains, the bedrock recedes and is replaced by a porous mixture of gravel, sand, mud, and rock, which the river meanders across. Much of the water, up to 20 percent, moves downward into the gravels beneath the floodplain. When the floodplain ends and bedrock again restricts the river's flow, those subterranean currents resurface, bubbling up in the form of springbrooks. The water returns to the river via overflow channels. Thus each river is really two rivers moving together and constantly interacting, one on the surface and one below.

The newly discovered community of invertebrates dwells in this subsurface flow. A film of fungi and nitrogen-fixing bacteria coats the alluvial gravels. Supported by dissolved organic matter carried by the river, this film is itself grazed by higher organisms—the archiannelids, bathynellids, and amphipods. They, in turn, are food for inch-and-a-quarter-long ivory-and-cream-colored stonefly larvae, ghostlike creatures that spend years hidden beneath the floodplain before emerging on the river as adults. As adults, the stoneflies live a few weeks, just long enough to mate.

This underground food-chain influences life within and adjacent to the aboveground portion of the river. As the organisms process the dissolved organic matter, they release large amounts of previously unavailable nutrients into the water, especially phosphates and nitrates. Relatively infertile water becomes charged with nutrients. When the currents emerge on the surface, they fertilize the riparian growth of the floodplain. Aerial photographs show that, generally, the most productive, vigorous plant communities coincide with upwellings and springbrooks.

By feeding the floodplain, this subterranean community nourishes hundreds of species. Riparian plant communities support more bird and mammal species than any other type of habitat. Trout, salmon, and whitefish favor the springbrooks as spawning habitat; the constant upwelling of nutrient-laden water nourishes the fry when they hatch. From Montana to Alaska, the combination of spawning trout and lush vegetation draws grizzly bears, bald eagles, cormorants, mink, and otters.

IN FOCUS: TARANTULAS

Distribution

About thirty species of tarantulas inhabit the U.S.; many more live in Mexico. Tarantulas occur only as far east as the Mississippi River, but they live as far north as Missouri, Colorado, Utah, southwestern Idaho, and southeastern Oregon.

Description

Tarantulas are large, hairy spiders. Their carapace is dimpled in the center with grooves that radiate outward like spokes. In the U.S., the largest of these spiders weigh up to two-thirds of an ounce and sport legs spanning 6 or 7 inches. After their final molt, males are easily distinguished from females by their darker colors and longer legs.

Life History

Tarantulas of the American southwest live solitary lives in the burrows they dig beneath large stones. Faithful to their dens, a single spider occupies the same hole for many years, if not its entire life. Except when males search for a mate, tarantulas seldom venture more than a few yards beyond the burrow entrance.

Tarantulas are sexually mature after eight to ten years. Males reaching this age molt for the final time. Mature males emerge from their burrows and wander in search of a mate from June to December; they show little interest in eating. When a male locates a female, the two spiders face each other, raise up, and entwine their front legs in a courtship ritual. The male, using the short arms near his mouth, deposits sperm in a furrow on the underside of the female's midsection. Then he scurries away.

If he is not fast enough, the female consumes him. Partly for this reason, males live only about ten years, while females live twenty.

The female encases the eggs in a silk sac and guards the package for six or seven weeks. Upon hatching, the spiderlings stay with their mother for a week or so, then disperse, each searching for its own burrow site.

Relations

Tarantulas of the southwest dine mostly on invertebrates—beetles, grasshoppers, millipedes—but have been known to catch and eat toads, mice, and lizards. Their prey is abundant in summer but scarce in winter. So the tarantulas must fast. They disappear inside their burrows after plugging the entrances with silk and leaves. Tarantulas can go without food for over two years.

A host of birds and mammals prey on tarantulas. The youngest of the spiders fall to birds, lizards, frogs, toads, and snakes. Adults are eaten by digging animals like skunks, coatimundis, and javelinas. The most serious tarantula predator, however, is an insect: a 2-inch-long, metallic-blue or greenish wasp with a stinger a third of an inch long. Called *Pepsis*, or, more descriptively, the tarantula hawk, the wasp hunts mostly females. The wasp stings the spider on its soft underbelly, paralyzing it. Then, dragging the tarantula to a hole, the wasp lays an egg on the carapace and pushes dirt over the top. The egg hatches, and the wasp larva feeds for a month or longer on the living-but-still-paralyzed tarantula.

Tarantulas are also plagued by small-headed flies, creatures that specialize in laying eggs on tarantulas. The eggs hatch into maggots that devour their host from the inside out.

This Invertebrate Begins Life on a Fish

Mussels mate when the male sheds sperm into the water and the female draws that sperm in with her inhalant current. The fertilized eggs incubate and hatch in the female's gills. Eventually, the larvae, or glochidia, which resemble miniature adults, leave the female and disperse in huge numbers, often on a web of mucous. Fish feed heavily on glochidia. Some of the larvae survive, however, and attach themselves to the fish where they form cysts and live as parasites. For example, the larvae of fat-mucket mussels, a 4-inch species found throughout the eastern U.S. and Canada, attach to the gills and fins of fish. After about twenty days, when the larvae are about one one hundredth of an inch in size, the cysts rupture, and the mussels drop free and attach themselves to the river or lake bottom. They reach full size two years later. The females of some mussels assist their larvae's search for hosts by luring predatory fish with their protruding, brightly colored, undulating, and sometimes fish-shaped mantle flaps.

Fish provide mussel larvae with nourishment, protection against bacterial and protozoan attack, and a means of dispersal (glochidia can't swim on their own). If a larva fails to attach to a fish, as most do, they fall to the bottom where they are eaten or smothered by sediment. Among the many North American fish species that serve as mussel hosts are salmon, trout, suckers, pike, gar, catfish, bullhead, bass, pumpkinseed, crappie, drum, sturgeon, perch, and sculpins.

Part Six
FISH

Part Six Fish

Numbers and Distribution

ROUGHLY 1,060 SPECIES OF NATIVE freshwater fish live in North America. Canada and the U.S. harbor about 800 species—the most diverse temperate freshwater fish fauna in the world. The Mississippi drainage alone possesses more species than all of Europe. Mexico hosts an estimated 384 freshwater fish species, which is also a high number for the size of the country.

North of Mexico, minnows and darters make up 48 percent of all fish species. Minnows account for about 30 percent. In Mexico, minnow species dominate as well. Along with livebearers and cichlids, the minnow family, Cyprinidae, accounts for half of all fish species. The charts that follow describe the relative proportions of the ten most diverse families of freshwater fish for both parts of North America.

Eight freshwater families—mooneyes, bullhead catfishes, trout-perches, pirate perches, cavefishes, splitfins, sunfishes, and pygmy sunfishes—and 966 species are endemic (indigenous and restricted) to North

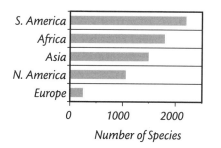

Freshwater fish diversity of the continents

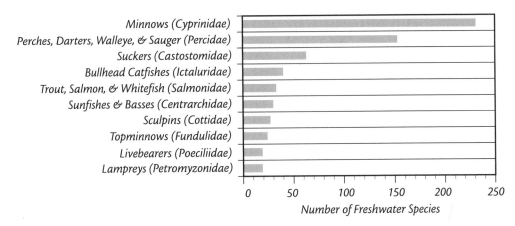

The ten most diverse families north of Mexico

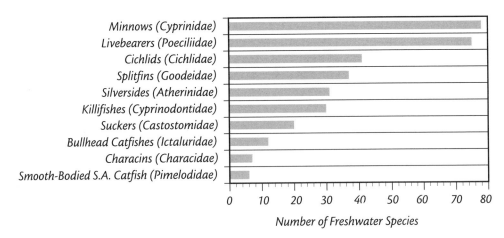

The ten most diverse families in Mexico

America; all are thought to have evolved on the continent. Areas with especially high proportions of endemic species include the Southeast, the West, and Mexico. The Mobile River basin in Mississippi, Alabama, and Georgia, for example, supports forty endemic species, the Tennessee River drainage, thirty-three. The twenty-two endemic species in the Colorado River drainage represent 67 percent of that system's total fish fauna. The Sacramento–San Joaquin drainage hosts twelve endemic species. Mexico's rivers also support high percentages (greater than 50 percent) of endemic species.

The Fish Faunas of North America: A Summary

Temperate North America divides into three fish regions: the Arctic-Atlantic, the oldest region, possessing the richest fauna; the Pacific, a smaller, arid, mountainous area with relatively few species; and the Mexican Transition, a zone where temperate North America meets the tropics. The Mexican Lowlands is tropical. This section describes the provinces within each of the temperate regions based on the distribution of three types of fish: *freshwater dispersing species*, like northern pike, that are restricted to fresh water; *diadromous species*, like salmon, that regularly move between fresh water and salt water and spend a part of their life cycle in each; and *freshwater representatives of marine families*, like sculpins, species in families dominated by marine species.

Fish provinces of North America

The Arctic-Atlantic Region

Mississippi Province

With some three hundred species, the Mississippi Province encompasses the Mississippi-Missouri River system and the Atlantic and Gulf Coast drainages south of the St. Lawrence River and east of the Rio Grande. The most diverse province in temperate North America, the Mississippi Province also includes the most ancient river system, the Mississippi-Missouri. Some of the province's tributary systems, such as the Tennessee and the Cumberland, support large numbers of endemic species (those restricted to a particular drainage); the province has been a major center of fish evolution in North America and has served as a refuge during glaciations. As a whole, the province shelters thirty-four endemic species. It also possesses species from some of the most ancient fish families, families of which few representatives remain in the world. Sturgeon, paddlefish, gar, mooneye, and goldeye are examples.

Minnows represent about 30 percent of the total number of species, perch 26 percent, suckers 9 percent, and sunfish 7 percent. Diadromous fishes make up 7 percent of the species, and freshwater representatives of marine families make up 5 percent.

Rio Grande Province

Comprised of the Rio Grande and its tributaries, this province harbors an estimated seventy-five species. Although small, this fauna is similar to that of the Mississippi Province. A third of the species belong to the minnow family. As many as a quarter of these are endemic. Two species, the Rio Grande perch (a cichlid) and the Mexican tetra (a characin), are more closely related to species found in the Mexican Transition Province than those of temperate North America.

Atlantic Coast Province

A series of independent drainages, the Atlantic Coast Province empties into the Atlantic and the Gulf of Mexico. The fish there are similar to those of the Mississippi Province, although the streams typically have more endemic species. Diadromous species, minnows, and suckers dominate the northern streams. The middle section of the province includes some ancient drainages that at one time connected to the Mississippi. Those that drain the more southern Appalachians are rich in endemic species. A single stream may host as many as eleven.

Great Lakes–St. Lawrence Province

This system, recently connected to the northern part of the Mississippi Province, shares a similar fauna with the Mississippi. The Great Lakes also have a large number of endemic species—whitefish, lake trout, and blue walleye are examples. Of the province's 162 species, 77 percent have little tolerance for salt water, 16 percent are diadromous, and 7 percent are members of marine families.

Hudson Bay Province

Encompassing most of central Canada, the Hudson Bay Province supports a fish fauna similar to that of the Mississippi Province. Of its roughly eighty-five species, just under a fifth are diadromous. Sculpins, freshwater representatives of a marine family, and diadromous species, like salmon, dominate the northern parts of the province.

Arctic Province
The Arctic encompasses all the streams that flow into the Arctic Ocean and holds fifty-six species of freshwater fish, many of which originated in the Mississippi or neighboring Pacific Provinces. The province is a transition zone between three regions: the Pacific and Atlantic parts of North America, and Eurasia. Four Arctic species—the inconnu, the Arctic cisco, the Arctic lamprey, and the least cisco—occur outside of the Arctic, in Siberia. Just under half the Arctic species are diadromous.

The Pacific Region
Alaska Coastal Province
Comprised mostly of short, fast-flowing streams issuing from the Coast Range, the Alaska Coastal Province supports only thirty-four species, 79 percent of which belong to diadromous families. Another 11 percent are freshwater representatives of marine families. The three species intolerant of salt water—northern pike, longnose sucker, and Alaska blackfish—are also found in Siberia.

Columbia Province
The Columbia Province extends southward from the Alaska Coastal Province to encompass the vast Columbia River drainage. With fifty-one species, it is richest of all the Pacific provinces, but remains species-poor compared to the Mississippi with three hundred. Nineteen Columbia-Province species tolerate only fresh water (seven of those are endemic). Of the fourteen diadromous species, eight are salmonids. The province also hosts twelve species of sculpin.

Great Basin Province
All the drainages of the arid Great Basin Province are internally drained; water does not leave except by evaporation. This physical oddity and a history in which large lakes inundated much of the basin during the last ice age lead to one of the most interesting fish faunas on the continent. Of the province's fifty species, 60 percent are minnows and suckers. Many are endemic. In Bear Lake, for example, 80 percent of the species are found nowhere else in the world. In many of the province's drainages, biologists continue to discover new species.

Klamath Province
The tiny Klamath Province is made up of only two rivers—the Klamath and the Rogue. Together they hold thirty freshwater species, eleven that are endemic. Only about one-quarter of the species—all minnows and suckers—are restricted to fresh water. The suckers are all endemic. Of the province's diadromous species, eight are salmonids and four are lampreys. Sculpins—freshwater representatives of marine families—comprise the balance.

Sacramento Province
The Sacramento Province, which includes the Sacramento–San Joaquin drainage and

minor coastal streams, encompasses most of the water flowing through California. Almost half of its forty-three species are endemic. The list includes the Sacramento perch, the most primitive member of the bass-sunfish family and the only native west of the Rocky Mountains. Twenty species are diadromous and eleven are freshwater representatives of marine families. The tule perch is the only freshwater fish in its family.

Colorado Province

This province includes the Colorado River and its tributaries. Almost three-quarters of the Colorado system's thirty species live only in fresh water; only five are diadromous, and three are freshwater representatives of marine families. A high percentage of the Colorado's fish fauna is endemic, the minnows particularly so.

South Coastal Province

Encompassing Baja California and the southwestern corner of California, the species-poor South Coastal Province takes in a series of unconnected, small, coastal drainages harboring thirteen native species. Only three, all endemic to the Los Angeles Basin, are restricted to fresh water.

The Mexican Transition Region

The river basins in the Mexican Transition Province hold 152 species. Lampreys, sturgeons, salmonids, suckers, minnows, springfishes, sunfishes, basses, and perches are among the common families represented. A clear gradation extends the length of the Coastal Plain, from Rio Soto La Marina, where 75 percent of the fish fauna are North American forms, to Papaloapan, where 95 percent of the species are Mesoamerican forms. The Yaqui River in northwest Mexico is itself a transition zone. Of the Yaqui's sixteen species restricted to fresh water, seven evolved from species found in the Rio Grande drainage, three from species in the Colorado drainage, and four from species in Central American drainages. South of the province, mostly neotropical (Mesoamerican) species dominate.

ENDEMIC SPECIES IN MEXICAN RIVERS

Drainage	Percent Endemic
Lerma-Santiago	66
Usumacinta-Grijalva	36
Panuco	40
Rio Balsas	35
Rio Ameca	32
Rio Papaloapan	21
Rio Coatzacoalcos	13
Rio Conchos	21
Rio Tunal	62
Cuatro Cienegas Depression	50
Chichankanab Lake	65
Media Luna Lake	65

Status of North American Freshwater Fish

North America's rich and unique freshwater fish fauna is in trouble. Fish biologists warn that, over the next few decades, the continent may lose a greater proportion of its aquatic fauna than tropical systems will lose. The trend in the U.S., typical for the rest of the continent, is worse than that for either birds or mammals, groups that get considerably more attention than aquatic organisms.

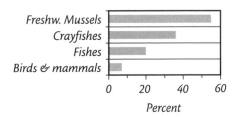

The percentage of species of imperiled or extinct by major taxonomic group

The percentages given in the chart below are conservative estimates. In 1979, the Endangered Species Committee of the American Fisheries Society developed a list of 251 freshwater fishes of North America judged to be in danger. Updating the list a decade later, the society noted 364 imperiled taxa. Both lists used the same endangered and threatened categories defined in the Endangered Species Act of 1973 but added a special-concern category: fishes that could become threatened or endangered with only minor habitat disturbances. The 1989 list reveals that as many as one-third of North American freshwater fish are in danger, and that figure does not include the twenty-seven species and thirteen subspecies known to have become extinct during this century (sixteen since 1964).

Overfishing, the introduction of nonnative species, disease, and other major problems are all secondary in importance to habitat destruction. Ninety-three percent of the imperiled species suffer from deteriorating habitats.

The relation between declining aquatic habitats and the waning of fish species is not a simple one. Obviously, species with limited distributions are more likely to be jeopardized by changes in their local habitats than are species with extensive ranges. Many fishes on the lists are restricted to

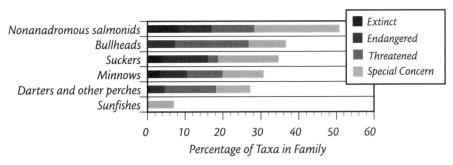

The percentage of imperiled species and subspecies in the six most diverse fish families in the U.S.

local distributions, and a few, such as the Clear Creek gambusia and Devil's Hole pupfish, are limited to a single spring. A single, isolated event could cause their extinction. Some of the more widespread species on the imperiled list depend on large rivers; their inclusion indicates that big-river habitats are also deteriorating.

In the U.S., the West and South list a higher percentage of imperiled fish than other regions (although the East has a greater number of species that are imperiled because it has more species to begin with). The Colorado River drainage is in particular trouble. All of its native fish fauna is extinct, endangered, or threatened. In California, two-thirds of the native taxa are either extinct or are declining in number.

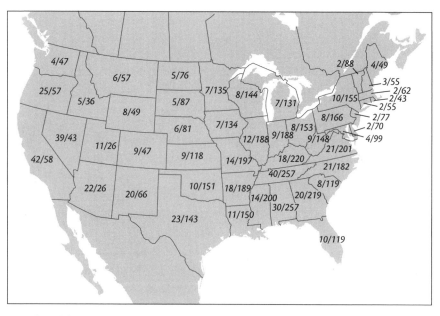

Number of freshwater fish species imperiled and the number of freshwater fish species in each state

NATURAL HISTORY

Fish West, Fish East: A Tale of Two Faunas

The difference in species diversity is perhaps the most striking of many dissimilarities between the fish faunas east and west of the Continental Divide. A roughly 4,000-square-mile drainage in Ontario, Canada, might host fifty species, a relatively low number for the eastern part of the continent. A West Coast drainage of equal size typically supports only about eighteen species; a western interior drainage, only five to ten.

The differences between the body sizes of the fish east and west is also significant, with larger varieties west. Body size is indicative of a number of physiological and behavioral traits. Larger species, those that grow to more than 12 inches long, live longer, experience longer reproductive spans, and produce more offspring. The juveniles of the larger species are more likely to live segregated from adults. In most western drainages, over half the species are longer than 12 inches, whereas fewer than 30 percent are under 4 inches. Even the western minnows are big; 36 percent grow longer than 12 inches. In the east, most adult stream fish are small- to medium-sized. In the Missouri River, for example, only 27 percent reach more than 12 inches in length. Farther east, in Ontario, the number drops to just 18 percent. Only 2 percent of the minnows fall into the large category.

Western fish, because of their size, generally employ different reproductive strategies than fish in the East. Most simply scatter their eggs on the bottom of the stream or lake and exhibit no postspawning care of embryos or young. In the East, over a third of the species guard their eggs. Even within families, this pattern holds; no species of western minnow cares for its young, whereas 33 percent of eastern minnows are considered brood hiders or guarders. This difference, in turn, has ramifications for migration patterns. Species that don't expend energy guarding young are more likely to migrate, because they accumulate fat stores. More species migrate in the West than in the East.

Biologists believe Pleistocene glaciation may account for these differences. Even though ice covered much of northeastern North America, the Missouri-Mississippi system remained intact and served as a refuge. Smaller tributaries, isolated and reconnected, developed a large number of small species; larger species died out when flows dropped. Meanwhile, in the West, ice covered most streams north of the Columbia. When the ice receded, fish—primarily large, migratory salmonids—recolonized. Species from other groups moved in from the East or South via meltwater channels. Fossil evidence suggests that streams south of the Columbia supported more species both before and during the Pleistocene. As the glaciers melted and rainfall dropped, many species died out. Conditions favored the ones able to live in cold, swift water or the ones that could migrate.

DIFFERENCES BETWEEN WESTERN AND EASTERN FISH

Trait	East of the Rockies	West of the Rockies
Diversity	High	Low
Size	Small species dominate	Large species dominate
Life History	Short lives, early maturation, low fecundity, short reproductive spans	Long lives, late maturation, high fecundity, long reproductive spans
Parental Care	Brood hiders and guarders common	Mostly no parental care
Migration	Most species have limited movements, some large species make spawning migrations	Spawning migrations common

Four- or Five-Fish Communities

The headwaters of rivers and streams that issue from mountains in North America share certain traits, particularly among their fish communities. If the streams are cold (under 68°F) and lack barriers to fish passage, they will generally host four or five dominant species—a trout, a sculpin, a sucker, a dace, and perhaps a drift-feeding minnow. The particular species may vary, but the four- or five-fish community structure is consistent, whether the streams occur north, south, east, or west. Cool- or warm-water streams do not fit this pattern.

COLDWATER FISH FAUNAS

Drainage	Trout	Sculpin	Dace	Sucker
Colorado	cutthroat trout	mottled sculpin	speckled dace	mountain sucker
Sacramento	rainbow trout	riffle sculpin or pit sculpin	speckled dace	Sacramento sucker
Columbia	rainbow trout, cutthroat trout	various sculpins (12 in drainage)	speckled dace, longnose dace	largescale sucker
Yukon	dolly varden, Arctic char	slimy sculpin		longnose sucker
New York	brook trout	mottled sculpin	blacknose dace	white sucker
Kentucky	rainbow trout	banded sculpin	blacknose dace	white sucker

Pupfish: In Some Very Hot Water

Deserts possess some of the world's harshest environments for fish. Among the most inhospitable are places in Death Valley like Devil's Hole, Salt Creek, and Tecopa Bore, small habitats—springs and ponds—where the water is hot, full of salt and minerals, low in oxygen, and bombarded by intense solar radiation. The only fish capable of tolerating such extreme conditions are a few pupfish of the genus *Cyprinodon*.

Just 1 to 3 inches long, pupfish have small, up-turned mouths, a single dorsal fin, and no lateral line. Although they mostly inhabit deserts and semideserts, the genus, which includes about thirty species, is one of the most widely distributed in North America and occupies the greatest range of aquatic habitats. Individual species, however, can have among the most restricted ranges of any organism. Often, a species will occur in a single spring. The Devil's Hole pupfish, for instance, has a range of about 215 square feet, the smallest known for any vertebrate animal.

Apparently the genus is not old. Ancestral pupfish probably originated in estuaries along the Atlantic Coast and moved into Death Valley only during the early part of the last ice age, when giant lakes covered much of the region. At that time, tributaries connected Death Valley to the Colorado River. As the climate grew more arid, the lakes and streams dried up, and fish were left high and dry or isolated in springs, ponds, and marshes. Most species died out. Pupfish, though, apparently pre-adapted to survive severe environments, persisted in the few, isolated water bodies that remained. Each population eventually evolved into a distinct species and survived for thousands of years sequestered within small, isolated habitats.

Devil's Hole is a typical pupfish habitat. A cavelike structure formed by faults and fed by ground water, the spring has no outlet. The water stays near 93°F. Although Devil's Hole is over 200 feet deep, the pupfish it supports, the Devil's Hole pupfish, is confined to a 215-square-foot, shallow limestone shelf. The shelf provides both spawning habitat and food (in the form of algae), neither of which occur elsewhere in Devil's Hole. The structure is estimated to be 10,000 years old, which means the Devil's Hole pupfish is a young species, probably descended from the Amaragosa pupfish in an adjacent series of springs. Irrigation practices have lowered

the water level in Devil's Hole, and the U.S. Fish and Wildlife Service lists the pupfish as endangered.

Another species, the Salt Creek pupfish, perhaps equally young, lives in a spring-fed creek, where, over the course of the year, the temperatures fluctuate from near freezing to over 104°F, and salinities reach those of seawater. The water of Salt Creek also contains high levels of an unusual ion—boron—and extremely high amounts of total dissolved solids (tap water in Los Angeles has 495 parts per million (ppm) dissolved solids, whereas Salt Creek carries 23,600 ppm).

The water from Salt Creek occasionally seeps into Cottonball Marsh, a series of salt-encrusted pools also with high salinities—up to 4.6 times that of seawater. Still, a species of pupfish, the Cottonball Marsh pupfish, thrives. Most freshwater animals have an upper salinity tolerance of between 3 and 10 parts per thousand (ppt). Many pupfish can easily handle 90 ppt. One survives at 142 ppt. In addition to tolerating the salt, Cottonball Marsh pupfish handle temperatures as high as 105°F (109°F in the lab) and daily fluctuations of as much as 30°F.

Temperatures range even higher in Tecopa Bore, an overflow from an artesian well. The water comes out of the well at almost 118°F but cools as it flows across the desert floor. Amaragosa pupfish, introduced to the overflow, congregate where water temperatures hover around 108°F, an upper limit for the species. The fish gather there to feed on rich algae beds that grow just upstream in hotter waters. They wait until a wind blows a plume of the 108° water upstream then dart in behind it to feed. When the water heats up again, they drift back downstream. The arrangement works well for the fish; with the exception of intensively managed fish farms, Tecopa Bore has the highest rate of fish productivity of any water anywhere in the world.

Amaragosa pupfish tolerate 108°F water

Pupfish are remarkably adapted in many ways. They handle extremely low dissolved oxygen levels, lower than those tolerated by any other fish that relies on gill-breathing. And they breed across a wide range of temperatures. For some species, successful spawning can occur over a 55-degree range.

Fish biologists believe pupfish in the Southwest originated from a single species preadapted to survive extreme and rapidly changing habitats. The descendants adapted physiologically to conditions lethal to almost all other fish species. Sadly, many of these survivors, unable to adapt to the activities of humans, are now on the verge of extinction.

Hermaphrodites and Sexual Parasites: Strange Reproductive Strategies in North American Fish

As the saying goes, it takes two to tango, and in most vertebrate species it does take the genetic material from two parents to produce offspring. But not in all. Certain fish (and some lizards) have found ways around this seemingly implacable equation. One brackish-water species, the rivulus (*Rivulus marmoratus*), is a self-fertilizing hermaphrodite. At least in Florida waters, males of the species are extremely rare and not often needed, because females fertilize themselves.

Even stranger is the Amazon molly (*Poecilia formosa*), a species with one of the most unusual sexual systems known. Entirely devoid of males, the species lives as a sexual parasite in sloughs and backwaters of extreme southern Texas and Mexico. To produce young, females mate with the males of one of two host species, the sailfin molly (*P. latipinna*) or the shortfin molly (*P. mexicanna*). But this is no ordinary mating; the host species' sperm merely stimulates the eggs of the Amazon molly; male genetic information is not passed on. Hence, the female gives birth to genetically identical females—clones. The result is an all-female species.

In *Poeciliopsis*, a more complicated process produces another all-female "species." Sperm from the host male fertilizes the egg, and a hybrid is produced. But when the females of these hybrids produce eggs, the chromosomes contributed by the host male are lost during meiosis.

Sometimes these females mate with a third species, and the union gives rise to off-spring that are hybrids between the original maternal species and the new species. In these hybrids, some chromosomal reassortment occurs, and eggs with genes from the third species are produced. These new hybrid females then mate with the original host (the second host species) producing what are, in essence, triple hybrids—females with traits of all three of the original species.

Some think that Amazon mollies started out as sailfin-shortfin hybrids but are ge-netically distinct enough to now be considered a separate species. They have managed to maintain genetic variability despite the absence of genetic recombination, because each population of Amazon molly appears to have arisen independently. In other words, this all-female species consists of a number of genetically distinct clones, each with a separate origin. What is curious is that the Amazons are, as a rule, more widespread and abundant than either of the two host species. Amazons tend to be larger and have higher survival rates than their hosts. Amazons also appear to be more adaptable—better able to survive changing environments than either host. All-female populations are also more fecund than bisexual ones.

How do the Amazons keep from becoming too successful—from outcompeting and ultimately eliminating the species they parasitize? Sailfin and shortfin males exhibit a strong dominance-hierarchy. Males that end up mating with the Amazons are actually excess males, unable to mate with females of their own species after more aggressive males displaced them. This hierarchy, however, breaks down when sailfin and shortfin population densities are low. Then all the host males are taken up by host females. The unisex Amazons have a tough time finding males, and their populations drop while the hosts' numbers increase.

In the Dark: The Adaptations of Cave Fish

Cave fish possess a number of adapta-tions—tiny eyes, a lack of pigmentation, reduced or absent pelvic fins, small bod-ies, and low metabolic rates—that allow them to live in pure darkness. The traits evolved in a number of different families independently. One family in particular, the cavefishes (Amblyopsidae), exhibits a clear evolutionary transition between the species that live on the surface in light and those that have dwelt beneath the ground in perpetual darkness.

The family, endemic to the eastern U.S, includes six species. The swampfish, the only one of the six that lives in full light, thrives in swamps, sloughs, and backwa-ters. Another, the spring cavefish, lives in springs issuing from the mouths of caves, in what might be called a twilight region. Living entirely within caves, the southern,

Swampfish live in full light.

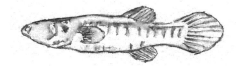

Cavefish live in total darkness.

northern, Ozark, and Alabama cavefishes flourish without light. In their general form and size, all six of these species resemble each other. The swampfish and spring cavefish, however, have pigmented skin. Although the swampfish is more bold, both species are dark brown above and yellowish on the belly, and sport vivid pink gills, black stripes on their sides, and black streaks running down their backs. The others—the four subterranean species—lack pigmentation and are a translucent pinkish white.

Swampfish and spring cavefish have eyes, although they are small. But the cave-dwelling species possess only vestigial eye tissue that lies just beneath the skin. On the other hand, their lateral line systems (the organ designed to detect water movement) are exceptionally well developed, as are the parts of the brain that deal with the lateral line system and with equilibrium. The cave dwellers also have bigger heads than the surface species.

Their metabolisms differ, too. Although the cave species possess metabolic rates about half that of the spring cavefish, they are extremely efficient at capturing scarce prey. They hunt small crustaceans by moving slowly but constantly, their long pectoral fins working almost like oars. The surface dwellers employ strategies most efficient when prey densities are high. The cave dwellers also respond to predators differently. They have no escape response; in their subterranean ecosystems, they reside at the top of the food chain. Birds and other fish prey on swampfish and spring cavefish, so they remain alert and show well-developed escape responses.

The females of both types of fish incubate their eggs in gill cavities, but the eggs of the cave dwellers are fewer, bigger, and slower in developing. Bigger eggs take less energy and minimize cannibalism, a major source of mortality in both spring cavefish and swampfish. Female northern cavefish also carry their young in their gills until the juveniles are old enough to care for themselves.

Other cave-dwelling fish live in North America. The widemouth blindcat and the toothless blindcat, for example, are pinkish white, four- to five-inch-long catfish that live deep (1,000 to 1,860 feet) beneath the earth's surface. They, too, are blind and have well-developed lateral lines. Another species, the Mexican tetra, is common in Texas and Mexico. It has both surface and subterranean populations. Underground varieties are blind and lack pigmentation.

IN FOCUS: CUTTHROAT TROUT

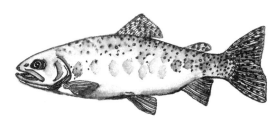

Westslope cutthroat trout

Westslope cutthroat trout distribution

Distribution

Cutthroat trout (*Oncorhynchus clarki*) range from Alaska to southern California and from the Pacific Coast to the inter-mountain area. Natural populations live east of the Continental Divide only in the headwaters of the Missouri and Rio Grande Rivers. Coastal cutthroats occur both as freshwater residents and as sea-run fish.

Description

Races and subspecies of cutthroat vary in appearance, especially in the number, size, and distribution of their spots. Freshwater forms have fewer spots than those that run to the sea, and all have a distinctive red or orange slash beneath the lower jaw. Many possess a reddish tinge on their head and sides. Sea-run cutthroats lose the orange slash and are silver when at sea. When they are inland, they take on a greenish gold to reddish tinge, and the slash becomes prominent. Adult cutthroat range in size from a few ounces (those inhabiting small streams) to in excess of 10 pounds. A 41-pound fish from Pyramid Lake, Utah, holds the record for the largest cutthroat ever caught.

Life History

Cutthroat trout follow several life strategies: some spend their entire lives in small tributary streams or lakes, some migrate between lakes and streams, others are anadromous or sea-going. All spawn in streams in the spring when water temperatures reach about 50°F. Eggs hatch anywhere from one to two months after being laid; the exact timing depends, again, on water temperatures. The hatchlings, called alevins, remain buried in their spawning gravels for up to two weeks. Once they emerge from the gravels, the fry seek the slower reaches of streams, where they suffer high rates of mortality. Five thousand eggs may yield only two to four spawning adults. Most inland forms of cutthroat feed principally on insects and other invertebrates. Large lake-dwelling and sea-run cutthroats consume small fish as well.

Status

Habitat loss has decimated freshwater populations. The U.S. Fish and Wildlife Service lists the Lahontan, Paiute, and greenback cutthroats as threatened. Most sea-run varieties remain abundant.

The White Sturgeon of the Columbia: North America's Largest Fish

White sturgeon (*Acipenser transmontanus*), North America's largest freshwater fish species, can weigh 1,500 pounds and can grow to be over 20 feet long. One of the world's most ancient fish, they are found on the West Coast from the Aleutian Islands to central California. Reproducing populations occur mostly in three river basins: the Sacramento–San Joaquin, the Fraser, and the Columbia, which has the largest.

At one time, white sturgeon thrived in the mainstem of the Columbia from the mouth all the way to Canada, in the Snake River to Shoshone Falls, and in the Kootenai River to Kootenai Falls in Montana, as well as in the lower reaches of many smaller tributaries. Today, however, this giant is found in just three places in the Columbia Basin: below the Bonneville Dam, which is the farthest downstream dam on the system; between dams, where populations are isolated from each other; and in a few large tributaries.

In the late 1800s, the Columbia supported a major commercial fishery. Five and a half million pounds of sturgeon were harvested, for example, in 1892. But by 1899, the sturgeon population had plummeted from overfishing. The harvest stayed low until the 1940s when the population started to recover. Commercial fishing increased, although the government enforced a 6-foot-maximum size restriction. The harvest doubled in the 1970s and again in the early 1980s. Then in 1983, concerned about the population, the federal government added more restrictions. The fish remains economically important to the region. Downstream from McNary Dam in Washington, fishing for sturgeon generated more than $10 million in 1992 alone.

White sturgeon are vulnerable to overfishing. Although they live as long as one hundred years, females do not reach sexual maturity until fifteen to thirty-two years of age, and then mature females spawn only once every two to eleven years. In the twenty-six dams on the Columbia System, sturgeon are hindered by impoundments

White sturgeon can reach 20 feet in length.

that have altered flows, depths, velocities, temperatures, turbidities, and even the bottom substrates of rivers. Moreover, the dams block sturgeon migration. White sturgeon are most abundant and grow the fastest in the lower Columbia, where they use estuarine and marine habitats as well as the river. But that population is also at risk of collapse. Upstream, on the mainstem of the Columbia, biologists consider healthy only three of the eleven populations between dams. The others show the deleterious effects of altered river flows, overfishing, and poaching.

The population in the Kootenai River in Montana is also declining; in 1994, the U.S. Fish and Wildlife Service listed Kootenai River sturgeon as endangered.

Today, fewer than one thousand are left, 80 percent of those over 20 years old. Almost no young have hatched since 1974, when the Libby Dam began altering the flow patterns of the river.

The Snake River is burdened with twelve dams from its mouth upstream to Shoshone Falls in Idaho. Sturgeon are abundant in only two stretches between dams, in those reaches where free-flowing river habitat still exists. Irrigators dewatering sections of streams have hurt sturgeon production in the Snake. Fishermen, too, contribute to the decline. Unless changes are made in how dams are operated and unless overharvesting ends, North America may lose its largest and one of its oldest fish.

Part Seven
AMPHIBIANS
AND REPTILES

Part Seven Amphibians and Reptiles

Numbers and Distribution

AMPHIBIANS ARE EASY TO MISS BECAUSE they are secretive and nocturnal or crepuscular (active at dusk and dawn). But that doesn't mean they're not plentiful. Take the night-loving red-backed salamanders in Shenandoah National Park in Virginia. They reach densities of seven to ten individuals per square yard! In the Shenandoah and in many other places, amphibians exceed reptiles, birds, and mammals in number and bulk-per-acre. Some examples of amphibian biomass:

• In a typical pond in Texas, the lesser sirens, an eel-like salamander that reaches two feet in length, has a greater biomass than that of the seven species of fish that live in the same pond.

• In northeastern forests, the total weight of salamanders is twice that of birds at their peak breeding time and about equal to that of small mammals. Salamanders produce more new tissue annually than either birds or mammals (tissue with a higher protein content than that produced by any other vertebrate). Farther south in eastern deciduous forests, salamanders generate more biomass than any other vertebrate—more than all the birds and mammals combined.

• Lungless salamanders in one redwood forest in the Berkeley Hills in California averaged six to seven hundred individuals per acre. Their biomass exceeds that of any other vertebrate.

Amphibians, with their great number and bulk, are the primary predators of invertebrates in many habitats. A thousand small frogs (northern cricket frogs) consume an estimated 4.8 million small arthropods (mostly insects) per year, for example. In turn, amphibians are one of the major sources of food energy for snakes, predatory birds, and mammals.

A Salamander Heaven

If North America has a salamander heaven, it's the Great Smoky Mountains. That southern, unglaciated region of the Appalachians, with its isolated peaks, cool, moist climate, and huge number of microhabitats, shelters the highest abundance and diversity of salamanders anywhere on the continent. Twenty-eight species from five different families thrive there. One large family, the lungless salamanders (Plethodontidae) evolved in the Appalachians. They are called lungless because the adults have neither gills nor lungs; they breathe through their skins.

HOW MANY AMPHIBIANS AND REPTILES?

	North of Mexico		Mexico†	
Group	Families	Species	Families	Species
Amphibians				
Salamanders	7	140	4	89
Frogs and Toads	9	90	8	194
Reptiles				
Crocodiles	2	2	2	3
Turtles	7	49*	9	38
Lizards	8	97	10	330
Snakes	5	125	7	319

†Mexico shares 6 salamanders, 37 frogs and toads, 70 lizards, 76 snakes, 19 turtles, and 1 crocodile species with the rest of North America.
*The turtle tally does not include sea turtles.

And We're Still Finding New Ones

New species of amphibians and reptiles are still being discovered in North America. Since 1978, fifty-three are new, in fact. Admittedly, most of those "new" species were known creatures reclassified into distinct species after molecular analyses of their DNA. Most of these new ones belonged to complex groups such as the lungless salamanders of the Appalachians. Many Appalachian mountaintops harbor their own species and subspecies. Species never before described by science are occasionally added to the list, even in well-populated places like California.

Mexico's Great "Herp" Diversity

Over 970 species of reptiles and amphibians are native to Mexico, more than the U.S. and Canada combined. Fifty-five percent of the species are endemic; they occur nowhere else in the world. Reptiles and amphibians, like almost everything else, reach their greatest diversity in the tropics. What's surprising is that Mexico hosts more species than all the Central American countries put together, a richness that does not extend to salamanders and turtles, however. Salamanders are restricted mostly to the temperate regions of the Northern Hemisphere, and the northern and southern limits of turtles are generally narrower than those of snakes and lizards.

In fact, except for Columbia in South America, Mexico houses the greatest diversity of herpetofauna of any area of equal size on earth. The great rainforests of South America and Africa harbor considerably more frogs and toads but are limited in reptilian diversity. Just about everywhere else on the globe hosts fewer than half the number of reptile and amphibian species that Mexico supports.

Why are So Many in Decline?

Habitat degradation and loss seems most harmful for amphibian and reptile populations. Other problems include timber harvesting; environmental pollutants such as toxic pesticides and herbicides and acid rain; nonnative species of gamefish introduced for sport; nonnative amphibians and reptiles such as bullfrogs in western states and anoline lizards in south Florida; and increased ultraviolet radiation, which lowers immunities to certain diseases. Amphibians are especially vulnerable to environmental contaminants for several reasons.

• Their life cycle requires favorable conditions on land and in water.

• Their skin is permeable to gas and water, two avenues for the entry of chemical contaminants.

• Their skin pigmentation and their habit of basking makes them especially vulnerable to increased ultraviolet light levels resulting from a loss of ozone.

• Many larval amphibians feed on plant and animal matter, material that attracts persistent chlorinated chemicals. As adults, amphibians feed on animals (mostly insects) and tend to accumulate concentrations of synthetic chemicals.

• Especially vulnerable to cold and drought, many species go without reproducing for several years.

• Because they depend on moist, cool environments, many species are patchy in distribution. That means populations are often isolated from other populations and, therefore, more susceptible to outside threats.

• During metamorphosis, amphibians—especially frogs—undergo profound reorganization of structure and physiology. The process is driven by hormones. Chemical contaminants stored in fat tissue are often released during metamorphosis.

Thus, hormone mimics—chemical contaminants such as pesticides that interfere with hormone signals—may be disrupting this crucial stage in their life cycle. Similar problems may occur during breeding periods when fatty tissues are metabolized.

Some well-documented amphibian declines are listed below.

REGIONAL AMPHIBIAN DECLINES

Region	Problem
Pacific Northwest	Tailed frogs (*Ascaphus truei*) and torrent salamanders (*Rhyacotriton*), two species that occupy small streams, have suffered severe declines because of timber harvesting practices that destroy streamside habitats.
Rocky Mountains, from southern Wyoming to northern New Mexico	The western toad (*Bufo boreas*) now occurs at fewer than 20% of the locations where it was known just a few decades ago. The reasons for the decline are not understood but are thought to be mostly human caused.
Southeastern U.S.	The degradation of stream habitats and the conversion of natural forests and their associated wetlands to forest plantations, farms and ranches, or urban landscapes have hurt salamander and frog populations.
Canada and the U.S.	Northern leopard frogs (*Rana pipiens*), once abundant, are now declining (some significantly) especially in the central Rocky Mountains and southwestern regions.

Other species in western North America with well-documented and serious declines in all or major portions of their ranges include the Yosemite toad (*Bufo canorus*) of the California Sierra Nevada; the Wyoming toad (*Bufo hemiophrys baxteri*) of the Laramie Basin, Wyoming; the Arroyo toad (*Bufo microscaphus californicus*) of southern California and northern Baja California; the Chiricahua leopard frog (*Rana chiricahuensis*) of southwest New Mexico, Arizona, and Mexico; the lowland leopard frog (*Rana yavapaiensis*) of the southwest U.S. and northwest Mexico; the plains leopard frog (*Rana blairi*) of the central U.S.; the spotted frog (*Rana pretiosa*) of western North America; the Cascades frog (*Rana cascadae*) of the

Cascade mountains; the mountain yellow-legged frog (*Rana muscosa*) of California and western Nevada; the foothill yellow-legged frog (*Rana boylii*) of western Oregon, California, and northern Baja California; the Tarahumara frog (*Rana tara-* *humarae*) of southern Arizona and Mexico; the California red-legged frog (*Rana aurora*) of the Pacific Coast; the California tiger salamander (*Ambystoma californiense*) of California; and the tiger salamander (*Ambystoma tigrinum*) of the Colorado Rockies.

The Status of Turtles

With the exception of the far north, turtles live just about everywhere in North America. Marine turtles swim coastal waters from Alaska to Mexico, and except for Alaska and the northern provinces of Canada, the rest of the continent is inhabited by nonmarine species. Among the nonmarine species with the widest ranges are the painted turtle (the only species that spans the continent east to west), the snapping turtle and the common musk turtle (both ranging from Canada to Mexico), the eastern mud turtle, the common map turtle, the slider, the eastern box turtle, and the diamondback terrapin.

Despite their broad distribution, North America's turtles are suffering serious declines. One recent study suggests that habitat destruction and collectors who market turtles as pets or sell them abroad for food threaten to wipe out all the species north of Mexico. The degradation of coastal marshes, for example, imperils the diamondback terrapin. Farther inland, logging destroys habitat for woodland species such as the box turtle. Pesticides and herbicides take their toll, as do highways across turtle habitats. Turtles are especially vulnerable to these kinds of threats. Relative to other animals, they reach sexual maturity late and suffer a high juvenile mortality rate. Most herpetologists believe that only aggressive and coordinated conservation efforts will see North America's turtles survive over the long term.

In the U.S. alone, populations of many of the fifty nonmarine species are in sharp decline. According to the U.S. Fish and Wildlife Service, 40 percent of the nation's turtle species require some form of conservation simply to maintain their present numbers. Twenty-eight percent are listed or are candidates for listing under the Endangered Species Act. All the tortoises and marine species require conservation action.

Although no turtle species have disappeared in the U.S. since European colonization, most have shrinking distributions. For instance, bog turtles no longer live in western Pennsylvania and portions of New York. Spotted turtles, too, have vanished from portions of their range. Among those with dwindling distributions are wide-ranging, formerly common species like the common box turtle, the desert tortoise, the gopher tortoise, the common slider, and the alligator snapping turtle. Members of the map turtle genus, *Graptemys*, are at extreme risk of extinction, because their ranges never were of great size.

Some of the best data on long-term population changes in turtles are for the diamondback terrapin, a species exploited heavily during the nineteenth century as a gourmet food. Terrapin populations declined rapidly—enough that some states set seasons and limits for their protection as early as 1878. The market for terrapin meat waned, and populations recovered somewhat, because the habitat remained intact. Now some populations are declining again because of renewed regional harvesting, increased habitat destruction, and mortality caused by vehicles and crab traps.

Five species of marine turtles—the loggerhead, green, Kemp's ridley, leatherback, and hawksbill—frequent the beaches and offshore waters of the southeastern U.S. All five nest on the coast, but only the loggerhead and green turtle do so in any numbers. Marine-turtle nesting concentrates on beaches from southern North Carolina to the middle west coast of Florida. The beaches of Florida, particularly in Brevard and Indian River Counties, host probably the world's largest population of loggerheads. Nearly the entire world population of Kemp's ridleys uses a single Mexican beach for nesting. Juveniles and subadult Kemp's ridleys spend much of their time in U.S. offshore waters.

Marine turtles, especially juveniles and subadults, feed in lagoons, estuaries, and bays. In North America, the most important feeding grounds include Chesapeake Bay, Virginia (for loggerheads and Kemp's ridleys); Pamlico Sound, North Carolina (for loggerheads); and Mosquito Lagoon, Florida, and Laguna Madre, Texas (for green turtles). Offshore waters such as Florida Bay and the Cedar Keys, Florida (for green turtles), and the mouth of the Mississippi River and the northeast Gulf of Mexico (for Kemp's ridleys) also feed turtles. Reefs provide resting and some feeding habitat for loggerheads, greens, and hawksbills, and offshore currents, especially the Gulf Stream, serve as migratory corridors, especially for leatherbacks.

Sea turtles are difficult to protect and manage because they live so long, reach sexual maturity late, and suffer high egg and juvenile mortality. Marine turtles also require a wide range of habitats and migrate enormous distances. Most spend only part of their lives in North America's waters. Hatchling loggerheads ride ocean currents for years before returning to feed as subadults in southeastern lagoons. They travel as far as Europe and the Azores and enter the Mediterranean Sea, where many are lost to the fishing industry. After nesting, adult loggerheads leave U.S. waters and spend years in feeding grounds in the Bahamas and Cuba, then return.

Today, marine turtle populations are threatened worldwide and are under intense pressure in the Caribbean Basin and the Gulf of Mexico. Fishermen capture subadult loggerheads extensively in the eastern Atlantic Ocean and the Mediterranean Sea. Those that hatch or nest on North American beaches or migrate to North American waters must be conserved through international efforts.

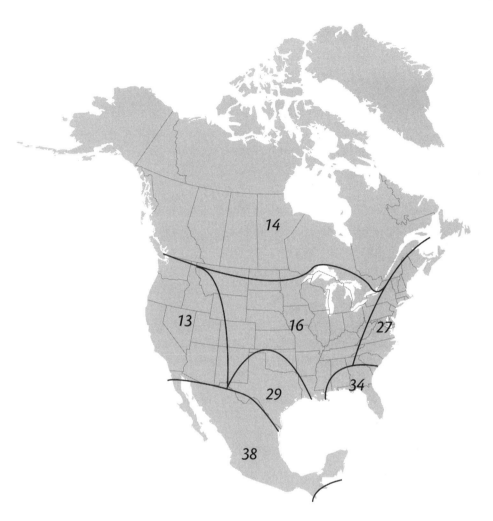

Turtle species density. The greatest number of turtle species occurs in the south and east.

The Demise of the Kemp's Ridley

Kemp's ridley turtles show extreme fidelity to their natal breeding site. At one time, more than 40,000 females nested in a single mass nesting (termed "*arribada*") in Tamaulipas, Mexico. Several *arribadas* probably occurred each year. But exploitation of nesting females since 1947 has nearly wiped out the species. Today, only about four to five hundred turtles nest, despite stringent protections. The principal threat today is incidental capture during shrimp fishing.

Status of Turtles in the U.S.

Common name	Status
Snapping turtles	
Alligator snapping turtle	Unknown but vulnerable; C2* candidate
Semiaquatic pond turtles	
Wood turtle	May become threatened if trade not brought under control
Western pond turtle	Declining; C2 candidate
Bog turtle	Unknown; are or may be threatened by international trade; C2 candidate
Blanding's turtle	Declining; C2 candidate
Barbour's map turtle	Unknown; C2 candidate
Cagle's map turtle	Unknown
Yellow–blotched map turtle	Threatened, but insufficiently known; may be threatened by trade
Ringed map turtle	Threatened; restricted distribution
Diamondback terrapin	Some populations unknown, others declining; some C2 candidates
Alabama red-bellied turtle	Endangered; restricted distribution
Red-bellied turtle	Endangered according to population or geographic area
Mud and musk turtles	
Yellow mud turtle	Unknown; C2 candidate; listing applies to population or geographic area
Mexican rough–footed mud turtle	Unknown; C2 candidate; listing applies to population or geographic area
Flattened musk turtle	Threatened
Tortoises	
Desert tortoise	Some populations threatened, others C2 candidates; may become threatened by trade; status of Sonoran Desert population unknown
Texas tortoise	May be threatened if trade not controlled; receives some conservation action
Gopher tortoise	Declining; some populations threatened, others are C2 candidates; may be threatened if trade not controlled; receiving some conservation help
Softshell turtles	
Spiny softshell turtle	Are or may be affected by international trade
Sea Turtles	
Loggerhead	Threatened
Green sea turtle	Endangered or threatened according to population or geographic area
Hawksbill	Endangered
Kemp's ridley	Endangered
Olive ridley	Endangered or threatened according to population or geographic area
Leatherback	Endangered

*C2 means the species may qualify for threatened or endangered status, but more information is needed.

NATURAL HISTORY

Desert Amphibians

From the standpoint of evolution, amphibians fall somewhere between fish and reptiles. Almost all amphibians lay their eggs in water. Most spend the larval stage of their lives swimming and breathing through gills. When adult amphibians leave the water, their skin remains moist and permeable, susceptible to desiccation. Even moderate temperatures and dryness can be lethal to amphibians that can't reach water. But there are exceptions. Some amphibians thrive in deserts.

Spadefoot toad

The California tree frog is one example of a desert amphibian. With a range extending from the Colorado Desert of California into northern Baja, the California tree frog survives because it never strays from permanent springs, seeps, or water holes. Still, it must cope with temperatures in excess of 105°F (anything above 95°F is deadly for most amphibians). By evaporating water from their skin, California tree frogs maintain a body temperature of below 86°F, regardless of the air temperature. They are able to replenish the moisture lost to evaporation by reclaiming water from urine. The frogs can store up to 25 percent of their body weight in the form of dilute urine.

Red-spotted toads also live in the Colorado Desert but not necessarily near water. Like California tree frogs, they cool themselves by evaporating water from their skins and are able to recycle water from urine, but red-spotted toads also burrow into the relatively cool soil in rock crevices. When air temperatures outside are searing, a red-spotted toad in its burrow will maintain a temperature of 88°F or below. And the species can endure long periods without visiting a water source, because they store up to 40 percent of their weight as urine and recycle it as needed. The toad also tolerates up to a 40 percent loss of body water. By comparison, camels, one of the most efficient mammals in this respect, can withstand only about a 20 percent loss.

Spadefoot toads take desert living one step further. They survive in southwest deserts without permanent water sources. By burrowing deep, up to 3 feet beneath the surface, they completely escape the hottest, driest season in the desert. In the soil, they escape evaporation losses while their bodies absorb moisture from the earth. And like the California tree frog and the red-spotted toad, the spadefoot retains and recycles large amounts of urine. A spadefoot can hold up to half its body weight in urine. When the summer rains arrive, the toads emerge from their burrows and journey to seasonal water sources. On the way, they eat termites and other insects. Famous for their appetites, spadefoots might consume half their weight in insects in a single night. Remarkably, that is enough to sustain a spadefoot toad for an entire year, if need be. Reaching water, the toads don't tarry. It takes them about a day to mate and lay eggs. Then it's back to the desert. Sometimes traveling for miles, a spadefoot eventually settles into a shallow summer burrow, from which it emerges periodically to feed. Then, in late summer, as the dry season returns, spadefoot toads excavate deep burrows where they await the next year's rains. During droughts, they can survive as long as two years underground, quite a feat for an amphibian.

IN FOCUS: WESTERN OR BOREAL TOAD

Boreal toad

Boreal toad distribution

Distribution

Boreal toads (*Bufo boreas*) range from western British Columbia and southern Alaska to northern Baja California, Mexico, and as far east as Montana, western and central Wyoming, Nevada, the mountains of Utah, and western Colorado.

Description

Squat and pudgy, the boreal toad is one of North America's largest toads. Adults can be 5 inches long. Their color varies from dusky brown to gray-green. Like other toads, they have warts; theirs are rust-colored and ringed with black. Often, a lighter stripe extends down the length of the back.

Habitat

Boreal toads inhabit the mountainous areas of northwestern North America, from sea level to elevations near or above treeline, although they are less common at higher elevations. They live in deserts near streams and springs, in grasslands and mountain meadows, aspen groves, and forests. Wherever they occur, they are usually found near ponds, lakes (including saline lakes), rivers, and streams.

Life History

Depending on latitude and elevation, boreal toads are active from January to October. Most are diurnal during the spring and fall and nocturnal during the summer. In winter they hibernate in natural chambers near streams. The high water table, the constantly flowing stream, and the snow help maintain air temperatures within their dens at or just above freezing.

A boreal toad may live nine to ten years. Their minimum breeding age is two to three years. The timing of their egg-laying varies with elevation and weather but can occur any time between January and July. Egg development depends partly on temperature, although metamorphosis is usually completed within three months of egg laying. Sex ratios differ according to habitat type; males are more numerous in wet areas, females in dry habitats.

Boreal toads eat mostly invertebrates—bees, beetles, ants, grasshoppers, spiders, crayfish, and sowbugs. They in turn often become prey to ravens and other birds, reptiles, and mammals, even though they produce skin toxins and are avoided by many predators. Tadpoles are eaten by fish, amphibians, birds, and mammals.

Status

Boreal toad populations are declining; the species has vanished in recent years from much of its range. Surveys find it at fewer than 20 percent of the locations where it was common a decade or two ago. In the U.S., the most widespread subspecies is listed as a Category 2 subspecies, one possibly qualifying for endangered or threatened status.

The Life of a Lizard

To find out how lizards make their living in the deserts of western North America, lizard researcher Eric Pianka and his assistants spent five years walking thousands of miles observing and collecting thousands of lizards. For each species, they determined the period of activity, the place of activity, and the foraging strategy. This is what they found:

Mode of Life	% of Species
Diurnal (active during daylight)	86
Ground-dwelling	74
Sit-and-wait foraging	60
Actively foraging	14
Arboreal (inhabiting trees)	12
Nocturnal (active at night)	14
Ground-dwelling	14
Arboreal	0
Subterranean	0
All ground dwelling	88
All arboreal	12

Pianka also looked at species density. How does the number of species of lizards and snakes inhabiting North American deserts compare with that of other kinds of vertebrates, specifically birds and small mammals? On his various study sites, Pianka found, perhaps not surprisingly, that reptiles make up most of the vertebrate species in the desert.

Type of Organism	Number of Spp. (mean)	Number of Spp. (range)
Lizards	7.4	(4–11)
Snakes	4.5	(2–9)
Total Reptiles	11.9	(6–20)
Birds	7.8	(3–16)
Small Mammals	5.3	(4–8)
Total	24.7	(14–40)

Crocodiles, Alligators, and Caimans

For nonexperts, the differences between crocodiles, alligators, and caimans can be subtle. In crocodiles, the fourth lower tooth fits into a notch on the outside of the upper jaw and is visible when the animal's mouth is closed. In alligators, the fourth tooth fits inside a socket on the upper jaw and is hidden. Alligators also have broader, shorter heads than crocodiles. Alligators and caimans look similar. Alligators, however, possess a bony septum that divides their nasal opening longitudinally, something caimans lack. And caimans sport twice as many plates on the backs of their necks as alligators have.

The American crocodile (Crocodylus acutus) ranges from southern Florida to northern Peru and Venezuela. Timid in disposition, crocodiles can grow to about 16 feet in length. When water temperatures drop to lower than 65°F, the American crocodile becomes torpid, sinks to the bottom, and drowns, which explains why crocodiles do not occur farther north than they do. The American crocodile, however, does tolerate high salinities; croc tongues bear twenty to forty salt glands that excrete excess sodium and potassium.

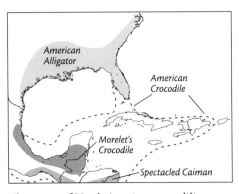

The ranges of North American crocodilians

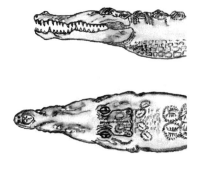

American crocodile

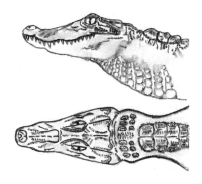

Spectacled caiman

Caimans are the Central and South American equivalents of alligators. The northernmost species of caiman, the spectacled caiman (*Caiman crocodilus*), occurs from southern Mexico to the northwestern tip of South America. Inadvertently introduced to Florida, the species now lives there in the wild. Spectacled caiman seldom reach 6 feet in length. They prefer quiet, open freshwater habitats, although they live in brackish waters too.

The Morelet's crocodile (*Crocodylus moreleti*) occurs along the Caribbean coast of Mexico from Tampico in the north to Campeche in the south and across the base of the Yucatan Peninsula to Belize and northern Guatemala. The Morelet's grows to just under 10 feet in length and is primarily a freshwater species that lives in savanna ponds and lakes. Like other crocodilians, it eats fish, amphibians, reptiles, water birds, small mammals, and mollusks.

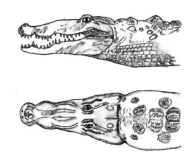

Morelet's crocodile

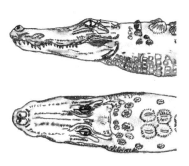

American alligator

The American alligator (*Alligator mississippiensis*) occurs widely across the southeastern U.S., its range extending northward to the point where the average annual minimum temperature drops to 15°F. (The northernmost record for siting an American alligator is on the Arkansas River, about 300 miles north of the Mississippi Delta.) Probably because alligators have a low tolerance for excessive heat, they do not range into Mexico. They live mostly in freshwater lakes and ponds and reach 19.5 feet in length.

Alligator Nannies

To nest, female American alligators build 6-foot-high mounds of plant debris and mud. Warmed by both the sun and decaying vegetation, the nests are ideal egg incubators that provide protection against floods and desiccation, which is why other types of reptiles—turtles, snakes, lizards—also nest in them. The squatters not only find alligator nests an easy place to dig but benefit by protection when female alligators aggressively defend their nests.

Most of the reptiles that parasitize the mounds do so irregularly, but Florida red-bellied turtles are regular customers. In many Florida swamps, fully half of the alligator nests contain red-bellied turtle eggs, often multiple clutches of them, laid by as many as ten or more turtles. One nest held two hundred red-bellied eggs in addition to the alligator's own twenty-five to sixty. Egg-eating predators like raccoons that visit the mounds usually eat only a fraction of the eggs they find; generally some survive. The arrangement therefore offers some benefit to the alligators. Chances are good the raccoons will be eating mostly turtle eggs. Still, alligators often attack turtles caught burrowing in their nests.

Beyond Genes: The Mother Chooses

High school biology students learn that, like other traits, the gender of individual humans is inherited. The same is true for other mammals and birds, but not for certain reptiles and amphibians—specifically frogs and toads, alligators and crocodiles, many turtles, and some lizards. Rather, temperature or, to be more precise, the temperature where the mother chooses to lay her eggs, dictates the sex of these cold-blooded creatures. With diamondback terrapins, for example, eggs laid in open sites that get lots of sun become females. Those laid in cooler places hatch into males. Among diamondback terrapins, the largest females claim the warmest nesting sites, and so they produce almost all the females. Because small females tend to lay their eggs in shaded places, they mother most or all of the males.

With American alligators and common caimans, just the opposite holds true: high temperatures (90° to 93°F) produce males, cool ones (82° to 86°F) females.

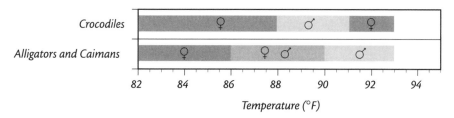

Temperature-dependent sex determination in some crocodilians

Temperatures between the two extremes yield a mix. Other crocodilian species produce all or mostly females at both high and low temperatures and males at midrange temperatures. As with terrapins, where a mother alligator or crocodile chooses to nest and when she lays her eggs determine the sex ratio of her offspring. Not surprisingly, both crocodiles and alligators are careful nesters. They construct several trial nests before settling into the one with the right thermal ambiance. For reasons not yet understood, different alligators in the same area show different preferences. Some choose nest sites on warm levees, others in cool marshes, for instance. Females usually dominate wild populations most years, but the ratio fluctuates. In these instances, mothers are making decisions beyond mate selection that affect the fundamental nature of their offspring. Such extra-genetic influences are termed "maternal effects."

A different kind of maternal effect operates in the side-blotched lizard, a 4- to 6-inch, voracious insect eater that ranges from Washington to Mexico. Male side-blotched lizards come in three genetically determined forms or morphs. Orange-throated morphs are aggressive, protect large breeding territories, and keep harems. Blue-throated morphs, less combative, keep smaller territories and guard a single mate. Yellow-throated morphs establish no territory, act like females, which they resemble, and move into the orange-throated lizard's territories clandestinely to mate with their females.

Remarkably, the dominant morph changes in any given population. The blue-throated males dominate for one or two years but are eventually supplanted by orange morphs. After several more years, the orange morphs decline, and the yellow increase. Then the yellow-throated give way to the blue, and the cycle begins again. Each morph, it seems, creates social conditions that lead to its downfall. Females mediate this cycle by adjusting their egg-laying patterns according to the dominant morph.

Female side-blotched lizards come in two morphs—an aggressive orange-throated and a more timid yellow-throated. When a female orange-throated morph is surrounded by other orange-throateds, she lays large eggs that hatch into females. The orange morphs tend to be pugnacious, and big eggs yield bigger, healthier female offspring that are better able to compete against their own kind. Yellow morphs surrounded by orange do just the opposite. They lay big, male eggs. Apparently, they count on their male offspring—the ones that sneak around the orange-throated males' territories disguised as females—to prevail over yellow-throated females when surrounded by aggressive orange morphs. The maternal effect eventually allows the yellow males to replace the orange ones.

Scientists observe similar effects among plants, insects, and mammals. Maternal effects counter the traditional view that only the genetic information stored in an egg counts when it comes to what an offspring looks like or does. They can enhance an individual's chance of survival, alter a population's sex ratios, or influence the size of a species' population. Sometimes, mothers know best.

Part Eight

BIRDS

Part Eight Birds

NUMBERS AND DISTRIBUTION

Of Distributions and Migrations

ZOOLOGISTS DIVIDE THE WORLD'S LAND-masses into six regions or realms based on similarities in the distribution of animals. North America falls mostly within the Nearctic realm. The tropical regions of Mexico and Florida lie within the Neotropical. When it comes to birds, the Nearctic is relatively species poor. The region represents 17 percent of the world's land area but supports only about 750 breeding species of birds, 8.7 percent of the world's total. The percentage is much lower in winter, when many species leave the continent for warmer climes. The dominant groups of the Nearctic are the wood warblers (Parulidae), the blackbirds and orioles (Icteridae), and the cardinals and grosbeaks (Cardinalini of the Emberizinae).

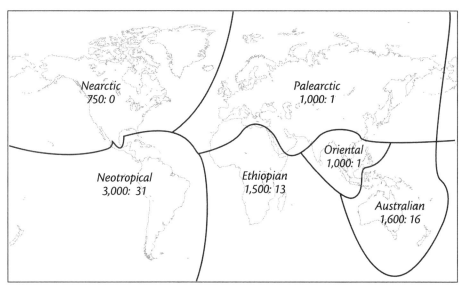

Biogeographic realms of the world. The first number is the number of bird species in the realm, the second is the number of endemic families.

Diversity increases toward the equator, and generally, more species live in the West than in the East. The first trend, however, is reversed in the deciduous and coniferous woodlands along the East Coast. Also, fewer species reside on peninsulas like Baja and Florida.

As few as nineteen species live in some tundra areas; most of the Arctic region supports fewer than forty. The coniferous forest, the prairie, and the deciduous forest host about twice as many species per unit area as the tundra; the desert and savanna harbor four to six times as many. The tropical rainforest of Mexico enjoys the greatest diversity. In its richest areas, tropical Mexico supports over four hundred species.

About 150 of the land and freshwater species that breed in North America fly south annually to winter in Central and South America and the West Indies. Why so many of North America's birds migrate is a matter of conjecture. One of the most accepted explanations suggests that migration patterns stem from Pleistocene glaciations; birds migrated to escape the cold. Migration patterns probably also stem from the fact that the continent offers abundant food in the summer but little in the winter. By migrating, the birds can take advantage of the spring flushes of insects and long summer days to raise their young and then escape the desolation of winter by flying to warmer climates in the south.

The major groups of North American birds wintering in the tropics are the insect-eaters. They include swallows and swifts, goatsuckers, tyrant flycatchers, wood warblers, vireos, and orioles. The birds that remain in the Nearctic during winter include loons, grebes, cormorants, grouse, quails, turkeys, cranes, woodpeckers, corvides, titmice, nuthatches, creepers, dippers, mockingbirds, the Old-World warblers, pipits, waxwings, and shrikes.

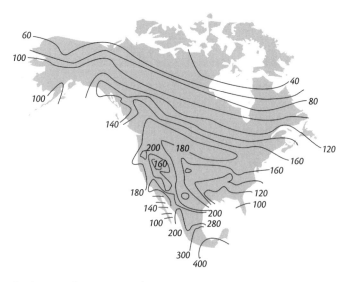

Bird species density across the continent

Seasonal Migration in Nearctic Breeding Birds

Family	Number of Nearctic Breeding Species	Number Wintering Entirely in Nearctica	Number Wintering in both Nearctica and Neotropica	Number Wintering Entirely in Neotropica
Loons	3	3	—	—
Grebes	6	5	1	—
Pelicans	2	1	1	—
Cormorants	5	4	1	—
Darters	1	—	1	—
Herons	13	1	12	—
Storks	1	—	1	—
Ibises and Spoonbills	5	—	5	—
Flamingos	1	—	1	—
Ducks	42	30	11	1
Vultures	4	1	3	—
Hawks	24	10	11	3
Ospreys	1	—	1	—
Falcons	7	2	4	1
Curassows	1	—	1	—
Grouse	9	9	—	—
Quails	6	6	—	—
Turkeys	1	1	—	—
Cranes	2	2	—	—
Limpkins	1	1	—	—
Rails	9	5	4	—
Jacanas	1	—	1	—
Plovers	10	3	5	2
Sandpipers	26	2	15	9
Stilts	2	1	1	—
Pigeons	12	3	8	1
Parrots	1	1	—	—
Cuckoos	6	1	3	2
Barn Owls	17	11	6	—
Owls	21	20	1	—
Goatsuckers	7	1	1	5
Swifts	4	—	1	3
Hummingbirds	17	10	4	3
Trogons	1	—	1	—
Kingfishers	2	—	2	—
Woodpeckers	22	18	4	—
Cotingas	1	—	1	—
Tyrant Flycatchers	30	9	8	13
Larks	1	—	1	—

SEASONAL MIGRATION IN NEARCTIC BREEDING BIRDS (CONT.)

Family	Number of Nearctic Breeding Species	Number Wintering Entirely in Nearctica	Number Wintering in both Nearctica and Neotropica	Number Wintering Entirely in Neotropica
Swallows	7	—	2	5
Jays and Crows	15	13	2	—
Titmice	14	14	—	—
Nuthatches	4	4	—	—
Creepers	1	1	—	—
Wrentits	1	1	—	—
Dippers	1	1	—	—
Wrens	10	9	1	—
Mockingbirds	11	10	1	—
Thrushes	12	9	—	3
Old World Warblers	4	4	—	—
Pipits	2	2	—	—
Waxwings	1	1	—	—
Silky Flycatchers	1	1	—	—
Shrikes	2	2	—	—
Vireos	11	3	2	6
Honeycreepers	1	1	—	—
Wood Warblers	54	14	10	30
Orioles and Blackbirds	21	11	7	3
Tanagers	4	—	1	3
Cardinals, Grosbeaks, Finches, and Sparrows	54	44	5	5

The North's Loss Is the South's Gain

In temperate North America, birds return in the spring and depart southward in the fall. In parts of Florida and the northern Bahamas, the number of bird species increases dramatically in winter—by 160 to 200 percent—as does the abundance of birds—densities jump from 2,300 birds per square mile in April to 4,100 per square mile in midwinter. A site in tropical Mexico with evergreen forest might support 4.2 small foliage gleaners per acre in summer but will host 165 in winter. Lowland areas typically sustain twenty-five times more warblers and vireos in winter than in summer. Fortunately, insects are also more plentiful in winter, roughly 1.6 times what they are in summer. In winter, across most of Mexico, migrants from the north comprise more than 30 percent of the bird population. The table that follows shows the types of habitats these migrants are using in Mexico (in terms of their abundance relative to the total bird population).

WINTERING NORTH AMERICAN BIRDS IN MEXICAN HABITATS

Habitat	% of Total Species that are Wintering Migrants	% of Total Individuals that are Wintering Migrants
Gallery Forest	20–22	64–69
Mangroves	50–74	75–83
Second Growth	51	59–63
Thorn Scrub	36–43	55–60
Tropical Deciduous	28–38	17–24
Oak Woodland	33–41	29–36
Pine-Oak Woodland	29–40	31–56
Pine Woodland	24	31

Farther south, the percentage of wintering northern migrants gradually drops off. Partly because fewer species migrate to the southern end of the wintering zone, the percentage of migrants is small there. In Ecuador, Peru, and Bolivia, the most species-rich bird habitat in the world, wintering northern migrants make up only 5 to 7 percent of the species.

The Birds of Mexico: A Neotropical-Nearctic Mix

Because Mexico is situated between the Nearctic and Neotropical realms, its bird fauna is a unique mixture. In Mexico, 769 species of birds breed, and another 257 occur as migrants, winter residents, or "accidentals." The total (1,026) is higher than that of the U.S. and Canada combined, even though the land area of Mexico amounts to less than 10 percent of the land area of those two nations.

Sixty percent of the seventy-two families of birds that breed in Mexico are considered widely distributed or common in North and South America. Ten percent are primarily of Nearctic distribution (reaching their southernmost limits in Mexico). Thirty-one percent are Neotropical (reaching their northernmost limits in Mexico). Some examples of the range limits of some species are shown below.

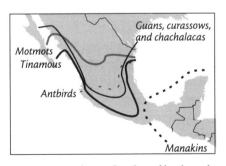
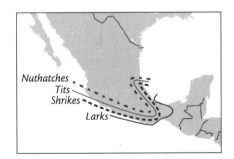

Range limits of some families of birds with primarily Neotropical (South American) distributions (left) and Nearctic (North American) distributions (right)

NORTH AMERICA'S FLYWAYS

Atlantic

Mississippi

Central

Pacific

Birds with Ancestors from the North Tend to Stay North

Ornithologists believe the ancestors of North American birds entered the continent in one of two ways: from the north (most likely from Eurasia via the Bering Land Bridge) or from the Neotropics to the south. The table that follows compares how far south the birds that are descended from each of these two groups migrate. Half of the north-originating species winter north of the U.S.–Mexico border, compared with only 5 percent of those descended from neotropical ancestors. Conversely, only 1 percent of the northern-descended species migrate to South America, compared with 36 percent of those with neotropical origins. Birds with northern roots tend to spend their winters farther north than those with neotropical origins.

Southern Limit of Migration	Number of Species	
	with Northern Origins	with Neotropic Origins
U.S.-Mex. Border	87	8
Central Mexico	44	30
Southern Mexico	7	16
Central America	13	56
Into South America	2	63
Totals	153	173

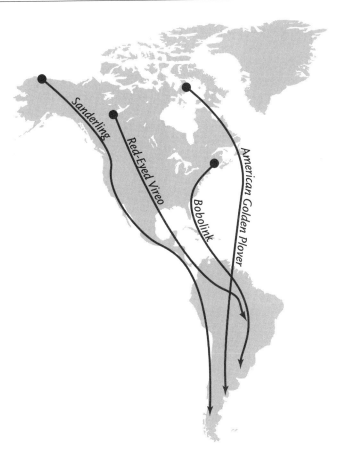

Long Distance Migrants

Among the long-distance migrants are Canadian bobolinks, which travel some 7,000 miles to Argentina. Some American golden plovers fly from northern Canada to Argentina. (Part of the trip is nonstop from Labrador to the northern coast of South America, a distance of over 3,000 miles. On their way back, the plovers fly an entirely different route to take advantage of favorable winds). Many of the longest-distance migrants are shorebirds like the plover. Two-thirds of the continent's shorebirds migrate from the Arctic, where they breed, to neotropical destinations, a roundtrip for most of over 15,000 miles. Hudsonian godwits fly 8,000 miles nonstop. The top long-distance migrant, however, is a seabird, the Arctic tern. It flies from its breeding grounds in the Arctic to its wintering homeland in Antarctica.

Other species head east or west before migrating, their patterns perhaps reflecting their species' origin. For instance, before migrating south, the Arctic warbler flies west—from Alaska across the Bering Sea to Siberia. From there it heads south, into the tropical regions of Asia.

Natural History

The Cowbird Threat

Brown-headed cowbirds, once limited to the plains region where they lived in close association with bison, have been expanding their range ever since the introduction of cattle. The species now occupies almost all of North America and is considered one of the greatest threats to several of the continent's songbirds. Cowbirds are brood parasites; that is, they don't build their own nests or take care of their own nestlings. Rather, they lay their eggs in the nests of other birds and let the other birds rear their young. Because cowbird nestlings hatch earlier and grow faster than the nestlings of their hosts, they crowd out or, at best, limit the food available for the host offspring. The result is that cowbirds have dramatically lowered the nest success of the host species.

Three species of cowbirds breed in North America: the brown-headed, which thrives in every state and province and in much of Mexico (see map); the bronzed, found mainly south of the U.S. from Mexico to Panama but also in Florida, the Gulf States, and the Southwest; and the shiny, once confined to South America but now found in the southeastern U.S. and the Caribbean. All three are brood parasites and are

Brown-headed cowbird

the only North American birds that rely entirely on other birds to raise their young.

Before Europeans arrived in North America, brown-headed cowbirds lived only on the shortgrass prairie west of the Mississippi, where there were large herds of bison. But as the East was settled and forests were cut, open habitats expanded, and the cowbird extended its range eastward. By the late 1800s, the species inhabited most cultivated parts of the east. During this century, conditions for cowbirds improved in the arid west as well, as farms and the numbers of livestock increased. Some of the range expansions have been recent. In the 1940s, no cowbirds could be found in the Sierra Nevada, but by the 1970s the bird had become one of the most common species there. Even so, brown-headed cowbirds are still most numerous on the shortgrass prairie where they evolved. Neighboring midwestern states hold the second largest concentration. Numbers drop off gradually to the east and west of these two regions, although cowbirds appear on more breeding bird censuses than any other species. And the bird continues to expand its range north (into the Yukon and northern Alberta) and south (into Florida and other southern states). The southeast, which supports the fastest growing brown-headed cowbird population, is also home to an expanding population of shiny cowbirds. The two parasites pose a double threat to the songbirds of the southeast.

Because North Americans provided more habitat for cowbirds by fragmenting and cutting forests and by bringing cows to nearly every corner of the continent, the brown-headed cowbird now enjoys the greatest breeding range of any North American passerine species. And because the bird does not waste time or energy building nests, sitting on eggs, or feeding young, it can travel farther than other species between locales where it lays its eggs and where it feeds—as far as 4.5 miles. Parental responsibilities require other birds to feed close to their nests.

Among the birds especially vulnerable to brown-headed cowbird parasitism are flycatchers, warblers, tanagers, thrushes, finches, and vireos. Kirkland's warblers, black-capped vireos, and least Bell's vireos are among the species most threatened.

Distribution of the brown-headed cowbird

Cowbird Facts

Brown-headed cowbirds parasitize the nests of some 240 species. Of these, 144 raise cowbird nestlings. Bronzed cowbirds are successful with about twenty-eight of the seventy-seven species that they parasitize.

Host species can be divided into those that accept cowbird eggs and rear their young and those that don't. The list of acceptors includes many warblers, vireos, phoebes, and songbirds. Among the rejectors: robins, catbirds, blue jays, kingbirds, waxwings, and brown thrashers.

Female brown-headed cowbirds lay up to forty eggs a year.

Brown-headed cowbirds usually take less than a minute to lay an egg. The mean laying time for host species ranges from 21 to 103 minutes. Rapid egg-laying allows cowbirds to deposit their eggs without being detected by the host.

Areas of heavy cowbird parasitism and notable effects: the fragmented forests of the Midwest (Wisconsin, Illinois, Missouri), where wood thrushes experience 80 to 100 percent parasitism levels; the grasslands of the northern Great Plains (North Dakota, Manitoba), where many species suffer 20 to 70 percent parasitism rates; the tallgrass prairie of Kansas (especially pastures), where multiple parasitism is the rule with species such as the dickcissel; and the riparian woodlands of southern California, where cowbirds threaten the survival of the least Bell's vireo and the southwestern willow flycatcher.

Neotropical Migrants: In Decline in Many Areas

Biologists have recently expressed concern over the fate of certain neotropical birds: species that migrate from the temperate parts of North America to the neotropical realm (areas south of the Mexican Plateau). The North American Breeding Bird Survey suggests that many neotropical migrant species are in decline—especially since 1980 and especially in the central and eastern regions of the continent. Three-quarters of the species in the east have declined since 1980. In Rock Creek and Glover-Archbold Parks in Washington D.C., formerly common songbirds are now rare or have disappeared entirely—species such as the Acadian flycatcher, the

Kentucky warbler, the black-and-white warbler, the American redstart, the ovenbird, the hooded warbler, the yellow-throated vireo, and the red-eyed vireo. The wood thrush, one of the most beloved songbirds in the east, has declined across much of its range. The scarlet tanager, a distinctive bird—the only one with a red body and black wings and tail—is also in trouble. Among the causes of the decline are deforestation of tropical habitats, habitat fragmentation in temperate North America, increased nest predation, and brood parasitism by cowbirds, although many local and regional factors play a part in the status of individual species.

Neotropical migrants (clockwise from top right): scarlet tanager, Acadian flycatcher, wood thrush, and black-and-white warbler

Forever Lost: North American Parrots and "Penguins"

The extinction of species ranks among the saddest changes European-Americans wrought upon North America. The destruction of habitat, the introduction of nonnative species, and the practice of overhunting and trapping account for most of the losses. Descriptions of birds lost follow. (Two—the Bachman's warbler and the ivory-billed woodpecker—may yet survive in some remote habitats, although it is unlikely.)

Carolina Parakeet

The Carolina parakeet, extinct in 1914, was the only member of the parrot family native to the U.S. Brilliantly colored—its head yellow and orange, its body green, its wings and tail blue—the Carolina parakeet flourished in the east in enormous flocks that feasted on fruit and grain crops. Farmers killed them by the thousands. Others hunted them for sport or trapped them for the pet trade. Carolina parakeets also suffered from the introduction of the honey bee. Wild colonies of bees appropriated the cavity nest-sites used by parakeets. Eventually the parakeet population grew too small for large flocks to form. Apparently, enormous social groupings were essential to the bird's survival. Perhaps the flocks were necessary for breeding, or detecting food, or escaping predators—no one knows for sure. But reduced to small numbers, the parakeet vanished, despite the presence of suitable habitat and abundant food.

Passenger Pigeon

Perhaps the best known of North America's extinct species, the passenger pigeon was at one time the world's the most abundant bird, its flocks exceeding 2 billion in number. James Audubon described a flock that took three days to pass overhead and estimated that as many as 300 million birds flew by each hour. Like the Carolina parakeet, the last passenger pigeon died in 1914.

Passenger pigeons inhabited the continent's eastern forests. They nested in huge, dense colonies that sometimes stretched for 40 miles. The combined effects of uncontrolled hunting and deforestation brought about the bird's demise. Ornithologists believe passenger pigeons, like Carolina parakeets, required enormous populations to survive. When their numbers dropped from in the billions to the tens of thousands and the nesting colonies had shrunk beyond a certain threshold, the species died out.

Labrador Duck

The Labrador duck, apparently rare before Europeans arrived in North America, disappeared around 1875. Most closely related to eiders, the Labrador duck resided along the East Coast. Whereas market hunting and commercial egg harvesting played a part in the species' death, pollution may have been the main cause. Labrador ducks depended on shellfish. Both duck and mollusk are especially sensitive to small amounts of pollutants.

Great Auk

The great auk, a large, flightless bird, vanished around 1852. The first bird to bear the name "penguin," the great auk stood two and a half feet tall and lived on fish. It lived in the North Atlantic in large colonies on offshore islands. Great auks moved slowly on land, so they were easy prey for fishermen and sailors who killed thousands of adults for food and feathers and who raided nests for their eggs and nestlings. These assaults contributed to the demise of a species already in decline. During the Little Ice Age, which lasted much of this millennium, ice formed around nesting colonies. Islands, previously isolated, became connected to the mainland and vulnerable to predation. Still, the bird probably would have survived had it not been for humans.

Great auk

Bachman's Warbler

This songbird is probably extinct, although it was once common in the low, wet forests of the southeastern U.S. By 1920, the species had declined enough to be considered rare. No confirmed breeding records have been reported from the U.S. since the mid-1960s. Several sightings have been made on Cuban wintering grounds during the last decade, however. Most authorities agree that if the Bachman's warbler is seen again in North America, it will most likely be in the swamps of South Carolina. Forest fragmentation, predation, brood parasitism, and severe storms played a part

in the bird's decline. Some ornithologists believe that this warbler fed in bamboo habitats, and they link its demise to the destruction of bamboo thickets across much of the bird's former range.

Ivory-Billed Woodpecker

At 18 inches high and with a 3-foot wingspan, the ivory-billed was North America's largest woodpecker. The species once resided across the southeastern U.S. but declined precipitously beginning in the 1880s, a victim of logging practices. By the mid-1900s, only about a dozen ivory-billed woodpeckers remained in North America, and it is unlikely any exist today. In 1996, The Nature Conservancy declared the bird extinct in the U.S. Vulnerable to habitat loss, ivory-billed woodpeckers required abundant pristine space. To breed successfully, each pair required several square miles of swampy, undisturbed old-growth forest.

Birds and Storms

Hurricanes may have contributed to the extinction of the Bachman's warbler. Natural phenomena like drought, fires, and storms can be catastrophic for birds, especially when birds are concentrated in small areas, a condition occurring during some migrations.

For example, in April 1993, a tornado hit Grand Isle, Louisiana, a low barrier island covered by sand dunes, marshes, and live oak thickets. This site is an important stopover point for neotropical species migrating from the Yucatan Peninsula or Central America. The tornado struck Grand Isle on April 8 at 2:30 in the afternoon. A day later, after hearing reports of dead birds, researchers from Louisiana State University surveyed the damage. The team estimated that 38,000 dead birds were washed up on the shore. The table below estimates the numbers killed of the ten species encountered in the greatest numbers. It also includes numbers for three species considered rare or with populations in serious decline.

Species	Estimated Number Killed
Ten species most frequently encountered	
Indigo bunting	4,207
Kentucky warbler	2,538
Wood thrush	2,362
Ovenbird	2,280
Red-eyed vireo	2,255
Worm-eating warbler	2,185
Hooded warbler	1,809
White-eyed vireo	1,800
Gray catbird	959
Orchard oriole	823
Species of special concern	
Cerulean warbler	583
Swainson's warbler	214
Seaside sparrow	111

Rain- and windstorms can also affect birds. In 1880 and 1909, residents along the Gulf of Mexico reported storms that drowned and killed "many thousands of northward migrating birds." Storms early in May of 1951 and 1976 killed an estimated 10,000 and 5,000 birds, respectively, along the coast of Texas. None of these storms was a tornado.

Hurricanes can decimate populations of migrating birds by destroying habitat or food resources. Four months after Hurricane Gilbert hit Jamaica, the populations of birds that fed on nectar, seeds, and fruit declined dramatically, while those that ate insects remained stable or increased.

A hurricane can be responsible for an extinction when the population of a species is already at low levels and its habitat is restricted to a small area, as may have happened to the Bachman's warbler. With its winter range limited to Cuba and the nearby Isle de Juventude and its habitat fragmented by agriculture, with its population already severely reduced, the species, which relied heavily on nectar, was vulnerable to hurricane damage.

On North America itself, hurricanes often affect species that require large old trees for nesting or roosting. Hurricane Hugo destroyed 44 percent of South Carolina's bald eagle nests. The storm also destroyed 87 percent of the active cavities used by red-cockaded woodpeckers in one forest. An estimated 63 percent of all the woodpeckers in that forest were killed by the storm.

Because storms can deal such devastating blows to birds, it is important to protect against the kinds of human activities that bring populations to fatally low levels. We can't stop storms, but we can mitigate their danger by saving habitat.

In Focus: Red-Cockaded Woodpecker

Red-cockaded woodpecker

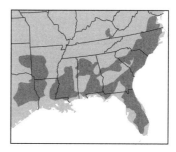

Red-cockaded woodpecker distribution

Distribution

In the mid-1800s, naturalist James Audubon reported that the red-cockaded woodpecker (*Picoides borealis*) thrived in the pine forests of the southeastern U.S.—the species ranged from Florida to New Jersey, as far west as Texas and Oklahoma, and inland to Missouri, Kentucky, and Tennessee. Today, only about 4,500 family units or groups of red-cockaded woodpeckers—roughly 10,000 to 14,000 birds—survive from Florida to Virginia and west to southeast Oklahoma and east Texas.

Description

About the size of the common cardinal, the red-cockaded woodpecker has a wingspan of 15 inches, a solid black cap and nape, white cheek patches, and a black-and-white ladder pattern on its back.

Habitat

Red-cockaded woodpeckers must inhabit mature pine forests, those with longleaf or loblolly pines averaging 70 to 120 years old. Whereas other woodpeckers bore cavities in dead trees with mostly soft, rotten wood, the red-cockaded excavates its holes exclusively in living pine trees, a single cavity taking one to three years to excavate.

Life History

Red-cockaded woodpeckers are a territorial, nonmigratory, cooperative-breeding species. A pair typically stays together for several years and raises a single brood each year. Upon fledging, two or three of the young males remain with their parents and help incubate the eggs and raise the young of the following year. Juvenile females, meanwhile, generally leave the group to search for males.

Rat snakes are a primary predator of red-cockaded woodpeckers. Agile tree climbers, rat snakes eat both eggs and nestlings. The bird defends itself by chipping small holes, called resin wells, in the bark of the cavity tree. Sap oozes down the trunk from the holes and adheres to the scales of climbing snakes. Faced with this fencelike obstacle, the snakes often abandon their efforts.

A number of other birds and small mammals use abandoned nest cavities of red-cockaded woodpeckers. Chickadees, bluebirds, titmice, and several other woodpecker species, including downy, hairy, and red-bellied, nest in the cavities. Larger woodpeckers enlarge the holes. Screech owls, wood ducks, and even raccoons later move in. Flying squirrels, several species of reptiles and amphibians, and insects (primarily bees and wasps) also use red-cockaded cavities.

Status

From the late 1800s to the mid-1900s, the red-cockaded woodpecker declined as logging companies and farmers cut mature pine forests. The U.S. government classified the species as endangered in 1970 under a law that preceded the Endangered Species Act. The red-cockaded woodpecker's current range is only 1 percent of the original.

The Recovery of the Wild Turkey

Wild turkeys, abundant in eastern bottomland-hardwood forests and pine woodlands before the days of European settlement, were a staple in the diets of the Indians. They also made clothing and ornamentation from the bird's feathers. Later, European-Americans relied on the bird for food. By only one vote in Congress, the wild turkey lost to the bald eagle as the national symbol of the U.S.

As the nation's human population grew, the turkey population plummeted.

Settlers logged and plowed large tracts of habitat. Entire populations fell to overhunting and introduced diseases spread by domestic poultry. By the mid-nineteenth century, the species, which had vanished from New England, survived only in remote parts of the Appalachian and Cumberland plateaus, the Ozarks, and the Gulf States. Numbers continued to drop into the early 1900s, and by 1920, wild turkeys lived in only eighteen of the thirty-nine states they originally occupied.

Wildlife agencies did not attempt to restore and manage wild turkeys until after World War II. Efforts to artificially propagate game-farm birds failed, because turkeys raised in captivity and not imprinted on wild hens lacked the necessary experience and survival skills. Eventually, biologists turned to trapping and relocating wild turkeys. With nets and immobilizing drugs, game managers moved thousands of birds successfully.

Early in this century, wild turkeys numbered in the tens of thousands, but by 1959, the population exceeded half a million. By 1994, almost all of the forested eastern U.S. and much of the forested West supported wild populations of turkeys. The population now approaches 4 million, and every state except Alaska offers turkey-hunting seasons. Alberta, southern Saskatchewan, southwestern Manitoba, and southern Ontario also now host populations.

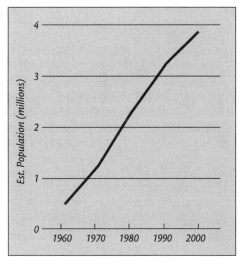

The turkey population in the U.S. since 1960

The Two North American Species of Turkey

The turkey originated 2 to 3 million years ago in the Pliocene epoch. The genus includes two species: the common wild turkey (*Meleagris gallopavo*) of the U.S., portions of southern Canada, and northern and central Mexico; and the ocellated turkey (*M. ocellata*) of the lowland tropical forests of the Yucatan in Mexico and Guatemala and Belize. The ocellated turkey is the smaller of the two and lacks the tuft of breast feathers characteristic of the common turkey. The ocellated is also more brilliantly colored, with reddish yellow bumps on a blue head topped by a yellow-tipped knob. The bright eyespots on its tail resemble those of the peacock. Unlike the common turkey, the ocellated has never been domesticated.

When Spaniards arrived in Mexico, Indians there had domesticated a subspecies of the common wild turkey. Conquistadors brought some of these tame birds back to Spain in 1519. The birds spread throughout Europe before 1600, and English colonists returned a slightly different European-bred strain to eastern North America in the seventeenth century. These turkeys spread in the wild. It is difficult to determine what subspecies originally populated North America. Today, biologists recognize six subspecies.

IN FOCUS: RUFFED GROUSE

Ruffed grouse

Ruffed grouse distribution

Distribution

The natural distribution of the ruffed grouse is almost identical to that of the quaking aspen, an indication of the extent to which the bird relies on the tree for food. Ruffed grouse (*Bonasa umbellus*) range from central Alaska to the eastern seaboard and south into the New England states, through the Carolinas, to the northern border of Georgia. In the West, their distribution extends south into the Rocky Mountains, through central Utah, and along the Pacific Coast into northern California. The bird has been introduced into Iowa, Newfoundland, and the Ruby Mountains of Nevada.

Description

A bantam chicken-sized bird, the ruffed grouse has a variegated plumage—shades of gray flecked with reds, browns, and black—an ideal camouflage for the habitats it occupies. Males bear a red patch of skin above the eye, and both sexes carry dark shoulder patches. The tail of the ruffed grouse is barred with tones of red or shades of gray.

Habitat

Ruffed grouse inhabit a variety of plant communities. They favor mixed hardwood and hardwood-conifer forests over pure stands of conifers, except in winter. Throughout their range, grouse prefer aspen stands and aspen mixed with other hardwoods or conifers.

Life History

Mating and courtship begin in April when males "drum" to attract mates. Drumming consists of a series of low-pitched, hollow-toned thumps generated by rapidly beating wings. Such low-pitched sounds are directional and carry well through the dense thickets the grouse inhabit.

Females nest on the ground in dense, pole-sized stands of aspen or other hardwoods. They lay from eight to fourteen eggs. The eggs hatch between May and June. Usually only three or four of the chicks survive their first summer. The chicks are precocial, meaning they are covered with down and are open eyed and mobile the minute they leave the egg.

Females range over about 100 acres, males only over about 10. Both sexes eat a variety of foods—fruits, nuts, twigs, leaves, and flowers from shrubs, forbs, grasses, and trees. The chicks feed heavily on insects and other small invertebrates. Ruffed grouse themselves fall prey to humans, wolves, coyotes, foxes, cougars, lynx, bobcats, hawks, falcons, owls, eagles, and snakes, and skunks, weasels, and other small carnivorous mammals—about 55 percent of the fall population dies each winter.

Raptors in the U.S.

Raptors, or birds of prey, include the hawks, falcons, eagles, vultures, and owls. Most are hunters, and because they reside at the top of the food chain, their populations are generally low and widely dispersed. Concentrations reflect changes in prey abundance. Raptors are also sensitive indicators of pesticide and heavy-metal contamination. The status of selected species follows.

Nesting **ospreys** concentrate along the Atlantic Coast, the Great Lakes, and the northern Rocky Mountains and in the Pacific Northwest. Most regional populations declined through the early 1970s, although the magnitude of decline varied. The North Atlantic Coast and Great Lakes populations plummeted. After the 1972 nationwide ban on DDT, populations rebounded in most areas. Ospreys also benefited from reservoir construction, especially in the West. Their numbers are stable now or increasing. Counts from most states in the early 1980s yielded an estimate of about 8,000 nesting pairs.

The endangered **snail kite** breeds in central and southern Florida in wetlands affected by drawdowns. From 1900 to 1960, populations declined; after 1960, they increased. Now relatively stable, the continent's snail kite population fluctuates between three and eight hundred individuals. The bird is very common in some areas outside the U.S.

Although the Bald Eagle Protection Act of 1940 protected **bald eagles** in the U.S., shooting, habitat destruction, and pesticides like DDT continued to affect many local populations, and numbers declined sharply between 1950 and the 1970s. In 1978, the U.S. Fish and Wildlife Service listed the species as endangered in forty-three states and threatened in five. After a nationwide ban on DDT in 1972, bald eagle reproduction improved, and populations rebounded. In 1981, about 1,300 pairs nested in the U.S. outside of Alaska. The active protection of nesting habitat and the release of hand-reared eagles contributed to the recovery. In 1993, at least 4,000 pairs of bald eagles nested in the contiguous U.S., and another 20,000 to 25,000 in Alaska.

Bald eagles nesting along the shorelines of Lakes Superior, Michigan, Huron, and Erie continue to suffer low reproductive rates due to relatively high concentrations of the toxins DDE and PCB. In Maine, relatively few young survive.

Habitat loss also remains a threat to bald eagles. Historically, the continent supported a continuous (though scattered) distribution of bald eagles in the Southwest. Now only a remnant population survives there.

Populations of **sharp-shinned hawks** in Midwest states might be increasing, but counts in the East reveal a drop in the numbers of juveniles. Blood samples collected in the Northeast contained high DDE pesticide concentrations. Other factors could be contributing to the decline. **Northern goshawk** counts in the East suggest a stable population, but analyses of counts from the West reveal declining numbers. Habitat loss has reduced the number of **Harris' hawks**. Their northern range extends up into the southwestern U.S., but searches reveal that Harris' hawks have vanished from the Colorado River Valley, California, and Arizona. The clearing of brush for agriculture in Texas caused a more than 50-percent reduction in the winter population there. The status of the **ferruginous hawk** is uncertain. Stable in some areas such as the Great Plains, the species is declining in half of the western states.

American **peregrine falcon** populations declined from DDT and other organochlorine pesticide contamination. The species vanished in the eastern U.S. and was declared endangered everywhere else. Biologists recovered peregrines in the East and have supplemented populations in the West (outside of Alaska) with the release of hundreds of captive-bred birds. Now several generations originating from released birds survive and produce young in the wild. In some locales, such as in parts of California, reproduction remains below normal. In Alaska, nesting numbers of the Arctic subspecies increased without intervention, and the Fish and Wildlife Service moved the subspecies from the endangered to the threatened list in 1984.

The distribution of the **ferruginous pygmy owl** extends north into southern Arizona and south Texas. The fragmentation and loss of deciduous riparian woodlands and remnant mesquite habitat threatens its survival there. Both the northern and Mexican subspecies of the **spotted owl** are threatened. The greatest threat to the species in the Pacific Northwest is the loss of old-growth forest; in the Southwest it is the general loss of forest habitat. Since 1968, the number of known owl nesting areas in Oregon has increased from 27 to about 2,700 separate sites occupied by pairs or single birds at some point within the last five years. The increase does not reflect a surge in the owl population but better surveying techniques.

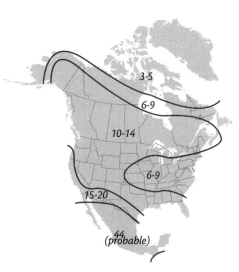

Hawk, falcon, and eagle species density

More Than Meets Our Eyes

Kestrels and other raptors seem to have an almost mystical ability to detect areas with lots of mice.

Often we make assumptions about the natural world based on our perceptions and miss what's actually happening. Hawks and falcons have long been recognized for their remarkable eyesight—their ability to discern even tiny animals at great distances. Visual creatures ourselves, we've assumed that birds of prey see the world as we do, only better. Large regions of the landscape may support only meager populations of mice and voles, while other places harbor concentrations. Raptors seem to possess a sixth sense in finding places where the populations of these creatures are highest. Many raptors hunt and build their nests in these areas. Until now, our assumption has been that birds of prey, at least those that hunt mice and voles, simply flew about until they spotted large numbers of rodents scurrying through the fields, or they looked for concentrations of other raptors as a signal.

But recent research on kestrels shows that raptors may be relying on a perception outside the realm of human experience. Voles, one of the kestrel's main prey, leave behind trails of urine and feces. Their inch-wide posteriors are soaked with urine. As they travel their complicated network of trails, the urine smells inform them who traveled where and when, much the way scent-posts signal information to packs of wolves.

These urine trails are visible in ultraviolet light at a part of the electromagnetic spectrum visible to kestrels but not to humans. Thus, for kestrels, and perhaps for a number of other rodent-hunting raptors, recently used vole runways stand out like neon—the equivalent of highway billboards. Ultraviolet vision enables them to evaluate large areas in a short time.

NORTH AMERICA'S FALCONS

Common Name	Scientific Name	Relative Size	Primary Habitat
Peregrine Falcon	*Falco peregrinus*	Large	Open lands; sea coasts
Gyrfalcon	*Falco rusticolus*	Large	Tundra; forest tundra
Prairie Falcon	*Falco mexicanus*	Large	Desert; open prairie
Aplomado Falcon	*Falco femoralis*	Medium	Tropical and desert scrub
Merlin	*Falco columbarius*	Small	Open lands; forest edge
American Kestrel	*Falco sparvarius*	Small	Open lands; scattered woods

Recovering the Rarest Bird in the World

California condors were probably never numerous in North America, although the species once ranged from British Columbia to Baja California and far to the east. Condors left fossils in Texas, Florida, and New York. Two thousand years ago, they nested in western Texas, Arizona, and New Mexico. Populations persisted in the Pacific Coast region, especially in the Columbia Gorge area, until the 1800s, and in northern Baja California until the early 1930s. Until 1987, when biologists took the last wild bird into captivity, a few California condors survived in the coastal ranges of California from Monterey and San Benito Counties south to Ventura County.

The California condor

For years, no one knew how many California condors existed, although birders understood they were in trouble as early as the 1890s. One estimate put their number at one hundred in the early 1940s; another counted fifty to sixty birds in the early 1960s; and by the late 1970s, the estimate was twenty-five to thirty.

Recognizing the California condor's perilous state, the U.S. Fish and Wildlife Service listed the species as endangered in 1967 (under a law preceding the Endangered Species Act of 1973). In 1979, several agencies and private groups initiated an effort to study and preserve the condor. They captured birds, weighed and measured them, and fitted some with tags and radio transmitters. They learned about the condors' feeding, mating, and chick-rearing habits, and studied habitat needs. In the course of that work, they learned that when California condors lost an egg, the female would lay a second and, sometimes, a third.

They were unable, however, to pinpoint the reason for the species' decline, although they suspected a combination of factors—direct mortality from shooting, egg collection, poisoning from substances put out by ranchers to eradicate livestock predators, poisoning from lead fragments of bullets embedded in animal carcasses that the condors feed on, an ever scarcer number of carcasses, and collisions with power lines. They also suspected that habitat losses to roads, cities, agriculture, housing tracts, and weekend mountain-retreats played a part.

To increase egg production, biologists removed eggs laid in the wild in 1983 and hatched them in captivity at the San Diego Wild Animal Park and the Los Angeles Zoo. They named the first California condor hatched in captivity "Sisquoc," and they raised it and subsequent chicks in boxes that simulated the caves the birds' parents used as nest sites. Zookeepers kept human contact to a minimum; they fed the chicks with hand puppets that mimed adult condors.

Meanwhile, researchers captured young, wild condors for a breeding program. Bringing immature, nonbreeding birds into captivity shortened the time necessary to create a viable breeding population. The Andean condor, a closely related species that inhabits areas in South America, had bred successfully in captivity. Some of those captive-born birds had been released into the wild, so American biologists had good reason to be optimistic about the California condor.

Until 1985, biologists planned to leave at least some condors in the wild. Free-flying condors might provide role models to captive-hatched birds. But members of four

of the five remaining breeding pairs disappeared over the winter of 1984–85, and the wild population dropped from fifteen to nine birds. With the number of wild condors continuing to plummet, the biologists decided in 1986 to capture all of those that remained in the wild and bring them into the breeding program. They trapped the last remaining wild California condor on April 19, 1987. Two of those wild birds successfully mated and produced the first captive-bred condor chick the following year.

In the fall of 1988, the U.S. Fish and Wildlife Service started a three-year reintroduction experiment using Andean condors as stand-ins for their endangered North American cousins. Between December and January, they released thirteen female Andean condors equipped with radio transmitters. To prevent reproduction in the wild, they freed

Condors: Big Birds That Reproduce Slowly

California condors are the largest birds in North America. They weigh up to 25 pounds; their wingspans stretch 9.5 feet. Magnificent flyers, condors soar on warm thermal updrafts for hours and reach altitudes of 15,000 feet.

Normally, California condors start breeding at age seven or eight. They nest in caves or clefts on cliffs with a clear approach for easy takeoff and landing and with nearby trees for roosting. Most nest sites known to be active since 1979 have been within a mix of chaparral and coniferous forests, although condors built two nests in giant sequoia trees in the Sierra Nevada. Typically, an adult pair lays one egg every other year; the fledgling depends on its parents through the next breeding season.

Like all vultures, condors eat carrion. They forage in grasslands and oak savannas, and although they prefer to eat large, dead animals like deer, cattle, and sheep, condors also feed on rodents and fish. After a particularly large meal, a bird may spend hours on the ground or on a low branch before it is able to take off again. Fastidious birds, condors clean their heads and necks after eating. They also bathe frequently and spend hours preening and drying their feathers.

only females. Those birds helped scientists perfect release techniques and identify environmental threats before they introduced the California birds. One of the Andean condors died from a collision with a power line. The rest were later recaptured and returned to their native habitat in South America.

In 1991, the team reintroduced two California condors and two Andean condors into the Los Padres National Forest's Sespe Condor Sanctuary in California. They included the Andean condors because studies indicated that California condors develop better in social groups. When they released six more California condors later that year, they relocated the Andean birds to South America. Biologists have made additional releases since, including six in Arizona. In December 1996, twenty-six California condors survived in the wild. All of the released birds are radio collared, and their diets are being supplemented with human-killed livestock.

A number of birds died. Power lines took at least five, poisoning took one. A golden eagle killed another. Biologists recaptured and returned to breeding facilities five other birds because they periodically perched on power lines and probably would not have survived in the wild.

The goal of the recovery program is to establish a minimum of three separate condor populations of 150 individuals and at least fifteen breeding pairs. Two of the populations would be in California and one in Arizona. If successful, the species might be downlisted from endangered to threatened. However, condor recovery will likely depend on a continuous supplemental feeding program, without which there would be too few carcasses to support the birds.

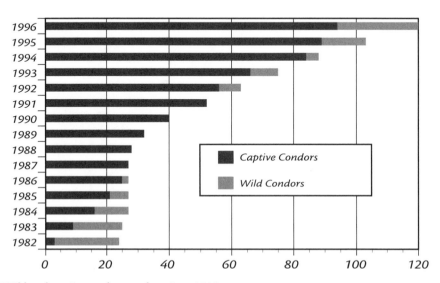

Wild and captive condor numbers since 1982

In Focus: Brown Pelican

Brown pelican

Brown pelican distribution

Distribution

The brown pelican (*Pelecanus occidentalis*) inhabits the Atlantic, Pacific, and Gulf Coasts of both North and South America. On the Atlantic Coast, brown pelicans can be found from Virginia southward; on the Pacific, from central California southward; and on the Gulf of Mexico, on the coasts of Alabama, Louisiana, and Texas.

Description

The smallest member of the pelican family, the brown pelican stands 42 to 54 inches tall, has a wingspan of 6.5 to 7.5 feet, and weighs 8 to 10 pounds. It has a brown and white neck, a white head capped in yellow, a grayish bill and pouch, a brown-streaked back, rump, and tail, and a dark brown belly. Its legs and feet are black.

Habitat

Rarely seen inland or far out at sea, brown pelicans prefer coastlines. They nest in open areas on islands free of mammal predators.

Life History

"A wonderful bird is the pelican,
his bill will hold more than his belican.
He can take in his beak
Food enough for a week,
But I'm darned if I see how the helican."
—Dixon L. Merrit, *The Pelican*

Indeed, the pelican's pouch holds up to three times more than its stomach. In addition to acting as a dipnet, the pouch keeps the pelican's catch until the water can be squeezed out. The pouch serves as a feeding trough for young pelicans and, in hot weather, as a cooling radiator. Primarily fish eaters, pelicans consume up to 4 pounds of fish a day, mostly "rough" fish such as menhaden, herring, sheepshead, pigfish, mullet, and minnows, species not considered important commercially.

Gregarious, male and female pelicans of all ages congregate in large flocks much of the year. They nest in colonies on the ground, in bushes, or in the tops of trees. Females lay two or three white eggs. Upon hatching, the young are altricial—blind, featherless, and completely dependent upon their parents. They fly about seventy-five days after hatching.

Brown pelicans have few natural enemies, although hurricanes and floods sometimes destroy their nests.

Status

People have hunted pelicans for their feathers. Fisherman, believing pelicans compete for fish, slaughtered them by the tens of thousands. Brown pelican populations also suffered from eggshell thinning caused by pesticides.

President Theodore Roosevelt designated Florida's Pelican Island as the first national wildlife refuge in 1903. In 1970, the U.S. Fish and Wildlife Service listed the bird as endangered. By 1985, brown pelican populations had recovered on the Atlantic Coast of the U.S., including all of Florida and Alabama, and the agency removed those populations from the Endangered Species List. Gulf and Pacific Coast populations are still classified as endangered.

North America's Most Familiar Goose

Canada geese (*Branta canadensis*), probably more abundant now than at any time in the last several hundred years, are the most widely distributed and variable species (in terms of visible characteristics) of bird in North America. Breeding populations inhabit every province and territory of Canada and forty-nine of the states in the U.S.

Market hunting and poor stewardship led to record low numbers of geese in the early 1900s and to the near extinction of several subspecies. But regulated seasons, closures, refuges, and stronger law enforcement led to restoration of most populations. The winter surveys of geese that started in 1936–37 are the oldest continuing index of migratory birds in North America.

The smaller subspecies of Canada geese nest farther north in the arctic and subarctic regions of Alaska and Canada, and, as a general rule, winter farther south (in the Gulf States and Mexico) than do larger subspecies. Hunters over-harvested most wintering populations of both subspecies in the early 1900s. By 1930, the giant Canada goose (*B. c. maxima*), which nested in the northern parts of the deciduous forest and tallgrass prairie, was considered extinct. Numbers of the large geese that nested in the Great Plains and Great Basin (*B. c. moffitti*) suffered serious declines. Small Canada geese from the remote arctic and subarctic breeding ranges fared better, but they too had been reduced in number.

While hunting depleted the number of Canada geese, agriculture and other human activities created new goose habitat. Farming led to the clearing of forests and the plowing of prairies. Cereal grains and pastures provided new sources of food, and the development of mechanical combines and pickers left behind waste grain. After the signing of the Migratory Bird

Treaty in 1916, uniform hunting regulations and improved wildlife law enforcement curtailed goose harvests. Most populations increased over the next several decades, and national wildlife refuges provided sanctuaries that aided the recovery.

Harold C. Hanson, a biologist with the Illinois Natural History Survey, rediscovered a population of the giant Canada goose, thought to have been extinct for decades. The publication of his book *The Giant Canada Goose* in 1965 initiated a large-scale restoration effort that eventually enabled the subspecies to reclaim its former range in the Mississippi and Central Flyways. Giant Canada geese now breed in all states east of the Mississippi River.

Research and scientific management in the 1970s led to a better understanding of

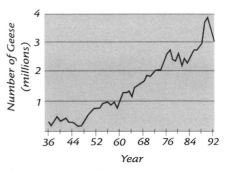

Canada goose population growth since the 1930s

the diversity, distribution, and population dynamics of Canada geese. Awareness of differences in distribution and migration patterns among the subspecies allowed managers to improve and control goose harvests. The Mississippi-Flyway–Giant, Hi-line, Rocky-Mountain, and Western-

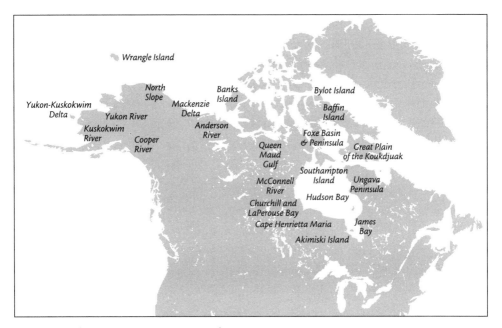

Major Canada goose nesting areas in North America

Prairie–Great-Plains populations, all composed mainly of large subspecies, grew at about twice the rate of populations of mainly smaller subspecies. The number of the large geese that breed in Atlantic Flyway states also increased dramatically.

Although small geese generally have not fared as well as large geese, which migrate shorter distances, some of the small subspecies have responded to more intensive management. Introduced Arctic foxes depleted island populations of the Aleu-

tian Canada goose (*B. c. leucopareia*), and the subspecies had nearly vanished by 1940. But biologists discovered about three hundred in the Aleutians, on Buldir Island, in 1962. The subsequent removal of foxes and transplants of wild geese boosted that population to 11,000 by 1993. Heavy hunting depleted numbers of cackling Canada geese. Populations plummeted to record lows in the early 1980s, but with intensive research and hunting controls, the geese recovered.

The Subspecies of Canada Geese (*Branta canadensis*)

The weights of the eleven recognized subspecies of Canada geese range from 3 pounds for the cackling Canada goose (*B. c. minima*) to 11 pounds for the giant Canada goose (*B. c. maxima*). The large-bodied subspecies are mainly continental in distribution, while the small-bodied ones breed in coastal Alaska and Arctic Canada. Recent genetic studies of the subspecies indicate that all subspecies shared a common ancestor about 1 million years ago. The twelve subspecies are listed below:

Large-Bodied Canada Geese

Atlantic Canada Geese (*Branta canadensis canadensis*)

Hudson Bay or Interior Canada Geese (*B. c. interior*)

Giant Canada Geese (*B. c. maxima*)

Western or Great Basin Canada Geese (*B. c. moffitti*)

Vancouver Canada Geese (*B. c. fulva*)

Dusky Canada Geese (*B. c. occidentalis*)

Small-Bodied Canada Geese

Baffin Island Canada Geese (*Branta canadensis hutchinsii*)

Taverner's or Alaskan Canada Geese (*B. c. taverneri*)

Cackling Canada Geese (*B. c. minima*)

Aleutian Canada Geese (*B. c. leucopareia*)

Lesser or Athabasca Canada Geese (*B. c. parvipes*)

Shorebird Staging Areas

Shorebirds—sandpipers, plovers, oyster-catchers, avocets, and stilts—inhabit more than the continent's shores. They visit desert, grassland, forest, mountain, tundra, and wetland habitats as well. Habitat losses over the past 150 years and unregulated and excessive hunting prior to 1918 hurt many populations. Today, some species remain in decline while others that did recover suffer new threats. During migration, shorebirds depend on a few critical "staging areas"—places where the birds pause to feed and replenish their energy reserves before continuing on their long-distance journeys. Because these areas are increasingly threatened by development, biologists consider all species of shorebirds vulnerable to extinction, even those with apparently healthy populations.

Habitat losses continue. The draining and degradation of wetlands is perhaps the most serious threat. On average, western states in the U.S. have lost 37 percent of their wetlands; many of those were areas vital to shorebirds. Grassland and coastline habitats, also key, have declined in similar proportions. The snowy plover, a species dependent on coastal habitats, has disappeared from almost two-thirds of its historic California nesting sites since 1970.

During migration, over 20 million shorebirds take to the air. Large proportions of all sanderlings, ruddy turnstones, red knots, dunlins, and white-rumped, Baird's, western, and semipalmated sandpipers visit a small number of staging areas. The Copper River Delta in Alaska, the Bay of Fundy in New Brunswick and Nova Scotia, the Cheyenne Bottoms in Kansas, and the Delaware Bay in New Jersey and Delaware are among the most important. Over the course of just two or three weeks, hundreds of thousands to millions of shorebirds—more than 80 percent of the entire North American population of some species—stop at any one of these staging areas, their arrival precisely synchronized with great "blooms" of invertebrates. Delaware Bay, a typical staging area, supports an enormous number of horseshoe crabs. Arriving precisely at the end of the crabs' breeding cycle, shorebirds gorge for weeks on crab eggs. They build energy reserves necessary for continuing their migration. An individual bird can gain up to 25 percent of its body weight in a few days of feeding. In recent decades, development has

Long-billed curlew

wiped out both feeding grounds and nearby roosting sites. Today, researchers report that 100,000 birds are often crammed into 200 to 300 yards of beach during high tide.

Shorebird populations show both increasing and decreasing trends. West of the Great Plains, populations of willets and upland sandpipers seem to have rebounded over the last twenty-five years, while many others, such as the black-necked stilt, the marbled godwit, and the spotted sandpiper, appear to have stabilized at lower levels. However, populations of snowy plovers, mountain plovers, American golden plo-

vers, killdeer, American avocets, long-billed curlews, common snipes, and Wilson's phalaropes have all dropped significantly. The status of other species in the West is unknown.

East of the Rockies, snowy, piping, and mountain plovers, killdeer, red knots, sanderlings, whimbrels, semipalmated and least sandpipers, short-billed dowitchers, phalaropes, and common snipes are all declining significantly, as is perhaps the black-bellied plover. Only a concerted effort to protect areas they use will allow North America's shorebirds to survive.

Number of shorebird species breeding and wintering in selected regions

In Focus: Marbled Murrelet

Marbled murrelet

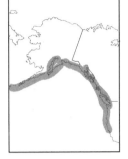

Marbled murrelet distribution

Distribution

In summer, marbled murrelets (*Brachyramphus marmoratus*) range from Alaska's Kenai Peninsula and the Barren and Aleutian Islands south along the coast to Point Sal in south-central California. In winter, their distribution shifts slightly to the south.

Description

Robin-sized, the marbled murrelet is a pelagic bird with a long, slender bill (relative to other murrelets) and a short tail. Its winter plumage is dark gray on the back and white on the scapulars, throat, and breast. In summer, the marbled murrelet's back feathers turn brown; the throat and breast become a mottled brown and white.

Habitat

In northern regions, where coniferous forests are unavailable, marbled murrelets nest on the tundra near the ocean. In Washington and Oregon, they nest in trees in old-growth stands of Douglas fir, mountain hemlock, western red cedar, or Sitka spruce; in California, in mixed redwood forests. The birds spend most of their time within a mile or so of the Pacific, although they have been found up to 60 miles inland. They forage in the ocean, near the shore, and in bays, sounds, and saltwater passages. Occasionally, marbled murrelets feed on freshwater lakes inland.

Life History

Marbled murrelets do not breed until they are at least two years old. Depending on latitude, they nest from mid-April to late September and are semicolonial in their nesting habits. Not all adults nest, and those that do lay only a single egg, which is incubated by both parents for about thirty days. Once the chicks hatch, adults fly from their ocean feeding grounds to nest sites at dusk and dawn. They feed their nestlings at least once and sometimes twice a day or night. The chicks fledge in twenty-eight days and fly directly from the nest to the ocean.

Marbled murrelets do not feed in large flocks, although loose aggregations occur in the winter. During the breeding season, the birds feed in pairs or as single individuals, their food consisting of small fish and underwater invertebrates.

Status

In the U.S., the marbled murrelet is listed as a threatened species. Both California and Oregon classify the bird as a critically imperiled species; Washington State, as rare or uncommon; Alaska, as widespread and abundant, but precarious over the long-term; and British Columbia, as rare or uncommon.

The cutting of old-growth forests is the principal factor threatening the marbled murrelet in the south. Gill nets kill some birds (for example, in Barkley Sound off Vancouver Island, British Columbia, fishermen's nets took an estimated 380 marbled murrelets in 1980, almost one-tenth of the fall population for that area). Marbled murrelets are also vulnerable to oil spills, perhaps more so than any other seabird in North America.

Part Nine
MAMMALS

Contents

NUMBERS AND DISTRIBUTION

WARMER CLIMATES TEND TO SUPPORT more species than cooler ones, so the diversity of mammals in North America increases from north to south. This trend is largely due to the number of bat species found in the tropics. Exclude bats, and the trend becomes much less apparent (see maps); only in Canada does the number of species really drop. The regions of highest diversity in temperate North America and tropical Mexico possess approximately the same number of species, between eighty and ninety.

In another trend, the West supports more species than the East. Compare the sixty to seventy species found in many of the eastern seaboard states with the ninety-plus species found across much of California. Repeated Pleistocene glaciations, which isolated many species on habitat "islands" in western mountain ranges, may explain the difference.

Wapiti or elk

In a third trend, mountainous areas, whether they occur east or west, host a higher number of species than hilly or flat terrains. Mountains contain a greater range of altitudes and exposures and offer more habitats. More habitats support more species. Speciation may also depend on land shape. Peninsulas like the Aleutian, Seward, Boothia, Melville, Nova Scotia, Baja, Florida, and Yucatan are relatively species poor. Generally, fingers of land are susceptible to local extinctions because immigration can occur in only one direction.

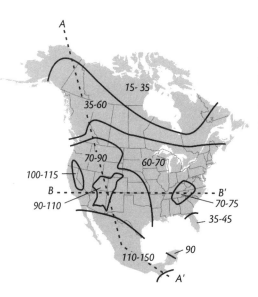

Mammal species density for all mammals

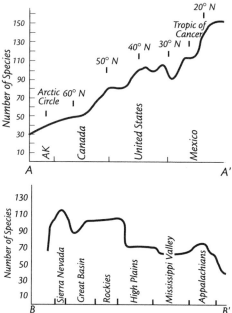

Species density north to south (A to A') is shown at top, and west to east (B to B') at bottom

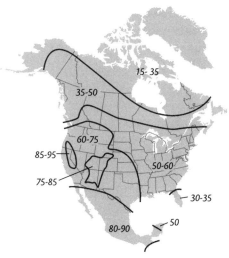

Mammal species density when bats are excluded

NUMBER OF MAMMALS BY SELECTED HABITATS

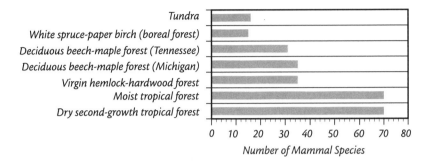

Tundra
White spruce-paper birch (boreal forest)
Deciduous beech-maple forest (Tennessee)
Deciduous beech-maple forest (Michigan)
Virgin hemlock-hardwood forest
Moist tropical forest
Dry second-growth tropical forest

0   10   20   30   40   50   60   70   80
Number of Mammal Species

MAMMALIAN DISTRIBUTION BY BIOGEOGRAPHIC REALM

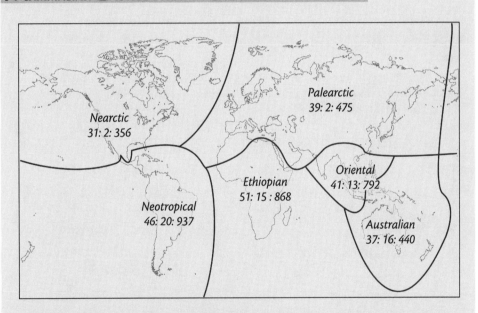

Palearctic
39: 2: 475

Nearctic
31: 2: 356

Oriental
41: 13: 792

Ethiopian
51: 15 : 868

Neotropical
46: 20: 937

Australian
37: 16: 440

This map of the world's biogeographic realms shows the number of families, the number of endemic families, and the number of species in each realm. The number of species is an approximation; the figures do not include mammal species found only in transitional areas. Other, more inclusive tallies put the number of mammal species found in the Nearctic, which includes all but the tropical parts of North America, at 423. The two endemic families in Nearctic (families that occur nowhere else) are those of the mountain beaver (Aplodontidae) and the pronghorn antelope (Antilocapridae).

Relations

The chart below describes the similarity of North America's temperate mammal fauna with that of other biogeographical realms. Not surprisingly, North America's fauna is most closely tied to the Neotropics and the Palearctic, both connected to North America by land bridges either currently or in the recent past. The continent is most distant from the Ethiopian and Australian realms.

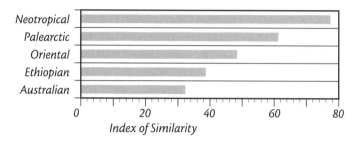

Index of Similarity

NORTH AMERICA'S LINKS WITH THE NEOTROPICS

Central America has acted as a filter regulating the north-south movement of species. Most of the migration has been from north to south; only a few South American species have managed to cross Central America to colonize the north.

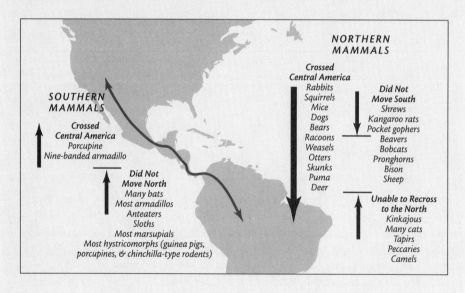

NORTHERN MAMMALS

Crossed
Central America
Rabbits
Squirrels
Mice
Dogs
Bears
Racoons
Weasels
Otters
Skunks
Puma
Deer

Did Not
Move South
Shrews
Kangaroo rats
Pocket gophers
Beavers
Bobcats
Pronghorns
Bison
Sheep

Unable to Recross
to the North
Kinkajous
Many cats
Tapirs
Peccaries
Camels

SOUTHERN MAMMALS

Crossed
Central America
Porcupine
Nine-banded armadillo

Did Not
Move North
Many bats
Most armadillos
Anteaters
Sloths
Most marsupials
Most hystricomorphs (guinea pigs,
porcupines, & chinchilla-type rodents)

Mostly Rodents and Bats

Fifty-six percent of the mammal species in temperate North America are rodents. In the warmest parts of the continent, the group dominates as well. Rodents comprise 48 percent of the mammal species in Mexico. The number of bat species in North America increases from north to south, a worldwide pattern. The temperate portion of the continent has about fifty species; Mexico, a much smaller area, has 133. Bats comprise about 30 percent of Mexico's mammalian fauna.

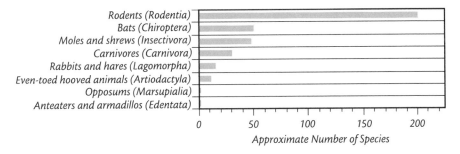

The number of species in each of the orders of temperate North American mammals

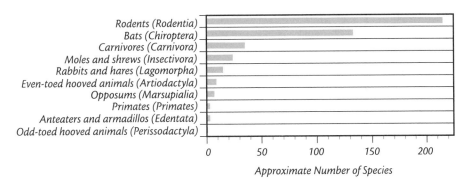

The number of species in each of the orders of Mexican mammals

Following the general pattern, the number of species in Mexico increases from north to south. Baja and the eastern foothills of the Sierra Madre Occidental support the fewest. Tropical species, like tapirs, monkeys, anteaters, and armadillos, are mostly restricted to parts of the Yucatan Peninsula and the coast. Rabbit, hare, mole, and shrew diversity is highest around central Mexico. Rodent species are numerous throughout most of Mexico, whereas bats reach their greatest diversity south of Mexico City.

NATURAL HISTORY

Grizzly Bears in the Continental U.S.

IN 1850, GRIZZLY BEARS ROAMED MOST of the western U.S., from the Great Plains to the Pacific Coast. By 1920, they had vanished from 95 percent of their original range. Unregulated hunting continued through the 1950s, and, by 1970, grizzly bears had suffered a further 52 percent decline in their range. They survived only in remote wilderness areas larger than 10,000 square miles.

Because of this dramatic decline and the uncertain status of the few remaining grizzly bear populations, the U.S. Fish and Wildlife Service listed the grizzly bear as a threatened species in 1975. Today, the species persists in only five areas: the Northern Continental Divide (NCDE), Greater Yellowstone (GYE), Cabinet-Yaak (CYE), Selkirk (SE), and North Cascade (NCE) Ecosystems. All these populations except Yellowstone's retain some biological con-

nection with grizzlies in southern Canada, although the future prospects of Canadian grizzly bears are subject to debate. The U.S. portions of these five populations exist in federally designated recovery areas, where they receive the full protection of the Endangered Species Act.

A few grizzly bears may also occur in the San Juan Mountains of southern Colorado and the Bitterroot Ecosystem of Idaho and Montana. The U.S. Fish and Wildlife Service has proposed reintroducing grizzlies into the Bitterroot Mountains but not the San Juans.

Recent research in the Northern Continental Divide, Yellowstone, and Selkirk Ecosystems estimates that the Northern Continental Divide Ecosystem harbors a minimum of 175 bears, the Yellowstone Ecosystem at least 142, and the Cabinet-Yaak, Selkirk, and North Cascade Ecosystems no more than 75 animals each.

There are few reliable estimates of population trends for any of the populations. In most cases, scientists lack the data necessary to make projections, and some populations are so small (for example, in the Selkirks) that the death of a few individuals can turn a growing population into a declining one. Current best estimates are that the largest populations—those in the Northern Continental Divide and Yellowstone areas—are stable or increasing slightly.

Among existing isolated populations of brown bears and grizzly bears worldwide, only populations above about 450 bears rebounded when given protection. Conversely, populations with fewer than two hundred bears continued to decline, even

after being protected. All of the smaller populations occupied areas of less than 3,900 square miles. This relationship between range size and vulnerability is consistent with the pattern seen in North America since 1920.

An exchange of genes among individuals and populations is important to the survival of populations. One geneticist estimated that populations of about five hundred interbreeding grizzlies may be required to maintain normal levels of genetic diversity. This "genetically effective" population size equates to total population sizes of around 2,000, because not all bears breed. Given that grizzly bears travel at most 28 to 65 miles from their mothers' range, it is unlikely that populations separated by greater distances exchange breeding animals. Bears may not move across large gaps where they are likely to get in trouble with humans.

Given these conditions, grizzly bear populations in the contiguous U.S. may not survive over the long term. The small populations in the North Cascade, Selkirk, and Bitterroot Ecosystems, the San Juan Mountains, and the U.S. portion of the Cabinet-Yaak Ecosystem are not viable. Even though the North Cascade Ecosystem encompasses almost 10,000 square miles, the bears there are isolated from other populations. The Cabinet-Yaak and Selkirk populations could mix with bears from Canada, but their ecosystems are small, about 2,000 square miles. Many of the U.S. populations that disappeared between 1920 and 1970 and many of the European populations currently in rapid decline live or lived in areas of this size.

Prospects for the larger Northern Continental Divide and Greater Yellowstone populations are better but still uncertain. The Yellowstone Ecosystem is isolated and contains at most 420 animals (the estimated maximum population); the long-term status of the population there seems tenuous. The Northern Continental Divide population probably has the best prospects; that population is the largest and is spread over the greatest area.

Bears in the Northern Continental Divide Ecosystem mingle with bears from other populations. Nonetheless, even the estimates of maximum population size place the Northern Continental Divide population near the threshold of 450 animals. The ecosystem approaches the 10,000-square-mile threshold size.

The future of the Selkirk, Cabinet-Yaak, and Northern Continental Divide populations hinges in large part on connections with Canadian grizzly populations. South-

ern Canadian grizzlies, however, lack protection; outside of national parks, they are hunted legally. There is also serious debate over the status of the Canadian populations, especially in southwestern Alberta and the northern Selkirks. Thus, Canadian grizzlies may not guarantee the long-term survival of those U.S. populations.

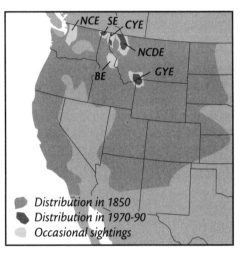

Distribution in 1850
Distribution in 1970-90
Occasional sightings

Grizzly bear distribution in 1850 and the populations that remain today

Recent Grizzly Bear Population Trends

Ecosystem	Pop. Size Est.	Viability
Northern Continental Divide	175–514	?
Greater Yellowstone	142–420	?
Cabinet-Yaak	9–55	Not Viable
Selkirk	26–36	Not Viable
North Cascade	10–20	Not Viable
Bitterroot	0–?	Not Viable
San Juan	0–?	Not Viable

Sculptor of the Boreal Forest

Moose are not ancient animals. They first appear in the fossil record about 2 million years ago, just after the last ice age started. Boreal forests, the primary habitat of moose, originated about the same time. The two have been shaping each other ever since.

Weighing over 1,000 pounds, moose possess big appetites and feed in many different plant communities—wetlands, wet coniferous forests, not-so-wet coniferous forests, and young deciduous forests. Of the trees that make up the boreal forest, moose prefer browsing on aspen, poplar, and birch over conifers like spruce and balsam fir. Deciduous species move in first after a disturbance like a fire, grow fast, and produce a leaf litter rich in nitrogen and quick to decompose—all traits conifers lack.

By browsing both voraciously and selectively, moose influence the composition and structure of boreal forest communities. Under certain conditions, they shift the makeup of the forest from deciduous to coniferous. They create what biologists refer to as "spruce-moose savannas." And because conifers produce a more sterile and recalcitrant leaf litter and less of it, moose alter soil formation. In heavily browsed areas, soil carbon and nitrogen drop, as does

In northern forests, moose shape everything from the soil on up.

the ability of the soil to exchange ions. The changes cause a decrease in soil microbial activity, processes that determine how much nitrogen is available in the soil for plants. Nitrogen is the limiting nutrient in boreal forest communities, so the productivity of spruce is affected, as are the natural processes that allow one plant community to succeed another. The populations of moose and most other animals in the boreal forest reflect these changes in soil and vegetation. Because they exert a disproportionately large effect on the environment, biologists call moose a keystone species. Without moose, the boreal forest would not be the same place.

The Ups and Downs of Snowshoe Hares and Aspen

In the boreal forest, populations of snowshoe hares fluctuate with extraordinary regularity and synchrony. Roughly every ten years their numbers increase by as much as two hundredfold, and it occurs simultaneously across several million square miles of country. Then, precipitously, the population crashes, dropping by as much as 50 to 90 percent in a single winter, the declines occurring even though the hares are continuously breeding throughout the summer and conditions for survival appear good. Most researchers attribute the collapses to high levels of predation helped along by food shortages, severe weather, and to a lesser extent, disease.

Food shortages probably affect predation more than anything else. When malnourished, snowshoe hares are much more vulnerable to predators than when well fed. Biologists were puzzled, however, that peak populations of hares became malnourished despite an abundance of food. The plants appeared to hold the key.

Snowshoe hares prefer willow and aspen as browse. Both are normally less resinous and, therefore, more palatable than other plants. Consequently, when hare populations peak, young aspen trees are overbrowsed. Without any defense, continuous overbrowsing would kill aspen. But heavy feeding stimulates the trees to sprout new shoots high in foul-tasting compounds—chemicals like terpenes and phenolic resins that hinder protein digestion and vitamin production in hares. Thus, just as the hare population peaks, the hares are robbed of one of their most important foods and must turn to other, less nutritious foods, which they quickly overbrowse. Starvation and malnutrition set in, predators gather, and the population crashes. Spared further overbrowsing, the aspen trees stop producing repellent chemicals, which are energy-expensive substances rich in carbon. The trees put those resources back into growth and renew themselves.

Mediated in part by aspen trees, snowshoe hare populations rise and fall in ten-year cycles.

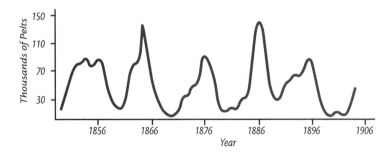

Snowshoe hare population levels as reflected in pelt collections by Hudson Bay Company posts along Hudson Bay

Cycles of Mammals, Trees, and Lyme Disease in Eastern Forests

Understanding how natural systems function is the work of community ecologists. As scientists, they typically focus their studies on the direct interactions of two or three major species within a community—for example, a predator and its primary prey. But organisms interact in indirect ways as well. Subtle connections often involve many species and can take years of study to reveal. Take, for example, research conducted by the Institute of Ecosystem Studies on the connections between oaks, deer, mice, ticks, and gypsy moths in North America's eastern deciduous forests.

Oaks are among the dominant trees in eastern forests. Certain of them—white oak, red oak, and chestnut oak—are mast seeders; that is, every two to six years, they produce enormous quantities of acorns. During off years, they produce few or none. Good mast years are a boon to insects, birds, and mammals; the populations of dozens of species ebb and flow with the oaks' cycles. Among the mammals most tied to mast are white-footed mice, east-

ern chipmunks, and white-tailed deer. Because of their sheer numbers or biomass, they in turn, affect the populations of many other species, including animals that may not feed on acorns. Chipmunks, for example, are major predators of the eggs and nestlings of ground-nesting birds. White-footed mice consume a large percentage of gypsy moth pupae. Both mice and chipmunks compete with birds for nonmast seeds, and both feed a host of predators such as raptors and foxes. Through overbrowsing, white-tailed deer inhibit the growth and survival of tree seedlings in the understory. That, in turn, adversely affects the abundance and diversity of songbirds. Good mast years can set off a cascade of interlocking events that determines how the forest and its inhabitants prosper.

During a good mast year, white-tailed deer move from the maple-woodland habitats they normally favor into oak-dominated stands. There, they feed almost exclusively on acorns. During the winters that

White-footed mouse and acorn

The stages in the lives of a tick: eggs, larvae, and adult

follow good mast years, female white-tailed deer bear more twins. A surge in the deer population typically follows a good mast year.

As the deer move through the forest, they collect adult ticks. The ticks feed and mate on the deer and then drop off into the leaf litter on the forest floor in the fall. There, ticks lay their eggs the following spring. So, during good mast years, they lay them in oak-dominated stands. In the summers following mast years, the oak stands see an eruption of larval ticks.

Fluctuations in acorn production also affect the white-footed mouse. During mast years, mice, like deer, gorge on acorns. They put on fat and gather caches of the nuts—enough to see them through the winter. The extra stores translate into higher survival rates and allow a considerable number of mice to breed during the winter. Mice seldom breed during the winters of nonmast years. The result is an explosion in the mouse population the following summer, just as the larval ticks are at their peak.

White-footed mice are not only the favored host of larval ticks but also carry the Lyme disease microbe in their blood. Mice are chiefly responsible for infecting ticks

with the disease. The larval ticks enter the nymph stage of their life cycle and seek hosts the following summer. Carried by mice dispersing from the oak stands, the nymphs spread across an ever wider area. As adults, ticks bite humans and transmit Lyme disease.

Gypsy moths play another part in this web. Accidentally introduced to the U.S. in the 1800s, gypsy moths are voracious herbivores that eat oak leaves. Like the mammals, their populations cycle. During peaks they defoliate vast expanses of the forest. They can kill mature oaks. In this way, gypsy moths alter the natural cycle of mast production. An outbreak can delay or even eliminate a mast year.

Scientists only recently discovered the reason for long lapses between gypsy moth population peaks. Apparently, white-footed mice, the major predator of the moth pupae, mediate the cycles and help maintain moth populations at low levels. It seems that gypsy moths cannot rebound until the mouse population collapses. Even at moderate levels, the populations of mice keep gypsy moths under control by eating 90 percent of the pupae. When the mice are at low densities, however, only about half the pupae get eaten, 20 percent of those by white-footed mice. Thus, gypsy moths, which manipulate the cycle of mast years, are themselves manipulated—via mouse predation—by the production of acorns. When gypsy moths defoliate a forest, more saplings grow in the understory. The acorn-mouse-gypsy-moth cycle ultimately changes the vegetative composition of the forest itself.

Beavers Build More Than Dams

Before Europeans arrived in North America, beavers numbered (depending on the expert consulted) between 60 and 400 million. Populating virtually every stream in North America from the Arctic to northern Mexico, beavers altered the courses and flows of streams and the composition and diversity of plant and animal communities.

Beavers build lots of dams when their populations are high—twenty or more beaver ponds per mile of stream is not unusual when the topography and food conditions are right. Beaver dams increase the amount of beaver habitat and reduce the threat posed to beavers by predators. The dams also trap sediment. A small beaver dam will contain as much as 230,000 cubic feet of sediment. Full of carbon and nutrients, the sediment helps to stabilize communities, which is partly why stream bottoms with beaver ponds respond more quickly after disturbances like fire.

Beaver ponds also affect aquatic organisms. Whereas an undammed stretch of stream might support mostly blackflies and the kinds of midges, mayflies, and caddisflies that favor moving water, an equivalent segment of stream with a beaver pond will harbor those same species along with an assortment of slack-water midges, dragonflies, aquatic worms, and filtering clams. A section of stream with beaver ponds will support two to five times the number of invertebrates.

Beavers harvest trees and shrubs to build dams. A single beaver family will cut over a metric ton of wood per year within 100 yards of their pond. In addition, the ponds themselves flood and kill many trees and shrubs. Removing all that vegetation transforms the riparian zone. In northern areas, the beavers cut trees like aspen, birch, and cottonwood. Shrubs like alder and hazel and young aspen trees sprout up in response. Ultimately, black spruce and balsam fir, species the beavers avoid, replace the shrubs. These changes in the plant community attract a different set of insects, birds, and mammals. Stream temperatures change too, because of reduced shading. Communities of aquatic organisms are altered in turn.

Beavers also influence the way nitrogen is cycled in and around streams. Research shows that plant-available nitrogen is four times greater under the kind of flooded and water-logged conditions beavers create. In one study, usable nitrogen, often a limiting nutrient, doubled over a forty-five-year period as a direct result of the wetlands created by beavers.

The fast-moving streams that we know today looked very different when beavers reigned. Ponds bordered by open canopies dotted the streams then, and along the stream banks stood flooded forests, marshes, and bogs. Although beaver populations in most areas are but a fraction of what they once were, the legacy of the animal remains in the stream channels and the plant and animal communities we see today.

Sometimes She Who Hesitates Has the Advantage

The pregnancies of a number of carnivores and an odd assortment of other mammals—armadillos, certain fruit bats, seals, walruses, bears, and roe deer—last much longer than would be expected on the basis of each animal's body size. The gestation period of the western spotted skunk (*Spilogale gracilis*), for example, extends 210 to 260 days. The gestation for the eastern spotted skunk (*Spilogale putorius*), until recently considered the same species as the western, endures just fifty days. Biologists attribute the western spotted skunk's prolonged pregnancy, and that of over a dozen other North American carnivores, to a special adaptation called delayed implantation.

Among most mammals, after ovulation occurs, the egg travels down the oviduct, where it is fertilized and begins to develop. A few days later, the egg enters the uterus, implants itself on the uterine wall, and continues to develop as an embryo. This is the normal sequence of events, but in animals that exhibit delayed implantation, development is halted. The fertilized egg, called a blastocyst, does not immediately attach to the uterus but floats free for a time—anywhere from a few days to ten months, depending on the species.

Researchers propose several theories to explain why delayed implantation developed. One speculates that in some species the adaptation enables the young to be born as early as possible in the spring so they are better able to face their first winter. Without delayed implantation, the young of some species would be born in late fall or winter, a difficult if not impossible time for them to survive. Among other animals, the delay may be a physiological response to the drop in body temperature that occurs during hibernation. But even for these animals, arresting embryo development might prove useful. By temporarily uncoupling breeding and birthing, each could occur at its optimum time.

Biologist Rodney Mead of the University of Idaho put forth a scenario for how delayed implantation developed among spotted skunks. The pygmy spotted skunk (*Spilogale pygmaea*), thought to be the oldest species in its genus, evolved in Central America or southern Mexico and migrated north. The species now ranges across much of Mexico. Pygmy spotted skunks give birth to two litters a year and show no evidence of delayed implantation. Their gestation period lasts forty-eight days. The eastern and western spotted skunks probably descended from the pygmy and invaded regions to the north after the last ice age. Like the pygmy, the eastern species, which occasionally has two litters a year, shows no evidence of delayed implantation. Pregnancy in the western species, on the other hand, lasts five times longer than that of either of the other two. The western spotted skunk mates in September. The fertilized egg undergoes normal development until the blastocyst stage then floats in the uterus for two hundred days before implanting, when gestation proceeds. Western spotted skunks give birth about thirty days later, in May.

In Mexico, the climate is warm enough for pygmy spotted skunks to enjoy an extended breeding season that allows for two litters a year. But the populations that ventured north into new habitats had to adapt to shorter summers and fewer hours of daylight in the spring. Shorter days delay the onset of spring breeding and push back the onset of a second estrus. For these skunks, the second pregnancy would occur in the fall of the year when the days grew shorter. With increasing hours of darkness, the pineal glands in the pregnant females increase their production of melatonin. That, in turn, causes a chain of events—altered hypothalamic-pituitary function, which leads to reduced ovarian function. Unprepared, the uterus cannot accept the blastocysts. They arrive but fail to attach, floating free until the days are longer again, and the production of melatonin drops off. Thus skunks conceiving in late summer or fall give birth in the spring. Lactation delays the onset of estrus until fall, and the cycle repeats. In the case of western spotted skunks, this was apparently a lucky circumstance, because delayed implantation meant the babies conceived the previous fall were born early in the spring, thirty days before the babies conceived in the spring. Those early skunks had an advantage because by the close of the summer they were better able to survive their first winter. Skunks with delayed implantation passed on more offspring than those without.

The chart below shows the length of time blastocysts remain dormant in some North American mammals with delayed implantation.

PERIOD OF DELAYED IMPLANTATION IN MAMMALS

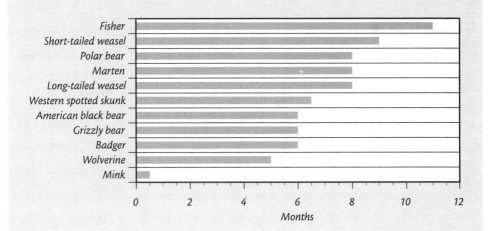

IN FOCUS: MOUNTAIN LION

Mountain lion

Mountain lion distribution

Distribution

Mountain lions (*Felis concolor*), also known as cougars, pumas, or panthers, inhabit more of the Western Hemisphere than any other native mammal. Before Europeans arrived, their distribution extended across almost all of the U.S. and Mexico and a large part of western Canada (the cats also occupied most of South America). Cougars still range from the Yukon Territory through most of South America, but their distribution is now patchy. Substantial populations remain only in the western U.S. and Canada, their numbers much reduced from pre-European times. At present, the only known mountain lion population east of Texas is in south Florida, although a small population may survive in western Arkansas and eastern Oklahoma. The Florida population is critically low; perhaps only fifty cats remain.

Description

Generally tawny-colored, mountain lion pelages vary from slate gray to reddish brown. The cat's size and weight also varies. Males average 7.8 feet in length and 175 to 200 pounds in weight; females, 6.5 feet and 75 to 175 pounds. Although mountain lions are large by most standards, zoologists classify them as "small cats," in part because their voice boxes are built like those of small cats—a series of bones connected so tightly that they are unable to vibrate enough to produce the kind of loud roars African lions make. Mountain lions also purr like domestic cats but with a lower tone.

Habitat

Perhaps the most adaptable native mammal in North America, mountain lions thrive in all types of habitats from deserts to coastal rainforests, from dry forests to grasslands, and from alpine areas to lowland swamps. Their preferred habitat is the same as that of deer, their primary prey. Mountain lions hunt in areas with cover. They travel along heavily vegetated stream courses and ridgetops; their dens are usually located in shallow hollows, in brushy thickets, or beneath logs. Perhaps no North American mammal is more reclusive than the cougar; the animal is seldom seen in the wild.

Life History

Mountain lions are polygamous. They first breed when they are two to three years old. Females are capable of breeding throughout the year. Litters range from one to four kittens, and usually a female delivers a litter every two or three years. The kittens gain weight rapidly. In ten to twenty days, they weigh over 2 pounds. After seven to eight weeks, the young cats follow their mother to her kills. She weans them days thereafter. Most young cougars can survive on their own after six months but typically stay with their mothers until they are one or two years old.

Mountain lions, one of the only solitary predators that consistently prey on animals larger than themselves, feed almost exclusively on deer, elk, and, sometimes, young moose. Depending on where mountain lions live, they may also take bighorn sheep, beavers, marmots, porcupines, snowshoe hares, wild hogs, peccaries, rac- coons, armadillos, domestic dogs, and an assortment of small mammals. Between 1890 and 1990, mountain lions attacked fifty-three people in Canada and the U.S.; nine of those people died as a result. Surprisingly, twenty of the attacks took place on Vancouver Island, British Columbia. Wolves occasionally kill adult lions; a number of predators, among them grizzly bears, black bears, and golden eagles, may prey on kittens.

Status

Most western populations have increased steadily over the past ten or fifteen years. The U.S. government, however, lists the Yuma puma as a Category 2 species, meaning they may qualify for endangered or threatened status once more information is collected. Wisconsin pumas share that status. Florida panthers are listed as endangered; according to the Nature Conservancy, the cat is critically imperiled in Florida, Arkansas, Louisiana, and South Carolina. Eastern cougars are also listed as endangered, although they may be extinct. Habitat loss poses the greatest threat to vulnerable mountain lion populations.

A Natural Arms-Race: Bats and Their Prey

Echolocation is the term used to describe the process by which animals use pulses of sound to orient themselves or to locate food. Besides bats, toothed (and possibly baleen) whales, porpoises, dolphins, and killer whales use echolocation, as do some species of birds and shrews. Rats, pack rats, seals, and humans use this form of sonar, too, although not as well. The best echolocators are dolphins and bats.

Insect-catching bats employ echolocation to determine the exact position of insects. A bat must capture an insect every three to five seconds while flying in order not to starve. Bats determine the distance to prey by measuring the time lag between their vocalizations and the returning echos. By comparing how each of their ears receives the echoes, they judge the angular position of the target.

Studies show that echolocation enables bats to distinguish between different kinds of insects, even similar ones. Apparently they detect wingbeat frequencies, flight angle, speed, wing size, body size, and shape. From this information, they construct auditory images, not unlike visual images. These sound pictures enable bats to select preferred prey.

To avoid being eaten by bats, insects possess their own set of tricks. Many—moths, crickets, katydids, lacewings, and mantids—evolved ears, some of which are tuned to the acoustic frequency of the bats that hunt them. They listen for the echolocation signals of hunting bats. When signaled, they either veer off or dive to the ground, depending on how far away the bat is.

Certain bats respond to this defensive tactic by garbling their signals—mismatching frequencies, emitting calls at low intensities, shortening the duration of the calls. In effect, they reduce the distance at which insects can detect them by as much as 92 percent. Other bats take this stealth strategy further. They use echolocation to direct them to the general vicinity of their prey, then become silent and rely on visual cues or wing sounds of the insects. Not only do these bats avoid alerting their quarry, they are less likely to attract the attention of their own brethren, potential competitors.

When attacked, tiger moths—small-to medium-sized moths usually with brightly spotted wings—emit chains of clicking sounds that mimic bat echolocation signals. Upon hearing the clicks, bats veer away. Perhaps the moth sounds interfere with or disrupt the bat's processing of its own signals, or perhaps they make the bat think the moth is another bat. Possibly the clicks startle the bat. In this last scenario, the moth sounds may operate like the large eyespots on the wings of some moths, which can scare potential predators. Lastly, the clicks may serve as a warning. Some species of tiger moths are poisonous. Painted lichen moths of Ontario, for example, do not evade swooping hoary bats or red bats but click instead. The bats abort their attack. When these tiger moths' noisemakers are damaged, the bats do not veer off but catch the moths then spit them out. Thus, the clicks might work like the bright colors on some poisonous butterflies or the rattles on rattlesnakes.

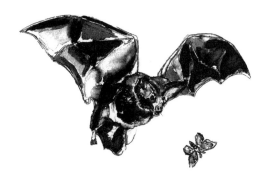

Fishing with Sound

Not all echolocating bats eat insects. Mexican fishing bats, which live in Mexico along the Gulf of California, use echolocation to find fish, their primary food. When their sonar picks up the dorsal fin of a fish breaking the water's surface, these bats swoop low, skim across the waves, and drag their extra-large hind feet through the water. Gaffing the fish with their sharp hind claws, the bats carry their catch back to land for consumption. Interestingly, Mexican fishing bats obtain all the water they need from the fish they eat. Because they spend most of their time over salt water, their kidneys are adapted to conserve water; the small amount of urine they do produce is highly concentrated.

THE DIVERSITY OF BATS

The diversity of bats at selected locations in North America. The first number is the number of families at that location, the second is the number of species. Bats are primarily tropical mammals, so diversity increases as one approaches the equator. Diversity increases east to west as well.

COMMON BATS OF NORTH AMERICA

Allen's big-eared bat	Long-legged myotis
Allen's yellow bat	Mexican big-eared bat
Big brown bat	Mexican fishing bat
Big free-tailed bat	Mexican free-tailed bat
California leaf-nosed bat	Mexican long-nosed bat
California myotis	Miller's myotis
Cave myotis	Northern yellow bat
Common vampire bat	Pallid bat
Eastern pipistrelle	Pocketed free-tailed bat
Evening bat	Rafinesque's big-eared bat
Flat-headed myotis	Red bat
Fringed myotis	Sanborn's long-nosed bat
Gray myotis	Seminole bat
Greater funnel-eared bat	Silver-haired bat
Hairy fruit-eating bat	Small-footed myotis
Hairy-legged vampire bat	Southeastern myotis
Highland fruit-eating bat	Southern yellow bat
Hoary bat	Southwestern myotis
Hog-nosed bat	Spotted bat
Indiana myotis	Townsend's big-eared bat
Keen's myotis	Underwood's mastiff bat
Leaf-chinned bat	Wagner's mastiff bat
Little brown myotis	Western pipistrelle
Long-eared myotis	Yuma myotis

Shrews: Small and Ancient

Although they look like little pointy-nosed rodents, shrews are members of the Insectivora order. They possess many early mammalian characteristics, those typical of dinosaur-era mammals: their brains are small (especially the portions we normally associate with intelligence), their skulls lack zygomatic arches, and their jaws bear a double articulating surface. Like reptiles, birds, and marsupials, most shrews possess cloacas; that is, their genital and urinary systems merge into a single opening. In addition, male shrews lack scrotums; their testicles remain inside their body cavity.

Successful mammals, shrews look much like they did 40 million years ago.

Shrews are known for their high-speed metabolism and the appetite that goes along with it. The average shrew respires at a rate twenty-five times that of a human. When they are excited, their hearts beat up to 1,320 times a minute. To feed the furnace that drives such an engine, shrews burn enormous quantities of food for their size. Most must eat every two or three hours or starve. Their diet encompasses just about any animals they can catch and eat—beetles, bugs, flies, butterflies, ants, earwigs, springtails, mites, spiders, harvestmen, wood lice, centipedes, millipedes, snails, slugs, and earthworms.

Some North American shrews use echolocation to navigate, much as bats do. The masked shrew, the wandering shrew, the water shrew, and the American short-tailed shrew all emit short, high-frequency sounds to find their way around new environments. One researcher trained wandering shrews to locate a small platform placed below them. The shrews leaped to the platform then ran along a narrow ramp to a box that contained a reward. Systematically precluding all other cues (such as visual and olfactory), the scientist showed that wandering shrews found their way with ultrasound.

Like bats, shrews consume enormous quantities of insects. Studies in pine plantations in Ontario found that masked and short-tailed shrews were the major predators controlling infestations of European and larch sawflies, major forest pests. Widespread, occupying a range of habitats, and exploiting a huge variety of prey species, shrews play a significant role in the continent's natural communities.

Shrews are among North America's most ancient mammals.

Shrew Diversity in North America

Genus	Common Name	No. of Species
Sorex	Red-toothed or long-tailed shrews	27
Blarina	Short-tailed shrews	4
Cryptotis	Small-eared shrew	1
Notiosorex	Desert shrew	1

The Physiology of Monogamy

Monogamy, not uncommon among birds, is rare in mammals; only 3 percent of mammals are monogamous. When it comes to forming long-lasting, male-female partnerships, humans are the exception, which is partly why researchers like C. S. Carter of the University of Maryland and L. L. Getz of the University of Illinois are interested in prairie voles (*Microtus ochrogaster*). Like us and just a few other mammals, prairie voles form long-lasting bonds with members of the opposite sex.

Scientists define monogamy as a lifelong association between a male and a female. They list a number of traits common to socially monogamous mammals, such as: males and females are generally similar in size and appearance; both parents participate in defending their young and their territories; both contribute to the rearing of the young; they live in elaborate social groups composed of extended family and offspring; and they avoid incest.

Socially monogamous behavior, however, does not necessarily include sexual fidelity. Prairie voles, like humans, sometimes seek sex with other partners.

Biologists have yet to discover the specific advantages that monogamy imparts to prairie voles—that is, the pressures in the environment that selected for monogamous behavior. But by comparing the physiology of prairie voles with that of other closely related, nonmonogamous species, they have identified some of the hormones that mediate the behavior.

Unlike the females of nonmonogamous vole species, female prairie voles do not enter estrus (sexual heat) until they smell a potential mate. Fathers and brothers do not trigger this reaction, only the pheromones of sufficiently unrelated males stimulate a female's ovaries and send her into heat. The smells induce the release of hormones affecting her receptivity. The same hormones operate in the females of nonmonogamous voles when they mate, but in prairie voles, the timing differs. Because the release of progesterone is delayed, a female prairie vole can engage in bouts of mating that last ten times longer than those of nonmonogamous voles (thirty to forty hours instead of two or three). Prairie vole sex extends beyond what is necessary to ensure the fertilization of their eggs. Carter and Getz believe that extended mating helps to establish lifelong bonds.

Nonmonogamous species of voles separate immediately after mating and may become aggressive toward each other if forced to remain in close proximity. After prairie voles mate, however, they keep touching and remain physically close. Previous research had associated the release of the hormone oxytocin with the bonding that occurs between a mother and her offspring (researchers call oxytocin the hormone of "mother love"). So Carter and Getz speculated oxytocin, which is produced in response to breast or genital stimulation, might also play a role in the bonding between monogamous pairs. Indeed, they found that in prairie voles, the receptors for oxytocin are much more numerous in those parts of the brain involved in sexual and social behavior than they are in polygamous voles' brains. By injecting oxytocin into female prairie voles and, conversely, administering drugs that block the action of oxytocin, scientists found evidence that the hormone plays a key role in the forming of monogamous social bonds.

Whereas prairie vole pairs remain socially close during nonreproductive periods, they can be vicious toward intruders—other voles looking to mate or steal food. The effects of oxytocin, it seems, do not extend beyond one's mate and offspring. Research shows that the structurally similar hormone vasopressin, also released during sexual behavior, is antagonistic toward oxytocin. Vasopressin appears to mediate defensive behavior and is associated with the aggression shown toward outsiders. Carter and Getz think a primary function of oxytocin is to block the more primitive, antisocial behavior caused by vasopressin.

Adrenal hormones may also come into play. Experiments show that male rats exposed to high levels of stress early in life (during the time they are undergoing sexual differentiation) tend to be more feminine in character and more inclined to care for their own offspring. The experiments suggest that the adrenal system, which is triggered during times of stress, inhibits the action of masculinizing hormones. In prairie voles, the adrenal glands are unusually reactive shortly after birth and may, in fact, be suppressing male hormones, which may account physiologically for the reduction in sexual differences between males and females and the higher level of parental care shown by males.

Hormones, of course, are not the ultimate cause of monogamous behavior in prairie voles. They simply mediate a design shaped by natural forces in the prairie vole's environment. Only by understanding those yet undescribed selection pressures will we grasp the significance of monogamy.

Prairie voles are among the 3 percent of mammals that are monogamous.

A Keystone of Desert Communities

Kangaroo rats, like pocket gophers, prairie dogs, snowshoe hares, pikas, beavers, wolves, and an assortment of other animals (and plants), are designated by ecologists as keystone species. They exist in relatively moderate numbers but exert an enormous influence on the communities in which they live. Loss of any species has an impact, but loss of a keystone species can disrupt or collapse an entire community.

Kangaroo rats are considered a keystone species.

In a recent study, James Brown and Edward Heske of the University of New Mexico removed three similar species of kangaroo rats from fenced plots in the Chihuahuan Desert of southeastern Arizona. The fences, low enough to allow large grazers to pass, were perforated with holes too small to let kangaroo rats back in but large enough to allow the passage of the desert's other rodents. Over the next twelve years, the researchers monitored the vegetation in the plots and compared them with the rest of the desert and with equivalent fenced plots containing kangaroo rats.

Over the long term, removing the rats caused dramatic changes in the desert's plant life. The vegetation community, in fact, changed from desert shrubland to grassland. The shift started when tall perennial and annual grasses invaded open spaces between shrubs. Some of these high grasses increased more than twentyfold, whereas short grasses became sparse. Over the longer term—about ten years—winter annuals with small seeds disappeared altogether, and those with large seeds multiplied. In fact, large-seeded annuals increased by as much as several thousand times. More leaf litter fell onto the desert floor, positively affecting soil formation and moisture levels. In winter, snow lasted longer in the plots without kangaroo rats.

Another change: seed-eating birds stopped visiting the plots without kangaroo rats, even though what had been bare ground with the kangaroo rats was now filled with grasses and forbs. Apparently, the birds, adapted to more open conditions, had trouble harvesting seeds in the denser conditions or felt too vulnerable to predators. Other faunal changes occurred as well. Six new species of rodents moved in, all characteristic of arid grasslands.

The researchers believe the changes came about in part because kangaroo rats are selective foragers. They eat mostly large seeds. Protected from that sort of foraging, the large-seeded plants multiplied at the expense of the small-seeded species. The changes created opportunities for other rodent species. Other effects relate to the runways that kangaroo rats make and to the large quantities of soil the rats move when they forage, cache food, and burrow. Evidently, these soil disturbances speed the decomposition of litter on the desert floor and encourage the establishment of certain plants. Altered vegetation affects the foraging of birds.

The eight other species of rodents that remained in the plots after the kangaroo rats had been removed did nothing to prevent the shift from shrubland to grassland. Clearly, not all animals are created equal. Some play disproportionately large roles in their communities. If maintaining particular ecosystems is the goal, identifying and protecting keystone species is crucial.

Up From Mexico: The Armadillo

While the ranges of many North American mammals are shrinking from habitat losses, a few species gain ground. Most of these increasers are generalists capable of adapting to human activities and developments; they fare better in human-altered settings than in purely natural ones. Among the most common examples are deer, foxes, coyotes, opossums, and rabbits. The nine-banded armadillo, a 2.5-foot-long armor-plated insect-eater, is another. The armadillo continues to increase its range by several hundred square miles each year.

Of twenty-one species of armadillo in the world, two occur in North America. The northern naked-tailed armadillo ranges from Ecuador into southern Mexico. The nine-banded, with the largest range of all the armadillos, lives from central Argentina into Kansas and Missouri. Common south of the U.S. border for thousands of years, the nine-banded armadillo first crossed into the U.S. about 150 years ago and has been expanding its range ever since.

Today, eight states—Texas, Louisiana, Arkansas, Oklahoma, Alabama, Mississippi, Florida, and Georgia—support healthy armadillo populations while the animal frequents six others—Tennessee, South Carolina, New Mexico, Kansas, Missouri, and Nebraska. It has even reached the barrier islands off South Carolina and Georgia. The armadillo continues to extend its range much faster than other mammals with expanding distributions. So why didn't the nine-banded armadillo invade this territory long ago, before European-Americans arrived? Why is the current dispersal proceeding so rapidly? And how far north will armadillos ultimately go?

Zoologists James Taulman and Lynn Robbins suggest that before 1850, Indian subsistence hunters took armadillos for

Over the last 150 years, the nine-banded armadillo has substantially expanded its range.

meat and materials and probably kept the nine-banded armadillo south of the Mexican border. By the 1850s, Indian hunting had stopped. Settlers farmed, grazed cattle, and suppressed fires. Those changes, combined with drought, led to the gradual replacement of tallgrass prairie with mesquite brushland. The brushlands produced more leaf litter, which increased habitat for insects and small vertebrates. Armadillos prefer brushlands over grasslands, and they forage in deep leaf litter.

Because armadillos generally won't cross wide rivers, lowering the water levels in south Texas rivers for agriculture probably contributed to the range expansion. Given droughts, irrigation withdrawals, and silt accumulations, the rivers could be forded. The armadillo also received some help from humans. Many populations, including those in Florida and Alabama, originated from released individuals.

Just how far north armadillos will go depends ultimately on climate. Taulman and Robbins argue the species is bounded by precipitation and temperature restrictions. Regions supporting wild populations will be those that receive at least 15 inches of precipitation a year and enjoy mean January temperatures higher than 28°F, or have fewer than twenty-four days a year in which the temperature falls below 32°F. Areas meeting these conditions are shown on the map below as the shaded area delineating potential armadillo distribution (the darker shading represents the animal's current distribution). Apparently, one day, armadillos will also populate the West Coast.

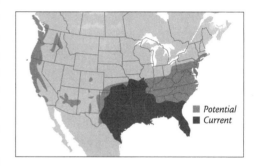

Present and potential armadillo distribution in the U.S.

Pocket Gophers: Churning the Prairie

Pocket gophers exert an enormous influence over the North American landscape and the biological community it supports. Relative to other rodents, pocket gophers are not abundant. Although they live in modest numbers, their digging influences everything from the diversity of the plant communities to the distribution of the animals. Some biologists even believe pocket gophers provide an explanation for the genesis of North America's fertile prairie soils.

An underground herbivore, pocket gophers are named for their fur-lined cheek pouches that they use to transport food. They reside only in the Western Hemisphere. North America possesses sixteen species: eight western, seven midwestern and eastern, and one in the southwestern U.S. and northern Mexico. Together, the ranges of these eight cover half the continent. Especially common in the West in grasslands and arid scrublands, pocket gophers are found as far east as Georgia. No two species coexist in the same area.

Pocket gophers excavate extensive tunnel systems from which they feed, year-round, on roots and the aboveground parts of plants harvested near their feeding holes. Burrowing requires much energy—360 to 3,400 times that of aboveground travel—and pocket gophers consume enormous quantities of food. On a per acre basis, energy flow through a typical population is comparable to that of large grazers.

Using their long front claws and, when necessary, their beaverlike incisors, they dig and shove loosened soil to the surface in mounds—yard-wide, foot-high piles of loose earth. They also backfill abandoned burrows. The result of all this activity is a thorough tilling of the soil and a reshuffling of nutrients. The mounds of fresh earth carry different amounts of nutrients than the surrounding surface soils and are exposed to more light (because they sit above the surrounding vegetation), so they offer another set of growing conditions to plants. Researchers report that when gophers are present on a plot of ground, nitrogen levels are higher and more variable. Light conditions vary more, too, and plant diversity is up to 50 percent greater. The abundance of annual leafy plants or forbs increases, while perennial prairie grasses decrease. Pocket gophers feeding on tree roots kill many trees, so openings are maintained. At the same time, productivity of land with pocket gophers is higher—about 5.5 percent above equivalent sites without pocket gophers. This occurs in spite of the fact that pocket gophers are both consuming plants and creating significant amounts of bare soil by pushing up new mounds.

The mounds, accumulating over many centuries, add up to some major changes in the landscape as well. Characteristic of North America's grasslands are features called mima mounds—6-foot-high, 150-foot-plus-diameter circular hills that number twenty to forty per acre. Mima mounds make for an undulating topography, one with a greater variety of growing sites, given the differences in exposure and drainage. Mima mounds also contain deeper, more fertile soils and support a richer plant community than surrounding flat areas. Scientists once thought these hills were the prod-

The pocket gopher is perhaps one of North America's most under-appreciated animals.

uct of wind or water erosion, wind deposition, or freezing and thawing during glaciations, but they now believe pocket gophers created the mounds by a long-term amassing of individual mounds.

Given that pocket gophers exert such a large influence over soils and plants, their significant effect on other herbivores is not surprising. Gopher mounds are ideal places for grasshoppers to lay their eggs. In a Minnesota study, pocket gopher mound density encouraged grasshopper abundance more than soil nitrogen, plant biomass, cover, or diversity. Pocket gophers also aid larger herbivores—deer, elk, antelope, buffalo—by improving soils. Pocket gophers serve as prey to birds (especially owls), mammals (coyotes, foxes, bobcats, badgers, skunks, and weasels), and snakes (gopher and bull snakes and rattlesnakes). Invertebrates, amphibians, reptiles, and other small mammals use their abandoned burrows.

EFFECTS OF POCKET GOPHERS

After One Week on 1 yd^2	After One Year on 100 yd^2	After Fifty Years on several acres
• More light penetration • Changed soil chemistry • Lowered plant biomass • More resources available to plants • More bare soil for plants to colonize	• Greater diversity of resources available to plants • More varied topography • Increased plant diversity and variability in biomass • More microhabitats available to plants	• Changed soil fertility • Changed rate and path of plant succession • Changed topography

A Steward of Wildflowers

Mountain meadows spangled with wildflowers owe a great deal to the pocket gophers busy in the soils beneath them. Pocket gophers maintain many meadows by preventing aspen clones and other trees from invading. Most aspen reproduce vegetatively. Roots send up suckers that form new trees. The clones expand, spreading outward from their centers to fill meadows, unless pocket gophers kill encroaching trees by eating the roots. Researchers in Arizona report that gophers live in meadows where soils are deep and where wildflowers, their preferred foods, are plentiful. Meanwhile, aspen clones are left to the rock outcrops, even though they would grow better in the meadows if pocket gophers were absent. In forested habitats, meadows increase diversity by providing habitat for plants, insects, birds, and mammals that depend on openings.

IN FOCUS: WHITE-NOSED COATI

White-nosed coati

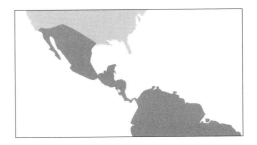

White-nosed coati distribution

Distribution

The white-nosed coati (*Nasua narica*) lives in southeast Arizona and Mexico south to western Columbia and Ecuador. The coati's family, Procyonidae, includes raccoons, olingos, the ringtail (which occurs from Oregon and Colorado to Mexico), the cacomistle, and the kinkajou.

Description

White-nosed coati weigh from 7.5 to 12 pounds; the males are 1 or 2 pounds heavier than females. Both sexes vary in length from 32 to 50 inches, with the tail providing about half of that length. Gray to brown in color, coati fur is often grizzled on the sides of the arms and white around the end of the muzzle. The animal also bears a small white spot above and below each eye, a large white spot on each cheek, a white throat and belly, black feet, and black rings on its tail.

Life History

Coatis are principally insectivores but eat lizards, frogs, mice, and fruit as well, and adult males will occasionally kill young coatis. Whereas the males are solitary animals, the females live in organized groups and care for each other's young. Most of the year, females chase males away from their band, but during the breeding season, females tolerate males.

Just before a coati gives birth, she leaves her band and builds a nest in a tree. The average litter size is three to five, and the young stay in the nest for five to six weeks. By the end of May, the mother escorts them out of the tree, and the families reunite with the original band. The males appear, cavort with, and groom the females and their young over several days. This activity, it's thought, enables a male to recognize his offspring so he will not inadvertently prey on them later.

Within bands, females groom each other, take turns watching for predators, work together to chase predators away, and groom and nurse each other's offspring. The behavior, termed "reciprocal altruism," allows each female to halve the time needed in caring for her young.

North America's Sea Cow

The Caribbean or West Indian manatee belongs to the ancient order Sirenia (the sea cows), the only living group of mammals both wholly aquatic and herbivorous. Their front limbs are flippers and they lack hind limbs: the posterior portions of their bodies are paddlelike structures. Worn teeth of manatees, like those of elephants, drop out and are replaced by others.

Whereas the largest manatees on record exceeded 12 feet in length and 3,500 pounds, most grow to 10 feet and weigh 800 to 1,200 pounds. Females are often larger than males. Manatee skin is tough, wrinkled, and grayish in color; it is continuously sloughing off. The sloughing may serve to shed accumulations of algae and microorganisms.

Although found primarily along the coast of Florida, Caribbean manatees range around the Caribbean and beyond. The southern end of their range is near Espirito Santo, Brazil. In Florida, manatees migrate between summer and winter feeding areas. Their movements, triggered by changes in water temperature, sometimes span large distances. During winter, Florida manatees congregate around warm springs and power plants that discharge warm water. During the summer, they migrate northward, some as far as Virginia and Maryland. Rarely, one will be reported as far north as New Jersey or as far west as Texas on the Gulf Coast.

Manatees thrive in freshwater, brackish, and saltwater environments but seem to prefer large, slow-moving rivers, river mouths, and shallow coastal areas such as coves and bays. They eat a variety of aquatic plants, including water hyacinth, water hydrilla, and wild celery in fresh water, and turtle grass, shoal grass, widgeon grass, and manatee grass in salt water. Manatees also pull vegetation from banks and eat the leaves and seeds of mangroves.

The Caribbean manatee

The digestive systems of manatees do not process food as thoroughly as those of other animals; adults must consume 4 to 9 percent of their weight every day, a task that requires five to eight hours of feeding. Although manatees eat while submerged, they surface periodically to breathe. They can remain underwater for as long as 12 minutes but average 4.5. Between meals, manatees rest, their bodies suspended just below the water's surface, their snouts above water.

Female manatees first breed between six and seven years of age. Several males, butting each other for position, follow females in estrus. Gestation lasts about thirteen months, and usually a female bears only one calf, or occasionally twins. A newborn manatee weighs 60 to 70 pounds and is 4 to 4.5 feet long. Nursing underwater on a nipple located behind the mother's forelimb and communicating through squeaks, squeals, whines and grunts, the baby periodically rides to the surface on its mother's back. Born with teeth, calves begin eating plants within a few weeks but nurse for as long as one year. They remain with their mothers for up to two years. Manatees may live forty to fifty years in the wild.

Indians once hunted manatees, as did the early colonists. They used manatee fat for lamp oil, their bones for medicinal purposes, and their hides for leather. Overhunting caused populations to plummet. Today, the largest problem facing manatees is speed boats, which can kill or injure animals submerged just below the surface. Many areas now post speed limit signs for boaters or bar motor boats from areas heavily populated by manatees. Sea cows also suffer harassment from skin divers, fishermen, and boaters who disrupt feeding and mating activities. During the winter, recreationists sometimes force manatees into cooler waters where the animals expend more energy and may die. Manatees are also killed by floodgates and canal locks and by fishing line and other trash that they consume or entangle themselves in.

Recently, natural events imperiled the manatee populations. In 1977, 1981, 1984, and 1989, unusually cold winters lowered water temperatures throughout Florida. Many manatees died, especially young ones. When the water drops to below 60°F, sea cows become sluggish and stop eating. Periodic red tide blooms also kill manatees. Red tide toxins accumulate in sea squirts, which in turn adhere to sea grasses ingested by feeding manatees.

Manatees are slow to rebound from any decline; their mortality rate may exceed the birth rate. In 1893, Florida passed a law to protect manatees, and since 1907, the state has fined people five hundred dollars for killing or harming the animal. In 1967, the U.S. federal government classified the species as endangered. Then, in 1978, the state of Florida designated itself a refuge and sanctuary for the manatee. The manatee is also protected under the Marine Mammal Protection Act of 1972.

IN FOCUS: RED FOX

Red fox

Red fox distribution

Distribution

Biologists still debate whether or not red foxes (*Vulpes vulpes*) are native to North America. Most believe they are, at least to the region north of latitude 40° N. But red foxes interbred with European red foxes, another race introduced during the mid-eighteenth century. Today, the species thrives in every state and province of the U.S. and Canada but is absent from Mexico. Both the distribution and population of the red fox increased after European settlement, primarily because agricultural practices increased habitat, and because European-Americans wiped out wolves, formerly the fox's chief predators.

Description

Red foxes are small, lightly built, catlike canines. Adults reach 3 feet in length, one-third of which is bushy tail, and weigh between 7 and 15 pounds. Their fur—dense, long, and soft—occurs in several color phases from reddish yellow to black to silver to bluish gray. Often, the fur of the shoulder region and back is slightly darker, and that of the belly, chin, and tip of the tail is white. The paws and muzzles are black.

Habitat

Red foxes are generalists, meaning they eat different kinds of food and exploit a variety of habitats—croplands, brushy thickets, pastures, woodlands, and open deciduous forests. But they favor areas with a mix of fields and woods and spend much of their time in "edge" habitats, such as where upland hardwoods meet croplands or where marsh meets woodland or thicket. Red foxes also use suburban areas, especially those with parks and golf courses.

Life History

Red foxes sometimes form monogamous bonds, although two or more males may court a single female. They breed from December to March, the pair digging a den or claiming an abandoned badger or marmot hole or dense thicket. The two may even establish multiple dens; presumably so that if one is threatened, they can move the pups to another. Litter size averages about five. The pups are weaned at one month, when they begin to play near the den entrance. Fox parents stalk mice, pocket gophers, and voles with their pups around the den site. When the young reach three months of age, they disperse, the males traveling as far as 150 miles. The mated pair may separate during the winter but reunites the next spring.

Red foxes eat voles, mice, lemmings, squirrels, hares, rabbits, ground-nesting birds, waterfowl, fish, insects, fruits such as berries, grasses, sedges, and grains. Occasionally they take raccoons, skunks, cats, dogs, and porcupines. When prey is scarce, red foxes establish food caches.

Humans are probably the red fox's chief predator—hunting, trapping, and automobiles are the primary causes of fox deaths in the Midwest. Wolves, coyotes, dogs, bobcats, lynxes, and cougars also kill foxes. Coyotes and foxes living in the same area compete; the coyotes usually displace the foxes. When humans remove coyotes from an area, foxes quickly move in.

North America's Wild Primates

Only a few monkeys—the spider monkey (*Ateles paniscus*) and the mantled and Guatemalan howler monkeys (*Alouatta palliata* and *A. pigra*, respectively)—live at North America's extreme southern and most tropical end. New World monkeys differ from Old World monkeys in that they have short muzzles; flat, naked faces; large, forward-facing eyes; widely spaced nostrils that open to the side; short necks and torsos; long hind legs; long digits; and, usually, long tails. North America's monkeys are members of a group called Cebids and are all large and possess tails with a naked, gripping surface at the tip. The spider monkey lacks a thumb and hangs and swings by its arms or tail; the two howlers climb but rarely swing by their arms.

In their tropical-rainforest habitats, these monkeys feed heavily on fruit and leaves. They are the most important seed dispersers for hundreds of plants, especially canopy trees and lianas.

Spider monkey

Spider monkeys, separated by some biologists into four species and lumped by others into a single species, range north into the southern part of the state of Tamaulipas, Mexico, and west into the state of Colima. With masks of unpigmented skin around their eyes and muzzle, spider monkeys in Mexico tend to be blackish or silvery on their backs and sides and paler beneath.

Their arms and tails are very long, and they weigh from 14 to 19 pounds. In Mexico, they favor mature rainforest but live in near rainforest, some dry forests, and mangrove swamps. Diurnal and arboreal, they eat mostly fruits. Although still abundant in some parts of Mexico, spider monkeys have disappeared from much of their former range. Where populations remain, they suffer from deforestation, habitat fragmentation, hunting, and the pet trade.

Mantled howler monkey

The mantled howler monkey lives as far north as the state of Tabasco, Mexico, and west into the eastern part of Oaxaca. The species is absent from the Yucatan. Weighing from 10.5 to 17 pounds, mantled howler monkeys are black with a fringe or saddle of long gold or buff-colored hair. The males sport white scrotums.

In Mexico, the species appears to be restricted to mature tropical rainforest and cloud forest where they live in the upper levels of the canopy. They avoid open country, although in Chiapas they occasionally visit low, thicketlike vegetation. Diurnal, arboreal, slow moving, and sedentary, mantled howlers live mostly on fruit and leaves. Named for their vocalizations, howlers roar and howl, their choruses lasting many minutes. Their droppings are strong smelling, and the monkeys are fa-mous for defecating on people walking below. Deforestation, road building, and hunting (the species is prized for its meat and pelt in Mexico) threaten Mexican populations.

The Guatemalan howler inhabits tropical southeastern Mexico from the Yucatan Peninsula to eastern Tabasco. Slightly larger than the mantled howler, this monkey bears longer hair and is entirely black except for the male's scrotum, which is white. Diurnal and arboreal, the species occupies little-disturbed rainforests in Mexico. Its howls and roars can be heard at dawn, in the late afternoon, and during rainstorms. At other times, this howler is quiet and inconspicuous. Mantled howlers, more tolerant of human disturbances, are replacing Guatemalan howlers where habitats have deteriorated.

Guatemalan howler monkey

The Gray Wolf: Returning to the Wilds of the West

Before Europeans arrived, gray wolves reigned as one of the continent's top predators. Early settlers moving west killed off prey populations—bison, deer, elk, and moose. Wolves turned to sheep and cattle. Ranchers and government trappers responded with an all-out campaign to eliminate wolves. They trapped, shot, and poisoned wolves. The indiscriminate and widespread use of strychnine also killed eagles, ravens, foxes, and bears.

Today, about 2,000 wolves survive in Minnesota, fewer than 20 on Isle Royale, 100 in Michigan's Upper Peninsula, 100 in Wisconsin, about 90 in Montana, and 50 in Wyoming. Fewer live in Idaho, Washington, North Dakota, and South Dakota. In Minnesota, where wolves are designated as threatened, a state program provides compensation for livestock killed by wolves, and a federal program provides for trapping of individual wolves guilty of depredation. The gray wolf is listed as endangered elsewhere in the lower forty-eight states. Canada has a stable or increasing population of around 50,000 to 60,000 wolves; Alaska has between 5,000 and 7,000. Wolves are not considered endangered or threatened in either Canada or Alaska. Greenland supports only a few wolves along its northeastern coast.

In 1994, the U.S. Fish and Wildlife Service (FWS) began an effort to reintroduce wolves into Yellowstone National Park and Forest Service lands in central Idaho. The wolves used in the reintroduction were trapped in Alberta and British Columbia. Once they were released, the FWS designated them as a "nonessential experimental population" under the Endangered Species Act. The classification allows the government to control the wolves under certain circumstances—for example, if they

The U.S. Fish and Wildlife Service has reintroduced wolves into several areas of the West and may do so in the East.

prey on livestock or if wild populations of deer, elk, and other large game are severely affected by wolf predation. A private organization established a fund to compensate landowners suffering losses to wolves.

Wolf recovery efforts represent an opportunity to redress past mistakes and to enhance our understanding of the complex interactions between an important predator and its environment.

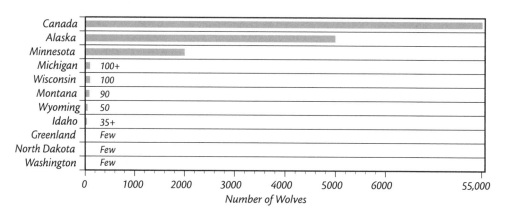

Status of gray wolf populations north of Mexico

Index

Credits

Original Art Commissioned

Janet McGahan: Pages 171 top right, 190 top right, 193, 197 middle, 199, 200, 201, 202, 203, 204, 206, 208, 213, 214, 218, 220, 225, 229, 231, 233, 235 top left, 236, 238, 239, 257, 259, 260 top left, 261, 273 bottom right, 275, 276 bottom left, 278 bottom right, 279, 294, 296, 297, 299, 301 middle left, 304 top left, 307, 308, 311 top left, 315, 317 top left, 323, 328, 331, 332 middle right, 333, 334, 335, 336, 338 top left, 340, 343, 345, 346, 347, 349, 351 top left, 352, 354 top left, 355, 356, 357.

Text, Tables, and Illustrations

Page 6, "Thickness of the crust..." map adapted from *The Geology of North America: An Overview* by A.W. Bally and R.A. Palmer ©1989 (Geological Society of America, Boulder, CO). Page 7, "The Earth's Layers" table adapted from *Planet Earth Cosmology, Geology, and the Evolution of Life and Environment* by Cesare Emiliani ©1992 (Cambridge University Press, Cambridge). Page 11, "Geologic Provinces of North America" map redrawn from *The Geology of North America: An Overview* by A.W. Bally and R.A. Palmer ©1989 (Geological Society of America, Boulder, CO). *Pages 18-22*, "Impact Craters" and "A Falling Star" text, table, and map adapted from information provided by the Geological Survey of Canada. Page 26, map modified from *Earth and Life through Time* by S. M. Stanley ©1989 (W. H. Freeman and Company, New York). Page 27, "Dance of the Continents" illustration adapted in part from the article "Earth Before Pangea" by Ian W. D. Dalziel in *Scientific American* (January, 1989). Page 28, "The Migration of North America" map redrawn from *The Geology of North America: An Overview* by A.W. Bally and R.A. Palmer ©1989 (Geological Society of America, Boulder, CO).

Page 29, illustration redrawn from *Earth and Life through Time* by S. M. Stanley ©1989 (W. H. Freeman and Company, New York). Page 30, "Exotic Terranes of the West" map redrawn from *The Evolution of North America* by Phillip B. King © 1977 (Princeton University Press, Princeton, New Jersey). Pages 31–32, "Most but not all..." and "Measuring Earthquakes" text and map adapted from publications of the U.S. Geological Survey. Pages 36–37, "The Next Big One in Northern California" and "The Stable Interior" text adapted from publications of the U.S. Geological Survey. Page 38, "Midplate Quakes" table adapted from *Neotectonics of North America* by D. B. Slemmons, E. R. Ehgdahl, M. D. Zoback, and D. D. Blackwell, eds. (Geological Society of America, Boulder, CO). Page 39, "Major earthquakes..." and "Clues to Prehistoric Quakes" text and map adapted from publications of the U.S. Geological Survey. Page 40, "Where Three Plates Meet" text and map adapted from an article by C. DeMets, et al. in *Eos* (October 1995). Page 42, "Major rifts..." map adapted from "Continental Rifting" by K. H. Olson, in *Encyclopedia of Earth System Science*, Volume 1, © 1992 (Academic Press, San Diego). Pages 43–49, tables and maps redrawn from publications of the U.S. Geological Survey. Pages 49–50, "Popocatépetl" and "The Mount St. Helens Experience" text and illustrations adapted from publications of the U.S. Geological Survey. Page 53, "The microcontinents..." after a map by Paul Hoffman ©1982 in *Decade of North American Geology Special Publication No. 1* (Geological Society of America, Boulder, CO). Page 65, "A Hot-Blooded Debate" table adapted from "The evidence for Endothermy in Dinosaurs" by J. H. Ostrum in *American Association for the Advancement of Science, Symposium No. 28*, R. D. K. Thomas and E. C. Olson, eds. Page 68, "Where Have All the Giant Mammals..." table from *Regional Stratigraphy of North America* by W. J. Frazier and D. R. Schwimmer ©1987 (Plenum Press, New York). Page 69, "Positions of North America" redrawn from *The Geology of North America: An Overview* by A.W. Bally and R.A. Palmer ©1989 (Geological Society of America, Boulder, CO). Pages 70–71, "Traditional Pleistocene..." and "Revised Chronology" tables adapted from *Regional Stratigraphy of North America* by W. J. Frazier and D. R. Schwimmer ©1987 (Plenum Press, New York). Pages 74–75, "A Brief History of the Cordilleran..." maps redrawn and adapted primarily from *Earth and Life through Time* by S. M. Stanley ©1989 (W. H. Freeman and Company, New York). Pages 79–80, "The Continent's Oldest..." and "Important Dinosaur Assemblages" tables adapted from *Regional Stratigraphy of North America* by W. J. Frazier and D. R. Schwimmer ©1987 (Plenum Press, New York). Page 86, "Three oceans receive runoff..." adapted from UNESCO. Page 87, "Principal river systems..." map redrawn from *Surface Water Hydrology*, H. S. Riggs and M. G. Wolman, eds. ©1990 (Geological Society of America, Boulder, CO). Page 87, "Largest Rivers" table from U.S. Geological Survey. Page 88, "Runoff" map redrawn and adapted from *Surface Water Hydrology*, H. S. Riggs and M. G. Wolman, eds. ©1990 (Geological Society of America, Boulder, CO). Page 88, "Ups and Downs..." map redrawn from *H. C. Riggs and K. D. Harvey* "Temporal and Spatial Variability of Streamflow" in *Surface Water Hydrology*, H. S. Riggs and M. G. Wolman, eds. ©1990 (Geological Society of America, Boulder, CO). Page 89, "Muddy Waters..." map and graph adapted from R. H. Meade, T. R. Yuzyk, and J. T. Day "Movement an Storage of Sediment in Rivers of the U.S. and Canada" in *Surface Water Hydrology*, H. S. Riggs and M. G. Wolman, eds. ©1990 (Geological Society of America, Boulder, CO). Page 90, "Pre-European vs. Modern Flows" map and table adapted from *Surface Water Hydrology*, H. S. Riggs and M. G. Wolman, eds. ©1990 (Geological Society of America, Boulder, CO). Page 92–93, "Lakes and Wetlands" map and table adapted from "Hydrology of Lakes and Wetlands" by

T. C. Winter and M. K. Woo in *Surface Water Hydrology*, H. S. Riggs and M. G. Wolman, eds. ©1990 (Geological Society of America, Boulder, CO). Page 95, "Percentage of large lakes..." and "Percentage of bogs..." from F. K. Hare, 1984, *Environment Canada Inland Water Directorate Research Paper 2* (Environment Canada, Ottawa). Page 96, "This profile of the Great Lakes..." redrawn from *Regulation of Great Lakes Water Levels, Report to the International Joint Commission* (International Great Lakes Levels Board, Washington, D.C.). Pages 96–97, "The Great Lakes" and "Closed Lakes" tables adapted from publications of the U.S. Geological Survey. Pages 98–101, "Groundwater Regions" table and map adapted from "Hydrogeologic Setting of Regions" by R. C. Heath in *Hydrogeology*, W. Black and J. S. Rosenshein, eds. ©1988 (Geological Society of America, Boulder, CO). Page 102, "Snow Regions" table adapted from "Snow and Ice" by R. H. Meier in *Surface Water Hydrology*, H. S. Riggs and M. G. Wolman, eds. ©1990 (Geological Society of America, Boulder, CO). Page 103, "The long-term probability..." map redrawn from an article by Dickson and Posey in *Monthly Weather Review,* 1967. Page 106, "Waterworld" adapted from the U.S. Geological Survey. Page 104, "Glaciers on Mount Rainier" adapted from the U.S. Geological Survey. Pages 108–111, "Soil Orders" table and map and "Soil Horizon" illustrations redrawn and adapted from "Soils" by D. Steila ©1993 in *The Flora of North America* (Oxford University Press, New York). Page 118, map adapted and simplified from *Map and Chart Series MC-36* ©1981 by the Geologic Society of America (Boulder, CO). Page 120, "Estimated changes in global temperatures..." adapted from the article "The Evolution of the Earth" by C. J. Alegre and S. H. Schneider in *Scientific American* (October, 1994). Pages 122–123, "Circulation of air and average..." maps redrawn and adapted from *The Atmosphere* by F. K. Lutgens and E. J. Tarbuck ©1989 (Prentice Hall, Englewood Cliffs, New

Jersey). **Pages 125–126** "*El Niño* and North America's Weather" adapted from publications of the National Oceanic and Atmospheric Administration. **Page 129**, "Air Masses and Source Regions" table from *The Atmosphere* by F. K. Lutgens and E. J. Tarbuck ©1989 (Prentice Hall, Englewood Cliffs, New Jersey). **Page 130**, "What the Wind Tells Us" text adapted from the U.S. Geological Survey. **Page 142**, "Record Temperatures" from *World Weather Extremes (with 1997 typed update)* (U.S. Army Engineer Topographic Laboratories, Ft. Belvoir, Virginia). **Page 144**, "Precipitation Patterns" map redrawn and adapted from *World Water Balance and Water Resources of the Earth*, 1978 (UNESCO Press, Paris). **Page 145**, "Record Precipitation" from *World Weather Extremes (with 1997 typed update)* (U.S. Army Engineer Topographic Laboratories, Ft. Belvoir, Virginia). **Pages 145–147**, "Major Droughts" text and table adapted from U.S. Geological Survey. **Page 148**, "Record Thunderstorms" and "Record Winds" text from *World Weather Extremes (with 1997 typed update)* (U.S. Army Engineer Topographic Laboratories, Ft. Belvoir, Virginia). **Page 148**, "Number of annual thunderstorm…" map adapted from World Meteorological Organization. **Page 149**, "Average number of tornadoes…" map adapted from the National Oceanic and Atmospheric Administration. **Page 158–162**, "The floristic richness…" and "Floristic Provinces" maps and table adapted from "Phytogeography" by R. F. Thorne ©1993 in *The Flora of North America* (Oxford University Press, New York). **Pages 174**, "Patterns of Change…" diagram redrawn and adapted from *North American Terrestrial Vegetation* by M. G. Barbour and W. D. Billings ©1988 (Cambridge University Press, New York). **Page 182**, "The Distribution of Communities" diagram redrawn from the article "A Gradient Perspective on the Vegetation of Sequoia National Park, California," by J. L. Vankat in *Madroño* (29). **Page 190**, "Coastal Marshes" map redrawn and adapted from *Physiological Ecology of North American Plant Communities*, B. F. Chabot and H. Mooney, eds. ©1985 (Chapman and Hall Publishers). **Pages 193–195**, "Fire-Dependent Plant Communities" text and maps adapted from U.S. National Biological Service. **Page 197**, "Weeds: An Enemy of Diversity" maps redrawn from the article "The Introduction and Spread of *Veronica beccabunga* (Sacrophulariacea) in Eastern North America" by D. H. Les and R. L. Stuckey in *Rhodora* (87). **Page 198**, "In Focus: Fire Moss" text adapted from U.S. Forest Service. **Page 203**, "In Focus: Northern Floodplain Forests" text adapted from U.S. Forest Service. **Page 205**, "What a Little Rust Can Do" text and map adapted from U.S. National Biological Service. **Page 208**, "In Focus: The Bluestem Prairie" text adapted from U.S. Forest Service. **Page 209**, "How Much Prairie" table adapted from the article "Roundtable: Prairie Conservation in North America" in *BioScience* (June, 1994). **Page 213**, "In Focus: The Conifer Bog" text adapted from U.S. Forest Service. **Pages 215–217**, "Native Plants of Commercial Value" table adapted from United Nations Food and Agricultural Organization. **Pages 218 and 220**, "No one knows…" and "Truffles Anyone?" text adapted from U.S. National Biological Service. **Pages 227–228**, "Insects by Vegetation Type" and "Families and Species Numbers…" adapted from *American Insects: A Handbook of the Insects of America North of Mexico* by A. H. Ross, Jr. ©1985 (Van Nostrand Reinhold Company, New York). **Page 230**, "Freshwater Mussels in Trouble" map adapted from U.S. National Biological Service. **Page 235**, "In Focus: Mountain Pine Beetle" text adapted from U.S. Forest Service. **Page 247**, map adapted from *An Introduction to Ichthyology* by P. B. Moyle ©1982 (Prentice Hall, Englewood Cliffs, New Jersey). **Page 250**, table adapted from *Biological Diversity of Mexico: Origins and Distribution* by T. P. Ramamoorthy et al. eds. ©1993 (Oxford University Press, New York). **Pages 251–252** map and table redrawn from the article "Status of Freshwater Fishes of the United States: Overview of an Imperiled Fauna" by M. L. Warren and B. M. Burr in *Fisheries* (19). Page 260, "In Focus: Cutthroat Trout" text adapted from U.S. Forest Service. Page 273, "The Status of Turtles" map and table adapted from U.S. National Biological Service. Page 276, "In Focus: Western or Boreal Toad" text adapted from U.S. Forest Service. Pages 278–279, "Crocodiles, Alligators and Caimans" text and map adapted from *Crocodiles* by R. Steel ©1989 (Christopher Helm, London). Page 288, "Of Distributions and Migrations" map adapted from *The Cambridge Encyclopedia of Ornithology* by M. Brooke and T. Birkhead, eds. ©1991 (Cambridge University Press, Cambridge). Pages 289–290, "Seasonal Migrations of Nearctic Breeding Birds" from the article "Synthesis: Ecological Basis and Evolution of Nearctic-Neotropical Bird Migration System" by Allen Keast in *Migrating Birds in the Neotropics: Ecology, Behavior, Distribution, and Conservation* © 1977 (Smithsonian Institution, Washington, D.C.) Page 291, "Wintering North American Birds in Mexican Habitats" data from an article by R. Hutto in *Migrating Birds in the Neotropics: Ecology, Behavior, Distribution, and Conservation*, Symposium Proceedings 1977 (Smithsonian Institution, Washington, D.C.) Page 291, maps adapted from *Biological Diversity of Mexico: Origins and Distribution* T. P. Ramamoorthy et al. eds. ©1993 (Oxford University Press, New York). Page 295, "The Cowbird Threat" map redrawn from "Brown-Headed Cowbird" by P. E. Lowther in *The Birds of North America*, A. Poole and F. Gill, eds. ©1993 (The Academy of Natural Sciences, The American Ornithologists Union, Washington, D.C.) Page 300, "Birds and Storms" table from an article by D. A. Wiedenfeld and M. G. Wiedenfeld in *The Journal of Field Ornithology*, Winter, 1995. Page 301, "In Focus: Red-Cockaded Woodpecker" Cowbird Threat" map redrawn from "Red-Cockaded Woodpecker" by J. A. Jackson in *The Birds of North America*, A. Poole and F. Gill, eds. ©1994 (The Academy of Natural Sciences,

The American Ornithologists Union, Washington, D.C.) Page 302, "The Recovery of the Wild Turkey" text and graph adapted from U.S. National Biological Service. Page 304, "In Focus: Ruffed Grouse" text adapted from U.S. Forest Service. Pages 305–306, "Raptors in the U.S." text adapted from U.S. National Biological Survey. Page 306, map adapted from *Hawks, Eagles, and Falcons of North America* by P. A. Johnsgard (Smithsonian Institution Press, Washington D.C.). Page 310, graph adapted from U.S. National Biological Survey. Pages 312–313, "North America's Most Familiar Goose" text, graph, and map adapted from U.S. National Biological Survey. Pages 315–316, "Shorebird Staging Areas" text and map adapted from U.S. National Biological Survey. Page 317, map adapted from U.S. National Biological Survey. Page 324, graphs and maps adapted from the article "Species Density of North American Recent Mammals" by G. G. Simpson in *Systematic Zoology* (June 1964). Page 326, "Relations" graph adapted from *Mammal Ecology* by M. J. Delaney ©1982 (Blackie and Son Limited, Glasgow and London). Page 326, "North America's Links…" map adapted from *The Geography of Evolution* by G. G. Simpson ©1965 (Chilton Books, Philadelphia). Page 328, text, table and map adapted from U.S. National Biological Survey. Page 332, graph adapted from *Current Mammalogy*, Volume 2, L. B. Kieth and H. H. Genoways, eds. (Plenum Press, New York). Page 337, graph adapted from "The Physiology and Evolution of Delayed Implantation in Carnivores" by R. A. Mead in *Carnivore Behavior, Ecology, and Evolution*, J. L. Gittleman, ed. ©1989 (Cornell University Press, Ithica). Page 348, map adapted from the article "Recent Range Expansion and Distributional Limits of the Nine-Banded Armadillo in the United States" by J. F. Tauman and L. W. Robbins in *Journal of Biogeography* (1996). Page 250, "Effects of Pocket Gophers" table adapted from the article "Pocket Gophers in Ecosystems: Patterns and Mechanisms" by N. Huntly and R.

Inouye in *BioScience* (December, 1988). **Page 354**, "In Focus: Red Fox" text adapted from U.S. Forest Service. **Page 354**, map adapted from "Foxes" by D. E. Samuel and B. B. Nelson in *Wild Mammals of North America: Biology, Management, and Economics*, J. A. Chapman and G. A. Feldhamer, eds. (The John Hopkins University Press, Baltimore). **Page 358**, "In Focus: The Gray Wolf…" text and graph adapted from U.S. National Biological Survey.

PENFIELD ACADEMY
7925, NADEAU
BROSSARD
J4Y 1X8
TÉL.: (514) 926-2202